GREENBOOK

es
05
EDITION

Includes All Buildings and Accessories for All Department 56® Villages.

✓ *The Original Snow Village® Series*
✓ *Dickens' Village Series®*
✓ *New England Village® Series*
✓ *Alpine Village Series®*
✓ *Christmas In The City® Series*
✓ *The Holy Land® Collection*
✓ *North Pole Series™*
✓ *Small Collections*

   (Includes: Historical Landmark Series®, Meadowland, Literary Classics® Collection, Disney Parks Village™ Series, North Pole Woods™ Collection, Seasons Bay® Series)

✓ *Profiles Department 56®*
✓ *And Other Related Series*

Featuring Secondary Market Values, Historical Facts, Information, and Trivia that will make collecting more enjoyable than ever.

Personal Collection of

_____

GREENBOOK®
The Definitive Reference & Secondary Market Guide To
Department 56® Villages

To order books: 1-877-212-4356 (Toll-Free Inside the U.S.)
Inquiries: 401-467-9343
Fax: 401-467-9359

www.greenbooks.com
www.villagechronicle.com

© Copyright 2005, The Collectible Source, Inc.

Published by The Collectible Source, Inc

All Rights Reserved. All of the information, photos, and illustrations within this publication are the property of The Collectible Source, Inc. No portion of this publication may be reproduced, stored in or introduced into a retrieval system or transmitted in any manner or by any means–including, but not limited to, electronic, mechanical, photocopying, recording or otherwise–without the prior written permission of the copyright owners.

This product depicting intellectual properties of Department 56, Inc. was produced by The Collectible Source, Inc. under license of Department 56, Inc. The Collectible Source, Inc., the Village Chronicle®, and Greenbook® are not affiliated with Department 56, Inc. or D56, Inc., and Department 56, Inc. and D56, Inc. make no representation as to the accuracy of any of the information or statements contained in this resource.

All uses of the following "Department 56®, Inc.," "Department 56®," "Dept. 56®," "D56, Inc.," "D56," "The Original Snow Village® Collection" "The Heritage Village Collection®," "The Dickens' Village Series®," "The New England Village Series," "The Alpine Village Series®," "The Christmas in the City® Series," "Little Town of Bethlehem™ Series," "North Pole Series™," "Disney Parks Village™ Series," "Seasons Bay® Series" Charles Dickens' Signature Series™," "The Historical Landmark Series™," "Literary Classics® Series," "Elf Land," "North Pole Woods™ Collection," "Bucks County®," and "Profiles Department 56®" are Trademarks of Department 56®, Inc. "Cadillac," "Chevy," Chevrolet," and "Corvette" are the Trademarks of General Motors. "Coca-Cola" is a Trademark of Coca-Cola Co. "Crayola" is the Trademark of Binney & Smith. "Disney" is the Trademark of Disney. "Duesenberg" is the Trademark of Duesenberg Motors, Inc. "Elvis Presley" and "Graceland" are the Trademarks of Elvis Presley Enterprises. "Ford" is the Trademark of Ford Motor Co. "Good Humor" is the Trademark of Good Humor-Breyers Ice Cream. "Goodyear" is the Trademark of Goodyear Tire & Rubber Co. "Heinz" is the Trademark of Heinz Food Co. "Habitat For Humanity" is the Trademark of Habitat For Humanity International. "Harley-Davidson" is the Trademark of Harley-Davidson Motor Co. "Harry Potter" is the Trademark of Warner Bros. "McDonald's is the Trademark of McDonald's, Inc. "Hershey's" is the Trademark of Hershey Foods Corporation. "John Deere" is the Trademark of Deere & Co. "Lionel" is the Trademark of Lionel LLC. "Looney Tunes" is the Trademark of Warner Bros. "Times Tower" is the Trademark of Jamestown One Times Square, L.P. "Rockefeller" is the Trademark of RCPI Trust. "Starbucks" is the Trademark of Starbucks Inc. "State Farm" is the Trademark of State Farm Insurance Co. "The Grinch Who Stole Christmas" is the Trademark of Dr. Seuss Enterprises. "The Sound of Music" is the Trademark of R&H Org., Argyle & Fox. "Timberlake Outfitters" is the Trademark of Bob Timberlake, Inc. "Russell Stover" is the Trademark of Russell Stover Candies, Inc. "Rudolph" is the Trademark of GTM&L. Major League Baseball trademarks and copyrights are used with the permission of Major League Baseball Properties, Inc. "LEGO" and the "LEGO logo" are Trademarks of the LEGO Group. "Caribou" and "Caribou logo" are Trademarks of Caribou coffee Co. "Krispy Kreme" and the "Krispy Kreme Bowtie" are Trademarks of HDN Development Corp. "Polaris" is the Trademark of Polaris Industries, Inc. "Mercury" is the Trademark of Ford Motor Co. "Play-Doh" is the Trademark of Hasbro Consumer Products. "Radio City," "Radio City Rockettes," and "Radio City Entertainment" are the Trademarks of Radio City Trademarks, LLC. "Red Owl" and the Fanciful Owl Head Design are Trademarks of Supervalu, Inc. "Barbie" is the Trademark of Mattel, Inc., "Hard Rock Cafe" is a Trademark of Hard Rock Cafe International (USA), Inc., "Pillsbury Doughboy" is the Trademark of Pillsbury Co., Spam is a Trademark of Hormel Food Co., "M&M's" is the Trademark of Mars, Inc, "Dick Clark" is the Trademark of Dick Clark Productions.

ISBN 0-9649032-7-X

First Printing, February, 2005

Printed and bound in U.S.A.

Table Of Contents

Getting The Most From This Guide 4
Original Snow Village 5
Original Snow Village Accessories 69
Original Snow Village - Halloween 113
Original Snow Village Accessories - Halloween 119
Dickens' Village 125
Dickens' Village Accessories 171
New England Village 199
New England Village Accessories 219
Alpine Village 231
Alpine Village Accessories 239
Christmas In The City 243
Christmas In The City Accessories 267
The Holy Land 285
The Holy Land Accessories 293
North Pole 299
North Pole Accessories 321
Small Collections 339
    (Includes: Historical Landmark Series, Meadowland, Literary Classics Collection, Disney Parks Village Series, North Pole Woods Collection, Seasons Bay Series)
Heritage Village 365
Special Designs 373
General Village Accessories 387
Item Number Index 423
Alphabetical Index 435

On the Cover...
(top to bottom) New England Village Jacob Adams Barn, Christmas In The City Heritage Museum Of Art, Snow Village Prairie House, North Pole Ginny's Cookie Treats, Dickens' Village Heathmoor Castle

Getting The Most From This Guide

Sections
Each village has its own section. Its accessories immediately follow the lighted pieces.

The **Heritage Village** section contains porcelain pieces that were not necessarily designed for a specific village series and may be appropriate for two or more Heritage Villages.

The **Small Collection** section consists of collections that are too small in number to warrant their own individual sections.

The **Special Design**s section features buildings and accessories that were produced for a particular retailer, company, or organization.

Chronological Order
We're often asked why the collections are placed in chronological order. There are several reasons. One is that its sequence follows that of printed materials produced by Department 56, Inc. such as its History List. Another is that it's the only way a collector can get a complete grasp of a collection. It allows one to see how the designs, creativity, and technology developed over the years. It also makes it possible to see all the pieces made in one year (or a series of years) at a glance. For instance, say you want to see all the Dickens' Village Series buildings from 1991…there they are.

Values
Another question that is often asked is how we determine values. Simply put, we don't…actual sales from around the country determine them. We canvass various sources of secondary market sales throughout the nation, from East to West, from auctions, to brokers to swap & sells, to the traditional retail stores. Pricing structures in each of these sources differ, making a one-price-fits-all value unrealistic.

With That In Mind, It's More Than Just A Secondary Market Guide
This guide is designed to do more than present a pictorial representation of the collection with current values to accompany them. It's meant to offer you the facts, data, background, and yes, trivia in a concise, easy-to-follow manner. It's our goal to provide a guide that makes collecting the villages more exciting than ever before. It's our hope that we have accomplished this goal. If you have comments or ideas, please contact us at 401-467-9343 or at www.greenbooks.com.

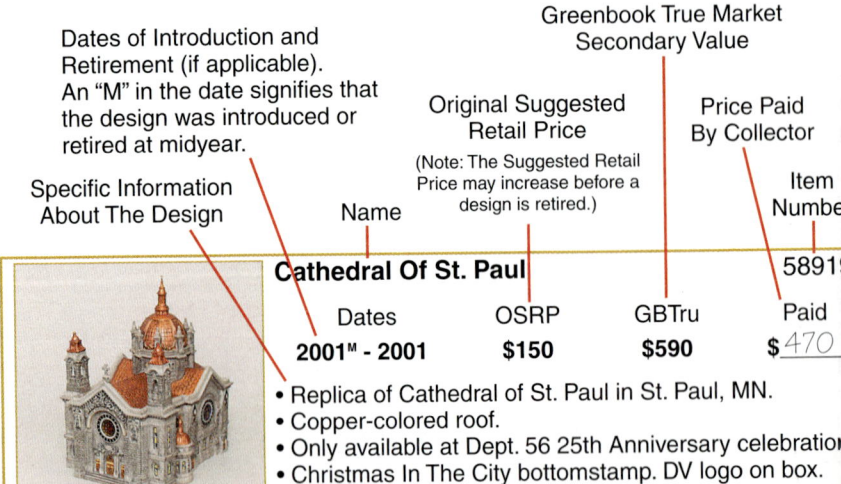

Dates of Introduction and Retirement (if applicable). An "M" in the date signifies that the design was introduced or retired at midyear.

Specific Information About The Design

Name

Original Suggested Retail Price
(Note: The Suggested Retail Price may increase before a design is retired.)

Greenbook True Market Secondary Value

Price Paid By Collector

Item Number

Cathedral Of St. Paul 58919

Dates | OSRP | GBTru | Paid
2001ᴹ - 2001 | $150 | $590 | $ 470

- Replica of Cathedral of St. Paul in St. Paul, MN.
- Copper-colored roof.
- Only available at Dept. 56 25th Anniversary celebration.
- Christmas In The City bottomstamp. DV logo on box.

The Original Snow Village® Collection

   The matriarch of the winter villages, the Original Snow Village® Collection debuted in 1976. The only ceramic community, it is the largest village, annually introducing and retiring the most pieces. The buildings are generally larger and more vividly colored than any of the porcelain villages. The detail and exceptional craftsmanship in recent years are in contrast to the early years.

   This is Americana through the years, and patriotic pieces and Classic Cars confirm that focus. Licensing agreements have resulted in buildings with such familiar names as Coca-Cola®, McDonald's®, Starbucks®, Harley-Davidson®, Lionel®, Ford®, and Krispy Kreme®. Among the most eye-catching buildings are several of an art deco nature. Retail establishments abound, but so do residences and churches. Among the homes is a subseries, the American Architecture Series that replicates various architectural styles. Popular pieces such as fire stations, lighthouses, and schools have been re-introduced to meet the demands of new collectors.

   While figures have never been in scale, the original contrast was even greater than today as downsizing took place in the late 1980s. Children are featured in the accessories to a much greater extent than any other village. Animals are also a very popular theme in the family-oriented designs. The Buck's County Series reflects an emphasis on the more rural lifestyle.

   The number of Halloween pieces has increased, and a separate section has been added to this publication at the end of the regular collection. Valentine's, Easter, and St. Patrick's Day have also expanded this village to more than a winter setting.

Snow Village

Mountain Lodge — 50013

Dates	OSRP	GBTru	Paid
1976 - 1979	$20	$355	$_____

- Colors on roof often vary.
- Must have a sunburst face on the end of the building to be authentic.
- Skis are sometimes broken or detached.

Gabled Cottage — 50021

Dates	OSRP	GBTru	Paid
1976 - 1979	$20	$290	$_____

- Color varies to the point where no two are alike.

The Inn — 50039

Dates	OSRP	GBTru	Paid
1976 - 1979	$20	$420	$_____

- Colors on roof often vary to the point where no two are alike.
- Watch for cracks in the porch supports.

Country Church — 50047

Dates	OSRP	GBTru	Paid
1976 - 1979	$18	$345	$_____

- Also known as Wayside Chapel.
- This is one of the most frequently imitated pieces in Snow Village. The lettering on the walls must be hand painted (as opposed to stamped on) to be authentic.

Steepled Church — 50054

Dates	OSRP	GBTru	Paid
1976 - 1979	$25	$585	$_____

- Colors on roof often vary.

Small Chalet — 50062

Dates	OSRP	GBTru	Paid
1976 - 1979	$15	$400	$_____

- Also known as Gingerbread Chalet.
- An often imitated design, it is difficult to authenticate.
- The color varies from tan to brown, and the number of flowers in window box varies.

Victorian House

50070

Dates	OSRP	GBTru	Paid
1977 - 1979	$30	$390	$_____

- Color of building varies among rust/white, salmon/white, pink/white, and orange/yellow (no tree attached).
- Birds are often broken off, leaving lack of paint and glazing where the birds should be.

Mansion

50088

Dates	OSRP	GBTru	Paid
1977 - 1979	$30	$520	$_____

- Color of roof often varies from forest green (first shipments) to turquoise.
- The amount of glaze on the forest green version varies while the turquoise version sometimes has flaking paint.

Stone Church (Version 1)

50096

Dates	OSRP	GBTru	Paid
1977 - 1979	$35	$645	$_____

- Pale mint green building with very glossy finish.
- Right sides of front steps are flush.
- Steeple is approximately 10½" high as opposed to the 1979 version which is approximately 8½" high.

(Version 2)

GBTru	Paid
$595	$_____

- Greenish-yellow building with less glossy finish.
- Right side of top front step is indented from bottom one.
- Both versions have felt glued to the bottom.
- The bell is sometimes missing from the bell tower.

Homestead

50112

Dates	OSRP	GBTru	Paid
1978 - 1984	$30	$210	$_____

- Sometimes not painted or glazed well.
- Porch pillars, garland, and chimney are easily damaged.

Snow Village

General Store — 50120

Dates	OSRP	GBTru	Paid
1978 - 1980	$25	See below	

- Variations: white with gray roof (first shipments), tan with red roof, and gold with brown roof.
- Signs: on white "General Store Y & L Brothers," on tan "General Store S & L Brothers," on gold "General Store."

	GBTru	Paid
White	$375	$_____
Tan	$440	$_____
Gold	$475	$_____

Cape Cod — 50138

Dates	OSRP	GBTru	Paid
1978 - 1980	$20	$350	$_____

- The snow around the bottom of the piece detaches easily.

Nantucket — 50146

Dates	OSRP	GBTru	Paid
1978 - 1986	$25	$225	$_____

- Some pieces were manufactured with garland above front windows; others were not. Still others had the garland broken off. This is usually easy to determine.

Skating Rink/Duck Pond Set — 5015

Dates	OSRP	GBTru	Paid
1978 - 1979	$16	$995	$_____

- The trees are attached directly to the bases where the size and weight caused frequent breakage.
- The pieces in this set are often sold separately on the secondary market.
- Do not confuse this set with the 1982 Skating Pond set
- Set of 2 includes the Skating Rink (features a snowman and a lighted tree) and the Duck Pond (features bench, blue birds, and a lighted tree).

Small Double Trees (Blue Birds) 50161

Dates	OSRP	GBTru	Paid
1978 - 1989	$13.50	$155	$_____

• Pieces with blue birds were shipped first.

(Red Birds Version)

		GBTru	Paid
		$40	$_____

• Pieces with red birds began to appear in late 1979.
• Throughout the years there were mold changes with the design becoming more and more detailed.
• Amount of snow on the trees varies greatly.

Victorian 50542

Dates	OSRP	GBTru	Paid
1979 - 1982	$30	See below	

• Peach (1st year) often has peeling paint.
• Gold with smooth walls (2nd year) ⎫ Defects are often
• Gold with clapboard walls (3rd year) ⎭ located along the bottom edges.

	GBTru	Paid
Peach	$345	$_____
Gold - S	$350	$_____
Gold - C	$365	$_____

Knob Hill (Gray) 50559

Dates	OSRP	GBTru	Paid
1979 - 1981	$30	$265	$_____

• This color is considered to be the first shipped.
• The paint on this version is commonly thin and bubbly.
• Cracks on the bottom are also common.
• Beware of chips along the steps.

(Yellow Version)

	GBTru	Paid
	$245	$_____

• Beware of chips along the steps.
• The chimneys on both colors are very fragile.

Snow Village

Brownstone — 50567

Dates	OSRP	GBTru	Paid
1979 - 1981	$36	See below	

	GBTru	Paid
• Gray roof (first year)	$495	$_____
• Red roof (second year)	$430	$_____

• Beware of cracks near windows and chipped steps.

Log Cabin — 50575

Dates	OSRP	GBTru	Paid
1979 - 1981	$22	$480	$_____

• The skis by the door are very fragile and are often broken off.

Countryside Church — 50583

Dates	OSRP	GBTru	Paid
1979 - 1984	$27.50	$225	$_____

Stone Church — 50591

Dates	OSRP	GBTru	Paid
1979 - 1980	$32	$875	$_____

• Similar to 1977 Stone Church, this steeple is approximately 8½" high.
• Felt was glued to the bottom at the factory to conceal cracks and chips.

School House — 50609

Dates	OSRP	GBTru	Paid
1979 - 1982	$30	$375	$_____

• Varies from reddish-brown to dark brown.
• American flag is separate in box.

Tudor House — 50617

Dates	OSRP	GBTru	Paid
1979 - 1981	$25	$295	$_____

• Another design with the same name was issued in this village in 2001.

Mission Church

50625

Dates	OSRP	GBTru	Paid
1979 - 1980	$30	$1650	$_____

- The bell is sometimes missing.

Mobile Home

50633

Dates	OSRP	GBTru	Paid
1979 - 1980	$18	$1595	$_____

- The paint is usually thin and bubbly.
- The trailer hitch is easily broken off and, therefore, is sometimes missing.

Giant Trees

50658

Dates	OSRP	GBTru	Paid
1979 - 1982	$20	$235	$_____

Adobe House

50666

Dates	OSRP	GBTru	Paid
1979 - 1980	$18	$2350	$_____

- Factory imperfections such as dents and fingerprints are common.
- The extended roof beams are fragile.

Cathedral Church

50674

Dates	OSRP	GBTru	Paid
1980 - 1981	$36	$2900	$_____

- Inspired by St. Paul Cathedral in St. Paul, MN.
- Prone to crazing.
- Felt is sometimes glued on at the factory to conceal chips and cracks.

Stone Mill House

50682

Dates	OSRP	GBTru	Paid
1980 - 1982	$30	$455	$_____

- Separate bag of oats (intended to be hung from block and tackle) is often missing and decreases value.
- Window areas are often thin and fragile.

Snow Village

Snow Village

Colonial Farm House 50709

Dates	OSRP	GBTru	Paid
1980 - 1982	$30	$240	$_____

- All Saints Church (1986) was also issued with this item number.

Town Church 50717

Dates	OSRP	GBTru	Paid
1980 - 1982	$33	$375	$_____

- Carriage House (1986) was also issued with this item number.

Train Station With 3 Train Cars 50856

Dates	OSRP	GBTru	Paid
1980 - 1985	$100	$325	$_____

- In the first year, the set included a Station with 6 windows in front (top, left). A year later, the Station was larger with 8 windows in front (bottom, left), and the OSRP increased to $110. Set of 4. All pieces light.

Train Station 50873

Dates	OSRP	GBTru	Paid
1980 - 1981	$42	$120	$_____

- Station has 6 windows in front and 1 in the door.
- It was sold individually as well as part of the above set.

3 Train Cars 50865

Dates	OSRP	GBTru	Paid
1980 - 1982	$65	$160	$_____

- It was sold individually as well as part of the above set.
- Set of 3. All pieces light.

Wooden Clapboard — 50725

Dates	OSRP	GBTru	Paid
1981 - 1984	$32	$235	$_____

English Cottage — 50733

Dates	OSRP	GBTru	Paid
1981 - 1982	$25	$290	$_____

- Toy Shop (1986) was also issued with this item number.

Barn — 50741

Dates	OSRP	GBTru	Paid
1981 - 1984	$32	$335	$_____

- The cow at the side of the barn often has its ears and/or horns broken off.

Corner Store — 50768

Dates	OSRP	GBTru	Paid
1981 - 1983	$30	$215	$_____

- Apothecary (1986) was also issued with this item number.

Bakery — 50776

Dates	OSRP	GBTru	Paid
1981 - 1983	$30	$220	$_____

- Bakery (1986) was also issued with this item number.

English Church — 50784

Dates	OSRP	GBTru	Paid
1981 - 1982	$30	$335	$_____

- Diner (1986) was also issued with this item number.
- Cross is separate in box.

Snow Village

Large Single Tree — 50806

Dates	OSRP	GBTru	Paid
1981 - 1989	$17	$40	$____

- Throughout the years there were mold changes with the design becoming more and more detailed.
- Amount of snow on the trees varies greatly.

Skating Pond — 50172

Dates	OSRP	GBTru	Paid
1982 - 1984	$25	$285	$____

- Snowman easily breaks off.
- Set of 2 includes pond and separate lighted trees.
- Do not confuse this piece with the 1978 Skating Pond/Duck Set.

Street Car — 50199

Dates	OSRP	GBTru	Paid
1982 - 1984	$16	$325	$____

- The "electrical hook-up" on roof often causes collectors to believe a pole should be included, but this is not so.
- Cathedral Church (1987) was also issued with this item number.

Centennial House — 50202

Dates	OSRP	GBTru	Paid
1982 - 1984	$32	$285	$____

- The front steps and extension are fragile.

Carriage House — 50210

Dates	OSRP	GBTru	Paid
1982 - 1984	$28	$220	$____

- Another design with the same name was issued in this village in 1986.

Pioneer Church — 50229

Dates	OSRP	GBTru	Paid
1982 - 1984	$30	$305	$____

- The front steps are fragile.

Swiss Chalet

50237

Dates	OSRP	GBTru	Paid
1982 - 1984	**$28**	**$385**	**$_____**

- Sometimes came from the factory with uneven and bubbly paint on the roof.

Bank

50245

Dates	OSRP	GBTru	Paid
1982 - 1983	**$32**	**$505**	**$_____**

- Check areas around the staircase and revolving door.
- Dentist sign at stairway is often broken off.
- Cumberland House (1987) was also issued with this item number.

Gabled House

50814

Dates	OSRP	GBTru	Paid
1982 - 1983	**$30**	**$310**	**$_____**

- Early samples are rust color; production pieces are white.
- Early release to GCC dealers.
- Red Barn (1987) was also issued with this item number.

Flower Shop

50822

Dates	OSRP	GBTru	Paid
1982 - 1983	**$25**	**$390**	**$_____**

- Window frames vary from brown to green.
- Flowers are fragile.
- Jefferson School (1987) was also issued with this item number.

New Stone Church

50830

Dates	OSRP	GBTru	Paid
1982 - 1984	**$32**	**$335**	**$_____**

- This is often not as glossy as most Snow Village pieces.
- Early release to GCC dealers.

Town Hall

50008

Dates	OSRP	GBTru	Paid
1983 - 1984	**$32**	**$285**	**$_____**

- Metal weathervane is separate in box. It is rare to find a Town Hall with its weathervane.

Snow Village

Snow Village

Grocery 50016

Dates	OSRP	GBTru	Paid
1983 - 1985	**$35**	**$275**	$_____

• The staircase is very fragile.

Victorian Cottage 50024

Dates	OSRP	GBTru	Paid
1983 - 1984	**$35**	**$310**	$_____

Governor's Mansion 50032

Dates	OSRP	GBTru	Paid
1983 - 1985	**$32**	**$255**	$_____

• The ironwork for the cupola is separate in box and is often missing.

Turn Of The Century 50040

Dates	OSRP	GBTru	Paid
1983 - 1986	**$36**	**$195**	$_____

• Bottom inscription reads "Turn The Time Of Century."
• The three chimneys are very fragile, especially the one on the center peak.

Gingerbread House 50253

Dates	OSRP	GBTru	Paid
1983 - 1984	**$24**	**$395**	$_____

• Besides lighted version, there is also a very rare non-lighted bank with a coin slot that was sold as a giftware item as opposed to part of Snow Village.

Village Church 50261

Dates	OSRP	GBTru	Paid
1983 - 1984	**$30**	**$415**	$_____

• Very similar to Parish Church (1984).
• Early release to GCC dealers.

Gothic Church — 50288

Dates	OSRP	GBTru	Paid
1983 - 1986	**$36**	**$215**	$_____

- The cross at the top is easily broken off.

Parsonage — 50296

Dates	OSRP	GBTru	Paid
1983 - 1985	**$35**	**$325**	$_____

- The cross atop the gable is easily broken off.

Wooden Church — 50318

Dates	OSRP	GBTru	Paid
1983 - 1985	**$30**	**$345**	$_____

Fire Station — 50326

Dates	OSRP	GBTru	Paid
1983 - 1984	**$32**	**$385**	$_____

- Varies with and without Dalmatian. Close examination should reveal whether a piece without a Dalmatian was made that way or if the dog was broken off.

English Tudor — 50334

Dates	OSRP	GBTru	Paid
1983 - 1985	**$30**	**$225**	$_____

- Chimneys are fragile.

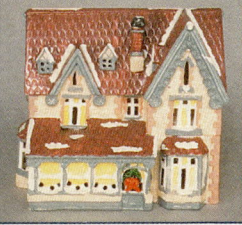

Chateau — 50849

Dates	OSRP	GBTru	Paid
1983 - 1984	**$35**	**$375**	$_____

- This is often not as glossy as most Snow Village pieces.
- Early release to GCC dealers.

Snow Village

Snow Village

Main Street House 50059

Dates	OSRP	GBTru	Paid
1984 - 1986	$27	$210	$_____

• Early release to GCC dealers.

Stratford House 50075

Dates	OSRP	GBTru	Paid
1984 - 1986	$28	$155	$_____

Haversham House 50083

Dates	OSRP	GBTru	Paid
1984 - 1987	$37	$200	$_____

• Early release to GCC dealers. These are larger, heavier, more impressive, and subject to more defects than those shipped later.   **GBTru: $215**   Paid: $_____

Galena House 50091

Dates	OSRP	GBTru	Paid
1984 - 1985	$32	$335	$_____

• The front steps are fragile.

River Road House 50105

Dates	OSRP	GBTru	Paid
1984 - 1987	$36	$170	$_____

• Early release to GCC dealers. These have window above door and transoms above lower front windows cut out. Later ones do not.

Delta House 50121

Dates	OSRP	GBTru	Paid
1984 - 1986	$32	$250	$_____

• Ironwork for the top of the tower is separate in box and is often missing.

Bayport 50156

Dates	OSRP	GBTru	Paid
1984 - 1986	**$30**	**$195**	$_____

Congregational Church 50342

Dates	OSRP	GBTru	Paid
1984 - 1985	**$28**	**$535**	$_____

- It is rare to find one with a straight steeple.
- The steeple is easily broken.

Trinity Church 50350

Dates	OSRP	GBTru	Paid
1984 - 1986	**$32**	**$285**	$_____

Summit House 50369

Dates	OSRP	GBTru	Paid
1984 - 1985	**$28**	**$350**	$_____

- The porch columns are crooked on almost all examples of this design.
- Do not handle by porch columns.

New School House 50377

Dates	OSRP	GBTru	Paid
1984 - 1986	**$35**	**$250**	$_____

- American flag is separate in box.

Parish Church 50393

Dates	OSRP	GBTru	Paid
1984 - 1986	**$32**	**$275**	$_____

- Very similar to Village Church (1993).

Snow Village

Stucco Bungalow 50458

Dates	OSRP	GBTru	Paid
1985 - 1986	**$30**	**$345**	$_____

Williamsburg House 50466

Dates	OSRP	GBTru	Paid
1985 - 1988	**$37**	**$125**	$_____

- Entryway attachment is fragile.
- The paint on the building is known to suddenly develop cracks under the glaze after a period of time.

Plantation House 50474

Dates	OSRP	GBTru	Paid
1985 - 1987	**$37**	**$95**	$_____

- Do not handle by porch columns.

Church Of The Open Door 50482

Dates	OSRP	GBTru	Paid
1985 - 1988	**$34**	**$120**	$_____

- Despite its name, the door on this design is closed.

Spruce Place 50490

Dates	OSRP	GBTru	Paid
1985 - 1987	**$33**	**$215**	$_____

- The area around the porch and steps is easily damaged.

Duplex 50504

Dates	OSRP	GBTru	Paid
1985 - 1987	**$35**	**$130**	$_____

Depot And Train With 2 Train Cars   50512

Dates	OSRP	GBTru	Paid
1985 - 1988	$65	$120	$_____

- There are 3 variations:
  1. Brown Depot with gray cornerstones (top) and Train Car with yellow windows.
  2. Brick Depot without cornerstones and Train Car with yellow windows (bottom).
  3. Brick Depot without cornerstones and Train Car with white windows.
- Though referred to as a set of 2, it includes the Depot, 2-piece train, and a ceramic track.

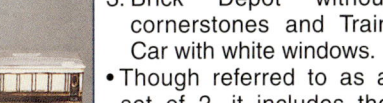

Ridgewood   50520

Dates	OSRP	GBTru	Paid
1985 - 1987	$35	$145	$_____

- Do not handle by porch columns.

Waverly Place   50415

Dates	OSRP	GBTru	Paid
1986 - 1986	$35	$295	$_____

- Inspired by Gingerbread Mansion in Ferndale, CA.
- Early release to GCC dealers.
- Squirrel is often missing.

Twin Peaks   50423

Dates	OSRP	GBTru	Paid
1986 - 1986	$32	$375	$_____

- The peaks are easily damaged.
- Early release to GCC dealers.

2101 Maple   50431

Dates	OSRP	GBTru	Paid
1986 - 1986	$32	$250	$_____

- The turret peak is easily damaged.
- Early release to GCC dealers.

Snow Village

Lincoln Park Duplex   50601

Dates	OSRP	GBTru	Paid
1986 - 1988	$33	$130	$_____

Sonoma House   50628

Dates	OSRP	GBTru	Paid
1986 - 1988	$33	$140	$_____

- Early release to GCC dealers.

Highland Park House   50636

Dates	OSRP	GBTru	Paid
1986 - 1988	$35	$140	$_____

- The chimney is fragile.
- Early release to GCC dealers.

Beacon Hill House   50652

Dates	OSRP	GBTru	Paid
1986 - 1988	$31	$160	$_____

- This design is often confused with the Pacific Heights House because they were mislabeled in the Department 56 Snow Village Collectors Album.

Pacific Heights House   50660

Dates	OSRP	GBTru	Paid
1986 - 1988	$33	$95	$_____

- This design is often confused with the Beacon Hill House because they were mislabeled in the Department 56 Snow Village Collectors Album.

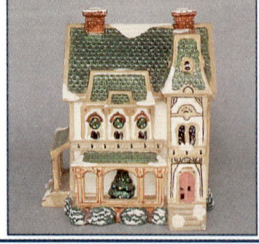

Ramsey Hill House   50679

Dates	OSRP	GBTru	Paid
1986 - 1989	$36	$95	$_____

- Early release to GCC dealers. Pieces in early release are brighter than those shipped later.

Saint James Church — 50687

Dates	OSRP	GBTru	Paid
1986 - 1988	$37	$130	$_____

• The cross on the center peak is easily broken off.

All Saints Church — 50709

Dates	OSRP	GBTru	Paid
1986 - 1997	$38	$50	$_____

• Colonial Farm House (1980) was also issued with this item number.

Carriage House — 50717

Dates	OSRP	GBTru	Paid
1986 - 1988	$29	$110	$_____

• Town Church (1980) was also issued with this item number.
• Another design with the same name was issued in this village in 1982.

Toy Shop — 50733

Dates	OSRP	GBTru	Paid
1986 - 1990	$36	$90	$_____

• Inspired by the Finch Building in Hastings, MN.
• Decorative attachments on the roof are fragile.
• English Cottage (1981) was also issued with this item number.

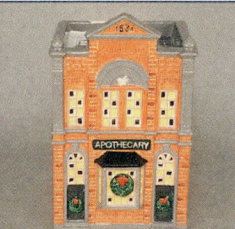

Apothecary — 50768

Dates	OSRP	GBTru	Paid
1986 - 1990	$34	$80	$_____

• Sleeves often read "Antique Shop."
• Inspired by the former City Hall in Hastings, MN.
• Corner Store (1981) was also issued with this item number.

Bakery — 50776

Dates	OSRP	GBTru	Paid
1986 - 1991	$35	$75	$_____

• Inspired by the Scofield Building in Northfield, MN.
• The awnings are fragile.
• Bakery (1981) was also issued with this item number.

Snow Village

Diner   50784

Dates	OSRP	GBTru	Paid
1986 - 1987	$22	$595	$_____

- Also known as Mickey's and Mickey's Diner.
- Inspired by Mickey's Diner in St. Paul, MN.
- English Church (1981) was also issued with this item number.

St. Anthony Hotel & Post Office   50067

Dates	OSRP	GBTru	Paid
1987 - 1989	$40	$90	$_____

- American flag is separate in box.

Snow Village Factory   50130

Dates	OSRP	GBTru	Paid
1987 - 1989	$45	$110	$_____

- Smokestack is a separate piece from building.
- The dark burgundy paint on the building is known to suddenly develop cracks under the glaze after a period of time.

Cathedral Church   50199

Dates	OSRP	GBTru	Paid
1987 - 1990	$50	$85	$_____

- Street Car (1982) was also issued with this item number.

Cumberland House   50245

Dates	OSRP	GBTru	Paid
1987 - 1995	$42	$55	$_____

- Do not handle by the columns.
- Bank (1982) was also issued with this item number.

Springfield House   50270

Dates	OSRP	GBTru	Paid
1987 - 1990	$40	$75	$_____

Lighthouse 50300

Dates	OSRP	GBTru	Paid
1987 - 1988	**$36**	**$415**	$_____

- There are 2 variations:
  Tower painted white and unglazed.
  Tower painted off-white and glazed.
- Do not handle by the tower.

Red Barn 50814

Dates	OSRP	GBTru	Paid
1987 - 1992	**$38**	**$90**	$_____

- Early release to GCC dealers.
- Gabled House (1982) was also issued with this item number.

Jefferson School 50822

Dates	OSRP	GBTru	Paid
1987 - 1991	**$36**	**$130**	$_____

- Early release to GCC dealers.
- Bell is sometimes missing from tower.
- Flower Shop (1982) was also issued with this item number.

Farm House 50890

Dates	OSRP	GBTru	Paid
1987 - 1992	**$40**	**$55**	$_____

- Do not handle by porch columns or railings.

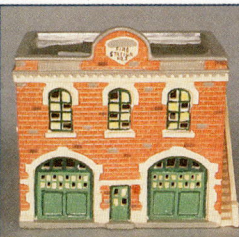

Fire Station No. 2 50911

Dates	OSRP	GBTru	Paid
1987 - 1989	**$40**	**$160**	$_____

- Staircase is easily damaged.
- Early release to GCC dealers.

Snow Village Resort Lodge 50920

Dates	OSRP	GBTru	Paid
1987 - 1989	**$55**	**$115**	$_____

Village Market — 50440

Dates	OSRP	GBTru	Paid
1988 - 1991	**$39**	**$80**	$_____

- Color varies from mint green to cream.
- Sisal tree on top of roof is packaged separately in the box and is often missing.
- Early release to GCC dealers.

Kenwood House — 50547

Dates	OSRP	GBTru	Paid
1988 - 1990	**$50**	**$125**	$_____

- Do not handle by porch columns.
- Early release to GCC dealers.

Maple Ridge Inn — 51217

Dates	OSRP	GBTru	Paid
1988 - 1990	**$55**	**$65**	$_____

- Inspired by the actual Maple Ridge Inn in Cambridge, NY. The home once belonged to relatives of painter Grandma Moses who visited there often.
- Early release to GCC dealers.

Village Station And Train — 51225

Dates	OSRP	GBTru	Paid
1988 - 1992	**$65**	**$85**	$_____

- Train cars do not light.
- Set of 4.

Cobblestone Antique Shop — 51233

Dates	OSRP	GBTru	Paid
1988 - 1992	**$36**	**$65**	$_____

- On rare occasion, the silk-screened windows detach.

Corner Cafe 51241

Dates	OSRP	GBTru	Paid
1988 - 1991	**$37**	**$85**	**$_____**

- On rare occasion, the silk-screened windows detach.

Single Car Garage 51250

Dates	OSRP	GBTru	Paid
1988 - 1990	**$22**	**$40**	**$_____**

- In many cases, the box must be broken in order to safely remove the piece.
- The tree attached to the back is indeed supposed to have holes drilled in it.

Home Sweet Home 51268

Dates	OSRP	GBTru	Paid
1988 - 1991	**$60**	**$95**	**$_____**

- Inspired by the East Hampton, NY historic home of John Howard Payne, composer of "Home Sweet Home."
- The windmill blades are packaged separately in the box and are made of metal.
- Set of 2.

Redeemer Church 51276

Dates	OSRP	GBTru	Paid
1988 - 1992	**$42**	**$60**	**$_____**

Service Station 51284

Dates	OSRP	GBTru	Paid
1988 - 1991	**$37.50**	**$165**	**$_____**

- Also known as Big Bill's Service Station which is the inscription on the bottom.
- Set of 2 includes Station and pumps.

Snow Village

Stonehurst House — 51403

Dates	OSRP	GBTru	Paid
1988 - 1994	**$37.50**	**$50**	$_____

Palos Verdes — 51411

Dates	OSRP	GBTru	Paid
1988 - 1990	**$37.50**	**$60**	$_____

• A small potted tree is packaged separately in the box.

Jingle Belle Houseboat — 51144

Dates	OSRP	GBTru	Paid
1989 - 1991	**$42**	**$180**	$_____

• Bell is packaged separately in box and is often missing.

Colonial Church — 51195

Dates	OSRP	GBTru	Paid
1989 - 1992	**$60**	**$70**	$_____

• The gray paint at steps and porch sometimes curls up and peels off.
• Do not handle by the columns.
• Early release to GCC dealers.

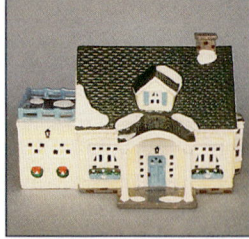

North Creek Cottage — 51209

Dates	OSRP	GBTru	Paid
1989 - 1992	**$45**	**$65**	$_____

• Do not handle by the columns.
• Early release to GCC dealers.

Paramount Theater — 51420

Dates	OSRP	GBTru	Paid
1989 - 1993	**$42**	**$145**	$_____

• Decals make cleaning this piece a delicate job.

Doctor's House 51438

Dates	OSRP	GBTru	Paid
1989 - 1992	**$56**	**$105**	$_____

- Do not handle by columns.

Courthouse 51446

Dates	OSRP	GBTru	Paid
1989 - 1993	**$65**	**$185**	$_____

- Inspired by the Gibson County Courthouse in Princetown, IN.
- Do not handle by tower.

Village Warming House 51454

Dates	OSRP	GBTru	Paid
1989 - 1992	**$42**	**$60**	$_____

- Includes 4 removable sisal trees.

J. Young's Granary 51497

Dates	OSRP	GBTru	Paid
1989 - 1992	**$45**	**$85**	$_____

Pinewood Log Cabin 51500

Dates	OSRP	GBTru	Paid
1989 - 1995	**$37.50**	**$55**	$_____

- Do not handle by porch columns.
- Early release to GCC dealers.

56 Flavors Ice Cream Parlor 51519

Dates	OSRP	GBTru	Paid
1990 - 1992	**$42**	**$165**	$_____

- Stem on cherry is often broken off and is often missing.
- "Parlor" decal comes off easily.
- Early release to GCC dealers.

Snow Village

Morningside House 51527

Dates	OSRP	GBTru	Paid
1990 - 1992	$45	$75	$_____

• Includes 5 removable sisal trees.

Mainstreet Hardware Store 51535

Dates	OSRP	GBTru	Paid
1990 - 1993	$42	$75	$_____

• Sample pieces have blue awnings and window trim. They were changed to green for the actual production.

Village Realty 51543

Dates	OSRP	GBTru	Paid
1990 - 1993	$42	$55	$_____

Spanish Mission Church 51551

Dates	OSRP	GBTru	Paid
1990 - 1992	$42	$80	$_____

• Inspired by the then-named Enga Memorial Chapel in Minneapolis, MN.
• Bell in tower is easily lost.
• Crosses on roof and in graveyard are fragile.

Prairie House 51560

Dates	OSRP	GBTru	Paid
1990 - 1993	$42	$75	$_____

• American Architecture Series.
• Includes 2 removable sisal trees.

Queen Anne Victorian 51578

Dates	OSRP	GBTru	Paid
1990 - 1996	$48	$65	$_____

• American Architecture Series.
• Do not handle by columns.

Snow Village

The Christmas Shop — 50970

Dates	OSRP	GBTru	Paid
1991 - 1996	**$37.50**	**$55**	$____

- Early release to GCC and Showcase dealers.

Snow Village

Oak Grove Tudor — 54003

Dates	OSRP	GBTru	Paid
1991 - 1994	**$42**	**$55**	$____

- Early release to Showcase dealers.

The Honeymooner Motel — 54011

Dates	OSRP	GBTru	Paid
1991 - 1993	**$42**	**$95**	$____

- The moon and stars symbol on the peak are easily damaged.
- Early release to Showcase dealers.

Village Greenhouse — 54020

Dates	OSRP	GBTru	Paid
1991 - 1995	**$35**	**$55**	$____

- The greenhouse "glass" often discolors with age.

Southern Colonial — 54038

Dates	OSRP	GBTru	Paid
1991 - 1994	**$48**	**$75**	$____

- American Architecture Series.
- 2 small sisal trees are separate in the box.
- Do not handle by columns or railings.

Gothic Farmhouse — 54046

Dates	OSRP	GBTru	Paid
1991 - 1997	**$48**	**$70**	$____

- American Architecture Series.
- Do not handle by columns.

Snow Village

Finklea's Finery: Costume Shop — 54054

Dates	OSRP	GBTru	Paid
1991 - 1993	$45	$65	$_____

• Some decals detach easily.

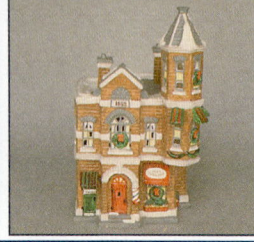

Jack's Corner Barber Shop — 54062

Dates	OSRP	GBTru	Paid
1991 - 1994	$42	$85	$_____

• The turret is easily damaged.

Double Bungalow — 54070

Dates	OSRP	GBTru	Paid
1991 - 1994	$45	$55	$_____

Grandma's Cottage — 54208

Dates	OSRP	GBTru	Paid
1992 - 1996	$42	$75	$_____

• Do not handle by columns or railings.
• Early release to GCC dealers.

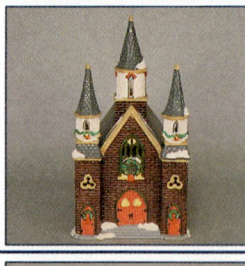

St. Luke's Church — 54216

Dates	OSRP	GBTru	Paid
1992 - 1994	$45	$55	$_____

• Early release to GCC dealers.

Village Post Office — 54224

Dates	OSRP	GBTru	Paid
1992 - 1995	$35	$70	$_____

• Early release to Showcase dealers.

Al's TV Shop 54232

Dates	OSRP	GBTru	Paid
1992 - 1995	**$40**	**$45**	$_____

- Television antenna is packaged separately in the box.

Good Shepherd Chapel & Church School 54240

Dates	OSRP	GBTru	Paid
1992 - 1996	**$72**	**$70**	$_____

- Though designed to do so, the two pieces do not always fit together well.
- Decals fall off easily.
- Set of 2.

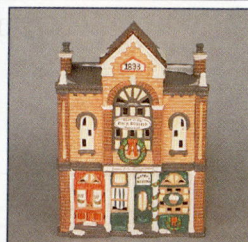

Print Shop & Village News 54259

Dates	OSRP	GBTru	Paid
1992 - 1994	**$37.50**	**$70**	$_____

- Do not handle by columns.

Hartford House 54267

Dates	OSRP	GBTru	Paid
1992 - 1995	**$55**	**$65**	$_____

- Do not handle by columns or railings.

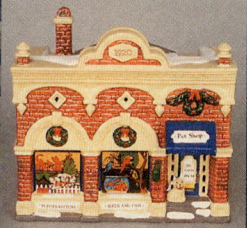

Village Vet And Pet Shop 54275

Dates	OSRP	GBTru	Paid
1992 - 1995	**$32**	**$75**	$_____

- Early pieces read "Vetrinary."
- Decals fall off easily.

Craftsman Cottage 54372

Dates	OSRP	GBTru	Paid
1992 - 1995	**$55**	**$65**	$_____

- American Architecture Series.

Snow Village

Village Station — 54380

Dates	OSRP	GBTru	Paid
1992 - 1997	$65	$85	$____

- Decals fall off easily.

Airport — 54399

Dates	OSRP	GBTru	Paid
1992 - 1996	$60	$95	$____

- Loudspeaker and propeller are easily damaged.
- Do not handle by tower.

Nantucket Renovation — 54410

Dates	OSRP	GBTru	Paid
1993 - 1993	$55	$65	$____

- First limited (year of production) Snow Village design.
- Concept is how a "remodeled" Nantucket might appear 15 years after the original one was issued.
- Packaged in special "blueprint" sleeve.

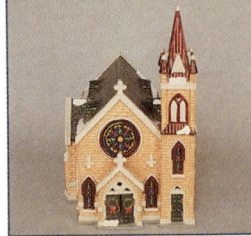

Mount Olivet Church — 54429

Dates	OSRP	GBTru	Paid
1993 - 1996	$65	$85	$____

- Crosses on peaks are easily damaged.

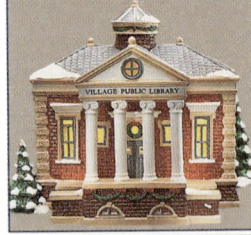

Village Public Library — 54437

Dates	OSRP	GBTru	Paid
1993 - 1997	$55	$75	$____

- Do not handle by columns.

Woodbury House — 54445

Dates	OSRP	GBTru	Paid
1993 - 1996	$45	$55	$____

- Do not handle by columns or railing.

Hunting Lodge   54453

Dates	OSRP	GBTru	Paid
1993 - 1996	**$50**	**$150**	$____

- Antlers are easily damaged.

Dairy Barn   54461

Dates	OSRP	GBTru	Paid
1993 - 1997	**$55**	**$75**	$____

- Weathervane is packaged separately in the box.

Dinah's Drive-In   54470

Dates	OSRP	GBTru	Paid
1993 - 1996	**$45**	**$105**	$____

- The name "Dinah" was inspired by the line "Someone's in the kitchen with Dinah" in the song "I've Been Working on the Railroad."
- The straw in the rooftop milk shake is easily damaged.

Snowy Hills Hospital   54488

Dates	OSRP	GBTru	Paid
1993 - 1996	**$48**	**$115**	$____

- A portion of the proceeds benefited AmFAR—the American Foundation for AIDS Research.
- Do not handle by columns.

Fisherman's Nook Cabins   54615

Dates	OSRP	GBTru	Paid
1994 - 1999	**$50**	**$70**	$____

- Cabins differ only by names "Bass" and "Trout."
- Railings are very fragile.
- Set of 2.

Snow Village

Fisherman's Nook Resort   54607

Dates	OSRP	GBTru	Paid
1994 - 1999	$75	$80	$____

- Sign on side is very fragile.

Snow Village Starter Set   54623

Dates	OSRP	GBTru	Paid
1994 - 1996	$50	$60	$____

- First available at GCC Open House event in November 1994.
- Set of 6 includes **Shady Oak Church** (named for street adjacent to Department 56's office complex), "Sunday School Serenade," trees, and snow.

Wedding Chapel   54640

Dates	OSRP	GBTru	Paid
1994 - 2001	$55	$60	$____

- Bell is attached in tower.

Federal House   54650

Dates	OSRP	GBTru	Paid
1994 - 1997	$50	$65	$____

- American Architecture Series.
- Do not handle by columns.

Carmel Cottage   54660

Dates	OSRP	GBTru	Paid
1994 - 1997	$48	$50	$____

Skate & Ski Shop 54674

Dates	OSRP	GBTru	Paid
1994 - 1998	$50	$60	$_____

- Sign and snow extending from front are easily damaged.

Glenhaven House 54682

Dates	OSRP	GBTru	Paid
1994 - 1997	$45	$60	$_____

- Do not handle by columns.

Coca–Cola® brand Bottling Plant 54690

Dates	OSRP	GBTru	Paid
1994 - 1997	$65	$100	$_____

- First pieces do not have soda cases on loading platform, though some later pieces have lost theirs. Close examination should reveal this.
- Licensed by Coca-Cola®.

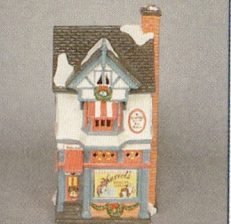

Marvel's Beauty Salon 54704

Dates	OSRP	GBTru	Paid
1994 - 1997	$37.50	$45	$_____

Christmas Cove Lighthouse 54836

Dates	OSRP	GBTru	Paid
1995ᴹ - 2001	$60	$75	$_____

- First lighthouse with separate bulb at top of tower.
- The top comes off easily and is susceptible to damage because it is a separate piece and does not fit tightly.

Coca–Cola® brand Corner Drugstore 54844

Dates	OSRP	GBTru	Paid
1995ᴹ - 1998	$55	$90	$_____

- Early samples have red "label" around the bottle at the top of the sign.
- Licensed by Coca-Cola®.

Snow Village

Snow Village

Peppermint Porch Day Care   54852

Dates	OSRP	GBTru	Paid
1995ᴹ - 1997	$45	$65	$____

- Early samples read "Peppermint Place."
- Do not handle by columns.

Snow Carnival Ice Palace   54850

Dates	OSRP	GBTru	Paid
1995 - 1998	$95	$125	$____

- Inspired by the snow castles constructed during carnivals in Minnesota.
- Acrylic turrets can become unglued or yellow with age.
- Set of 2 includes building and gate.

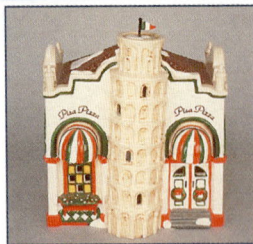

Pisa Pizza   5485

Dates	OSRP	GBTru	Paid
1995 - 1998	$35	$65	$____

Village Police Station   5485

Dates	OSRP	GBTru	Paid
1995 - 1998	$48	$65	$____

- Acrylic light globes are easily dislodged.
- Do not handle by attached doughnut shop.

Holly Brothers Garage   5485

Dates	OSRP	GBTru	Paid
1995 - 1998	$48	$65	$____

- Do not handle by columns or gas pumps.

Ryman Auditorium   548

Dates	OSRP	GBTru	Paid
1995 - 1997	$75	$100	$____

- Inspired by country music's Ryman Auditorium Nashville, TN, once home to the Grand Ole Opry.
- Licensed by Opryland USA, Inc.

Dutch Colonial — 54856

Dates	OSRP	GBTru	Paid
1995 - 1996	**$45**	**$55**	$_____

- American Architecture Series.

Beacon Hill Victorian — 54857

Dates	OSRP	GBTru	Paid
1995 - 1998	**$60**	**$70**	$_____

- Do not handle by columns or railing.

Bowling Alley — 54858

Dates	OSRP	GBTru	Paid
1995 - 1998	**$42**	**$55**	$_____

Starbucks Coffee® — 54859

Dates	OSRP	GBTru	Paid
1995 - 2000	**$48**	**$95**	$_____

- Do not handle by roof pediment.
- Licensed by Starbucks Coffee®.

Nick's Tree Farm — 54871

Dates	OSRP	GBTru	Paid
1996ᴹ - 1999	**$40**	**$50**	$_____

- Set of 10 includes Nick, hut, and 8 sisal trees.
- The coat, hat, and lantern hanging on the hut often come unglued.

Smokey Mountain Retreat — 54872

Dates	OSRP	GBTru	Paid
1996ᴹ - 2000	**$65**	**$75**	$_____

- Chimney "smokes" when used with Village Magic Smoke®. Smoking element sometimes leaks, requiring something being placed under it for protection.
- Do not handle by railings or columns.

Snow Village

Snow Village

Boulder Springs House   54873

Dates	OSRP	GBTru	Paid
1996^M - 1997	$60	$60	$_____

• Do not handle by columns or railing.

Reindeer Bus Depot   54874

Dates	OSRP	GBTru	Paid
1996^M - 1997	$42	$65	$_____

• Do not handle by columns, sign, or bench.

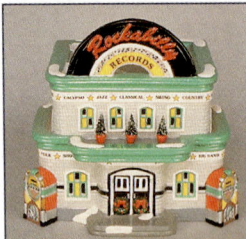

Rockabilly Records   54880

Dates	OSRP	GBTru	Paid
1996 - 1998	$45	$55	$_____

Christmas Lake High School   54881

Dates	OSRP	GBTru	Paid
1996 - 1999	$52	$75	$_____

• Attached basketball hoop is easily damaged.

Birch Run Ski Chalet   54882

Dates	OSRP	GBTru	Paid
1996 - 1999	$60	$75	$_____

• Do not handle by columns or railings.

Rosita's Cantina   5488

Dates	OSRP	GBTru	Paid
1996 - 1999	$50	$65	$_____

• Lighting fixtures are easily damaged when removing piece from box.

Shingle Victorian 54884

Dates	OSRP	GBTru	Paid
1996 - 1999	$55	$65	$_____

- American Architecture Series.
- Do not handle by columns or railings.

The Secret Garden Florist 54885

Dates	OSRP	GBTru	Paid
1996 - 2001	$50	$55	$_____

- The awning is cloth.
- Sign is separate in box.
- A similar design was produced for Bachman's in 1997. See the Special Design section.

Harley-Davidson® Motorcycle Shop 54886

Dates	OSRP	GBTru	Paid
1996 - 2002	$65	$85	$_____

- The gray paint on the front overhang's supports often peels. They are also very fragile.
- Licensed by Harley-Davidson®.

Mainstreet Gift Shop 54887

Dates	OSRP	GBTru	Paid
1997ᴹ - 1997	$50	$60	$_____

- To commemorate the 20th Anniversary of GCC, this design was available only through GCC member stores.
- Two signs are included—one with the GCC logo, and a blank one so dealers could personalize the design.

Snow Village Start A Tradition Set 54902

Dates	OSRP	GBTru	Paid
1997ᴹ - 1998	$100	$100	$_____

- It was first available for $75 during the 1997 Homes for the Holidays event.
- Set of 8 includes **Kringles Toy Shop**, **Nikki's Cocoa Shop**, "Saturday Morning Downtown" accessory, trees, snow, and road.
- Nikki's Cocoa Shop's hangtag reads "Kringle's Cocoa Shop."
- The handle on the mug is fragile.

Snow Village

Snow Village

Old Chelsea Mansion 54903

Dates	OSRP	GBTru	Paid
1997ᴹ - 1998	$85	$90	$_____

• Inspired by the New York, NY home of Clement C. Moore, author of "A Visit from St. Nicholas." Includes a book containing the classic poem and information about Moore and the mansion.

New Hope Church 54904

Dates	OSRP	GBTru	Paid
1997ᴹ - 1998	$60	$70	$_____

Ronald McDonald® House, The House That ♥ Built 08960

Dates	OSRP	GBTru	Paid
1997ᴹ - 1997	Promo	$260	$_____

• A limited edition design, this was made available as a fund raiser during the November 1997 Homes for the Holidays event. Proceeds benefited Ronald McDonald House Charities.

Christmas Barn Dance 5491

Dates	OSRP	GBTru	Paid
1997 - 1999	$65	$75	$_____

Italianate Villa 5491

Dates	OSRP	GBTru	Paid
1997 - 2001	$55	$75	$_____

• American Architecture Series.
• Spire is separate in box.
• Do not handle by columns.

Farm House 549

Dates	OSRP	GBTru	Paid
1997 - 2000	$50	$60	$_____

• Do not handle by columns.

Hershey's® Chocolate Shop — 54913

Dates	OSRP	GBTru	Paid
1997 - 2000	$55	$75	$_____

- The billboard on the roof is very fragile.
- Licensed by Hershey Foods.

McDonald's® — 54914

Dates	OSRP	GBTru	Paid
1997 - 1999	$65	$115	$_____

- First time people were included as an attachment.
- Because of the attachments and the arches, extra care should be taken when handling this piece.
- Licensed by McDonald's®.

Gracie's Dry Goods & General Store — 54915

Dates	OSRP	GBTru	Paid
1997 - 2000	$70	$85	$_____

- Do not handle by columns.
- Set of 2 includes Store and gas pumps.
- Licensed by Rapala.

Rollerama Roller Rink — 54916

Dates	OSRP	GBTru	Paid
1997 - 1999	$56	$65	$_____

- The lights on the building are functional.
- Do not handle by the front entryway.

Linden Hills Country Club — 54917

Dates	OSRP	GBTru	Paid
1997 - 2001	$60	$75	$_____

- Metal lanterns light from within.
- Linden Hills is an area near downtown Minneapolis, close to Lake Harriet.
- Set of 2 includes building and sign.

The Brandon Bungalow — 54918

Dates	OSRP	GBTru	Paid
1997 - 1999	$55	$65	$_____

- Brandon is a small resort town in northern Minnesota.

Snow Village

Rock Creek Mill House   54932

Dates	OSRP	GBTru	Paid
1998ᴹ - 1998	$64	$75	$_____

- Early samples have a glossy finish. Production pieces have a matte finish.
- The water wheel comes loose on occasion.

    Glossy Edition GBTru = $95 $_____

Carnival Carousel   54933

Dates	OSRP	GBTru	Paid
1998ᴹ - 2001	$150	$150	$_____

- Images on screen created by carousel inside building.
- Plays 30 songs.
- Includes AC adapter. Optional lights enhance appearance.

Snowy Pines Inn Exclusive Gift Set   54934

Dates	OSRP	GBTru	Paid
1998ᴹ - 1998	$65	$105	$_____

- Available during the 1998 Homes for the Holiday event.
- Set of 9 includes building, a 2 piece accessory "Decorate The Tree," trees, road, and snow.

Ronald McDonald® House, The House That ♥ Built   02210

Dates	OSRP	GBTru	Paid
1998ᴹ - 1998	Promo	$285	$_____

- Limited to only 5,600 pieces, this was made available as a fund raiser during the November 1998 Homes for the Holidays event. Proceeds benefited Ronald McDonald House Charities.

Center For The Arts   54940

Dates	OSRP	GBTru	Paid
1998 - 2000	$64	$70	$_____

- Sign for Art Center is separate in box.

Uptown Motors Ford® — 54941

Dates	OSRP	GBTru	Paid
1998 - 2002	$95	$110	$_____

- Working turntable inside building displays red Mustang.
- Set of 3 incudes building, car, and sign.
- Pennants and hanging sign packaged separately in box.
- Licensed by Ford Motor Co.

Fire Station #3 — 54942

Dates	OSRP	GBTru	Paid
1998 - 2003	$70	$85	$_____

- Turret peak is susceptible to damage when removing the piece from its box.

Stick Style House — 54943

Dates	OSRP	GBTru	Paid
1998 - 2000	$60	$70	$_____

- American Architecture Series.
- Do not handle by columns.

Hidden Ponds House — 54944

Dates	OSRP	GBTru	Paid
1998 - 2001	$50	$55	$_____

…Another Man's Treasure Garage — 54945

Dates	OSRP	GBTru	Paid
1998 - 2001	$60	$65	$_____

- Set of 22 includes building, items to be sold, and a string of pennants.

Snow Village

The Farmer's Co-Op Granary 54946

Dates	OSRP	GBTru	Paid
1998 - 2000	$64	$70	$_____

• Lamp is separate in box.

Lionel® Electric Train Shop 54947

Dates	OSRP	GBTru	Paid
1998 - 2000	$55	$75	$_____

• A similar design was produced for Allied Model Trains. See the Special Design section.
• Licensed by Lionel®.

Harley-Davidson® Manufacturing 54948

Dates	OSRP	GBTru	Paid
1998 - 2000	$80	$120	$_____

• The address reflects that of Harley-Davidson's Milwaukee, WI headquarters.
• Set of three includes building and two motorcycles.
• Licensed by Harley-Davidson®.

The Secret Garden Greenhouse 54949

Dates	OSRP	GBTru	Paid
1998 - 2001	$60	$65	$_____

• In addition to bulb and cord arrangement, interior lights along ceiling also light.
• A similar design was produced for Bachman's. See the Special Design section.

2000 Holly Lane 54977

Dates	OSRP	GBTru	Paid
1999ᴹ - 1999	$65	$105	$_____

• Limited to year of production.
• This is the first Snow Village design to include a three dimensional scene in the house.
• First available during the November 1999 Discover Department 56 event.
• Set of 11 includes house, gate, hedges, and snowman.

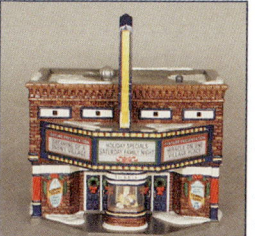

Cinema 56 — 54978

Dates	OSRP	GBTru	Paid
1999ᴹ - 2001	$85	$125	$____

- Marquee is interchangeable with optional accessory marquees.
- The lights around the marquee are functional.
- Do not handle by marquee.

A Home In The Making — 54979

Dates	OSRP	GBTru	Paid
1999ᴹ - 2001	$95	$90	$____

- A portion of the proceeds benefited Habitat for Humanity.
- Midyear introduction to select stores.
- Set of 5 includes the house, man climbing ladder, two men cutting board, two women carrying lumber, and sign.

Champsfield Stadium — 55001

Dates	OSRP	GBTru	Paid
1999 - 2001	$195	$200	$____

- Set of 24 includes two seating sections; two teams; two referees; fans; field; two goal posts; two billboards; U.S., Canadian, NFC, and AFC flags; and stickers and lettering for collector customization.
- Players' arms and waists move.
- Licensed by NFLP.

Village Bank & Trust — 55002

Dates	OSRP	GBTru	Paid
1999 - 2001	$75	$85	$____

- Lanterns on either side of the main entrance are functional.

Snow Village

Holy Spirit Church 55003

Dates	OSRP	GBTru	Paid
1999 - 2002	$70	$75	$_____

- Cross and plaque that can be personalized are separate in box.
- Do not handle by columns.
- Set of 2 includes church and sign.

Super Suds Laundromat 55006

Dates	OSRP	GBTru	Paid
1999 - 2001	$60	$60	$_____

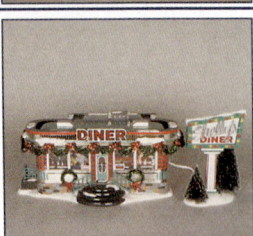

Shelly's Diner 55008

Dates	OSRP	GBTru	Paid
1999 -	$110	-	$_____

- Set of 2 includes Diner and lighted sign.

Cedar Point Cabin 55009

Dates	OSRP	GBTru	Paid
1999 - 2002	$66	$75	$_____

- A bird house is separate in box.

WSNO Radio 5501

Dates	OSRP	GBTru	Paid
1999 - 2002	$75	$80	$_____

- The light at the top of the antenna is functional.
- Lamp is separate in box.
- Customized version WCCO used as a promotional item at Twin Cities radio station.

Lucky Dragon Restaurant 5501

Dates	OSRP	GBTru	Paid
1999 - 2000	$75	$80	$_____

- Early sample reads "The Golden Dragon Restaurant."
- 8 lanterns are separate in box.
- The hanging lanterns are fragile.

Last Stop Gas Station   55012

Dates	OSRP	GBTru	Paid
1999 - 2001	$72	$75	$_____

- Set of 2 includes building and pumps.

Carpenter Gothic Bed & Breakfast   55043

Dates	OSRP	GBTru	Paid
2000ᴹ - 2003	$75	$95	$_____

- American Architecture Series.
- Do not handle by columns or railings.
- Set of 2 includes building and sign.

Silver Bells Christmas Shop Gift Set   55040

Dates	OSRP	GBTru	Paid
2000ᴹ - 2000	$75	$85	$_____

- Sold during the 2000 Discover Department 56 event.
- Limited to year of production.
- Silver bells commemorate Dept. 56's 25th anniversary.
- The lamppost at the tree lot is functional.
- Set of 4 includes Shop, "Oh, Christmas Tree" accessory, tree, and snow.

Elvis Presley's Graceland Gift Set   55041

Dates	OSRP	GBTru	Paid
2000ᴹ - 2001	$165	$175	$_____

- Sold during the 2000 Discover Department 56 event.
- Retired on January 8, 2001, Elvis' 66th birthday.
- Set of 6 includes Graceland, 1955 Pink Cadillac Fleetwood, wrought iron gate, original lawn decorations, and 2 sets of mylar twinkling trees.
- Licensed by EPE and GM.

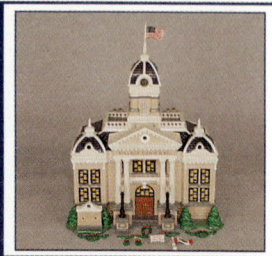

Village Town Hall — 55044

Dates	OSRP	GBTru	Paid
2000 - 2003	$96	$100	$_____

- 6 "add-on" garland pieces and sign allow holiday decor to be added to this non-snow building.
- U. S. and Canadian flags are separate in box.
- Spires and lampposts are fragile.

Candlerock Lighthouse Restaurant — 55045

Dates	OSRP	GBTru	Paid
2000 - 2001	$110	$125	$_____

- 25th Anniversary Limited Edition of 30,000.
- The top of the light tower is separate and can easily fall and be damaged.
- Flag and 3 lanterns are separate in box.

Palm Lounge Supper Club — 55046

Dates	OSRP	GBTru	Paid
2000 - 2001	$95	$100	$_____

- Set of 2 includes building and walkway.
- Posts on the walkway are fragile.

Frost And Sons 5 & Dime — 55047

Dates	OSRP	GBTru	Paid
2000 - 2002	$68	$70	$_____

- Do not handle by sign.
- Licensed by SWIMC, Inc. and Eveready Battery Co., Inc.

The Holiday House — 55048

Dates	OSRP	GBTru	Paid
2000 -	$90	-	$_____

- Santa and 4 reindeer are separate in box.

Buck's County™ Horse Barn — 55049

Dates	OSRP	GBTru	Paid
2000 - 2002	$72	$80	$_____

- Weathervane and lantern are separate in box.

Buck's County™ Farmhouse — 55051

Dates	OSRP	GBTru	Paid
2000 - 2002	**$75**	**$80**	$_____

- Weathervane is separate in box.
- Tree limbs are very fragile and are easily broken when removing or putting the piece in its box.

Abner's Implement Co. — 55052

Dates	OSRP	GBTru	Paid
2000 - 2003	**$85**	**$85**	$_____

- Buck's County Series.
- Set of 2 includes building and gas pump.
- Flag and lantern are separate in box.
- Licensed by Deere & Co.

Totem Town Souvenir Shop — 55053

Dates	OSRP	GBTru	Paid
2000 - 2002	**$68**	**$70**	$_____

- Sign and lantern are separate in box.

Timberlake Outfitters — 55054

Dates	OSRP	GBTru	Paid
2000 - 2002	**$75**	**$80**	$_____

- Block and tackle is separate in box.
- Oars are extremely fragile.
- Licensed by Bob Timberlake, Inc.

Crosby House — 55056

Dates	OSRP	GBTru	Paid
2000 - 2002	**$50**	**$55**	$_____

Lowell Inn — 55059

Dates	OSRP	GBTru	Paid
2001ᴹ - 2001	**$85**	**$145**	$_____

- Depicts the Stillwater, MN inn where the concept of the villages was conceived.
- Only available at Dept. 56's silver anniversary event.
- 16 flags (13 colonies, MN, US, D56) are separate in box.

Snow Village

Snow Village

Christmas Lake Chalet — 55061

Dates	OSRP	GBTru	Paid
2001ᴹ - 2001	$75	$85	$_____

- First available during the 2001 Holiday Discover Department 56 event.
- Fireplace flickers, and lanterns on porch light.
- Set of 5 includes Chalet, "The Final Touch" accessory, 2 sisal trees, and a bag of snow.

Tudor House — 55062

Dates	OSRP	GBTru	Paid
2001ᴹ - 2002	$60	$65	$_____

- American Architecture Series.
- Another design with the same name was issued in this village in 1979.

Stardust Drive-In Theater — 55064

Dates	OSRP	GBTru	Paid
2001ᴹ - 2003	$68	$75	$_____

- Animated screen with 12 different images.

Stardust Refreshment Stand — 55065

Dates	OSRP	GBTru	Paid
2001ᴹ - 2003	$50	$60	$_____

- Set of 7 includes Refreshment Stand and 6 speakers.

Juliette's School Of French Cuisine — 55063

Dates	OSRP	GBTru	Paid
2001 - 2002	$65	$75	$_____

- Mother's Day Spring promotion.
- Set of 4 includes School, sign, 2 potted shrubs, and extra sign which can be personalized.
- 5% of proceeds goes to fight against breast cancer.

McGuire's Irish Pub 55066

Dates	OSRP	GBTru	Paid
2001 - 2004	**$50**	**$55**	$____

- Designed to celebrate St. Partick's Day.
- Front banner is removable.
- Two lanterns are separate in the box.

Gus's Drive-In 55067

Dates	OSRP	GBTru	Paid
2001 - 2003	**$95**	**$105**	$____

- Set of 7 includes Drive-In, "Car Hop" accessory, 2 trays, 2 menus, and a sandwich board.

Woodlake Chapel Starter Set 55068

Dates	OSRP	GBTru	Paid
2001 - 2003	**$65**	**$70**	$____

- Set of 2 includes Chapel and 2 piece accessory "On Our Wedding Day."
- Cross and brass plaque which can be engraved are separate in the box.
- Cross attached to roof is very fragile.

Cedar Ridge School 55070

Dates	OSRP	GBTru	Paid
2001 - 2004	**$60**	**$60**	$____

- Flag, lantern, and brass plaque which can be engraved are separate in the box.

Snow Village

Snow Village

Krispy Kreme Doughnut Shop — 55071

Dates	OSRP	GBTru	Paid
2001 - 2004	$85	$85	$_____

- Set of 2 includes Shop and sign.
- Licensed by HDN Development Corporation.

Country Quilts And Pies — 55072

Dates	OSRP	GBTru	Paid
2001 - 2004	$65	$65	$_____

- Buck's County Series.
- Set of 2 includes building and "Handmade Quilts For Sale" accessory.

Polaris Snowmobile Dealership — 55078

Dates	OSRP	GBTru	Paid
2001 - 2003	$85	$80	$_____

- Sign is separate in the box.
- Licensed by Polaris Industries, Inc.

Village Legion Hall — 55080

Dates	OSRP	GBTru	Paid
2001 - 2003	$55	$55	$_____

- Set of 2 includes Hall and 2-piece accessory "Cannon And Flag."
- Second flag (with short staff) and lamppost are separate in the box.

Armed Forces Recruiting Station   55081

Dates	OSRP	GBTru	Paid
2001 - 2002	**$55**	**$65**	$_____

• Two signs and 2 flags are separate in the box.

Happy Easter House   55090

Dates	OSRP	GBTru	Paid
2001 -	**$50**	-	$_____

• Easter Series.
• "Happy Easter" sign is removable.
• Set of 3 includes house, 2-piece accessory "Egg Hunt."

Moonlight Bay Bunk And Breakfast   55074

Dates	OSRP	GBTru	Paid
2002ᴹ - 2004	**$75**	**$75**	$_____

• Set of 2 includes building and sign.

1224 Kissing Claus Lane   55091

Dates	OSRP	GBTru	Paid
2002ᴹ - 2002	**$75**	**$95**	$_____

• Holiday 2002 Special Edition.
• Animated and musical. Plays "I Saw Mommy Kissing Santa Claus."
• Set of 4 includes house, "Christmas Eve Delivery" accessory, a frosted topiary, and a bag of snow.
• Spires on roof are fragile.

Snow Village

Snow Village

Lily's Nursery & Gifts 55095

Dates	OSRP	GBTru	Paid
2002ᴹ - 2004	$65	$65	$_____

- Easter Series.
- Set of 3 includes building and 2 piece accessory, "Gifts For Easter."

Hearts & Blooms Cottage 55097

Dates	OSRP	GBTru	Paid
2002ᴹ -	$50	-	$_____

- Intended to be used as a Valentine's Day design.
- Set of 2 includes Cottage and "Young Love" accessory.

The Cocoa Stop 55096

Dates	OSRP	GBTru	Paid
2002ᴹ - 2002	$65	$145	$_____

- Club 56 dealer exclusive. Limited to 5,600 pieces.
- Many boxes and sleeves have a rippled effect.
- Certificate of authenticity and hot cocoa recipe are included in the box.

Red Owl Grocery Store 55303

Dates	OSRP	GBTru	Paid
2002 - 2003	$70	$75	$_____

- Named after a Midwest grocery store.
- Licensed by Supervalu, Inc.

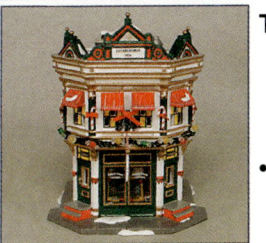

The Sweet Shop (Regular Issue)   55300

Dates	OSRP	GBTru	Paid
2002 - 2004	$65	$65	$____

• The Shop's hanging sign is extremely fragile.

(Early Release)   05923

Dates	OSRP	GBTru	Paid
2002ᴹ - 2002	$75	$105	$____

• This was an early release to department stores.
• Set of 5 includes the Shop, 2-piece lit accessory "Sampling The Treats" (pictured at left), frosted topiary with candy canes, and snow.

Harmony House   55302

Dates	OSRP	GBTru	Paid
2002 - 2004	$50	$50	$____

• Set of 3 includes the House, and 2 piece accessory, "Snowman Sonata And Fence."
• Can be personalized.

Rocky's 56 Filling Station   55305

Dates	OSRP	GBTru	Paid
2002 - 2004	$80	$80	$____

• Set of 3 includes the Station and 2 piece accessory, "56 Gasoline Pump And Sign."

Snow Village

Snow Village

Bungalow — 55304

Dates	OSRP	GBTru	Paid
2002 - 2004	$55	$55	$_____

- American Architecture Series.

Main Street Medical — 55306

Dates	OSRP	GBTru	Paid
2002 - 2004	$68	$70	$_____

- Can be personalized.

Jonathan The Bear Man's Carving Studio — 55307

Dates	OSRP	GBTru	Paid
2002 - 2003	$75	$80	$_____

- Limited to year of production.
- Named for an artist in Wyoming.

Dairy Land Creamery — 55308

Dates	OSRP	GBTru	Paid
2002 - 2004	$75	$75	$_____

Campbell's® Soup Counter — 55309

Dates	OSRP	GBTru	Paid
2002 - 2004	$60	$60	$_____

- Licensed by The Campbell Soup Co®.

The Frozen Swirl — 55318

Dates	OSRP	GBTru	Paid
2002 - 2004	$65	$65	$_____

Wright Bike Shop 55314

Dates	OSRP	GBTru	Paid
2002 - 2003	$65	$75	$_____

- Spring Gift Set.
- Set of 5 includes the Shop, "Let's Get A New Bike" accessory, 2 shrubs, and a summer tree.
- Can be personalized.
- Named for the Wright brothers.

Home For The Holidays Express 55320

Dates	OSRP	GBTru	Paid
2003ᴹ - 2003	$110	$135	$_____

- Holiday 2003 Special Edition.
- Musical. Plays "Home For The Holidays" and train sounds.
- Set of 11 includes train, station, "Welcoming Christmas To Town" accessory, vinyl track, birch tree, and a bag of snow.
- A special edition Home For The Holidays Caboose was issued in 2004 as a complementary piece.

Year Round Holiday House 55321

Dates	OSRP	GBTru	Paid
2003ᴹ - 2004	$75	$75	$_____

- Christmas Lane Series.
- Includes attachable decorations for five holidays.

American Hero Comics 55322

Dates	OSRP	GBTru	Paid
2003ᴹ - 2003	$65	$95	$_____

- Club 56 dealer exclusive. Limited to 5,600 pieces.

Snow Village

Sweetheart Candy Shop 55323

Dates	OSRP	GBTru	Paid
2003^M -	$50	-	$_____

• Valentine's Series.
• Candy decorations light up and flash.

Hard Rock Café Snow Village 55324

Dates	OSRP	GBTru	Paid
2003^M -	$85	-	$_____

• Includes pin.
• Licensed by Hard Rock Cafe International (USA), Inc.

Happy Easter Church 55325

Dates	OSRP	GBTru	Paid
2003^M -	$65	-	$_____

• Easter Series.
• Set of 3 includes Church, "Joyful Greetings" accessory, and 2 removable banners.

High Roller Riverboat Casino 55330

Dates	OSRP	GBTru	Paid
2003^M -	$110	-	$_____

• Special lighting effect on paddle wheel.

Village Train Station 55331

Dates	OSRP	GBTru	Paid
2003 -	$85	-	$_____

Mission Style House 55332

Dates	OSRP	GBTru	Paid
2003 -	$75	-	$____

• American Architecture Series.

Woody's Woodland Crafts 55333

Dates	OSRP	GBTru	Paid
2003 -	$45	-	$____

• Set of 2 includes building and "Wood Carvings For Sale" accessory.

Midtown Shops 55334

Dates	OSRP	GBTru	Paid
2003 -	$70	-	$____

Lot 56, Christmas Court 55335

Dates	OSRP	GBTru	Paid
2003 -	$65	-	$____

KBRR TV 55337

Dates	OSRP	GBTru	Paid
2003 -	$80	-	$____

• Can be personalized.
• Includes adapter.

Snow Village

Snow Village

Roosevelt Park Band Shell — 55338

Dates	OSRP	GBTru	Paid
2003 -	$65	-	$_____

- Set of 2 includes Band Shell and "Village Musicians" accessory.
- Adapter included.
- Christmas and Fourth Of July decorations are separate in box.

Vineland Estates Winery — 55339

Dates	OSRP	GBTru	Paid
2003 - 2004	$70	$70	$_____

- Numbered limited edition of 20,000.
- Can be personalized.

Friendly Used Car Sales — 55340

Dates	OSRP	GBTru	Paid
2003 -	$60	-	$_____

Pillsbury Doughboy™ Bake Shop — 55342

Dates	OSRP	GBTru	Paid
2003 -	$75	-	$_____

- Set of 2 includes Bake Shop and "Pillsbury Doughboy™" accessory.
- Licensed by The Pillsbury Company.

The Noel House 55341

Dates	OSRP	GBTru	Paid
2003 -	$85	-	$_____

• Christmas Lane Series.
• Includes an adapter.

Home For The Holidays Caboose

Dates	OSRP	GBTru	Paid
2004 - 2004	n/a	$795	$_____

• Limited to 1,000 pieces, it was distributed to collectors whose 2003 Homes For The Holidays Gift Set boxes contained special Department 56 holograms.

City Lights Christmas Trimmings 55348

Dates	OSRP	GBTru	Paid
2004^M -	$75	-	$_____

• Early release for City Lights in San Diego, CA.

Meadowbrook Church 55349

Dates	OSRP	GBTru	Paid
2004^M -	$65	-	$_____

• Can be personalized.
• Removeable Christmas decorations.

The Peppermint House 55350

Dates	OSRP	GBTru	Paid
2004^M - 2004	$75	$75	$_____

• Christmas Lane Series.
• Set of 5 includes building, "Buster Helps Out" accessory, lit tree, tree, and snow.
• Limited to year of production.

Snow Village

Snow Village

Winter Park Warming House   5535

Dates	OSRP	GBTru	Paid
2004^M - 2004	$65	$65	$____

• Club 56 dealer exclusive. Limited edition of 5,000.

American Bandstand   5535

Dates	OSRP	GBTru	Paid
2004^M -	$95	-	$____

• Animated.
• Plays "Bandstand Boogie."
• Licensed by Dick Clark Productions.

Chapel Of Love   5535

Dates	OSRP	GBTru	Paid
2004^M -	$50	-	$____

• Valentine's Series.
• Set of 2 includes the Chapel and "The Happy Couple" accessory.

Chocolate Bunny Factory   5535

Dates	OSRP	GBTru	Paid
2004^M -	$65	-	$____

• Easter Series.
• Set of 2 includes building and "The Best Part Of Easter" accessory.

Thanksgiving At Grandmother's House — 55358

Dates	OSRP	GBTru	Paid
2004 -	$75	-	$____

- Decorating set.
- Long Life Cordless Lighting.
- Set of 12 includes building, "Dinner Guests" accessory, tree, hay bale, pumpkins, gourds, and leaves.

Snow Village

Santa's Wonderland House — 55359

Dates	OSRP	GBTru	Paid
2004 -	$120	-	$____

- Christmas Lane Series.
- Adapter included.
- Train moves around house.

Budweiser Brewery — 55361

Dates	OSRP	GBTru	Paid
2004 -	$75	-	$____

- Inspired by real brewery in St. Louis, Missouri.
- Licensed by Anheuser-Busch, Inc.

Richardsonian Romanesque House — 55362

Dates	OSRP	GBTru	Paid
2004 -	$70	-	$____

- American Architecture Series.
- Limited to year of production.

Main Street Office Building — 55363

Dates	OSRP	GBTru	Paid
2004 -	$55	-	$____

- Can be personalized.

Snow Village

Christmas Time Post Office — 55364

Dates	OSRP	GBTru	Paid
2004 -	$60	-	$_____

• Can be personalized.

Village Pets - Sales & Service — 55365

Dates	OSRP	GBTru	Paid
2004 -	$60	-	$_____

St. Nick's Toy Land — 55366

Dates	OSRP	GBTru	Paid
2004 -	$75	-	$_____

• Decorating set.
• Long Life Cordless Lighting.

Hope Chest Consignment Shop — 55367

Dates	OSRP	GBTru	Paid
2004 -	$65	-	$_____

Long Haul Truck Stop — 55368

Dates	OSRP	GBTru	Paid
2004 -	$80	-	$_____

• Adapter included.
• Coffee cup sign blinks.

Grandpap's Cabin — 55369

Dates	OSRP	GBTru	Paid
2004 -	$50	-	$_____

• Weekend At The Lake Series.
• Includes a boat.

Cascades Marina			55370
Dates	OSRP	GBTru	Paid
2004 -	**$65**	-	$____

- Weekend At The Lake Series.
- Includes a boat.

Snow Village

Use the space(s) below to update your guide when the midyear introductions are announced.

_____ _____

	Dates	OSRP	GBTru	Paid
	____ - ____	$____	-	$____

_____ _____

	Dates	OSRP	GBTru	Paid
	____ - ____	$____	-	$____

_____ _____

	Dates	OSRP	GBTru	Paid
	____ - ____	$____	-	$____

_____ _____

	Dates	OSRP	GBTru	Paid
	____ - ____	$____	-	$____

Snow Village

	Dates	OSRP	GBTru	Paid
	___ - ___	$___	-	$___

	Dates	OSRP	GBTru	Paid
	___ - ___	$___	-	$___

	Dates	OSRP	GBTru	Paid
	___ - ___	$___	-	$___

	Dates	OSRP	GBTru	Paid
	___ - ___	$___	-	$___

	Dates	OSRP	GBTru	Paid
	___ - ___	$___	-	$___

	Dates	OSRP	GBTru	Paid
	___ - ___	$___	-	$___

Carolers

50641 - Set of 4
1979 - 1986
OSRP: $12
GBTru: $125
Paid: $_____

Ceramic Car

50690
1980 - 1986
OSRP: $5
GBTru: $45
Paid: $_____

Ceramic Sleigh

50792
1981 - 1986
OSRP: $5
GBTru: $45
Paid: $_____

Snowman With Broom

50180
1982 - 1990
OSRP: $3
GBTru: $2
Paid: $_____

• This is the first mixed media accessory. It's made of ceramic and straw.

Monks-A-Caroling

64599
1983 - 1984
OSRP: $6
GBTru: $45
Paid: $_____

• Blush on cheeks is lighter and diffused.
• 1982 giftware line had unglazed set (64602) w/paper books and cord sashes. **GBTru: $175**

Monks-A-Caroling

50407
1984 - 1988
OSRP: $6
GBTru: $45
Paid: $_____

• 1st: Bright red speckled rash on cheeks. 2nd: Blush on cheeks is a defined dot. Taller.

Scottie With Tree

50385
1984 - 1985
OSRP: $3
GBTru: $225
Paid: $_____

• Is also available with a white star on top of the tree.

Singing Nuns

50539
1985 - 1987
OSRP: $6
GBTru: $115
Paid: $_____

Auto With Tree

(Squashed Version)

50555

1985 - 2001

OSRP: $5

GBTru: $10

Paid: $_____

GBTru: $95

Paid: $_____

• The first pieces are less round and less detailed. See picture to the right.

Snow Kids Sled, Skis

50563 - Set of 2

1985 - 1987

OSRP: $11

GBTru: $40

Paid: $_____

• In 1987, this set was reduced in size and combined with Girl/Snowman, Boy to form Snow Kids.

Family Mom/Kids, Goose/Girl

50571 - Set of 2

1985 - 1988

OSRP: $11

GBTru: $40

Paid: $_____

• The first year's pieces were larger and less detailed than those produced in the later years.

Santa/Mailbox

50598 - Set of 2

1985 - 1988

OSRP: $11

GBTru: $40

Paid: $_____

• The first year's pieces were larger and less detailed than those produced in the later years.

Kids Around The Tree

50946

1986 - 1990

OSRP: $15

GBTru: $30

Paid: $_____

• The first year's pieces were larger and less detailed than those produced in the later years.

Girl/Snowman, Boy

50954 - Set of 2

1986 - 1987

OSRP: $11

GBTru: $40

Paid: $_____

• In 1987, this set was reduced in size and combined with Snow Kids Sled, Skis to form Snow Kids.

Shopping Girls With Packages

50962 - Set of 2

1986 - 1988

OSRP: $11

GBTru: $25

Paid: $_____

• The first year's pieces were larger and less detailed than those produced in the later years.

Snow Village Accessories

3 Nuns With Songbooks

51020
1987 - 1988
OSRP: $6
GBTru: $125
Paid: $_____

Praying Monks

51039
1987 - 1988
OSRP: $6
GBTru: $35
Paid: $_____

Children In Band

51047
1987 - 1989
OSRP: $15
GBTru: $20
Paid: $_____

Caroling Family

51055 - Set of 3
1987 - 1990
OSRP: $20
GBTru: $30
Paid: $_____

Taxi Cab

51063
1987 - 2000
OSRP: $6
GBTru: $6
Paid: $_____

Christmas Children

51071 - Set of 4
1987 - 1990
OSRP: $20
GBTru: $25
Paid: $_____

House For Sale Sign

51080
1987 - 1989
OSRP: $3.50
GBTru: $5
Paid: $_____

• A similar design with no writing was produced for GCC and given to collectors who made $100 purchases.

Snow Kids

51136 - Set of 4
1987 - 1990
OSRP: $20
GBTru: $30
Paid: $_____

• This set combines smaller versions of Snow Kids Sled, Skis (1985) and Girl/Snowman, Boy (1986).

Snow Village House For Sale Sign

Promo
1987 - 1987
OSRP: Promo
GBTru: $25
Paid: $_____

• This was free to dealers who placed their orders at Department 56 showrooms. It is a very rare accessory.

Man On Ladder Hanging Garland

51160
1988 - 1992
OSRP: $7.50
GBTru: $12
Paid: $_____

• Includes mixed media —ceramic man, wooden ladder, and sisal garland.

Hayride

51179
1988 - 1990
OSRP: $30
GBTru: $45
Paid: $_____

School Children

51187 - Set of 3
1988 - 1990
OSRP: $15
GBTru: $24
Paid: $_____

Apple Girl/Newspaper Boy

51292 - Set of 2
1988 - 1990
OSRP: $11
GBTru: $21
Paid: $_____

Woodsman And Boy

51306 - Set of 2
1988 - 1991
OSRP: $13
GBTru: $24
Paid: $_____

Doghouse/Cat In Garbage Can

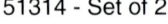

51314 - Set of 2
1988 - 1992
OSRP: $15
GBTru: $22
Paid: $_____

• Box reads "Cat And Dog."

Fire Hydrant & Mailbox

51322 - Set of 2
1988 - 1998
OSRP: $6
GBTru: $12
Paid: $_____

Water Tower

51330

1988 - 1991

OSRP: $20

GBTru: $55

Paid: $_____

• Similar designs were produced for retailers. See the Special Design section.

Nativity

51357

1988 - 2000

OSRP: $7.50

GBTru: $10

Paid: $_____

Woody Station Wagon

51365

1988 - 1990

OSRP: $6.50

GBTru: $20

Paid: $_____

School Bus, Snow Plow

51373 - Set of 2

1988 - 1991

OSRP: $16

GBTru: $52

Paid: $_____

Tree Lot

51381

1988 - 1999

OSRP: $33.50

GBTru: $36

Paid: $_____

• Includes mixed media —small ceramic shed, wooden fence, and 7 sisal trees.

Sisal Tree Lot

81833

1988 - 1991

OSRP: $45

GBTru: $65

Paid: $_____

Village Gazebo

51462

1989 - 1995

OSRP: $27

GBTru: $30

Paid: $_____

Choir Kids

51470

1989 - 1992

OSRP: $15

GBTru: $24

Paid: $_____

Snow Village Accessories

Snow Village Accessories

Special Delivery

51489 - Set of 2
1989 - 1990
OSRP: $16
GBTru: $65
Paid: $_____

• Retired after one year due to unauthorized use of red, white, and blue colors of U.S. Postal Service.

For Sale Sign

51667
1989 - 1998
OSRP: $4.50
GBTru: $5
Paid: $_____

• Similar designs were produced for retailers. See the Special Design section.

Street Sign

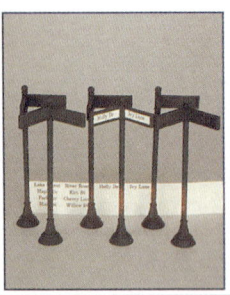

51675 - Set of 6
1989 - 1992
OSRP: $7.50
GBTru: $8
Paid: $_____

• Includes stickers (with street names and blank ones) for signs.
• Metal.

Kids Tree House

51683
1989 - 1991
OSRP: $25
GBTru: $36
Paid: $_____

• This was the first all resin accessory.

Bringing Home The Tree

51691
1989 - 1992
OSRP: $15
GBTru: $26
Paid: $_____

• Includes mixed media —ceramic sleigh and people with sisal tree.

Skate Faster Mom

51705
1989 - 1991
OSRP: $13
GBTru: $22
Paid: $_____

Crack The Whip

51713 - Set of 3
1989 - 1996
OSRP: $25
GBTru: $28
Paid: $_____

Through The Woods

51721 - Set of 2
1989 - 1991
OSRP: $18
GBTru: $26
Paid: $_____

Statue Of Mark Twain

51730
1989 - 1991
OSRP: $15
GBTru: $24
Paid: $_____

Calling All Cars

51748 - Set of 2
1989 - 1991
OSRP: $15
GBTru: $55
Paid: $_____

Village Stop Sign

51764 - Set of 2
1989 - 1998
OSRP: $5
GBTru: $5
Paid: $_____

• Metal.

Flag Pole

51772
1989 - 1999
OSRP: $8.50
GBTru: $10
Paid: $_____

• Metal, ceramic, and cloth.

Village Parking Meter

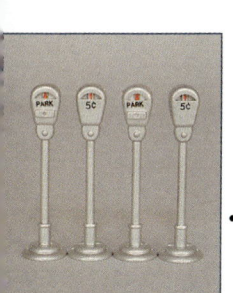

51780 - Set of 4
1989 - 1999
OSRP: $6
GBTru: $9
Paid: $_____

• Metal.

Mailbox

51799
1989 - 1990
OSRP: $3.50
GBTru: $15
Paid: $_____

• Retired after one year due to unauthorized use of red and blue colors of U.S.P.S.

Snow Village Promotional Sign

99481
1989 - 1990
OSRP: Promo
GBTru: $20
Paid: $_____

• Used as a promotional piece by Dept. 56 retailers.

Kids Decorating The Village Sign

51349
1990 - 1993
OSRP: $12.50
GBTru: $22
Paid: $_____

Snow Village Accessories

Down The Chimney He Goes

51586
1990 - 1993
OSRP: $6.50
GBTru: $7
Paid: $_____

• Adhesive strip allows this piece to be mounted on a building's roof.

Sno-Jet Snowmobile

51594
1990 - 1993
OSRP: $15
GBTru: $22
Paid: $_____

Sleighride

51608
1990 - 1992
OSRP: $30
GBTru: $45
Paid: $_____

Here We Come A Caroling

51616 - Set of 3
1990 - 1992
OSRP: $18
GBTru: $24
Paid: $_____

Home Delivery

51624 - Set of 2
1990 - 1992
OSRP: $16
GBTru: $30
Paid: $_____

Fresh Frozen Fish

51632 - Set of 2
1990 - 1993
OSRP: $20
GBTru: $30
Paid: $_____

A Tree For Me

51640 - Set of 2
1990 - 1995
OSRP: $7.50
GBTru: $12
Paid: $_____

• Ceramic with sisal trees.

A Home For The Holidays

51659
1990 - 1996
OSRP: $6.50
GBTru: $9
Paid: $_____

Special Delivery

51977 - Set of 2
1990 - 1992
OSRP: $16
GBTru: $28
Paid: $_____

• Re-issue of first Special Delivery (1989) after changing the color of the truck to red, white, and green.

Village Mail Box

51985
1990 - 1998
OSRP: $3.50
GBTru: $6
Paid: $_____

• Re-issue of Mailbox (1989) after changing the colors to red and green and putting "S.V. Mail" on front.

Christmas Trash Cans

52094 - Set of 2
1990 - 1998
OSRP: $7
GBTru: $10
Paid: $_____

• Metal, paper, and plastic.

Wreaths For Sale

54089 - Set of 4
1991 - 1994
OSRP: $27.50
GBTru: $34
Paid: $_____

• Ceramic with sisal wreaths.

Winter Fountain

54097
1991 - 1993
OSRP: $25
GBTru: $42
Paid: $_____

• Includes mixed media —ceramic and acrylic.

Cold Weather Sports

54100 - Set of 4
1991 - 1994
OSRP: $27.50
GBTru: $35
Paid: $_____

Come Join The Parade

54119
1991 - 1992
OSRP: $12.50
GBTru: $18
Paid: $_____

Village Marching Band

54127 - Set of 3
1991 - 1992
OSRP: $30
GBTru: $50
Paid: $_____

Snow Village Accessories

Snow Village Accessories

Christmas Cadillac

54135
1991 - 1994
OSRP: $9
GBTru: $15
Paid: $_____

Snowball Fort

54143 - Set of 3
1991 - 1993
OSRP: $27.50
GBTru: $36
Paid: $_____

Country Harvest

54151
1991 - 1993
OSRP: $13
GBTru: $18
Paid: $_____

Village Used Car Lot

54283 - Set of 5
1992 - 1997
OSRP: $45
GBTru: $45
Paid: $_____

Village Phone Booth

54291
1992 -
OSRP: $7.50
GBTru: -
Paid: $_____

Nanny And The Preschoolers

54305 - Set of 2
1992 - 1994
OSRP: $27.50
GBTru: $35
Paid: $_____

Early Morning Delivery

54313 - Set of 3
1992 - 1995
OSRP: $27.50
GBTru: $30
Paid: $_____

Christmas Puppies

54321 - Set of 2
1992 - 1996
OSRP: $27.50
GBTru: $33
Paid: $_____

Round & Round We Go! 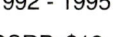 54330 - Set of 2 1992 - 1995 OSRP: $18 GBTru: $22 Paid: $_____	**A Heavy Snowfall**  54348 - Set of 2 1992 - 2001 OSRP: $16 GBTru: $22 Paid: $_____
We're Going To A Christmas Pageant 54356 1992 - 1994 OSRP: $15 GBTru: $18 Paid: $_____	**Winter Playground**  54364 1992 - 1995 OSRP: $20 GBTru: $32 Paid: $_____
Spirit Of Snow Village Airplane 54402 1992 - 1996 OSRP: $32.50 GBTru: $40 Paid: $_____ • This is very difficult to put back in box. See 1993 for item by the same name.	**Safety Patrol**  54496 - Set of 4 1993 - 1997 OSRP: $27.50 GBTru: $32 Paid: $_____
Christmas At The Farm  54500 - Set of 2 1993 - 1996 OSRP: $16 GBTru: $25 Paid: $_____	**Check It Out Bookmobile**  54518 - Set of 3 1993 - 1995 OSRP: $25 GBTru: $32 Paid: $_____

Snow Village Accessories

Tour The Village

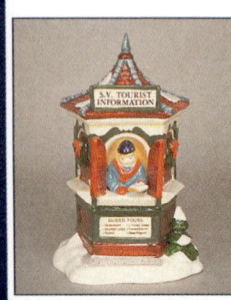

54526
1993 - 1997
OSRP: $12.50
GBTru: $18
Paid: $_____

• Bayport on sign is spelled "Bay**q**ort."

Pint-Size Pony Rides

54534 - Set of 3
1993 - 1996
OSRP: $37.50
GBTru: $45
Paid: $_____

Pick-up And Delivery

54542
1993 - 2001
OSRP: $10
GBTru: $12
Paid: $_____

• See Special Design section.

A Herd Of Holiday Heifers

54550 - Set of 3
1993 - 1997
OSRP: $18
GBTru: $28
Paid: $_____

Windmill

54569
1993 - 1993
OSRP: $20
GBTru: $25
Paid: $_____

Classic Cars

54577 - Set of 3
1993 - 1998
OSRP: $22.50
GBTru: $24
Paid: $_____

Spirit Of Snow Village Airplane

54585
1993 - 1996
OSRP: $12.50
GBTru: $50
Paid: $_____

• Available in blue or yellow. See 1992 for another item by the same name.

Village News Delivery

54593 - Set of 2
1993 - 1996
OSRP: $15
GBTru: $24
Paid: $_____

Caroling At The Farm

54631
1994^M - 2000
OSRP: $35
GBTru: $40
Paid: $_____

Stuck In The Snow

54712 - Set of 3
1994 - 1998
OSRP: $30
GBTru: $32
Paid: $_____

Pets On Parade

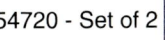

54720 - Set of 2
1994 - 1998
OSRP: $16.50
GBTru: $22
Paid: $_____

Feeding The Birds

54739 - Set of 3
1994 - 1997
OSRP: $25
GBTru: $30
Paid: $_____

Mush!

54747 - Set of 2
1994 - 1997
OSRP: $20
GBTru: $25
Paid: $_____

Skaters & Skiers

54755 - Set of 3
1994 - 2001
OSRP: $27.50
GBTru: $33
Paid: $_____

Going To The Chapel

54763 - Set of 2
1994 - 2001^M
OSRP: $20
GBTru: $24
Paid: $_____

Santa Comes To Town, 1995

54771
1994 - 1995
OSRP: $30
GBTru: $30
Paid: $_____

- Limited to year of production.
- First in a series.

Snow Village Accessories

Marshmallow Roast

54780 - Set of 3
1994 - 2002
OSRP: $32.50
GBTru: $38
Paid: $_____

• The fire is battery or adapter operated.

Coca–Cola® brand Delivery Truck

54798
1994 - 1998
OSRP: $15
GBTru: $30
Paid: $_____

• Licensed by Coca-Cola.

Coca–Cola® brand Delivery Men

54801 - Set of 2
1994 - 1998
OSRP: $25
GBTru: $32
Paid: $_____

• Licensed by Coca-Cola.

Coca–Cola® brand Billboard

54810
1994 - 1997
OSRP: $18
GBTru: $24
Paid: $_____

• Licensed by Coca-Cola.

Sunday School Serenade

54623
1994 - 1996
OSRP: *
GBTru: *

• Accessory contained in The Original Snow Village Starter Set.

Frosty Playtime

54860 - Set of 3
1995 - 1997
OSRP: $30
GBTru: $37
Paid: $_____

Poinsettias For Sale

54861 - Set of 3
1995 - 1998
OSRP: $30
GBTru: $35
Paid: $_____

Santa Comes To Town, 1996

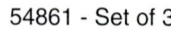

54862
1995 - 1996
OSRP: $32.50
GBTru: $40
Paid: $_____

• Limited to year of production.
• Second in a series.

Chopping Firewood

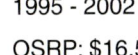

54863 - Set of 2
1995 - 2002
OSRP: $16.50
GBTru: $20
Paid: $_____

• This includes mixed media —ceramic and wood.

Firewood Delivery Truck

54864
1995 - 1999
OSRP: $15
GBTru: $22
Paid: $_____

• This includes mixed media —ceramic and wood.

Service With A Smile

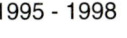

54865 - Set of 2
1995 - 1998
OSRP: $25
GBTru: $30
Paid: $_____

Pizza Delivery

54866 - Set of 2
1995 - 1998
OSRP: $20
GBTru: $26
Paid: $_____

Grand Ole Opry Carolers

54867
1995 - 1997
OSRP: $25
GBTru: $36
Paid: $_____

• Licensed by Opryland USA, Inc.

Snow Carnival Ice Sculptures

54868 - Set of 2
1995 - 1998
OSRP: $27.50
GBTru: $30
Paid: $_____

• Includes mixed media—ceramic and acrylic.

Snow Carnival King & Queen

54869
1995 - 1998
OSRP: $35
GBTru: $40
Paid: $_____

Starbucks Coffee® Cart

54870 - Set of 2
1995 - 2000
OSRP: $27.50
GBTru: $38
Paid: $_____

• Licensed by Starbucks Coffee.

Snow Village Accessories

Snow Village Accessories

Just Married

54879 - Set of 2
1995 -
OSRP: $25
GBTru: -
Paid: $_____

A Ride On The Reindeer Lines

54875 - Set of 3
1996ᴹ - 1997
OSRP: $35
GBTru: $40
Paid: $_____

Treetop Tree House

54890
1996 - 2004
OSRP: $35
GBTru: $35
Paid: $_____

• Resin.

On The Road Again

54891 - Set of 2
1996 - 2002
OSRP: $20
GBTru: $22
Paid: $_____

Moving Day

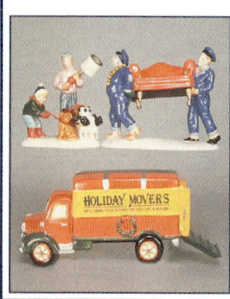

54892 - Set of 3
1996 - 1998
OSRP: $32.50
GBTru: $36
Paid: $_____

Holiday Hoops

54893 - Set of 3
1996 - 1999
OSRP: $20
GBTru: $30
Paid: $_____

Men At Work

54894 - Set of 5
1996 - 1998
OSRP: $27.50
GBTru: $30
Paid: $_____

Terry's Towing

54895 - Set of 2
1996 - 1999
OSRP: $20
GBTru: $26
Paid: $_____

Caroling Through The Snow

54896
1996 - 1999
OSRP: $15
GBTru: $22
Paid: $_____

Heading For The Hills

54897
1996 - 2002
OSRP: $8.50
GBTru: $10
Paid: $_____

• Available in blue or yellow.

A Harley-Davidson® Holiday

54898 - Set of 2
1996 - 1999
OSRP: $22.50
GBTru: $28
Paid: $_____

• Licensed by Harley-Davidson.

Santa Comes To Town, 1997

54899
1996 - 1997
OSRP: $35
GBTru: $40
Paid: $_____

• Limited to year of production.
• Third in a series.

Harley-Davidson® Fat Boy & Softail

54900
1996 - 2001^M
OSRP: $16.50
GBTru: $25
Paid: $_____

• Licensed by Harley-Davidson.

Harley-Davidson® Sign

54901
1996 - 2002
OSRP: $18
GBTru: $22
Paid: $_____

• Licensed by Harley-Davidson.

Saturday Morning Downtown

54902 - Set of 2
1997^M - 1998
OSRP: *
GBTru: *

* Accessory contained in The Original Snow Village Start A Tradition Set.

The Whole Family Goes Shopping

54905 - Set of 3
1997^M - 1999
OSRP: $25
GBTru: $28
Paid: $_____

Snow Village Accessories

Snow Village Accessories

A Holiday Sleigh Ride Together
54921
1997 - 2001^M
OSRP: $32.50
GBTru: $38
Paid: $_____

Christmas Kids
54922 - Set of 5
1997 - 1999
OSRP: $27.50
GBTru: $32
Paid: $_____

Let It Snow, Let It Snow
54923
1997 - 2000
OSRP: $20
GBTru: $24
Paid: $_____

Kids Love Hershey's!
54924 - Set of 2
1997 - 2000
OSRP: $30
GBTru: $32
Paid: $_____
• Licensed by Hershey Foods.

McDonald's...Lights Up The Night
54925
1997 - 1999
OSRP: $30
GBTru: $36
Paid: $_____
• Sign is battery/adapter operated.
• Licensed by McDonald's.

Kids, Candy Canes...& Ronald McDonald
54926 - Set of 3
1997 - 1999
OSRP: $30
GBTru: $35
Paid: $_____
• Licensed by McDonald's.

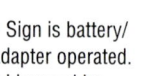

He Led Them Down The Streets Of Town
54927 - Set of 3
1997 - 1999
OSRP: $30
GBTru: $32
Paid: $_____

Everybody Goes Skating At Rollerama
54928 - Set of 2
1997 - 1999
OSRP: $25
GBTru: $28
Paid: $_____

Snow Village Accessories

At The Barn Dance, It's Allemande Left

54929 - Set of 2
1997 - 1999
OSRP: $30
GBTru: $36
Paid: $_____

Hitch-Up The Buckboard

54930
1997 - 1999
OSRP: $40
GBTru: $40
Paid: $_____

Farm Accessory Set

54931 - Set of 35
1997 - 2002
OSRP: $75
GBTru: $85
Paid: $_____

- Includes 8 trees, 12 hay bales, 4 fence, and 11 ceramic pieces.

Santa Comes To Town, 1998

54920
1997 - 1998
OSRP: $30
GBTru: $36
Paid: $_____

- Limited to year of production.
- Fourth in a series.

Snow Village Utility Accessories

52775
1998 - 2001
OSRP: $15
GBTru: $15
Paid: $_____

Decorate The Tree

54934 - Set of 2
1998^M - 1998
OSRP: *
GBTru: *

* Accessory contained in the Snowy Pines Inn Gift Set.

First Round Of The Year

54936 - Set of 3
1998^M - 2001^M
OSRP: $30
GBTru: $35
Paid: $_____

Carnival Tickets & Cotton Candy

54938 - Set of 3
1998^M - 2000
OSRP: $30
GBTru: $33
Paid: $_____

- Ceramic and cloth.

Two For The Road

54939

1998ᴹ - 2002

OSRP: $20

GBTru: $28

Paid: $_____

• Available in three color schemes—red, yellow, and blue.
• Licensed by Harley-Davidson.

Uptown Motors Ford® Billboard

52780

1998 - 2001ᴹ

OSRP: $20

GBTru: $22

Paid: $_____

• Licensed by Ford.

1955 Ford® Automobiles

54950

1998 - 2001

OSRP: $10 ea.

GBTru: $14

Paid: $_____

• 6 assorted, each with a sign.
• Licensed by Ford.

1964½ Ford® Mustang

54951

1998 - 2001

OSRP: $10 ea.

GBTru: $20

Paid: $_____

• 3 assorted, each with a sign.
• Licensed by Ford.

Village Fire Truck

54952

1998 - 2003

OSRP: $22.50

GBTru: $26

Paid: $_____

• Lighted headlights and emergency beacon are battery operated.

Fireman To The Rescue

54953 - Set of 3

1998 - 2001ᴹ

OSRP: $30

GBTru: $34

Paid: $_____

Fun At The Firehouse

54954 - Set of 2

1998 - 2004

OSRP: $27.50

GBTru: $28

Paid: $_____

Farmer's Flatbed

54955

1998 - 2000

OSRP: $17.50

GBTru: $18

Paid: $_____

The Catch Of The Day

54956
1998 - 2001^M
OSRP: $30
GBTru: $34
Paid: $_____

• Fishing line is easily broken.

Christmas Visit To The Florist

54957 - Set of 3
1998 - 2001
OSRP: $30
GBTru: $35
Paid: $_____

• A similar design was also produced for Bachman's. See the Special Design section.

Santa Comes To Town, 1999

54958
1998 - 1999
OSRP: $30
GBTru: $32
Paid: $_____

• Limited to year of production.
• Fifth in a series.

Village Service Vehicles

54959
1998 - 2001
OSRP: $15 ea.
GBTru: $16
Paid: $_____

• 3 assorted—garbage truck, tow truck, and snow plow were often sold separately.

Quality Service At Ford®

54970 - Set of 2
1998 - 2001^M
OSRP: $27.50
GBTru: $28
Paid: $_____

• Licensed by Ford.

Patrolling The Road

54971
1998 - 2001^M
OSRP: $20
GBTru: $24
Paid: $_____

• Licensed by Harley-Davidson.

Couldn't Wait Until Christmas

54972
1998 - 2000
OSRP: $17
GBTru: $22
Paid: $_____

• Licensed by Lionel.

Uncle Sam's Fireworks Stand

54974 - Set of 2
1998 - 2000
OSRP: $45
GBTru: $45
Paid: $_____

• July 1999 event piece.

Snow Village Accessories

Snow Village Accessories

Harley-Davidson® Water Tower

54975
1998 - 2002
OSRP: $32.50
GBTru: $45
Paid: $_____

• Licensed by Harley-Davidson.

Another Man's Treasure Accessories

54976 - Set of 3
1998 - 2001^M
OSRP: $27.50
GBTru: $34
Paid: $_____

A Home In The Making Accessories

54979 - Set of 4
1999^M - 2001
OSRP: *
GBTru: *

* This accessory is contained in A Home In The Making.
• Licensed by Habitat For Humanity

Looney Tunes® Film Festival

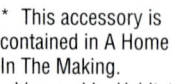

54983 - Set of 4
1999^M - 2001^M
OSRP: $40
GBTru: $44
Paid: $_____

• Marquee can be placed on Cinema 56.
• Licensed by Warner Bros.

The Backyard Patio

52836 - Set of 2
1999 - 2002
OSRP: $40
GBTru: $42
Paid: $_____

It's Time For An Icy Treat

55013 - Set of 2
1999 - 2001
OSRP: $30
GBTru: $30
Paid: $_____

• Licensed by Good Humor-Breyers Ice Cream.

Welcome To The Congregation

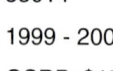

55014
1999 - 2001^M
OSRP: $15
GBTru: $18
Paid: $_____

Santa Comes To Town, 2000

55015
1999 - 2000
OSRP: $37.50
GBTru: $38
Paid: $_____

• Limited to year of production.
• Sixth in a series.

Laundry Day

55017
1999 - 2001ᴹ
OSRP: $13
GBTru: $18
Paid: $_____

Before The Big Game

55019 - Set of 4
1999 - 2001
OSRP: $37.50
GBTru: $40
Paid: $_____

Finding The Bird's Song

55020 - Set of 2
1999 - 2001ᴹ
OSRP: $25
GBTru: $26
Paid: $_____

Send In The Clown!

55021
1999 - 2001ᴹ
OSRP: $13.50
GBTru: $16
Paid: $_____

• Stickers are included so plaque can be personalized.

Holy Spirit Baptistery

55022
1999 - 2001
OSRP: $37.50
GBTru: $40
Paid: $_____

• Music box plays "Jesus Loves The Little Children."

First Deposit

55023
1999 - 2001
OSRP: $14
GBTru: $17
Paid: $_____

Angels In The Snow

55024 - Set of 2
1999 -
OSRP: $30
GBTru: -
Paid: $_____

Santa's Little Helpers

55025
1999 - 2001
OSRP: $27.50
GBTru: $32
Paid: $_____

Snow Village Accessories

Snow Village Accessories

Is That Frosty?

55030
1999 -
OSRP: $22.50
GBTru: -
Paid: $_____

On The Way To Ballet Class

55031 - Set of 3
1999 - 2001^M
OSRP: $27.50
GBTru: $30
Paid: $_____

The Dragon Parade

55032
1999 - 2001
OSRP: $35
GBTru: $40
Paid: $_____

Gifts On The Go

55035 - Set of 2
1999 - 2001^M
OSRP: $30
GBTru: $30
Paid: $_____

Backwoods Outhouse

55036
1999 -
OSRP: $20
GBTru: -
Paid: $_____

• Battery operated.

Oh, Christmas Tree

55040
2000^M - 2000
OSRP: *
GBTru: *

* Accessory contained in the Silver Bells Christmas Shop Gift Set.

1955 Pink Cadillac® Fleetwood™

55041
2000^M - 2000
OSRP: *
GBTru: *

* Accessory contained in the Elvis Presley's Graceland Gift Set.
• Licensed by GM.

Sitting In The Park

55100 - Set of 4
2000^M - 2002
OSRP: $28
GBTru: $26
Paid: $_____

How The Grinch Stole Christmas - Movie Premiere

55103 - Set of 2
2000ᴹ - 2001
OSRP: $17.50
GBTru: $24
Paid: $_____

• Marquee can be placed on Cinema 56.
• Licensed by Dr. Seuss Enterprises.

Windmill By The Chicken Coop

52867
2000 - 2003
OSRP: $55
GBTru: $48
Paid: $_____

• Buck's County Series.

The Old Pickup Truck

52868
2000 - 2002
OSRP: $30
GBTru: $30
Paid: $_____

• Buck's County Series.

Yesterday's Tractor

52869
2000 - 2002
OSRP: $30
GBTru: $30
Paid: $_____

• Buck's County Series.

The Tree Lighting Ceremony

55104 - Set of 3
2000 - 2002
OSRP: $65
GBTru: $65
Paid: $_____

• Lights are battery/adapter operated.

Now Showing - Elvis Presley Sign

55105
2000 - 2001
OSRP: $30
GBTru: $32
Paid: $_____

• Licensed by Elvis Presley Enterprises.
• Adapter operated.

Elvis Presley's Autograph

55106 - Set of 3
2000 - 2001
OSRP: $25
GBTru: $28
Paid: $_____

• Licensed by Elvis Presley Enterprises.

Pedal Cars For Christmas

55108 - Set of 2
2000 - 2003
OSRP: $27.50
GBTru: $32
Paid: $_____

Snow Village Accessories

Snow Village Accessories

Roadside Billboards

55109 - Set of 3
2000 - 2003
OSRP: $40
GBTru: $38
Paid: $_____
• Licensed by the Campbell Soup Co., SWIMC, Inc., and Eveready Batt. Co, Inc.
• Battery/adapter.

Christmastime Trimming

55110
2000 -
OSRP: $15
GBTru: -
Paid: $_____

Buck's County™ Water Tower

55111
2000 - 2003
OSRP: $32.50
GBTru: $40
Paid: $_____
• Buck's County Series.

Buck's County™ Stables

55112 - Set of 9
2000 - 2002
OSRP: $65
GBTru: $70
Paid: $_____
• Buck's County Series

Family Canoe Trip

55116 - Set of 3
2000 - 2002
OSRP: $48
GBTru: $48
Paid: $_____

2001 Space Oddity

55118 - Set of 11
2000 - 2001
OSRP: $125
GBTru: $125
Paid: $_____
• Includes adapter.

On The Beat

55119 - Set of 2
2000 -
OSRP: $35
GBTru: -
Paid: $_____
• Battery/adapter operated.

Santa Comes To Town, 2001

55120
2000 - 2001
OSRP: $40
GBTru: $40
Paid: $_____
• Limited to year of production.
• Seventh in a series.
• Batt./adapt. operate

The Abandoned Gas Pump

55121
2000 - 2002
OSRP: $37.50
GBTru: $38
Paid: $_____

• Buck's County Series.

1958 Corvette® Roadster

55281
2000 -
OSRP: $20
GBTru: -
Paid: $_____

• Classic Cars Series.
• Licensed by General Motors.

'50's Hot Rod

55282
2000 -
OSRP: $20
GBTru: -
Paid: $_____

• Classic Cars Series.

1957 Chevrolet® Bel Air

55283
2000 -
OSRP: $20
GBTru: -
Paid: $_____

• Classic Cars Series.
• Licensed by General Motors.

1958 John Deere® 730 Diesel Tractor

55284
2000 - 2003
OSRP: $20
GBTru: $24
Paid: $_____

• Classic Cars Series.
• Licensed by Deere & Co.

1950 Ford® F-1 Pickup

55285
2000 - 2003
OSRP: $20
GBTru: $22
Paid: $_____

• Classic Cars Series.
• Licensed by Ford Motor Co and Deere & Co.

Buck's County™ Horse Trailer

55286
2000 - 2002
OSRP: $17.50
GBTru: $18
Paid: $_____

• Buck's County Series.
• Coordinates with 1950 Ford F-1 Pickup.

1954 Willy's CJ3 Jeep®

55287
2000 - 2002
OSRP: $20
GBTru: $22
Paid: $_____

• Classic Cars Series.
• Licensed by Daimler-Chrysler Corp.

Snow Village Accessories

1949 Ford® Woody Wagon

55288
2000 -
OSRP: $20
GBTru: -
Paid: $_____

- Classic Cars Series.
- Licensed by Ford Motor Co.

1959 Chevrolet® Impala Convertible

55289
2000 -
OSRP: $20
GBTru: -
Paid: $_____

- Classic Cars Series.
- Licensed by General Motors.

The Final Touch

55061
2001^M - 2001
OSRP: *
GBTru: *

* The accessory contained in the Christmas Lake Chalet Gift Set.

Happy New Year

55124 - Set of 4
2001^M - 2002
OSRP: $25
GBTru: $26
Paid: $_____

- Includes sign that can be placed on Town Hall (#55044).

Fun In The Snow

55125 - Set of 2
2001^M -
OSRP: $25
GBTru: -
Paid: $_____

Holiday Reindeer Run

55126
2001^M - 2002
OSRP: $25
GBTru: $28
Paid: $_____

- Originally was titled Holiday Fun Run.

Car Hop

55067
2001 - 2003
OSRP: *
GBTru: *

* The accessory contained in Gus's Drive-In.

On Our Wedding Day

55068
2001 -
OSRP: *
GBTru: *

* The accessory contained in the Woodlake Chapel Starter Set.

Handmade Quilts For Sale

55072
2001 - 2004
OSRP: *
GBTru: *

* The accessory contained in Country Quilts And Pies.

Cannon And Flag

55080
2001 - 2003
OSRP: *
GBTru: *

* The accessory contained in Village Legion Hall.

Egg Hunt

55090
2001 -
OSRP: *
GBTru: *

* The accessory contained in Happy Easter House.

Feeding The Ducks

55122
2001 - 2003
OSRP: $40
GBTru: $44
Paid: $_____

- Buck's County Series.

Santa Comes To Town, 2002

55127
2001 - 2002
OSRP: $85
GBTru: $70
Paid: $_____

- Limited to year of production, 2002.
- Eighth in a series.
- Battery operated.

Bringing The Irish Cheer

55128
2001 -
OSRP: $12.50
GBTru: -
Paid: $_____

School's Out!

55129
2001 - 2003
OSRP: $20
GBTru: $20
Paid: $_____

Start Your Engines

55132 - Set of 2
2001 - 2003
OSRP: $25
GBTru: $26
Paid: $_____

Snow Village Accessories

Hiking In The North Woods

55133
2001 - 2003
OSRP: $20
GBTru: $20
Paid: $_____

Main Street Villagers

55134 - Set of 3
2001 -
OSRP: $25
GBTru: -
Paid: $_____

College Kids At Krispy Kreme

55135
2001 - 2004
OSRP: $17.50
GBTru: $18
Paid: $_____

• Licensed by HDN Development Corp.

Snowmobile Racers

55136 - Set of 2
2001 -
OSRP: $15
GBTru: -
Paid: $_____

Oh, Brother!

55137 - Set of 2
2001 - 2003
OSRP: $18
GBTru: $20
Paid: $_____

Door-To-Door Sales

55139 - Set of 2
2001 - 2003
OSRP: $20
GBTru: $20
Paid: $_____

4th of July Celebration

55141 - Set of 3
2001 -
OSRP: $25
GBTru: -
Paid: $_____

Rest Stop?

55142
2001 - 2003
OSRP: $15
GBTru: $16
Paid: $_____

Sunday Football With Dad

55143
2001 - 2003
OSRP: $15
GBTru: $17
Paid: $_____

Ben & Buddy's Lemonade Stand

55144
2001 - 2003
OSRP: $20
GBTru: $28
Paid: $_____

Brand New Recruit

55152
2001 - 2003
OSRP: $20
GBTru: $22
Paid: $_____

Congratulations…Recruit!

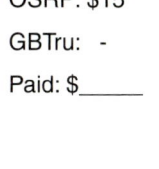

55153 - Set of 2
2001 - 2002
OSRP: $17.50
GBTru: $20
Paid: $_____

Snow Village Raising The Flag

55154
2001 -
OSRP: $15
GBTru: -
Paid: $_____

Welcome To Snow Village Population Sign

55155
2001 -
OSRP: $10
GBTru: -
Paid: $_____

School Bus

55292
2001 - 2004
OSRP: $20
GBTru: $20
Paid: $_____

• Classic Cars Series.

1950 Studebaker

55293
2001 - 2004
OSRP: $20
GBTru: $20
Paid: $_____

• Classic Cars Series.

Snow Village Accessories

1951 Custom Mercury

55294
2001 - 2004
OSRP: $20
GBTru: $20
Paid: $_____

• Classic Cars Series.
• Licensed by Ford Motor Co.

1959 Cadillac Eldorado

55295
2001 - 2003
OSRP: $20
GBTru: $20
Paid: $_____

• Classic Cars Series.
• Licensed by General Motors.

Sampling The Treats

05923 - Set of 2
2002^M - 2002
OSRP: *
GBTru: *

* The accessory contained in The Sweet Shop.

Christmas Eve Delivery

55091
2002^M - 2002
OSRP: *
GBTru: *

* The accessory contained in 1224 Kissing Claus Lane.

Gifts For Easter

55095 - Set of 2
2002^M -
OSRP: *
GBTru: *

• Easter Series.
* The accessory contained in Lily's Nursery & Gifts.

Young Love

55097
2002^M -
OSRP: *
GBTru: *

* The accessory contained in Hearts & Blooms Cottage.

Nature Walk

55156 - Set of 2
2002^M - 2004
OSRP: $27.50
GBTru: $28
Paid: $_____

Lucky's Irish Souvenirs

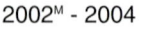
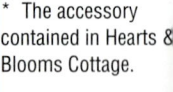

55157 - Set of
2002^M - 2004
OSRP: $45
GBTru: $40
Paid: $_____

• Battery/adapter operated.

Mainstreet Snowman

55159

2002^M - 2002

OSRP: $32.50

GBTru: $34

Paid: $_____

- Limited to year of production.
- Available only at Gold Key dealers.

One Hop Walk

55160

2002^M - 2004

OSRP: $40

GBTru: $40

Paid: $_____

- Easter Series.

It's The Easter Bunny!

55164 - Set of 2

2002^M - 2004

OSRP: $17.50

GBTru: $18

Paid: $_____

- Easter Series.

Krispy Kreme Doughnut Deliveries

55165

2002^M - 2004

OSRP: $20

GBTru: $20

Paid: $_____

- Licensed by HDN Development Corp. and General Motors.

1956 Hook & Ladder

55296

2002^M -

OSRP: $30

GBTru: -

Paid: $_____

- Classic Cars Series.

1956 Mainline Police Sedan

55297

2002^M -

OSRP: $20

GBTru: -

Paid: $_____

- Classic Cars Series.
- Box reads "1956 Ford Mainline Police Sedan."
- Licensed by Ford.

Village Snow Clown

55161

2002 - 2003

OSRP: $17.50

GBTru: $18

Paid: $_____

At Your Service

55168

2002 - 2004

OSRP: $12.50

GBTru: $13

Paid: $_____

Snow Village Accessories

Violin Serenade

55169
2002 - 2004
OSRP: $17.50
GBTru: $18
Paid: $_____

Making A House Call

55170
2002 - 2004
OSRP: $12.50
GBTru: $13
Paid: $_____

Home Away From Home

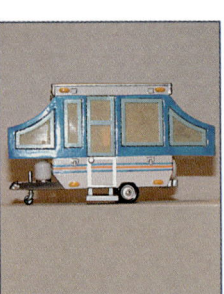

55171
2002 -
OSRP: $27.50
GBTru: -
Paid: $_____

• Battery/adapter operated.

Weekend Getaway

55172 - Set of 2
2002 - 2004
OSRP: $25
GBTru: $25
Paid: $_____

Let's Play House

55173
2002 -
OSRP: $22.50
GBTru: -
Paid: $_____

• Lighted.

Village Utilities

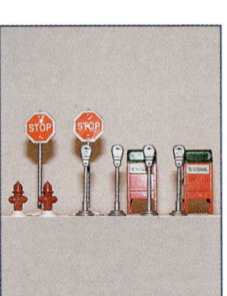

55175 - Set of 1
2002 -
OSRP: $15
GBTru: -
Paid: $_____

Best Friends

55176
2002 -
OSRP: $20
GBTru: -
Paid: $_____

Car Wash Fundraiser

55177 - Set of
2002 - 2004
OSRP: $20
GBTru: $20
Paid: $_____

• Can be personalize

Carry Out Boy

55178
2002 - 2003
OSRP: $17.50
GBTru: $18
Paid: $_____

Mm! Mm! Good!

55179
2002 - 2004
OSRP: $25
GBTru: $25
Paid: $_____

• Licensed by the Campbell Soup Co.

Summertime Family Picnic

55180 - Set of 3
2002 - 2004
OSRP: $37.50
GBTru: $38
Paid: $_____

Kiddie Parade

55181 - Set of 3
2002 - 2004
OSRP: $30
GBTru: $30
Paid: $_____

Merrily Round We Go

55183
2002 - 2004
OSRP: $45
GBTru: $45
Paid: $_____

• Animated.
• Battery/adapter operated.

Santa Comes To Town, 2003

55194
2002 - 2003
OSRP: $45
GBTru: $47
Paid: $_____

• Limited to year of production, 2003.
• Ninth in a series.

Fresh Dairy Delivery

55195 - Set of 2
2002 - 2004
OSRP: $25
GBTru: $25
Paid: $_____

Ice Cream For Everyone

55196 - Set of 2
2002 - 2004
OSRP: $22.50
GBTru: $23
Paid: $_____

Snow Village Accessories

Sitting In The Village

55197 - Set of 3
2002 -
OSRP: $25
GBTru: -
Paid: $_____

• Benches are not included.

Animals On The Farm

55199 - Set of 9
2002 - 2004
OSRP: $25
GBTru: $25
Paid: $_____

Jonathan The Bear Man

55202
2002 - 2003
OSRP: $12.50
GBTru: $16
Paid: $_____

• Named for a Wyoming artist.

1957 Ambulance

55299
2002 -
OSRP: $20
GBTru: -
Paid: $_____

• Classic Cars Series.

Snowman Sonata And Fence

55302
2002 -
OSRP: *
GBTru: *

* The accessory contained in Harmony House.

56 Gasoline Pump And Sign

55305
2002 -
OSRP: *
GBTru: *

* The accessory contained in Rocky's 56 Filling Station.

Let's Get A New Bike

55314
2002 - 2003
OSRP: *
GBTru: *

* The accessory contained in Wright Bike Shop.

1961 Ford Ranchero

55532
2002 - 2004
OSRP: $20
GBTru: $20
Paid: $_____

• Classic Cars Series
• Licensed by Ford Motor Co.

Snow Village Accessories

Main Street Christmas Tree

55205

2003^M - 2003

OSRP: $35

GBTru: $40

Paid: $_____

- Adapter included.
- Limited to year of production.
- Available only at Gold Key dealers.

St. Patrick's Day Parade

55207

2003^M - 2004

OSRP: $20

GBTru: $20

Paid: $_____

- Can be personalized.

Work A Little, Play A Little

55208 - Set of 4

2003^M - 2004

OSRP: $25

GBTru: $25

Paid: $_____

- Includes two sets of figures dressed for four seasons.

I'm Home!

55209

2003^M -

OSRP: $13.50

GBTru: -

Paid: $_____

Kisses - 25 Cents

55215 - Set of 2

2003^M -

OSRP: $25

GBTru: -

Paid: $_____

- Valentine's Day design.
- Special lighting effects.

Welcoming Christmas To Town

55320

2003^M - 2003

OSRP: *

GBTru: *

* The accessory contained in Home For The Holidays Express.

Joyful Greetings

55325

2003^M -

OSRP: *

GBTru: *

- Easter Series.
* The accessory contained in Happy Easter Church.

Easter Egg Hunt

55326 - Set of 3

2003^M -

OSRP: $50

GBTru: -

Paid: $_____

- Easter Series.
- Includes adapter.

Dressed In Our Easter Best

55327 - Set of 2
2003^M -
OSRP: $25
GBTru: -
Paid: $_____

• Easter Series.

1956 Pumper

55533
2003^M -
OSRP: $25
GBTru: -
Paid: $_____

• Classic Cars.

Personalized School Bus

55534
2003^M -
OSRP: $20
GBTru: -
Paid: $_____

• Classic Cars.

No Girls Allowed

55217
2003 -
OSRP: $20
GBTru: -
Paid: $_____

We're Going By Train!

55218 - Set of 2
2003 -
OSRP: $25
GBTru: -
Paid: $_____

Santa Comes To Town, 2004

55222
2003 - 2004
OSRP: $50
GBTru: $50
Paid: $_____

• Limited to year of production, 2004.
• Tenth in a series.

Brand New Shoes!

55224 - Set of 2
2003 -
OSRP: $17.50
GBTru: -
Paid: $_____

News Flash!

55225
2003 -
OSRP: $17.50
GBTru: -
Paid: $_____

Listening To A Summer Concert  55227 - Set of 2 2003 - OSRP: $20 GBTru: - Paid: $_____	**A Day At The Beach** 55228 2003 - OSRP: $25 GBTru: - Paid: $_____ 
Billboard Surprise  55229 2003 - OSRP: $22.50 GBTru: - Paid: $_____	**Here Comes The Birdie!**  55230 2003 - OSRP: $17.50 GBTru: - Paid: $_____
More Decorations?  55231 - Set of 2 2003 - OSRP: $17.50 GBTru: - Paid: $_____ • Chrsitmas Lane Series.	**Pleasing The Palate!**  55232 2003 - OSRP: $20 GBTru: - Paid: $_____
Christmas Is Coming  55233 2003 - OSRP: $25 GBTru: - Paid: $_____	**Neighborhood Poinsettia Salesman**  55235 - Set of 2 2003 - OSRP: $22.50 GBTru: - Paid: $_____

Snow Village Accessories

Snow Village Accessories

Wood Carvings For Sale

55333
2003 -
OSRP: *
GBTru: *

* The accessory contained in Woody's Woodland Crafts.

Village Musicians

55338
2003 -
OSRP: *
GBTru: *

* The accessory contained in Roosevelt Park Band Shell.

The Pillsbury Doughboy™

55342
2003 -
OSRP: *
GBTru: *

* The accessory contained in Pillsbury Doughboy Bake Shop.
• Licensed by The Pillsbury Company.

1955 Ford Thunderbird

55535
2003 -
OSRP: $20
GBTru: -
Paid: $_____

• Classic Cars Series.
• Licensed by Ford Motor Co.

1957 Cadillac Eldorado Brougham

55536
2003 -
OSRP: $20
GBTru: -
Paid: $_____

• Classic Cars Series.
• Licensed by General Motors.

We'll Win For Sure!

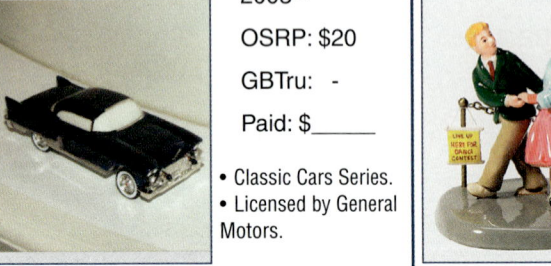

55251
2004ᴹ -
OSRP: $15
GBTru: -
Paid: $_____

Townspeople

55252 - Set of 4
2004ᴹ -
OSRP: $32.50
GBTru: -
Paid: $_____

Neighborhood Christmas Scene

55253
2004ᴹ - 2004
OSRP: $50
GBTru: $50
Paid: $_____

• Limited to year of production.

Main Street Town Santa

55254
2004^M - 2004
OSRP: $32.50
GBTru: $35
Paid: $_____

• Limited to year of production.

Buster Helps Out

55350
2004^M - 2004
OSRP: *
GBTru: *

* The accessory contained in The Peppermint House.

The Happy Couple

55354
2004^M -
OSRP: *
GBTru: *

* The accessory contained in Chapel Of Love.

The Best Part Of Easter

55355
2004^M -
OSRP: *
GBTru: *

* The accessory contained in Chocolate Bunny Factory.

1965 Ford Mustang 2+2 Fastback

55537
2004^M -
OSRP: $20
GBTru: -
Paid: $_____

• Classic Cars Series.
• Licensed by Ford Motor Co.

Budweiser Clydesdales

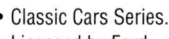

55256
2004 -
OSRP: $65
GBTru: -
Paid: $_____

• Licensed by Anheuser-Busch, Inc.

Harvest Yard Fun

55258 - Set of 2
2004 -
OSRP: $25
GBTru: -
Paid: $_____

Who's Walking Who?

55260
2004 -
OSRP: $20
GBTru: -
Paid: $_____

Snow Village Accessories

Snow Village Accessories

We Have A Deal!

55261
2004 -
OSRP: $17.50
GBTru: -
Paid: $_____

Something For Me?

55262
2004 -
OSRP: $17.50
GBTru: -
Paid: $_____

Can I Open One Now?

55264
2004 -
OSRP: $18.50
GBTru: -
Paid: $_____

What A Great Find!

55265
2004 -
OSRP: $17.50
GBTru: -
Paid: $_____

Santa Comes to Town - 2005

55266
2004 -
OSRP: $35
GBTru: -
Paid: $_____

- Limited to year of production.
- Licensed by Coca-Cola.

Christmas Lights Tour

55267
2004 -
OSRP: $25
GBTru: -
Paid: $_____

- Christmas Lane Series.

Future Hockey Stars

55268
2004 -
OSRP: $17.50
GBTru: -
Paid: $_____

Gone Fishing

55269
2004 -
OSRP: $20
GBTru: -
Paid: $_____

- Weekend At The Lake Series.

Snow Village Accessories

Dinner Guests

55358 - Set of 2
2004 -
OSRP: *
GBTru: *

* The accessory contained in Thanksgiving at Grandmother's House.

Freight Truck

55538
2004 -
OSRP: $20
GBTru: -
Paid: $_____

- Classic Cars Series.

Use the following space(s) to update your guide when the midyear introductions are announced.

_____
_____
____ - ____
OSRP: $_____
GBTru: -
Paid: $_____

_____
_____
____ - ____
OSRP: $_____
GBTru: -
Paid: $_____

_____
_____
____ - ____
OSRP: $_____
GBTru: -
Paid: $_____

_____
_____
____ - ____
OSRP: $_____
GBTru: -
Paid: $_____

_____
_____
____ - ____
OSRP: $_____
GBTru: -
Paid: $_____

Snow Village Accessories

____ - ____
OSRP: $_____
GBTru: -
Paid: $_____

____ - ____
OSRP: $_____
GBTru: -
Paid: $_____

____ - ____
OSRP: $_____
GBTru: -
Paid: $_____

____ - ____
OSRP: $_____
GBTru: -
Paid: $_____

____ - ____
OSRP: $_____
GBTru: -
Paid: $_____

____ - ____
OSRP: $_____
GBTru: -
Paid: $_____

____ - ____
OSRP: $_____
GBTru: -
Paid: $_____

____ - ____
OSRP: $_____
GBTru: -
Paid: $_____

Haunted Mansion (Green Roof) — 54935

Dates	OSRP	GBTru	Paid
1998ᴹ - 2000ᴹ	$110	$465	$_____

- This is the SV version.
- Images on screen created by carousel inside building.
- Includes AC adapter.

(Black Roof) — 34050

Dates	OSRP	GBTru	Paid
1998ᴹ - 1999	$110	$1695	$_____

- This is the giftware version and came in a black box.
- Images on screen created by carousel inside building.
- Includes AC adapter.

Grimsly Manor — 55004

Dates	OSRP	GBTru	Paid
1999 -	$120	-	$_____

- Features special effects including horror sounds and lightning supplied by separate unit in box.
- The earliest pieces have a jack-o'-lantern on the porch. Later ones do not. Care must be taken in selecting one with a jack-o'-lantern since some collectors have added it to a piece that originally did not have one.
- Four bats hang from eaves, rocker is on porch, and a tree is attached in back. Matte finish.
- The box can separate even while in the sleeve so the box must be carried by the bottom.

Creepy Creek Carriage House — 55055

Dates	OSRP	GBTru	Paid
2000 - 2003	$75	$85	$_____

- Bat mobile is separate in box.

Hauntsburg House — 55058

Dates	OSRP	GBTru	Paid
2000 - 2002	$95	$110	$_____

- Grass platform is separate in box.
- Be careful removing from box; the tree is easily broken.

Snow Village Halloween

Haunted Barn — 55060

Dates	OSRP	GBTru	Paid
2001ᴹ - 2001	$75	$115	$_____

- Halloween Discover Department 56 design. Limited to year of production.
- Set of 4 includes Barn, "Scarecrow Jack" accessory, fence, and tree.

The Spooky Schooner — 55087

Dates	OSRP	GBTru	Paid
2001 - 2002	$95	$90	$_____

- Limited to year of production, 2002.
- Has sound effects and green light.

Shipwreck Lighthouse — 55088

Dates	OSRP	GBTru	Paid
2001 - 2003	$110	$120	$_____

- Features animated ghost that glows in the dark.

Haunted Fun House Gift Set — 55094

Dates	OSRP	GBTru	Paid
2002ᴹ - 2002	$75	$95	$_____

- Limited to year of production.
- Several features are animated.
- Set of 4 includes the Fun House, "Dressed Up For Fun" accessory, tree, and leaves.

Snow Village Halloween

Spooky Farmhouse   55315

Dates	OSRP	GBTru	Paid
2002 - 2004	$55	$55	$_____

Helga's House Of Fortunes   55316

Dates	OSRP	GBTru	Paid
2002 - 2004	$95	$95	$_____

• Tells fortunes.

Ghostly Carousel   55317

Dates	OSRP	GBTru	Paid
2002 -	$130	-	$_____

• Animated with sounds.

Black Cat Diner   55319

Dates	OSRP	GBTru	Paid
2002 - 2003	$75	$95	$_____

• Holiday Program.
• Limited to year of production.
• Set of 4 includes the Diner, "You Go First!" accessory, 10" tree, and leaves.

Haunted Windmill   55345

Dates	OSRP	GBTru	Paid
2003 -	$95	-	$_____

• Working windmill.
• Makes horror sounds.

Snow Village Halloween

1031 Trick-Or-Treat Drive   55343

Dates	OSRP	GBTru	Paid
2003 - 2004	$75	$75	$_____

- Limited to year of production.
- Set of 8 includes the house, "Just Treats, No Tricks, Please" accessory, and Halloween decorations.

Castle Blackstone   55346

Dates	OSRP	GBTru	Paid
2003 -	$125	-	$_____

- Makes horror sounds.

Witch Way? Flight School   55347

Dates	OSRP	GBTru	Paid
2003 - 2004	$75	$75	$_____

- Limited to year of production.
- Set of 7 includes the School, "Practice Makes Perfect" accessory, and Halloween decorations.

Mickey's Haunted House   55375

Dates	OSRP	GBTru	Paid
2004 -	$85	-	$_____

- Licensed by Disney.

LaGhosti Movie Theater   55374

Dates	OSRP	GBTru	Paid
2004 -	**$75**	-	**$____**

- Set of 7 includes the Theater and "Hurry - The Movie's About To Start!" accessory, tree, bench, fence, and leaves.
- Limited to year of production.
- Plays scary movie sounds, and threater marquee lights.

Witchs' Brew Pub   55376

Dates	OSRP	GBTru	Paid
2004 -	**$80**	-	**$____**

- Adapter included.
- Multi-color effect in caldron.

Dead End Motel   55377

Dates	OSRP	GBTru	Paid
2004 -	**$60**	-	**$____**

- Adapter included.
- Motel Sign lights and blinks.

Use the space(s) below to update your guide when the midyear introductions are announced.

_____   _____

Dates	OSRP	GBTru	Paid
___ - ___	$____	-	$____

Snow Village Halloween

Snow Village Halloween

	Dates	OSRP	GBTru	Paid
	____ - ____	$____	-	$____
	____ - ____	$____	-	$____
	____ - ____	$____	-	$____
	____ - ____	$____	-	$____
	____ - ____	$____	-	$____
	____ - ____	$____	-	$____

Trick Or Treat Kids

54937 - Set of 3
1998^M -
OSRP: $33
GBTru: -
Paid: $_____

Costumes For Sale

54973 - Set of 2
1998 - 2002
OSRP: $60
GBTru: $70
Paid: $_____

• Pumpkin lights are battery/adapter operated.

Preparing For Halloween

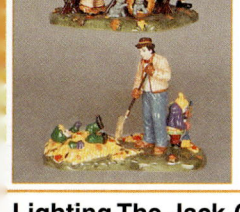

54982 - Set of 2
1999^M - 2002
OSRP: $40
GBTru: $45
Paid: $_____

Treats for The Kids

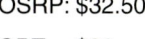

55016 - Set of 3
1999 - 2002
OSRP: $33
GBTru: $35
Paid: $_____

Lighting The Jack-O'-Lanterns

55117 - Set of 3
2000 - 2003
OSRP: $32.50
GBTru: $32
Paid: $_____

• Battery/adapter operated.

Scarecrow Jack

55060
2001^M - 2001
OSRP: *
GBTru: *

* This accessory is contained in the Haunted Barn Gift Set.

Halloween Hayride

55148
2001 -
OSRP: $45
GBTru: -
Paid: $_____

Captain Black Bart's Ghost

55149
2001 - 2002
OSRP: $18
GBTru: $22
Paid: $_____

Snow Village Halloween Acc.

Haunted Tree House

55150
2001 -
OSRP: $45
GBTru: -
Paid: $_____

Dressed Up For Fun

55094
2002^M - 2002
OSRP: *
GBTru: *

* The accessory contained in Haunted Fun House Gift Set.

Bobbing For Apples

55185
2002 - 2004
OSRP: $22.50
GBTru: $23
Paid: $_____

Halloween Kids

55186 - Set of 3
2002 - 2004
OSRP: $27.50
GBTru: $28
Paid: $_____

Halloween Dance

55189
2002 - 2004
OSRP: $85
GBTru: $85
Paid: $_____

• Musical and animated.

Strangers Beware

55192
2002 -
OSRP: $17.50
GBTru: -
Paid: $_____

Campbell's® Trick-Or-Treat

55198
2002 - 2003
OSRP: $17.50
GBTru: $20
Paid: $_____

• Licensed by The Campbell Soup Co.

Gathering Pumpkins

55200
2002 - 2004
OSRP: $30
GBTru: $30
Paid: $_____

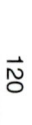

Costume Parade

55201
2002 - 2003
OSRP: $50
GBTru: $65
Paid: $_____

• Limited to year of production.
• Musical and animated.

Building The Scarecrow

55203
2002 - 2003
OSRP: $32.50
GBTru: $38
Paid: $_____

• Limited to year of production.

You Go First!

55319
2002 - 2003
OSRP: *
GBTru: *

* The accessory contained in Black Cat Diner.

Lighting Up Halloween

55238
2003 -
OSRP: $27.50
GBTru: -
Paid: $_____

• Lights up; battery operated.

A Gravely Haunting - 2004

55240 - Set of 2
2003 - 2004
OSRP: $22.50
GBTru: $23
Paid: $_____

• Limited to year of production, 2004.

Canine Trick-Or-Treaters

55241 - Set of 2
2003 -
OSRP: $20
GBTru: -
Paid: $_____

Pick Your Own Pumpkin

55244
2003 -
OSRP: $30
GBTru: -
Paid: $_____

Haunted Harvest

55245
2003 -
OSRP: $17.50
GBTru: -
Paid: $_____

Creative Carvings

55246
2003 -
OSRP: $32.50
GBTru: -
Paid: $_____

• Battery/adapter operated.

Forever On Guard

55248
2003 -
OSRP: $17.50
GBTru: -
Paid: $_____

• Battery/adapter operated.

Just Treats, No Tricks, Please

55343
2003 -
OSRP: *
GBTru: *

* The accessory contained in 1031 Trick-Or-Treat Drive.

Practice Makes Perfect

55347
2003 -
OSRP: *
GBTru: *

* The accessory contained in Witch Way? Flight School.

Haunted Coal Car

53156
2004^M -
OSRP: $85
GBTru: -
Paid: $_____

• Animated

Haunted Tower Tours

55257
2004 -
OSRP: $35
GBTru: -
Paid: $_____

• Adapter included.

A Gravely Haunting - 2005

55270
2004 -
OSRP: $20
GBTru: -
Paid: $_____

• Limited to year of production.

Can't Wait For Halloween!

55272 - Set of 2
2004 -
OSRP: $20
GBTru: -
Paid: $_____

Happy Haunting

55273
2004 -
OSRP: $22.50
GBTru: -
Paid: $_____

• Licensed by Disney.

Brew Ha-Ha

55274
2004 -
OSRP: $15
GBTru: -
Paid: $_____

Caramel Apple Stand

55275
2004 -
OSRP: $27.50
GBTru: -
Paid: $_____

• Battery/adapter compatible.

Black Kittens For Sale

55276
2004 -
OSRP: $10.00
GBTru: -
Paid: $_____

Halloween Hot Rod

55277
2004 -
OSRP: $18.50
GBTru: -
Paid: $_____

Hurry The Movie's About To Start!

Photo Not Available

55347 - Set of 7
2004 -
OSRP: *
GBTru: *

* The accessory contained in LaGhosti Movie Theater.

Use the following space(s) to update your guide when the midyear introductions are announced.

Snow Village Halloween Acc.

Snow Village Halloween Acc.

_____

_____

____ - ____

OSRP: $_____

GBTru: -

Paid: $_____

_____

_____

____ - ____

OSRP: $_____

GBTru: -

Paid: $_____

_____

_____

____ - ____

OSRP: $_____

GBTru: -

Paid: $_____

_____

_____

____ - ____

OSRP: $_____

GBTru: -

Paid: $_____

_____

_____

____ - ____

OSRP: $_____

GBTru: -

Paid: $_____

_____

_____

____ - ____

OSRP: $_____

GBTru: -

Paid: $_____

_____

_____

____ - ____

OSRP: $_____

GBTru: -

Paid: $_____

_____

_____

____ - ____

OSRP: $_____

GBTru: -

Paid: $_____

Dickens' Village Series®

This English village owes a great deal of its popularity to the author after whom it was named. Six of his novels are portrayed in at least one building within the collection, although technically the Satis Manor from Great Expectations is part of the Literary Classics® Series. But references to David Copperfield, Nicholas Nickleby, Oliver Twist, The Old Curiosity Shop, and—most especially—A Christmas Carol have been among the most popular pieces in the village. Some have even been reissued in updated forms following their retirement. Furthermore, the pieces in the Charles Dickens' Signature Series™ depict buildings from the life of the novelist.

But there is much more to this collection than just the entertaining stories of one prolific author. Rural countryside pieces with thatched roofs and small town shops dominated for many years, while more recent buildings seem to reflect an urban London from the past. Maritime pieces pay tribute to England's history as a nation of seafarers. There are beautiful churches, formidable castles and palaces, and—before they were designated as Historical Landmark Series™ pieces—representations of some of the nation's most famous structures.

Several accessories are characters from Dickens' works, and there are even images of the man himself reading from his works, writing, and raising a flag. In addition to figures and small non-lit structures, there are exquisite coaches, a variety of mongers, the Twelve Days of Dickens' Village characters, and links to rail lines that crossed the country. The Abington Canal Series and Queens Port pieces prove that it is a diverse country with a diverse history that has been captured brilliantly.

Dickens' Village

THE ORIGINAL SHOPS OF DICKENS' VILLAGE - Set of 7   65153

Dates	OSRP	GBTru	Paid
1984 - 1988	$175	$950	$_____

• None of the seven buildings have names on the bottom.

Crowntree Inn   65153

Dates	OSRP	GBTru	Paid
1984 - 1988	$25	$170	$_____

Candle Shop   65153

Dates	OSRP	GBTru	Paid
1984 - 1988	$25	$140	$_____

• Early pieces have gray roofs. Later ones have blue.

Green Grocer   65153

Dates	OSRP	GBTru	Paid
1984 - 1988	$25	$165	$_____

• Though there is snow at the base and above the front window, there is no snow on the roof.

Golden Swan Baker   65153

Dates	OSRP	GBTru	Paid
1984 - 1988	$25	$130	$_____

Bean And Son Smithy Shop   65153

Dates	OSRP	GBTru	Paid
1984 - 1988	$25	$150	$_____

Abel Beesley Butcher   65153

Dates	OSRP	GBTru	Paid
1984 - 1988	**$25**	**$95**	**$_____**

Jones & Co. Brush & Basket Shop   65153

Dates	OSRP	GBTru	Paid
1984 - 1988	**$25**	**$198**	**$_____**

Dickens' Village Church   65161

Dates	OSRP	GBTru	Paid
1985 - 1989	**$35**	**See below**	

- There are 5 recognized versions of the Village Church.
- White: Very pale walls and brown cornerstones and roof.
  GBTru: **$285**   Paid: $_____
- Yellow: Yellowish walls with butterscotch stones and roof.
  GBTru: **$135**   Paid: $_____
- Green: Pale green walls with butterscotch stones and roof.
  GBTru: **$220**   Paid: $_____
- Tan: Tan walls with butterscotch stones and roof.
  GBTru: **$110**   Paid: $_____
- Butterscotch: Walls and roof are nearly the same butterscotch color. Only sleeve to read "Village Church." All others read "Shops of Dickens' Village."
  GBTru: **$90**   Paid: $_____

Dickens' Village Mill   65196

Dates	OSRP	GBTru	Paid
1985 - 1986	**$35**	**$4725**	**$_____**

- Limited Edition of 2,500.
- Early pieces have sleeves that read "Dickens' Village Cottage."
- Early release to GCC dealers.

DICKENS' COTTAGES - Set of 3   65188

Dates	OSRP	GBTru	Paid
1985 - 1988	$75	$625	$_____

- None of the three buildings have names on the bottom.
- Early release to GCC dealers.

Thatched Cottage   65188

Dates	OSRP	GBTru	Paid
1985 - 1988	$25	$145	$_____

- Early release to GCC dealers.

Stone Cottage   65188

Dates	OSRP	GBTru	Paid
1985 - 1988	$25	See below	

- The Tan version is considered to be the first shipped.
- The Green version's walls vary from light green to a pea green.
- The chimneys are very fragile.
- Early release to GCC dealers.

	GBTru	Paid
Tan	$330	$_____
Green	$275	$_____

Tudor Cottage   6518

Dates	OSRP	GBTru	Paid
1985 - 1988	$25	$225	$_____

- The chimneys are very fragile and are often crooked.
- Early release to GCC dealers.

Norman Church   6502

Dates	OSRP	GBTru	Paid
1986 - 1987	$40	$2985	$_____

- Limited Edition of 3,500.
- Early Churches are light gray, and they got increasing darker as production continued.
- Early release to GCC dealers.

Dickens' Village

CHRISTMAS CAROL COTTAGES - Set of 3   65005

Dates	OSRP	GBTru	Paid
1986 - 1995	$75	$95	$_____

• Originally marketed as its own sub-series of Dickens' Village with sleeves and hangtags that read "A Christmas Carol." The early pieces were made in Taiwan, and later ones were made in the Philippines.

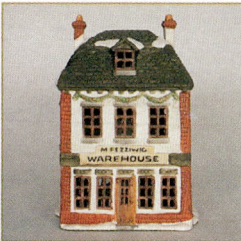

Fezziwig's Warehouse   65005

Dates	OSRP	GBTru	Paid
1986 - 1995	$25	$25	$_____

• Early pieces have panes cut out of the front door. Later ones have a solid front door.

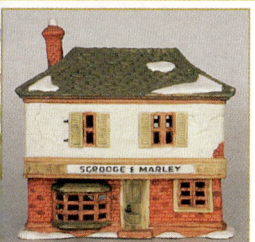

Scrooge & Marley Counting House   65005

Dates	OSRP	GBTru	Paid
1986 - 1995	$25	$40	$_____

• First of two pieces with this name. Re-issued in 2000.

The Cottage of Bob Cratchit & Tiny Tim   65005

Dates	OSRP	GBTru	Paid
1986 - 1995	$25	$45	$_____

• Many scholars believe that Dickens modeled his version of this home after his own childhood home on Bayham St. in Camden Town.

Blythe Pond Mill House   65080

Dates	OSRP	GBTru	Paid
1986 - 1990	$37	See below	

• Early shipments are commonly referred to as the "Correct" version. "Blythe Pond" is correctly inscribed in the bottom of the building.
• This is the rarer of the two versions.
• Later shipments are commonly referred to as the "By The Pond" version. "BY THE POND" is incorrectly inscribed in the bottom of the building.
• The sign above the door is correct on both versions.

	GBTru	Paid
Blythe Pond	$165	$_____
By The Pond	$55	$_____

Dickens' Village

DICKENS' LANE SHOPS - Set of 3   65072

Dates	OSRP	GBTru	Paid
1986 - 1989	$80	$315	$_____

Thomas Kersey Coffee House   65072

Dates	OSRP	GBTru	Paid
1986 - 1989	$27	$135	$_____

• Bottomstamp reads "Coffee House."

Cottage Toy Shop   65072

Dates	OSRP	GBTru	Paid
1986 - 1989	$27	$125	$_____

• Bottomstamp reads "Toy Shop."

Tuttle's Pub   65072

Dates	OSRP	GBTru	Paid
1986 - 1989	$27	$100	$_____

• Bottomstamp reads "Pub."

Chadbury Station And Train - Set of 4   65285

Dates	OSRP	GBTru	Paid
1986 - 1989	$65	$195	$_____

• The front of the platform on the first version of the station is 9" wide.
• The front of the platform on the second version is 9½" wide.
• Early sleeve reads "Train And Lighted Station." The late sleeve reads "Chadbury Station And Train."

BARLEY BREE - Set of 2   59005

Dates	OSRP	GBTru	Paid
1987 - 1989	$60	$215	$_____

- Though the pieces of this set were originally priced at $30 each, they are boxed together. It is extremely rare for them to be sold separately on the secondary market.
- Early pieces have dark roofs. Later ones have lighter roofs.

The Old Curiosity Shop   59056

Dates	OSRP	GBTru	Paid
1987 - 1999	$32	$30	$_____

- Designed after the Old Curiosity Shop on Portsmouth Street in London.
- First of two pieces with this name. Re-issued in 2000.

Kenilworth Castle   59161

Dates	OSRP	GBTru	Paid
1987 - 1988	$70	$425	$_____

- Bottom reads "Castle."
- Early pieces are approx. 9" tall, later ones approx. 8½".
- It's not unusual for this piece to have concave walls. One with straight walls is considered more valuable.

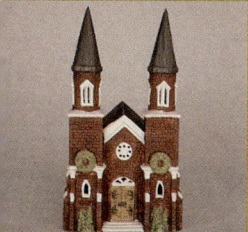

Brick Abbey   65498

Dates	OSRP	GBTru	Paid
1987 - 1989	$33	$195	$_____

- Many pieces have spires that lean inward. One with straight spires is considered more valuable.

Chesterton Manor House   65684

Dates	OSRP	GBTru	Paid
1987 - 1988	$45	$915	$_____

- Limited Edition of 7,500.
- Both the bottomstamp and box read "Manor."
- Early release to GCC dealers.

Dickens' Village

Counting House & Silas Thimbleton Barrister — 59021

Dates	OSRP	GBTru	Paid
1988 - 1990	$32	$70	$_____

- Early pieces have lamps with natural porcelain panes. Later ones have lamps with panes painted yellow.
- Box reads "Silas Thimbleton Barrister." Bottomstamp reads "Counting House."

C. Fletcher Public House — 59048

Dates	OSRP	GBTru	Paid
1988 - 1989	$35	$325	$_____

- Limited Edition of 12,500.
- Box and bottomstamp read "Public House."
- There are some proofs available, though they are rare.
- Early release to GCC dealers.

COBBLESTONE SHOPS - Set of 3 — 59242

Dates	OSRP	GBTru	Paid
1988 - 1990	$95	$250	$_____

The Wool Shop — 59242

Dates	OSRP	GBTru	Paid
1988 - 1990	$32	$135	$_____

Booter And Cobbler — 59242

Dates	OSRP	GBTru	Paid
1988 - 1990	$32	$70	$_____

- Some sleeves picture T. Wells Fruit & Spice Shop though they read "Booter & Cobbler" as they should.
- Some others picture Booter & Cobbler as they shoul and read "T. Wells Fruit & Spice Shop."

T. Wells Fruit & Spice Shop — 59242

Dates	OSRP	GBTru	Paid
1988 - 1990	$32	$65	$_____

- Some sleeves picture Booter & Cobbler though the read "T. Wells Fruit & Spice Shop" as they should.
- Some others picture T. Wells Fruit & Spice Shop as the should and read "Booter & Cobbler."

MERCHANT SHOPS - Set of 5   59269

Dates	OSRP	GBTru	Paid
1988 - 1993	$150	$155	$_____

Poulterer   59269

Dates	OSRP	GBTru	Paid
1988 - 1993	$32.50	$40	$_____

Geo. Weeton Watchmaker   59269

Dates	OSRP	GBTru	Paid
1988 - 1993	$32.50	$35	$_____

The Mermaid Fish Shoppe   59269

Dates	OSRP	GBTru	Paid
1988 - 1993	$32.50	$45	$_____

White Horse Bakery   59269

Dates	OSRP	GBTru	Paid
1988 - 1993	$32.50	$35	$_____

Walpole Tailors   59269

Dates	OSRP	GBTru	Paid
1988 - 1993	$32.50	$30	$_____

Dickens' Village

Dickens' Village

NICHOLAS NICKLEBY - Set of 2   59250

Dates	OSRP	GBTru	Paid
1988 - 1991	$72	$100	$_____

Set with the "K" version of Nicholas Nickleby Cottage: $115 $_____

Nicholas Nickleby Cottage   59250

Dates	OSRP	GBTru	Paid
1988 - 1991	$36	$50	$_____

- Early pieces have a bottomstamp that reads "Nick**o**las Nickleby."   **GBTru: $70** $_____

Wackford Squeers Boarding School   59250

Dates	OSRP	GBTru	Paid
1988 - 1991	$36	$60	$_____

- Dickens based his version of the school on the Bowes Academy that once stood in Yorkshire.
- The majority of these have a sagging roof.

Ivy Glen Church   59277

Dates	OSRP	GBTru	Paid
1988 - 1991	$35	$60	$_____

Victoria Station   55743

Dates	OSRP	GBTru	Paid
1989 - 1998	$100	$100	$_____

- Inspired by the famous station in London.
- Early release to Showcase and NALED dealers.

Knottinghill Church   5582

Dates	OSRP	GBTru	Paid
1989 - 1995	$50	$55	$_____

DAVID COPPERFIELD - Set of 3   55506

Dates	OSRP	GBTru	Paid
1989 - 1992	$125	$130	$_____

Set with the Tan version of Peggotty's Seaside Cottage: $175 $_____

• Early release to Showcase dealers.

Mr. Wickfield Solicitor   55506

Dates	OSRP	GBTru	Paid
1989 - 1992	$42.50	$55	$_____

• Dickens based his version of this house on one that stands at 71 St. Dunstan's St. in Canterbury, England.
• Early release to Showcase dealers.

Betsy Trotwood's Cottage   55506

Dates	OSRP	GBTru	Paid
1989 - 1992	$42.50	$45	$_____

• Dickens based his version of this cottage on one owned by Mary Strong in Broadstairs, England. It is now a Dickens museum.
• Early release to Showcase dealers.

Peggotty's Seaside Cottage   55506

Dates	OSRP	GBTru	Paid
1989 - 1992	$42.50	See below	

• The Tan version was the earlier of the two. Its hull is not painted. Department 56 stated that the green paint it intended to use would not adhere to the porcelain.
• The problem was resolved by using a different green paint.
• This was an early release to Showcase dealers.
• Dickens based his version of the cottage on an actual boat-turned dwelling at the canal at Gravesend.

	GBTru	Paid
Tan	$90	$_____
Green	$45	$_____

Cobles Police Station   55832

Dates	OSRP	GBTru	Paid
1989 - 1991	$37.50	$90	$_____

Dickens' Village

Theatre Royal — 55840

Dates	OSRP	GBTru	Paid
1989 - 1992	$45	$60	$_____

- Inspired by the Theatre Royal in Rochester, England where Dickens saw his first Shakespearean play.

Ruth Marion Scotch Woolens — 55859

Dates	OSRP	GBTru	Paid
1989 - 1990	$65	$250	$_____
		$150	$_____

- Limited Edition of 17,500.
- Proofs have "Proof" stamped on the bottom and on the sleeve instead of a number.
- Early release to GCC dealers.

Green Gate Cottage — 55867

Dates	OSRP	GBTru	Paid
1989 - 1990	$65	$175	$_____
		$125	$_____

- Limited Edition of 22,500.
- Proofs have "Proof" stamped on the bottom and on the sleeve instead of a number.
- Early release to Showcase Dealers.

The Flat Of Ebenezer Scrooge — 55875

Dates	OSRP	GBTru	Paid
1989 - 2001	$37.50	See below	

- Version 1:
- Window panes on the second and third floor are painted yellow. The fourth floor's far left shutter is slightly open.
- Gray trim is darker than on subsequent editions.
- Early release to NALED dealers.

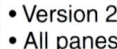

- Version 2:
- All panes have been cut out of the windows on the second and third floors.
- Like Version 1, this was made in Taiwan.

- Version 3:
- Window panes are yellow. The far left shutter on the 4th floor is closed. Made in Philippines and China.
- Christmas Carol Series.
- Ebenezer Scrooge's House introduced in 2001.

	GBTru	Paid
Version 1	$85	$_____
Version 2	$45	$_____
Version 3	$40	$_____

Dickens' Village

Bishops Oast House — 55670

Dates	OSRP	GBTru	Paid
1990 - 1992	**$45**	**$55**	$_____

- "Bishops" refers to a surname, not a religious figure.
- Oast houses dot the Kent countryside. Many have been converted into private homes.

KING'S ROAD - Set of 2 — 55689

Dates	OSRP	GBTru	Paid
1990 - 1996	**$72**	**$60**	$_____

Tutbury Printer — 55690

Dates	OSRP	GBTru	Paid
1990 - 1996	**$36**	**$35**	$_____

C. H. Watt Physician — 55691

Dates	OSRP	GBTru	Paid
1990 - 1996	**$36**	**$35**	$_____

Fagin's Hide-A-Way — 55522

Dates	OSRP	GBTru	Paid
1991 - 1995	**$68**	**$70**	$_____

- Dickens based his Fagin's Hide-A-Way and its characters in Oliver Twist on the people who frequented the series of underground passages in London.

Ashbury Inn — 55557

Dates	OSRP	GBTru	Paid
1991 - 1995	**$55**	**$60**	$_____

Dickens' Village

OLIVER TWIST - Set of 2 — 55530

Dates	OSRP	GBTru	Paid
1991 - 1993	$75	$65	$_____

Brownlow House — 55530

Dates	OSRP	GBTru	Paid
1991 - 1993	$37.50	$40	$_____

- Early samples have charcoal gray roof and trim.
- Dickens based his version of this house on the one at 39 Craven Street in London.

Maylie Cottage — 55530

Dates	OSRP	GBTru	Paid
1991 - 1993	$37.50	$40	$_____

Nephew Fred's Flat — 55573

Dates	OSRP	GBTru	Paid
1991 - 1994	$35	$60	$_____

- Christmas Carol Series.
- Early pieces were manufactured in Taiwan and are darker than the later ones from China.
- Later version, Fred Holiwell's House, introduced in 2001.

Crown & Cricket Inn — 57509

Dates	OSRP	GBTru	Paid
1991 - 1992	$100	$105	$_____

- Limited to year of production.
- The first of the Charles Dickens' Signature Series.
- Early pieces have light trim, later ones darker gray trim.

Old Michaelchurch — 55620

Dates	OSRP	GBTru	Paid
1992 - 1996	$42	$45	$_____

- Early release to Showcase and GCC dealers.

The Pied Bull Inn — 57517

Dates	OSRP	GBTru	Paid
1992 - 1993	**$100**	**$100**	$_____

- Limited to year of production.
- Charles Dickens' Signature Series.
- Sign is separate in box.

Hembleton Pewterer — 58009

Dates	OSRP	GBTru	Paid
1992 - 1995	**$72**	**$60**	$_____

- The right side of the early pieces is composed of two small additions. On the later ones it is one large addition.

King's Road Post Office — 58017

Dates	OSRP	GBTru	Paid
1992 - 1998	**$45**	**$40**	$_____

- Flag is separate in box.

Boarding & Lodging School - #18 — 58092

Dates	OSRP	GBTru	Paid
1992 - 1993	**$48**	**$75**	$_____

- Limited to year of production. See also 1994 release.
- This Signature Series piece commemorates the 150th anniversary of the publishing of *A Christmas Carol*.
- Early release to Showcase dealers and buying groups.

Dedlock Arms — 57525

Dates	OSRP	GBTru	Paid
1993 - 1994	**$100**	**$90**	$_____

- Limited to year of production.
- Charles Dickens' Signature Series.
- Dickens based his version of this tavern from *Bleak House* on the Sondes Arms in Rockingham, England.

Kingsford's Brew House — 58114

Dates	OSRP	GBTru	Paid
1993 - 1996	**$45**	**$50**	$_____

- Sign is separate in box.

Dickens' Village

PUMP LANE SHOPPES - Set of 3 — 58084

Dates	OSRP	GBTru	Paid
1993 - 1996	$112	$110	$_____

Bumpstead Nye Cloaks & Canes — 58085

Dates	OSRP	GBTru	Paid
1993 - 1996	$37.50	$40	$_____

Lomas Ltd. Molasses — 58086

Dates	OSRP	GBTru	Paid
1993 - 1996	$37.50	$40	$_____

W. M. Wheat Cakes & Puddings — 58087

Dates	OSRP	GBTru	Paid
1993 - 1996	$37.50	$45	$_____

• The name on the front of the building reads "WM," the abbreviation of William.

Great Denton Mill — 58122

Dates	OSRP	GBTru	Paid
1993 - 1997	$50	$55	$_____

Whittlesbourne Church — 5821?

Dates	OSRP	GBTru	Paid
1994^M - 1998	$85	$80	$_____

Dickens' Village

Giggelswick Mutton & Ham — 58220

Dates	OSRP	GBTru	Paid
1994ᴹ - 1997	$48	$50	$_____

Boarding & Lodging School - #43 — 58106

Dates	OSRP	GBTru	Paid
1994 - 1998	$48	$50	$_____

- This School with 43 as its address is similar to the 1992 limited edition that has 18 as its address. Putting the addresses together forms 1843, the year *A Christmas Carol* was published.

PORTOBELLO ROAD THATCHED COTTAGES - Set of 3 — 58246

Dates	OSRP	GBTru	Paid
1994 - 1997	$120	$110	$_____

Mr. & Mrs. Pickle — 58247

Dates	OSRP	GBTru	Paid
1994 - 1997	$40	$40	$_____

Cobb Cottage — 58248

Dates	OSRP	GBTru	Paid
1994 - 1997	$40	$40	$_____

Browning Cottage — 58249

Dates	OSRP	GBTru	Paid
1994 - 1997	$40	$45	$_____

Dickens' Village

Sir John Falstaff Inn 57533

Dates	OSRP	GBTru	Paid
1994 - 1995	**$100**	**$85**	$_____

- Limited to year of production.
- Charles Dickens' Signature Series.
- Inspired by the inn across from Dickens' last home, Gad's Hill Place.

Hather Harness 58238

Dates	OSRP	GBTru	Paid
1994 - 1997	**$48**	**$40**	$_____

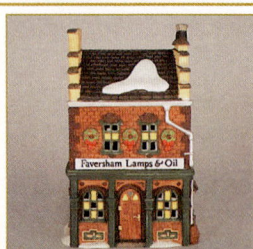

Dickens' Village Start A Tradition Set 58327

Dates	OSRP	GBTru	Paid
1995ᴹ - 1996	**$85**	**$80**	$_____

- First available at the 1995 Homes for the Holidays event.
- During that event and the 1996 Homes for the Holidays event, it was specially priced at $65.

- Set of 13 includes the "Town Square Shops"— **Faversham Lamps & Oil** (top) and **Morston Steak And Kidney Pie** (bottom)—the 3 piece accessory "Town Square Carolers," 6 trees, Cobblestone Road, and a bag of snow.

The Maltings 58335

Dates	OSRP	GBTru	Paid
1995ᴹ - 1998	**$50**	**$50**	$_____

Dudden Cross Church 58343

Dates	OSRP	GBTru	Paid
1995ᴹ - 1997	**$45**	**$50**	$_____

- Early pieces have a bell that hangs in actual cutout in bell tower. Later ones have bell as part of porcelain.

The Grapes Inn — 57534

Dates	OSRP	GBTru	Paid
1995 - 1996	$120	$100	$_____

- Limited to year of production.
- Charles Dickens' Signature Series.
- Dickens based the Porters in *Our Mutual Friend* on this inn located in the Limehouse section of London.

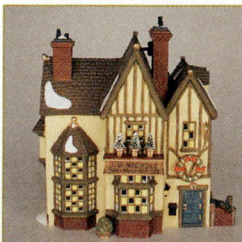

J. D. Nichols Toy Shop — 58328

Dates	OSRP	GBTru	Paid
1995 - 1998	$48	$50	$_____

- Sign is separate in box.

Dursley Manor — 58329

Dates	OSRP	GBTru	Paid
1995 - 1999	$50	$55	$_____

Blenham Street Bank — 58330

Dates	OSRP	GBTru	Paid
1995 - 1998	$60	$70	$_____

WRENBURY SHOPS - Set of 3 — 58331

Dates	OSRP	GBTru	Paid
1995 - 1997/98	$100	$100	$_____

Wrenbury Baker — 58332

Dates	OSRP	GBTru	Paid
1995 - 1997	$35	$35	$_____

- Sign is separate in box.

Dickens' Village

The Chop Shop — 58333

Dates	OSRP	GBTru	Paid
1995 - 1997	$35	$40	$_____

- Sign is separate in box.

T. Puddlewick Spectacle Shop — 58334

Dates	OSRP	GBTru	Paid
1995 - 1998	$35	$40	$_____

- Sign is separate in box.

Ramsford Palace — 58336

Dates	OSRP	GBTru	Paid
1996ᴹ - 1996	$175	$250	$_____

- Limited Edition of 27,500.
- Inspired by the Castle Howard in York, England.
- Set of 17 includes the Palace, the 2 piece accessory "Palace Guards," gate, fountain, 8 wall hedges, and 4 corner topiaries.

Butter Tub Farmhouse — 58337

Dates	OSRP	GBTru	Paid
1996ᴹ - 1999	$40	$60	$_____

- Butter Tub refers to the Buttertub Pass in Yorkshire, England where pools known as buttertubs form in potholes.

Butter Tub Barn — 58338

Dates	OSRP	GBTru	Paid
1996ᴹ - 1999	$48	$55	$_____

- Butter Tub refers to the Buttertub Pass in Yorkshire, England where pools known as buttertubs form in potholes.

The Christmas Carol Cottage — 58339

Dates	OSRP	GBTru	Paid
1996ᴹ - 2000	$60	$60	$_____

- Christmas Carol Revisited Series.
- Uses Magic Smoke to create smoking effect rising from the chimney.
- Sign is separate in box.

Gad's Hill Place — 57535

Dates	OSRP	GBTru	Paid
1996 - 1997	$98	$100	$_____

- Limited to year of production.
- Inspired by Dickens' last home, Gad's Hill Place.
- Sign is separate in box.
- Charles Dickens' Signature Series.

Nettie Quinn Puppets & Marionettes — 58344

Dates	OSRP	GBTru	Paid
1996 - 2001	$50	$55	$_____

- This is the first Heritage Village Collection design to feature multiple weathervanes, and they are very fragile.
- Sign and 2 marionettes are separate in box.

Mulberrie Court Brownstones — 58345

Dates	OSRP	GBTru	Paid
1996 - 1999	$90	$100	$_____

- This piece is frequently adopted into Christmas In The City by collectors.
- Includes 7 sisal bushes to be placed around building.

The Olde Camden Town Church — 58346

Dates	OSRP	GBTru	Paid
1996 - 1999	$55	$60	$_____

- Dickens may have based his version of the Church on St. Stephen's Church in Camden, England.
- Christmas Carol Revisited Series.

The Melancholy Tavern — 58347

Dates	OSRP	GBTru	Paid
1996 - 1999	$45	$45	$_____

- Dickens may have based his version of the Tavern on the Baker's Chop Shop that once stood in London.
- First of two pieces with this name. Re-issued in 2003.
- Christmas Carol Revisited Series. Sign is separate in box.

Dickens' Village

Quilly's Antiques — 58348

Dates	OSRP	GBTru	Paid
1996 - 1999	$46	$50	$_____

Dickens' Village Start A Tradition Set — 58322

Dates	OSRP	GBTru	Paid
1997ᴹ - 1998	$100	$95	$_____

- First available during the November 1997 Homes for the Holidays event. The price was reduced to $65 during the event.

- Set of 13 includes **Sudbury Church** (top), **Old East Rectory** (bottom), a 3 piece accessory "The Spirit Of Giving," 6 sisal trees, Cobblestone Road, and a bag of snow.

J. Lytes Coal Merchant — 58323

Dates	OSRP	GBTru	Paid
1997ᴹ - 1999	$50	$50	$_____

- Early pieces have bottomstamps that read "Dickens' **Vallage** Series."

Tower Of London — 58500

Dates	OSRP	GBTru	Paid
1997ᴹ - 1997	$165	$225	$_____

- Limited to year of production.
- The first Historical Landmark Series design. See this series in the Small Collection section.
- This, the White Tower, is one of the many towers that comprise the Tower of London, famous for housing a prison as well as the Crown Jewels. Legend says six ravens must be at the tower to preserve the monarchy.
- The actual Tower of London is located along the Thames River in London.
- Set of 5 includes the Tower, a gate with tower, the raven master, a sign, and a wall with ravens.

Barmby Moor Cottage 58324

Dates	OSRP	GBTru	Paid
1997ᴹ - 2000	**$48**	**$50**	$_____

• Barmby Moor is a village located east of York, England.

Manchester Square 58301

Dates	OSRP	GBTru	Paid
1997 - 2000	**$250**	**$245**	$_____

• Early pieces have bottomstamps that read "Dickens' Village **Seires**."
• Set of 25 includes **Custom House** (top), **Frogmore Chemist** (center), **G. Choir's Weights & Scales** (bottom), **Lydby Trunk & Satchel Shop** (below), the 7 piece accessory "Manchester Square Accessory Set," 12 trees, Cobblestone Road, and a bag of snow.
• Frogmore's sign and G. Choir's scales are separate in box.
• Man's walking stick is fragile.

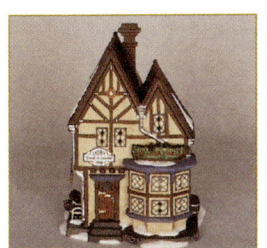

East Indies Trading Co. 58302

Dates	OSRP	GBTru	Paid
1997 - 1999	**$65**	**$70**	$_____

• Similar to the Canadian Trading Co., but with a change of colors.

Canadian Trading Co. 58306

Dates	OSRP	GBTru	Paid
1997 - 1998	**$65**	**$125**	$_____

• Similar to the East Indies Trading Co., but with a slight change of colors.
• Available only in Canada.
• Sign is separate in box.

Leacock Poulterer 58303

Dates	OSRP	GBTru	Paid
1997 - 1999	$48	$50	$_____

• Christmas Carol Revisited Series.

Crooked Fence Cottage 58304

Dates	OSRP	GBTru	Paid
1997 - 2000	$60	$60	$_____

• Early pieces have bottomstamps that read "Dickens' Village **Seires**."
• Bird cage is separate in box.
• The tree branches in front are very fragile.

Ashwick Lane Hose & Ladder 58305

Dates	OSRP	GBTru	Paid
1997 -	$54	-	$_____

• 2 ladders are separate in box.
• This design was also the primary piece in a special GCC gift set in 2000.

The Old Globe Theatre 58501

Dates	OSRP	GBTru	Paid
1997 - 1998	$175	$165	$_____

• Limited to year of production.
• The second Historical Landmark Series design. See this series in the Small Collection section.
• First samples of the building were made as two pieces. For production it is one piece.
• Some early pieces have "The City Globe" stamped on the bottom.
• The Globe Theatre, located along the Thames River in London, was demolished in 1644 and was rebuilt in 1996 near the original site.
• Set of 4 includes the Theatre, two trumpeters, and a sign.

Thomas Mudge Timepieces 58307

Dates	OSRP	GBTru	Paid
1998ᴹ - 2000	$60	$70	$_____

• Clock is separate in box.
• Lamppost is fragile.

Seton Morris Spice Merchant Gift Set 58308

Dates	OSRP	GBTru	Paid
1998ᴹ - 1998	$65	$65	$_____

- Limited to year of production.
- First available during the November 1998 Homes for the Holidays event.
- Set of 10 includes the shop, a 3 piece accessory "Christmas Apples," 4 sisal trees, Cobblestone Road, and a bag of snow.

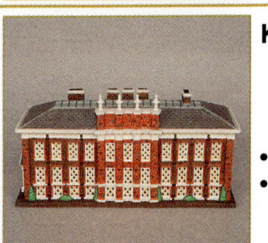

Kensington Palace 58309

Dates	OSRP	GBTru	Paid
1998ᴹ - 1998	$195	$180	$_____

- Limited to year of production.
- Introduced during the 1998 International Collectible Expo, this special edition of the famous London royal residence was first available during the November 1998 Homes for the Holidays event.
- A portion of the proceeds benefited the Ronald McDonald Houses across the U.S. and Canada.
- Early pieces had boxes that read "Princess of Whales." When discovered, stickers that read "Princess of Wales" were placed over the mistake.
- Set includes the Palace, palace gates, a statue of William III, a flag of Great Britain, 4 sisal trees, 4 sisal hedges, adhesive adornments, and Cobblestone Road.

Tattyeave Knoll 58311

Dates	OSRP	GBTru	Paid
1998ᴹ - 1999	$55	$55	$_____

Heathmoor Castle 58313

Dates	OSRP	GBTru	Paid
1998 - 1999	$90	$90	$_____

- Limited to year of production.
- 2 pennants are separate in box.
- 1 lion on each of the two center turrets is supposed to appear as if it is broken.

Dickens' Village

Teaman & Crupp China Shop — 58314

Dates	OSRP	GBTru	Paid
1998 - 2003	**$64**	**$65**	$_____

- Sign is separate in box.

Lynton Point Tower — 58315

Dates	OSRP	GBTru	Paid
1998 - 2001	**$80**	**$80**	$_____

- 2 small attachments are separate in box.
- Oars at boat are fragile.

North Eastern Sea Fisheries Ltd. — 58316

Dates	OSRP	GBTru	Paid
1998 - 1999	**$70**	**$70**	$_____

The Horse And Hounds Pub — 58340

Dates	OSRP	GBTru	Paid
1998 - 2004	**$70**	**$70**	$_____

- Two signs are separate in box.

Great Expectations Satis Manor — 58310

Dates	OSRP	GBTru	Paid
1998 - 2001	**$110**	**$110**	$_____

- The first Literary Classics design. See this series in the Small Collection section.
- Charles Dickens used Restoration House in Rochester England as the model for his Satis Manor.
- Set of 4 plus book includes the Manor and the accessory "Miss Havisham, Estella, and Pip."

Dickens' Village

Big Ben   58341

Dates	OSRP	GBTru	Paid
1998 - 2003	$95	$115	$____

- The fourth Historical Landmark Series design. See this series in the Small Collection section.
- It is a replica of London's Big Ben along the Thames River.
- Set of 2 includes Big Ben with working clock and sign.

Chancery Corner   58352

Dates	OSRP	GBTru	Paid
1999ᴹ - 1999	$65	$75	$____

- Limited to year of production.
- This was the first Dickens' Village design to include a three-dimensional scene in the house.
- First available during the 1999 Discover Department 56 event.
- Set of 8 includes the house, 2 sisal trees, 2 fence sections with gate, walkway, birdbath, and snow.

Dudley Docker   58353

Dates	OSRP	GBTru	Paid
1999ᴹ - 2000	$70	$75	$____

Old Queensbridge Station   58443

Dates	OSRP	GBTru	Paid
1999 - 2002	$100	$95	$____

- 6 hanging plants and a clock are separate in box.
- Do not handle by the metal canopies.
- Set of 2 includes the Station and a platform.

Dickens' Village

Margrove Orangery 58440

Dates	OSRP	GBTru	Paid
1999 - 2001	$98	$90	$_____

Aldeburgh Music Box Shop 58441

Dates	OSRP	GBTru	Paid
1999 - 2000	$60	$65	$_____

- Dream House Sweepstakes Grand Prize winner assisted in the design.
- Music box plays "Chopin's "Fantaisie-Impromptu."
- Named after a seaside town in England.

Aldeburgh Music Box Shop Gift Set 58442

Dates	OSRP	GBTru	Paid
1999 - 2000	$85	$95	$_____

- Limited Edition of 35,000.
- First available during the Spring 2000 Discover Department 56 event.
- Music box plays "Heindenroselin."
- Set of 3 includes Shop, "The Mother's Gift" accessory, walkway with pediments, floral hedges and topiaries, and 2 hanging baskets.
- Sign is separate in box for this and the design above.

McShane Cottage 58444

Dates	OSRP	GBTru	Paid
1999 - 2001	$55	$55	$_____

- Set of 2 includes the Cottage and a duck house.

Staghorn Lodge 58445

Dates	OSRP	GBTru	Paid
1999 - 2002	$72	$75	$_____

- Early pieces have brown antlers above the front door o antlers that were simply painted on. Later ones have gold antlers.

Dickens' Village

Leed's Oyster House — 58446

Dates	OSRP	GBTru	Paid
1999 - 2001	**$68**	**$70**	$____

- The positions of the holes for the signs are reversed from the ones shown on the sleeve. This requires that the location of the signs be switched.

The China Trader — 58447

Dates	OSRP	GBTru	Paid
1999 - 2000	**$72**	**$75**	$____

The Spider Box Locks — 58448

Dates	OSRP	GBTru	Paid
1999 - 2001	**$60**	**$60**	$____

- Sign and key are separate in box.

Wingham Lane Parrot Seller — 58449

Dates	OSRP	GBTru	Paid
1999 - 2001	**$68**	**$65**	$____

- Sign and 5 bird cages are separate in box.
- This shop derives its name from the Wingham Bird Park located near Canterbury, England.

The Old Royal Observatory Gold Dome Edition — 58451

Dates	OSRP	GBTru	Paid
1999 - 2000	**Promo**	**$365**	$____

- Limited to 5,500, Department 56 sent one to its valued retailers as a thank you for their support.
- The fifth Historical Landmark Series design. See this series in the Small Collection section.

The Old Royal Observatory — 58453

Dates	OSRP	GBTru	Paid
1999 - 2000	**$95**	**$105**	$____

- Limited Edition of 35,000.
- The fifth Historical Landmark Series design. See this series in the Small Collection section.
- Set of 2 includes Observatory and sign.

Dickens' Village

Fezziwig's Ballroom Animated Gift Set   58470

Dates	OSRP	GBTru	Paid
2000ᴹ - 2000	$75	$105	$_____

- First available during the 2000 Discover Dept. 56 event.
- The silver bell honors Department 56's 25th anniversary.
- The dancers inside the building spin on a revolving turntable.
- Set of 6 includes the warehouse, the accessory "Scrooge At Fezziwig's Ball," 3 sisal trees, and a bag of snow.
- Christmas Carol Series.

St. Martin-In-The-Fields Church   58471

Dates	OSRP	GBTru	Paid
2000ᴹ - 2002	$96	$100	$_____

- Inspired by the famous church in London's Trafalgar Sq.
- The Roman numerals on the portico of Department 56's version read 1716 instead of 1726.
- Ornamental top for spire is separate in box.

Ashwick Lane Gift Set   05700

Dates	OSRP	GBTru	Paid
2000ᴹ - 2000	$65	$75	$_____

- Gold accents have been added to the hinges and rail posts of the 1997 version of this building.
- This set is an exclusive for GCC dealers.
- Set of 10 includes the fire house, a 3 piece accessory "At The Firehouse" that has a brass plaque that can be personalized, 4 trees, Cobblestone Road, and a bag of snow.

Crowntree Freckleton Windmill   58472

Dates	OSRP	GBTru	Paid
2000 - 2001	$80	$105	$_____

- 25th Anniversary Limited Edition of 30,000.
- Abington Canal Series.
- Windmill is animated.
- The open door and fence are very fragile.

Abington Lockside Inn — 58473

Dates	OSRP	GBTru	Paid
2000 - 2003	$68	$65	$_____

- Abington Canal Series.

Abington Lockkeeper's Residence — 58474

Dates	OSRP	GBTru	Paid
2000 - 2002	$58	$60	$_____

- Abington Canal Series.
- Bell is separate in box.

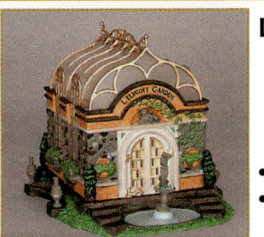

Lilycott Garden Conservatory — 58475

Dates	OSRP	GBTru	Paid
2000 - 2001	$65	$70	$_____

- Discover Department 56 Spring Event Piece.
- Set of 5 includes building, "Sweet Roses" accessory, and 3 topiary trees.
- Fountain is separate in box.

Hedgerow Garden Cottage — 58476

Dates	OSRP	GBTru	Paid
2000 - 2002	$57	$55	$_____

Burwickglen Golf Clubhouse — 58477

Dates	OSRP	GBTru	Paid
2000 - 2002	$96	$95	$_____

- Sign, 9 pennants, and "pin" are separate in box.

Dickens' Village

Dickens' Village

Glendun Cocoa Works — 58478

Dates	OSRP	GBTru	Paid
2000 - 2003	$80	$85	$_____

• Lantern is separate in box.
• Smokestack and ironwork brace are fragile.

Rockingham School — 58479

Dates	OSRP	GBTru	Paid
2000 - 2002	$85	$85	$_____

• Sign is separate in box.
• Spires and small stacks are fragile.

Royal Stock Exchange — 58480

Dates	OSRP	GBTru	Paid
2000 - 2001	$110	$115	$_____

• Urns are fragile.

Royal Staffordshire Porcelains — 58481

Dates	OSRP	GBTru	Paid
2000 - 2002	$65	$70	$_____

• Sign is separate in box.

The Old Curiosity Shop — 58482

Dates	OSRP	GBTru	Paid
2000 -	$50	-	$_____

• This is the updated version of the same piece originally issued in 1987.
• Do not handle by hitching posts.

Scrooge & Marley Counting House — 58483

Dates	OSRP	GBTru	Paid
2000 -	$80	-	$_____

• This is the updated version of the same piece originally issued in 1986.
• Sign is separate in box.
• Christmas Carol Series.

Sherlock Holmes - 221B Baker Street　　58601

Dates	OSRP	GBTru	Paid
2000 - 2003	$90	$100	$_____

- This is the fifth Literary Classics piece. See this series in the Small Collection section.
- Inspired by Arthur Conan Doyle's famous works, this is Department 56's interpretation of the home of England's greatest fictional detective.
- Set of 3 plus book includes the house and 2 piece accessory "Elementary My Dear Watson."

Brightsmith & Sons, Queens Jewellers　　58484

Dates	OSRP	GBTru	Paid
2001ᴹ - 2001	$75	$495	$_____

- Special Swarovski crystals are featured on the building.
- Only available at Dept. 56 25th Anniversary celebration.
- Sign separate in box.

Somerset Valley Church　　58485

Dates	OSRP	GBTru	Paid
2001ᴹ - 2001	$75	$80	$_____

- First available during the 2001 Holiday Discover Department 56 event.
- Church bell can be set to chime hourly.
- Set of 9 includes the Church, the accessory "Christmas Eve Celebration," 3 sisal trees, 2 fieldstone wall sections, and a bag of snow.

Cratchit's Corner　　58486

Dates	OSRP	GBTru	Paid
2001ᴹ -	$80	-	$_____

- Christmas Carol Series.

Dickens' Village

Dickens' Village

Mrs. Brimm's Tea Room Gift Set — 58487

Dates	OSRP	GBTru	Paid
2001 - 2002	$65	$70	$_____

- First available during the Mother's Day Spring Program.
- Set of 4 includes building, sign that can be personalized, tree, and accessory "High Tea."
- Hanging sign and 2 hanging plants are separate in box.
- 5% of proceeds goes to fight against breast cancer.

Dickens' Gad's Hill Chalet — 58488

Dates	OSRP	GBTru	Paid
2001 - 2003	$65	$70	$_____

- Set of 2 includes Chalet and "Dickens Writing" accessory.

"Bidwell Windmill" #2 — 58489

Dates	OSRP	GBTru	Paid
2001 - 2003	$80	$85	$_____

- Abington Canal Series.
- Windmill is animated.

Ebenezer Scrooge's House — 5849

Dates	OSRP	GBTru	Paid
2001 -	$85	-	$_____

- Christmas Carol Series.
- Hanging sack is separate in the box.
- This is an updated version of The Flat of Ebenezer Scrooge (1989).

Fred Holiwell's House — 58492

Dates	OSRP	GBTru	Paid
2001 - 2004	$62	$62	$_____

- Christmas Carol Series.
- This is an updated version of Nephew Fred's Flat (1991).

Sheffield Manor — 58493

Dates	OSRP	GBTru	Paid
2001 - 2002	$130	$150	$_____

- Limited to year of production, 2002.

The Slone Hotel — 58494

Dates	OSRP	GBTru	Paid
2001 - 2003	$90	$90	$_____

- Set of 2 includes includes Hotel and "Doorman" accessory.
- Spire is separate in the box.
- Awning supports are very fragile.

Bayly's Blacksmith — 58495

Dates	OSRP	GBTru	Paid
2001 - 2004	$70	$70	$_____

- Sign is separate in the box.

St. Ives Lock House — 58496

Dates	OSRP	GBTru	Paid
2001 - 2003	$75	$80	$_____

- Abington Canal series.
- The ladder is extremely fragile.

Dickens' Village

Piccadilly Gallery   58498

Dates	OSRP	GBTru	Paid
2001 - 2002	$75	$75	$_____

• Lamps are fragile.

Thornbury Chapel   58502

Dates	OSRP	GBTru	Paid
2001 - 2003	$60	$60	$_____

Christmas At Codington Cottage   05925

Dates	OSRP	GBTru	Paid
2002ᴹ - 2002	$75	$70	$_____

• Department store exclusive.
• Limited to year of production.
• The "Winter Frolic" accessory is animated.
• The railing and water pump are very fragile.
• Set of 7 includes the Cottage, "Winter Frolic" accessory, 3 Natural Evergreens, a Bare Branch Tree, and snow.
• A similar design, Codington Cottage with a different accessory and no trees or snow, was released as a regular issue in 2002.

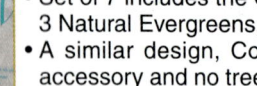

1 Royal Tree Court   58506

Dates	OSRP	GBTru	Paid
2002ᴹ - 2002	$75	$95	$_____

• Holiday 2002 Special Edition.
• Limited to year of production.
• Animated.
• Set of 8 includes the house, "Bearing Gifts" accessory, 2 riverstone walls, 2 frosted topiaries, a Bare Branch Tree, and snow.
• Spires are fragile.

Dickens' Village

Norfolk Biffins Bakery 58491

Dates	OSRP	GBTru	Paid
2002ᴹ - 2004	$65	$65	$_____

- Christmas Carol Series.

Hop Castle Folly 58633

Dates	OSRP	GBTru	Paid
2002ᴹ - 2002	$65	$125	$_____

- Club 56 dealer exclusive.
- Limited to 5,600 numbered pieces.
- Inspired by an actual building in northern England.
- Set of 2 includes the building and "Lord Of The Follies" accessory.
- Weathervane is separate in the box.
- Certificate of authenticity is included in the box.

Regent Street Coffeehouse 58507

Dates	OSRP	GBTru	Paid
2002 - 2004	$70	$70	$_____

Antiquarian Bookseller 58508

Dates	OSRP	GBTru	Paid
2002 - 2004	$57	$60	$_____

Mordecai Mould Undertaker 58509

Dates	OSRP	GBTru	Paid
2002 - 2004	$70	$70	$_____

- All Hallow's Eve design.
- Named for the undertaker in Dickens' "Life And Adventures Of Martin Chuzzlewit."

Dickens' Village

Collyweston Post Office 58510

Dates	OSRP	GBTru	Paid
2002 - 2003	$50	$55	$_____

The Leather Bottle 58511

Dates	OSRP	GBTru	Paid
2002 - 2003	$65	$70	$_____

- Abington Canal Series.
- Charles Dickens frequented a pub named The Leather Bottle.

Belle's House 58512

Dates	OSRP	GBTru	Paid
2002 - 2004	$55	$55	$_____

- Christmas Carol Series.
- A special 20th Anniversary edition of this design was issued in 2004.

The Daily News 58513

Dates	OSRP	GBTru	Paid
2002 - 2004	$75	$75	$_____

- Set of 2 includes the building and "The First Edition" accessory.
- Named after the newspaper where Charles Dickens was the editior.

Westminster Abbey 5851?

Dates	OSRP	GBTru	Paid
2002 -	$95	-	$_____

- This is a replica of one of England's most famous landmarks.
- Historical information is printed on the back of facade.

Codington Cottage 58514

Dates	OSRP	GBTru	Paid
2002 - 2003	**$65**	**$70**	**$_____**

- Set of 2 includes the Cottage and "Bringing Home The Holly" accessory.
- A similar design, Christmas At Codington Cottage with a different accessory, trees, and snow, was released as a department store exclusive in 2002.

Shakespeare's Birthplace 58515

Dates	OSRP	GBTru	Paid
2002 - 2003	**$85**	**$85**	**$_____**

- Limited to 25,000 numbered pieces.
- Inspired by the author's birthplace in Stratford-Upon-Avon.
- Set of 4 includes the building and "All The World's A Stage" accessory.

Sweetbriar Cottage 58518

Dates	OSRP	GBTru	Paid
2002 - 2003	**$65**	**$65**	**$_____**

- Spring Gift Set.
- Set of 3 includes the Cottage, "Rose Garden Beauty" accessory, and a spring tree.

Dickens' Village

London Skating Club 58700

Dates	OSRP	GBTru	Paid
2003^M - 2003	$75	$75	$_____

- Holiday Gift Set.
- Set of 5 includes "Victorian Skaters" accessory, birch tree, and snow.
- Skaters move around rink.

Gunnersbury Park Folly 58702

Dates	OSRP	GBTru	Paid
2003^M - 2003	$65	$70	$_____

- Club 56 dealer exclusive. Limited to 5,600 pieces.

Melancholy Tavern 58703

Dates	OSRP	GBTru	Paid
2003^M -	$65	-	$_____

- This is the updated version of the piece originally issued in 1996.

Green's Park Nosegays 58704

Dates	OSRP	GBTru	Paid
2003 -	$65	-	$_____

- Spring Gift Set.
- Set of 2 includes the building and "For You, My Lady" accessory.

Dickens' Village

Tower Bridge Of London — 58705

Dates	OSRP	GBTru	Paid
2003 - 2004	$165	$225	$____

- Historical Landmark Series. Numbered ltd. edition of 20,000.
- Dickens' Village 20th Anniversary Series. Includes pin.
- It is a replica of London's Tower Bridge.
- Set of 4.

Theatre Of The Macabre — 58706

Dates	OSRP	GBTru	Paid
2003 -	$65	-	$____

- All Hallow's Eve Series.

All Saints Church — 58707

Dates	OSRP	GBTru	Paid
2003 -	$70	-	$____

- All Hallow's Eve Series.

Notting Hill Water Tower — 58708

Dates	OSRP	GBTru	Paid
2003 -	$55	-	$____

- Spire and lamp are separate in box.

Williams Gas Works — 58709

Dates	OSRP	GBTru	Paid
2003 -	$70	-	$____

Dickens' Birthplace — 58710

Dates	OSRP	GBTru	Paid
2003 - 2004	$50	$50	$____

- Limited to year of production. Includes lantern and plaque.
- Dickens' Village 20th Anniversary Series. Includes pin.
- It is a replica of the house in which Dickens was born in Portsmouth, England.

Dickens' Village

Stump Hill Gatehouse — 58711

Dates	OSRP	GBTru	Paid
2003 -	$50	-	$_____

Hospital For Sick Children At Ormond Street — 58712

Dates	OSRP	GBTru	Paid
2003 - 2004	$65	$65	$_____

- Limited to year of production.
- Dickens' Village 20th Anniversary Series. Includes pin.
- This was inspired by the hospital in London.

Naval Academy, Queens Port — 58713

Dates	OSRP	GBTru	Paid
2003 -	$75	-	$_____

Lighthouse, Queens Port — 58714

Dates	OSRP	GBTru	Paid
2003 -	$70	-	$_____

Belle's House - Special Edition — 0297?

Dates	OSRP	GBTru	Paid
2004ᴹ - 2004	n/a	$975	$_____

- Numbered limited of 500 pieces.
- This edition differs from the original (2002) in that it ha? a Dickens' Village 20th Anniversary stamp on the bo? tom, has an intricate bay window, and features Bel? looking out an upper window at Scrooge.
- A number limited of 500 pieces, the first 250 were di? tributed when Department 56 randomly drew name? from its *celebrations* magazine subscription list. Anothe? 200 were sold on eBay in late 2004.

The Red Lion Pub — 58715

Dates	OSRP	GBTru	Paid
2004ᴹ - 2004	$65	$65	$_____

- Limited to year of production.
- Dickens' Village 20th Anniversary Series.
- Includes pin.

Canadian Pub — 58716

Dates	OSRP	GBTru	Paid
2004ᴹ - 2004	$91 CA	$85	$_____

- Limited to year of production.
- Available only in Canada.
- Includes pin.

Victorian Family Christmas House — 58717

Dates	OSRP	GBTru	Paid
2004ᴹ - 2004	$75	$75	$_____

- Limited to year of production.
- A Victorian Christmas Series.
- Set of 6 includes the House, "Kissing Under The Mistletoe" accessory, sign, two trees, and snow.

T. Smith Christmas Crackers — 58719

Dates	OSRP	GBTru	Paid
2004ᴹ -	$65	-	$_____

- Limited to year of production.
- A Victorian Christmas Series.
- Set of 2 includes the building and "Popping The Cracker" accessory.

Dickens' Village

Windsor Castle — 58720

Dates	OSRP	GBTru	Paid
2004 -	$95	-	$_____

- Historical Landmark Series.
- This lighted facade is a replica of the world's largest occupied castle.

Tower Bridge Of London — 58721

Dates	OSRP	GBTru	Paid
2004 -	$135	-	$_____

- Re-issue of the Historical Landmark Series limited edition that was issued in 2003.

St. Stephen's Church — 58722

Dates	OSRP	GBTru	Paid
2004 -	$75	-	$_____

- A Victorian Christmas Series.
- Decorating Set.
- Long Life Cordless Lighting.
- Set of two includes building and tree.

J. Horsley Christmas Cards — 5872?

Dates	OSRP	GBTru	Paid
2004 -	$65	-	$_____

- A Victorian Christmas Series.

Turner's Spice & Mustard Shop — 5872?

Dates	OSRP	GBTru	Paid
2004 -	$60	-	$_____

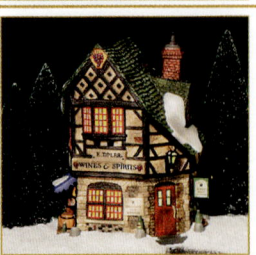

E. Tipler, Agent For Wines & Spirits — 5872?

Dates	OSRP	GBTru	Paid
2004 -	$60	-	$_____

- Sign separate in box.

T. C. Chester Clocks & Watches — 58726

Dates	OSRP	GBTru	Paid
2004 -	**$55**	-	$_____

• Sign separate in box.

Customs House, Queens Port — 58727

Dates	OSRP	GBTru	Paid
2004 -	**$65**	-	$_____

Howard Street Row Houses — 58728

Dates	OSRP	GBTru	Paid
2004 -	**$70**	-	$_____

• Removable Christmas decorations.

Hollyberry Cottage — 58729

Dates	OSRP	GBTru	Paid
2004 -	**$45**	-	$_____

Scotland Yard Station — 58730

Dates	OSRP	GBTru	Paid
2004 -	**$70**	-	$_____

• Limited to year of production.
• Named for the famous home to the Metropolitan Police Department.

Barleycorn Manor — 58731

Dates	OSRP	GBTru	Paid
2004 -	**$70**	-	$_____

• All Hallow's Eve Series.

Dickens' Village

Use the following space(s) to update your guide when the midyear introductions are announced.

Dickens' Village

_____ _____

Dates   OSRP   GBTru   Paid
____ - ____ $_____   - $_____

_____ _____

Dates   OSRP   GBTru   Paid
____ - ____ $_____   - $_____

_____ _____

Dates   OSRP   GBTru   Paid
____ - ____ $_____   - $_____

_____ _____

Dates   OSRP   GBTru   Paid
____ - ____ $_____   - $_____

_____ _____

Dates   OSRP   GBTru   Paid
____ - ____ $_____   - $_____

Carolers (White Post Version)   (Black Post Version)

65269 - Set of 3
1984 - 1990
OSRP: $10
GBTru: $60
Paid: $_____

• Made for a short time, the white post set includes a viola that is very light with dark brown trim.

65269 - Set of 3
GBTru: $40
Paid: $_____

• Early pieces of the black post set have a viola that is one color and made in Taiwan. The second viola has dark trim and was made in the Philippines.

Village Train

65277 - Set of 3
1985 - 1985
OSRP: $12
GBTru: $345
Paid: $_____

• Also called the "Brighton Train" due to the name on the side of the middle car.

Christmas Carol Figures

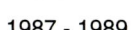

65013 - Set of 3
1986 - 1990
OSRP: $12.50
GBTru: $45
Paid: $_____

• A Christmas Carol Series. Sleeve shows Tiny Tim with crutch, but there isn't one in the figurine.

Farm People & Animals

59013 - Set of 5
1987 - 1989
OSRP: $24
GBTru: $60
Paid: $_____

• Early pieces had box that read "Heritage Village Farm Set."

Blacksmith

59340 - Set of 3
1987 - 1990
OSRP: $20
GBTru: $55
Paid: $_____

Silo & Hay Shed

59501 - Set of 2
1987 - 1989
OSRP: $18
GBTru: $110
Paid: $_____

• Early versions have roofs with rust, gold, and brown stripes. Later ones are brown.

Dickens' Village Sign

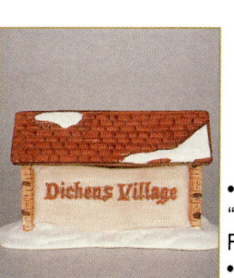

65692
1987 - 1993
OSRP: $6
GBTru: $10
Paid: $_____

• Bottomstamp reads "Handcrafted by Jiean Fung Porcelains, Taiwan."
• The early signs have a dark background.

Dickens' Village Accessories

Ox Sled (Tan Pants)

59510
1987 - 1989
OSRP: $20
GBTru: $125
Paid: $_____

• The driver has tan pants and is seated on a green cushion.

(Blue Pants Version)

GBTru: $65
Paid: $_____

• The driver has blue pants and is seated on a black cushion.

(Blue Pants/Mold Change Version)

GBTru: $75
Paid: $_____

• Blue pants, black cushion, and the snow under the oxen is not attached to hind legs.

Dover Coach (Version 1)

65900
1987 - 1990
OSRP: $18
GBTru: $55
Paid: $_____

• The coachman is clean shaven, and the wheels are very crude. Made in Taiwan.
• Box reads "Horse With Coach."

(Version 2)

GBTru: $50
Paid: $_____

• The coachman has a mustache; the wheels are more round. Made in Taiwan.

(Version 3)

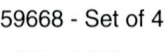

GBTru: $45
Paid: $_____

• The coachman has a mustache, and the wheels are round. Made in Sri Lanka.

Shopkeepers

59668 - Set of 4
1987 - 1988
OSRP: $15
GBTru: $25
Paid: $_____

• One of only two accessories to have "snow" sprinkled on them.

City Workers

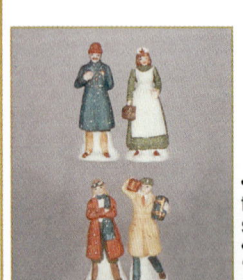

59676 - Set of 4
1987 - 1988
OSRP: $15
GBTru: $24
Paid: $_____

• One of only two acc to have "snow" sprinkled on them.
• Some boxes read "City People"; some have no name.

Village Well & Holy Cross

65471 - Set of 2
1987 - 1989
OSRP: $13
GBTru: $90
Paid: $_____

• Early versions have blue water, dark birds. Later ones have colorless water, light birds.

Childe Pond And Skaters

59030 - Set of 4
1988 - 1991
OSRP: $30
GBTru: $45
Paid: $_____

• Color of the warming hut varies, but does not affect the value.

Fezziwig And Friends

59285 - Set of 3
1988 - 1990
OSRP: $12.50
GBTru: $35
Paid: $_____

• Christmas Carol Series.

Nicholas Nickleby Characters

59293 - Set of 4
1988 - 1991
OSRP: $20
GBTru: $28
Paid: $_____

• Sleeves have misspelling—"Nicholas Nickelby."

David Copperfield Characters

55514 - Set of 5
1989 - 1992
OSRP: $32.50
GBTru: $28
Paid: $_____

Lamplighter With Lamp

55778 - Set of 2
1989 - 2004
OSRP: $9
GBTru: $9
Paid: $_____

Royal Coach

55786
1989 - 1992
OSRP: $55
GBTru: $60
Paid: $_____

• Early release to NALED dealers.

Constables

55794 - Set of 3
1989 - 1991
OSRP: $17.50
GBTru: $50
Paid: $_____

Dickens' Village Accessories

Violet Vendor/Carolers/Chestnut Vendor

55808 - Set of 3
1989 - 1992
OSRP: $23
GBTru: $28
Paid: $_____

King's Road Cab

55816
1989 - 1998
OSRP: $30
GBTru: $28
Paid: $_____

Christmas Carol Christmas Morning Figures

55883 - Set of 3
1989 - 2002
OSRP: $18
GBTru: $20
Paid: $_____

• Christmas Carol Series.
• Early release to NALED dealers.

Christmas Carol Christmas Spirits Figures

55891 - Set of 4
1989 - 2001
OSRP: $27.50
GBTru: $26
Paid: $_____

• Christmas Carol Series.

Town Crier & Chimney Sweep

55697 - Set of 2
1990 - 2001ᴹ
OSRP: $15
GBTru: $16
Paid: $_____

Carolers On The Doorstep

55700 - Set of 4
1990 - 1993
OSRP: $25
GBTru: $20
Paid: $_____

Holiday Travelers

55719 - Set of 3
1990 - 1999
OSRP: $22.50
GBTru: $24
Paid: $_____

The Flying Scot Train

55735 - Set of 4
1990 - 1998
OSRP: $48
GBTru: $45
Paid: $_____

Victoria Station Train Platform

55751
1990 - 1999
OSRP: $20
GBTru: $24
Paid: $_____

• Porcelain and metal.
• Reads "Platform 1" on one side; "Platform 2" on the other.

Oliver Twist Characters

55549 - Set of 3
1991 - 1993
OSRP: $35
GBTru: $30
Paid: $_____

Bringing Home The Yule Log

55581 - Set of 3
1991 - 1998
OSRP: $27.50
GBTru: $25
Paid: $_____

Poultry Market

55590 - Set of 3
1991 - 1995
OSRP: $30
GBTru: $33
Paid: $_____

• Early samples have patches on the left hand side of the drape.
• 3 geese are separate in box.

Come Into The Inn

55603 - Set of 3
1991 - 1994
OSRP: $22
GBTru: $24
Paid: $_____

Holiday Coach

55611
1991 - 1998
OSRP: $68
GBTru: $70
Paid: $_____

• Early pieces have gold chains, and later ones have silver chains.

Gate House

55301
1992 - 1992
OSRP: $22.50
GBTru: $25
Paid: $_____

• Brick varies from gray to blue.
• Event piece for 1992 dealer Open Houses.

The Old Puppeteer

58025 - Set of 3
1992 - 1995
OSRP: $32
GBTru: $33
Paid: $_____

• 2 marionettes are separate in box and can easily be lost.

Dickens' Village Accessories

The Bird Seller

58033 - Set of 3
1992 - 1995
OSRP: $25
GBTru: $24
Paid: $_____

Village Street Peddlers

58041 - Set of 2
1992 - 1994
OSRP: $16
GBTru: $18
Paid: $_____

English Post Box

58050
1992 - 2000
OSRP: $4.50
GBTru: $8
Paid: $_____

• Metal.

Lionhead Bridge

58645
1992 - 1997
OSRP: $22
GBTru: $20
Paid: $_____

Chelsea Market Fruit Monger & Cart

58130 - Set of 2
1993 - 1997
OSRP: $25
GBTru: $24
Paid: $_____

• Lantern and staff are separate in box.

Chelsea Market Fish Monger & Cart

58149 - Set of 2
1993 - 1997
OSRP: $25
GBTru: $24
Paid: $_____

• Lantern and staff are separate in box.

Chelsea Market Flower Monger & Cart

58157 - Set of 2
1993 - 2000
OSRP: $27.50
GBTru: $24
Paid: $_____

• A similar design was produced for Lord & Taylor. See the Special Design section.

Chelsea Lane Shoppers

58165 - Set of 4
1993 - 1999
OSRP: $30
GBTru: $28
Paid: $_____

Vision Of A Christmas Past

58173 - Set of 3
1993 - 1996
OSRP: $27.50
GBTru: $25
Paid: $_____

• Christmas Carol Series.

C. Bradford, Wheelwright & Son

58181 - Set of 2
1993 - 1996
OSRP: $24
GBTru: $25
Paid: $_____

Bringing Fleeces To The Mill

58190 - Set of 2
1993 - 1998
OSRP: $35
GBTru: $40
Paid: $_____

Dashing Through The Snow

58203
1993 - 2002
OSRP: $32.50
GBTru: $32
Paid: $_____

Winter Sleighride

58254
1994 - 2001
OSRP: $18
GBTru: $22
Paid: $_____

• In early samples, the handle is attached to the sleigh with wires that curl before entering the sleigh.

Chelsea Market Mistletoe Monger & Cart

58262 - Set of 2
1994 - 1998
OSRP: $25
GBTru: $24
Paid: $_____

• Lantern and staff are separate in box.

Chelsea Market Curiosities Monger & Cart

58270 - Set of 2
1994 - 1998
OSRP: $27.50
GBTru: $24
Paid: $_____

• Violin is separate in box.

Portobello Road Peddlers

58289 - Set of 3
1994 - 1998
OSRP: $27.50
GBTru: $30
Paid: $_____

Dickens' Village Accessories

Thatchers

58297 - Set of 3
1994 - 1997
OSRP: $35
GBTru: $38
Paid: $_____

• Frequently displayed with Cobb Cottage which has its roof undergoing repair.

A Peaceful Glow On Christmas Eve

58300 - Set of 3
1994 - 2003
OSRP: $30
GBTru: $30
Paid: $_____

Christmas Carol Holiday Trimming Set

58319 - Set of 21
1994 - 1997
OSRP: $65
GBTru: $60
Paid: $_____

• Christmas Carol Series.

Postern

98710
1994 - 1994
OSRP: $17.50
GBTru: $15
Paid: $_____

• Special imprint on bottom commemorates the village's 10th anniversary.

A Partridge In A Pear Tree - #I

58351
1995 - 1999
OSRP: $35
GBTru: $35
Paid: $_____

• 12 Days of Dickens' Village Series.
• 3 sets of bells are separate in box.

Two Turtle Doves - #II

58360 - Set of 4
1995 - 1999
OSRP: $32.50
GBTru: $35
Paid: $_____

• 12 Days of Dickens' Village Series.

Three French Hens - #III

58378 - Set of 3
1995 - 1999
OSRP: $32.50
GBTru: $35
Paid: $_____

• 12 Days of Dickens' Village Series.

Four Calling Birds - #IV

58379 - Set of 2
1995 - 1999
OSRP: $32.50
GBTru: $38
Paid: $_____

• 12 Days of Dickens' Village Series.

Five Golden Rings - #V

58381 - Set of 2
1995 - 1999
OSRP: $27.50
GBTru: $42
Paid: $_____

• 12 Days of Dickens' Village Series.

Six Geese A-Laying - #VI

58382 - Set of 2
1995 - 1999
OSRP: $30
GBTru: $42
Paid: $_____

• 12 Days of Dickens' Village Series.

Brixton Road Watchman

58390 - Set of 2
1995 - 1999
OSRP: $25
GBTru: $24
Paid: $_____

• Man's walking stick is fragile.

Tallyho!

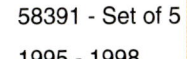

58391 - Set of 5
1995 - 1998
OSRP: $50
GBTru: $45
Paid: $_____

Chelsea Market Hat Monger & Cart

58392 - Set of 2
1995 - 2000
OSRP: $27.50
GBTru: $28
Paid: $_____

• Lantern and staff are separate in box.

Ye Olde Lamplighter Dickens' Village Sign

58393
1995 - 2001ᴹ
OSRP: $20
GBTru: $24
Paid: $_____

Cobbler & Clock Peddler

58394 - Set of 2
1995 - 1997
OSRP: $25
GBTru: $22
Paid: $_____

• Though designed for Dickens', many collectors believe it more appropriate for Alpine.

Dickens' Village Accessories

Town Square Carolers

58327 - Set of 3
1995 - 1996
OSRP: *
GBTru: *

* Accessory contained in the Dickens' Village Start A Tradition Set.

Palace Guards

58336 - Set of 2
1996^M - 1996
OSRP: *
GBTru: *

* Accessory contained in the Ramsford Palace Set.

Tending The New Calves

58395 - Set of 3
1996^M - 1999
OSRP: $33
GBTru: $33
Paid: $_____

Caroling With The Cratchit Family

58396 - Set of 3
1996^M -
OSRP: $37.50
GBTru: -
Paid: $_____

• Christmas Carol Revisited Series.

Yeomen Of The Guard

58397 - Set of 5
1996^M - 1997
OSRP: $30
GBTru: $50
Paid: $_____

• Lances and swords are fragile.

Seven Swans A-Swimming - #VII

58383 - Set of 4
1996 - 2000
OSRP: $27.50
GBTru: $45
Paid: $_____

• 12 Days of Dickens' Village Series.

Eight Maids A-Milking - #VIII

58384 - Set of 2
1996 - 2000
OSRP: $25
GBTru: $38
Paid: $_____

• 12 Days of Dickens' Village Series.

The Fezziwig Delivery Wagon

58400
1996 -
OSRP: $32.50
GBTru: -
Paid: $_____

• Christmas Carol Revisited Series.
• Similar design made for Lord & Taylor. See Special Design section

Red Christmas Sulky

58401
1996 - 2001
OSRP: $30
GBTru: $28
Paid: $_____

Gingerbread Vendor

58402 - Set of 2
1996 - 2001
OSRP: $22.50
GBTru: $24
Paid: $_____

A Christmas Carol Reading By Charles Dickens

58403 - Set of 4
1996 - 2001
OSRP: $45
GBTru: $35
Paid: $_____

- Christmas Carol Revisited Series.
- Sign is separate in box.

A Christmas Carol Reading By Charles Dickens

58404 - Set of 7
1996 - 1997
OSRP: $75
GBTru: $75
Paid: $_____

- Limited to 42,500.
- Christmas Carol Revisited Series.
- 4 lanterns and 2 signs separate in box.

Delivering Coal For The Hearth

58326 - Set of 2
1997ᴹ - 1999
OSRP: $32.50
GBTru: $35
Paid: $_____

- Early pieces have maroon wheels and buckets attached. Later ones have red wheels and buckets on hooks.

Nine Ladies Dancing - #IX

58385 - Set of 3
1997 - 2000
OSRP: $30
GBTru: $42
Paid: $_____

- 12 Days of Dickens' Village Series.

Ten Pipers Piping - #X

58386 - Set of 3
1997 - 2000
OSRP: $30
GBTru: $50
Paid: $_____

- 12 Days of Dickens' Village Series.

Ashley Pond Skating Party

58405 - Set of 6
1997 - 1999
OSRP: $70
GBTru: $80
Paid: $_____

- One side of hanging sign reads "Ashley Pond," the other "Ashley Road Pond."

Dickens' Village Accessories

The Fire Brigade Of London Town

58406 - Set of 5
1997 -
OSRP: $70
GBTru: -
Paid: $_____

Father Christmas's Journey

58407 - Set of 2
1997 - 2001
OSRP: $30
GBTru: $30
Paid: $_____

• A similar design was produced for North Pole City. See the Special Design section.

Christmas Pudding Costermonger

58408 - Set of 3
1997 - 2001^M
OSRP: $32.50
GBTru: $33
Paid: $_____

• Lantern is separate in box.

The Spirit Of Giving

58322 - Set of 3
1997 - 1998
OSRP: *
GBTru: *

* Accessory contained in the Dickens' Village Start A Tradition Set.

Manchester Square Accessory Set

58301 - Set of 7
1997 - 2000
OSRP: *
GBTru: *

* Accessory contained in the Manchester Square Set.
• Man's walking stick is fragile.

Christmas Apples

58308 - Set of 3
1998^M - 1998
OSRP: *
GBTru: *

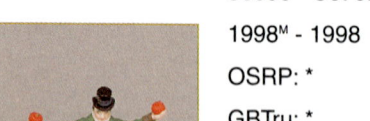

* Accessory contained in the Seton Morris Spice Merchant Set.

Miss Havisham, Estella, And Pip

58310 - Set of 3
1998 - 2001
OSRP: *
GBTru: *

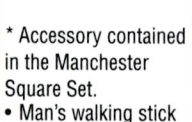
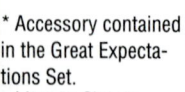

* Accessory contained in the Great Expectations Set.
• Literary Classic Series.

Here We Come A-Wassailing

58410 - Set of 5
1998 - 2001^M
OSRP: $45
GBTru: $50
Paid: $_____

Sitting In Camden Park

58411 - Set of 4
1998 -
OSRP: $35
GBTru: -
Paid: $_____

Eleven Lords A-Leaping - #XI

58413
1998 - 2000
OSRP: $27.50
GBTru: $55
Paid: $_____

• 12 Days of Dickens' Village Series.

Until We Meet Again

58414 - Set of 2
1998 - 2001
OSRP: $27.50
GBTru: $33
Paid: $_____

Child's Play

58415 - Set of 2
1998 - 2001ᴹ
OSRP: $25
GBTru: $28
Paid: $_____

Tending The Cold Frame

58416 - Set of 3
1998 - 1999
OSRP: $32.50
GBTru: $40
Paid: $_____

• A similar design was also produced for Bachman's. See the Special Design section.

Ale Mates

58417 - Set of 2
1998 - 2004
OSRP: $25
GBTru: $25
Paid: $_____

Twelve Drummers Drumming - #XII

58387
1999ᴹ - 2000
OSRP: $65
GBTru: $175
Paid: $_____

• 12 Days of Dickens' Village Series.

A Good Day's Catch

58420 - Set of 2
1999ᴹ - 2000
OSRP: $27.50
GBTru: $34
Paid: $_____

Dickens' Village Accessories

The Mother's Gift

58442

1999 - 2000

OSRP: *

GBTru: *

* Accessory contained in the Aldeburgh Music Box Shop Gift Set.

The Queen's Parliamentary Coach

58454

1999 - 2000

OSRP: $60

GBTru: $60

Paid: $_____

• Limited to year of production.

Members Of Parliament

58455 - Set of 2

1999 - 2000

OSRP: $19

GBTru: $24

Paid: $_____

• Paper in man's hand is real.

King's Road Market Cross

58456

1999 - 2000

OSRP: $25

GBTru: $26

Paid: $_____

• Dream House Sweep-stakes Deluxe Prize winner assisted in the design.

Meeting Family At The Railroad Station

58457 - Set of 4

1999 - 2001ᴹ

OSRP: $32.50

GBTru: $34

Paid: $_____

Master Gardeners

58458 - Set of 2

1999 - 2001ᴹ

OSRP: $30

GBTru: $33

Paid: $_____

Under The Bumbershoot

58460

1999 - 2002

OSRP: $20

GBTru: $28

Paid: $_____

• Similar designs were produced for the NCC. See the Special Design section.

A Treasure From The Sea

58461 - Set of 2

1999 - 2001ᴹ

OSRP: $22.50

GBTru: $25

Paid: $_____

Fine Asian Antiques

58462 - Set of 2
1999 - 2001^M
OSRP: $27.50
GBTru: $28
Paid: $_____

Busy Railway Station

58464 - Set of 3
1999 - 2001^M
OSRP: $27.50
GBTru: $30
Paid: $_____

• Red and green lights are battery/adapter operated.

Locomotive Shed & Water Tower

58465
1999 - 2001
OSRP: $32.50
GBTru: $35
Paid: $_____

Queensbridge Railroad Yard Acc.

58466 - Set of 3
1999 - 2001^M
OSRP: $37.50
GBTru: $38
Paid: $_____

12 Days Of Dickens' Village Sign

58467
1999 - 2000
OSRP: $20
GBTru: $34
Paid: $_____

• 12 Days of Dickens' Village Series.

Scrooge At Fezziwig's Ball

58470
2000^M - 2000
OSRP: *
GBTru: *

* Accessory contained in the Fezziwig's Ballroom Gift Set.

Holiday Quintet

58520 - Set of 6
2000^M -
OSRP: $37.50
GBTru: -
Paid: $_____

• Lamppost is battery/adapter operated.
• Bow and baton are fragile.

At The Fire House

05700 - Set of 3
2000^M - 2000
OSRP: *
GBTru: *

* Accessory contained in the GCC Ashwick Lane Gift Set.

Sweet Roses

58475 - Set of 5
2000 - 2001
OSRP: *
GBTru: *

* Accessory contained in the Lilycott Garden Conservatory Gift Set.

Abington Locks

58521 - Set of 2
2000 - 2003
OSRP: $48
GBTru: $50
Paid: $_____

• Abington Canal Series.

Abington Canal Boat

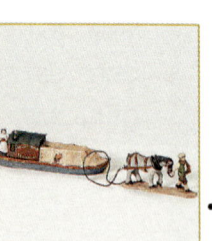

58522 - Set of 2
2000 - 2002
OSRP: $35
GBTru: $40
Paid: $_____

• Abington Canal Series.

Gourmet Chocolates Delivery Wagon

58523
2000 - 2003
OSRP: $45
GBTru: $50
Paid: $_____

Hedgerow Dovecote

58524 - Set of 2
2000 - 2002
OSRP: $32.50
GBTru: $35
Paid: $_____

Par For The Course

58525 - Set of 3
2000 - 2002
OSRP: $27.50
GBTru: $28
Paid: $_____

Following The Leader

58526 - Set of 2
2000 - 2002
OSRP: $32.50
GBTru: $34
Paid: $_____

Master Potter

58527
2000 - 2002
OSRP: $18
GBTru: $22
Paid: $_____

Sliding Down Cornhill With Bob Cratchit

58528
2000 -
OSRP: $25
GBTru: -
Paid: $_____

• Christmas Carol Series.

Polo Players

58529 - Set of 2
2000 - 2002
OSRP: $40
GBTru: $40
Paid: $_____

These Are For You

58530 - Set of 2
2000 - 2002
OSRP: $25
GBTru: $30
Paid: $_____

Horses At The Lampguard

58531 - Set of 3
2000 -
OSRP: $45
GBTru: -
Paid: $_____

Keeping The Streets Clean

58532 - Set of 2
2000 - 2002
OSRP: $18
GBTru: $24
Paid: $_____

Merry Go Roundabout

58533
2000 - 2004
OSRP: $32.50
GBTru: $35
Paid: $_____

Sherlock Holmes-The Hansom Cab

58534
2000 - 2003
OSRP: $35
GBTru: $45
Paid: $_____

Abington Canal

58535 - Set of 2
2000 - 2003
OSRP: $30
GBTru: $35
Paid: $_____

• Abington Canal Series.

Dickens' Village Accessories

Abington Bridge

58536
2000 - 2003
OSRP: $37.50
GBTru: $40
Paid: $_____

• Abington Canal Series.

Elementary My Dear Watson

58601
2000 - 2003
OSRP: *
GBTru: *

* Accessory contained in Sherlock Holmes - 221B Baker Street set.
• Literary Classic Series.

Christmas Eve Celebration

58485
2001ᴹ - 2001
OSRP: *
GBTru: *

* Accessory contained in the Somerset Valley Church Gift Set.

Bob Cratchit And Tiny Tim

58537
2001ᴹ -
OSRP: $15
GBTru: -
Paid: $_____

• Christmas Carol Series.

Ghost Of Christmas Present Visits Scrooge

58538
2001ᴹ - 2001
OSRP: $15
GBTru: $22
Paid: $_____

• Christmas Carol Series.

High Tea

58487
2001 - 2002
OSRP: *
GBTru: *

* The accessory contained in Mrs. Brimm's Tea Room Gift Set.

Dickens Writing

58488
2001 - 2003
OSRP: *
GBTru: *

* The accessory contained in the Dickens' Gad's Hill Chalet.

Doorman

58494
2001 - 2003
OSRP: *
GBTru: *

* The accessory contained in The Sloane Hotel.

The Big Prize Turkey

58539 - Set of 2

2001 -

OSRP: $27.50

GBTru: -

Paid: $_____

- Christmas Carol Series.

Cobbler's Corner Stand

58540 - Set of 2

2001 - 2004

OSRP: $27.50

GBTru: $28

Paid: $_____

Blacksmith To The Rescue

58541

2001 - 2004

OSRP: $22.50

GBTru: $23

Paid: $_____

- Originally was named "Shoeing The Horse."

A Christmas Carol Visit

58542 - Set of 4

2001 -

OSRP: $27.50

GBTru: -

Paid: $_____

- Christmas Carol Series.

Taking Grain To The Mill

58545

2001 - 2003

OSRP: $20

GBTru: $22

Paid: $_____

- Abington Canal Series.

A Family Tradition

58546 - Set of 2

2001 - 2002

OSRP: $20

GBTru: $24

Paid: $_____

Lock Keeper

58547

2001 - 2003

OSRP: $12.50

GBTru: $15

Paid: $_____

- Abington Canal Series.

Chimney Sweep & Son

58548

2001 - 2004

OSRP: $18.50

GBTru: $19

Paid: $_____

Dickens' Village Accessories

An Elegant Ride

58549
2001 -
OSRP: $30
GBTru: -
Paid: $_____

Street Merchants

58550 - Set of 3
2001 - 2004
OSRP: $17.50
GBTru: $18
Paid: $_____

Formal Gardens

58551
2001 - 2003
OSRP: $65
GBTru: $70
Paid: $_____

Holiday Joy

58552
2001 - 2003
OSRP: $32.50
GBTru: $40
Paid: $_____

• Battery/ adapter operated.

Dickens' Raising The Flag

58555
2001 - 2003
OSRP: $15
GBTru: $18
Paid: $_____

• Includes British and Canadian flags.

Winter Frolic

05925
2002^M - 2002
OSRP: *
GBTru: *

* The accessory contained in Christmas At Codington Cottage.

Bearing Gifts

58506
2002^M - 2002
OSRP: *
GBTru: *

* The accessory contained in 1 Royal Tree Court.

Lord Of The Follies

58633
2002^M - 2002
OSRP: *
GBTru: *

* The accessory contained in Hop Castle Folly.

Chestnut Vendor

58557

2002^M -

OSRP: $32.50

GBTru: -

Paid: $_____

• Battery/ adapter operated.

The First Edition

58513

2002 - 2004

OSRP: *

GBTru: *

* The accessory contained in The Daily News.

Bringing Home The Holly

58514

2002 - 2003

OSRP: *

GBTru: *

* The accessory contained in Codington Cottage.

All The World's A Stage

58515

2002 - 2003

OSRP: *

GBTru: *

* The accessory contained in Shakespeare's Birthplace.

Rose Garden Beauty

58518

2002 - 2003

OSRP: *

GBTru: *

* The accessory contained in Sweetbriar Cottage.

A Gentleman and Lady

58559

2002 -

OSRP: $15

GBTru: -

Paid: $_____

London Newspaper Stand

58560 - Set of 2

2002 -

OSRP: $25

GBTru: -

Paid: $_____

Jack-Of-The-Lantern

58561

2002 -

OSRP: $25

GBTru: -

Paid: $_____

• All Hallow's Eve design.

Last Mail Call Of The Day

58562
2002 - 2004
OSRP: $10
GBTru: $10
Paid: $_____

Love or Money?

58563
2002 - 2004
OSRP: $15
GBTru: $15
Paid: $_____

• Christmas Carol Series.

Temple Bar

58564
2002 - 2003
OSRP: $60
GBTru: $65
Paid: $_____

• Historical Landmark Series.

Covered Bridge At The Manor

58565
2002 - 2004
OSRP: $45
GBTru: $45
Paid: $_____

The Charitable Vicar

58566 - Set of 2
2002 -
OSRP: $25
GBTru: -
Paid: $_____

A Rare Find

58567
2002 - 2004
OSRP: $15
GBTru: $15
Paid: $_____

• Battery/ adapter operated.

A Christmas Beginning

58568
2002 -
OSRP: $17.50
GBTru: -
Paid: $_____

Omnibus

58569
2002 -
OSRP: $55
GBTru: -
Paid: $_____

The Coffee-Stall

58571 - Set of 2
2003ᴹ -
OSRP: $27.50
GBTru: -
Paid: $_____

Victorian Skaters

58700 - Set of 3
2003ᴹ -
OSRP: *
GBTru: *

* The accessory contained in London Skating Club.

The Halfpenny Showman

58572
2003 -
OSRP: $17.50
GBTru: -
Paid: $_____

The Strange Case Of Dr. Jekyll & Mr. Hyde

58573
2003 -
OSRP: $15
GBTru: -
Paid: $_____

• All Hallow's Eve Series.
• Inspired by Robert Louis Stevenson's novel.

Horse Drawn Hearse

58574
2003 -
OSRP: $35
GBTru: -
Paid: $_____

• All Hallow's Eve Series.

Christmas Morning Parade

58575 - Set of 2
2003 -
OSRP: $17.50
GBTru: -
Paid: $_____

London Gas Worker

58576
2003 -
OSRP: $15
GBTru: -
Paid: $_____

Dickens Learns To Read

58577
2003 -
OSRP: $12.50
GBTru: -
Paid: $_____

• Dickens' Village 20th Anniversary Series.

Dickens' Village Accessories

A Story For The Children

58578
2003 -
OSRP: $12.50
GBTru: -
Paid: $_____

• Dickens' Village 20th Anniversary Series.

Ready For Duty, Queens Port

58579
2003 -
OSRP: $15
GBTru: -
Paid: $_____

Bringing Christmas Cheer, Queens Port

58580
2003 -
OSRP: $20
GBTru: -
Paid: $_____

A Busy Day In Town

58581 - Set of 3
2003 -
OSRP: $25
GBTru: -
Paid: $_____

• Dickens' Village 20th Anniversary Series.

A Basket Full Of Blooms

58583
2003 -
OSRP: $16.50
GBTru: -
Paid: $_____

For You, My Lady

58704
2003 -
OSRP: *
GBTru: *

* The accessory contained in Green's Park Nosegays.

Scrooge

02973
2004 - 2004
OSRP: *
GBTru: *

* The accessory contained in Belle's House - Special Edition.

Decorating With Holiday Greenery

58584 - Set of
2004ᴹ -
OSRP: $18.50
GBTru: -
Paid: $_____

• A Victorian Christmas Series.

Victorian Father Christmas

58585
2004^M - 2004
OSRP: $32.50
GBTru: $33
Paid: $_____

- Limited to year of production.
- A Victorian Christmas Series.

A Toast To Our Anniversary

58587
2004^M -
OSRP: $15
GBTru: -
Paid: $_____

- Dickens' Village 20th Anniversary Series.

Victorian Christmas Scene

58588
2004^M - 2004
OSRP: $50
GBTru: $50
Paid: $_____

- Limited to year of production, 2004.
- A Victorian Christmas Series.

Kissing Under The Mistletoe

58717
2004^M - 2004
OSRP: *
GBTru: *

* The accessory contained in Victorian Family Christmas House.

Popping The Cracker

58719
2004^M -
OSRP: *
GBTru: *

* The accessory contained in T. Smith's Christmas Crackers.

Strolling Down Howard Street

58409
2004 -
OSRP: $17.50
GBTru: -
Paid: $_____

Begging For Soul Cakes

58412 - Set of 2
2004 -
OSRP: $17.50
GBTru: -
Paid: $_____

- All Hallow's Eve Series.

A Caroling We Shall Go

58589
2004 -
OSRP: $80
GBTru: -
Paid: $_____

- Animated.
- Plays "Good King Wenceslas."

Dickens' Village Accessories

Town Square Market

58590
2004 -
OSRP: $70
GBTru: -
Paid: $_____

• Animated.

HMS Britannia

58591
2004 -
OSRP: $55
GBTru: -
Paid: $_____

• Queensport Series.
• AC/DC adapter compatible.

Our Best Vintage, Sir

58593
2004 -
OSRP: $15
GBTru: -
Paid: $_____

Guarding The Castle

58594
2004 -
OSRP: $17.50
GBTru: -
Paid: $_____

• Historical Landmark Series.

A Boxing Day Tradition

58595
2004 -
OSRP: $17.50
GBTru: -
Paid: $_____

• A Victorian Christmas Series.

One More Christmas Card To Post, Please

58596
2004 -
OSRP: $15
GBTru: -
Paid: $_____

• A Victorian Christmas Series.

Get Your Spices 'Ere!

58597
2004 -
OSRP: $10
GBTru: -
Paid: $_____

On Time Delivery

58598
2004 -
OSRP: $12.50
GBTru: -
Paid: $_____

Dickens' Village Accessories

Checking The Ship's Manifest

58599
2004 -
OSRP: $17.50
GBTru: -
Paid: $_____

Use the following space(s) to update your guide when the midyear introductions are announced.

_____

_____

____ - ____

OSRP: $_____
GBTru: -
Paid: $_____

_____

_____

____ - ____

OSRP: $_____
GBTru: -
Paid: $_____

_____

_____

____ - ____

OSRP: $_____
GBTru: -
Paid: $_____

_____

_____

____ - ____

OSRP: $_____
GBTru: -
Paid: $_____

_____

_____

____ - ____

OSRP: $_____
GBTru: -
Paid: $_____

_____

_____

____ - ____

OSRP: $_____
GBTru: -
Paid: $_____

Dickens' Village Accessories

Enjoy collecting the villages more than ever. Visit

The Marketplace

on pages 462 thru 464

_ _ _ _ _ _ _ _ _ _ _ _ _ _ _

For copies of the photos of the 2005 midyear introductions, send $3 and a self-addressed stamped envelope to:

Greenbook
56 Freeway Drive
Cranston RI 02920

The pages will be mailed in June or as orders are received after June.

New England Village® Series

In its diversity, there is also its charm. The northeastern corner of the country contains the six states jointly known as New England. Blazing colors of autumn grace the pages of innumerable calendars, but nature's glory is only part of New England's fame. It is not an overlooked part, though, for Autumn Birches and Maples enhance many displays, and the accompanying activity of Tapping the Maples is another highlight. Some of the recent village pieces lack snow, further enabling collectors to create year round scenes.

Agriculture once dominated the area, and multiple barns, farmhouses, and livestock depict that segment of the region's past. Even cranberry bogs are represented. Equally a part of the area's history and economy was the maritime industry. The Atlantic's waters provided livelihood to Lobster Trappers, boat builders, and fish canneries. Its rugged coast accounts for the several lighthouses that have been captured in miniature. An expanding Seaside Series enables collectors to truly develop this aspect of New England life.

The rushing streams generated power for the start of America's industrial age, a period captured in the imposing Smythe Woolen Mill. Many New England towns grew up around these economic centers. If the mills were one symbol of the area in the 1800s, another was certainly its churches. Vivid scenes of fall foliage often include the stately white steeple of a local church. Church bazaars were a highlight of these small towns, loosely connected by rail stations, but strongly unified by the work ethic and patriotic spirit such as that demonstrated by Paul Revere.

NEW ENGLAND VILLAGE- Set of 7   65307

Dates	OSRP	GBTru	Paid
1986 - 1989	$170	$1010	$_____

• None of the seven buildings have names on the bottom.

Apothecary   65307

Dates	OSRP	GBTru	Paid
1986 - 1989	$25	$110	$_____

General Store   65307

Dates	OSRP	GBTru	Paid
1986 - 1989	$25	$240	$_____

• Do not handle by porch posts; they are very fragile.

Nathaniel Bingham Fabrics   6530

Dates	OSRP	GBTru	Paid
1986 - 1989	$25	$120	$_____

Livery Stable & Boot Shop   6530

Dates	OSRP	GBTru	Paid
1986 - 1989	$25	$115	$_____

Brick Town Hall   6530

Dates	OSRP	GBTru	Paid
1986 - 1989	$25	$115	$_____

Steeple Church (Version 1)   65307

Dates	OSRP	GBTru	Paid
1986 - 1989	$25	$125	$_____

- Front tree is attached with porcelain slip.
- Sleeve is open on sides.

(Version 2)

		GBTru	Paid
		$80	$_____

- Front tree is attached with glue.
- Sleeve is open at top and bottom.
- This design was re-issued in 1989 with item # 65390.

Red Schoolhouse   65307

Dates	OSRP	GBTru	Paid
1986 - 1989	$25	$265	$_____

Jacob Adams Farmhouse & Barn   65382

Dates	OSRP	GBTru	Paid
1986 - 1989	$65	$425	$_____

- Early pieces have sleeves that read "New England Village Farm." Later ones read "Jacob Adams Farmhouse and Barn."

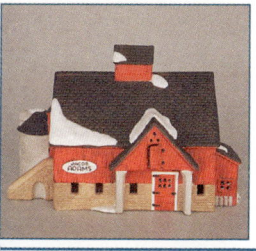

- Because the animals were simply in tissue and placed in the box with no separate compartments, they are often damaged.
- Set of 5 includes Farmhouse, Barn, 2 cows, and a horse.
- Do not handle house by columns.

Craggy Cove Lighthouse   59307

Dates	OSRP	GBTru	Paid
1987 - 1994	$35	$50	$_____

- Early pieces have a drain hole at the bottom of the tower. Later ones do not. Not only does the hole help collectors decide how early their piece was manufactured, but it also allows them to insert a "beacon."

Weston Train Station 59315

Dates	OSRP	GBTru	Paid
1987 - 1989	$42	$225	$_____

- This station looks very much like the now-dilapidated station in the Boston, MA suburb of Weston.

Smythe Woolen Mill 65439

Dates	OSRP	GBTru	Paid
1987 - 1988	$42	$910	$_____

- Limited Edition of 7,500.

Timber Knoll Log Cabin 65447

Dates	OSRP	GBTru	Paid
1987 - 1990	$28	$135	$_____

- Bottomstamp reads "Log Cabin."
- Do not handle by columns.

Old North Church 59323

Dates	OSRP	GBTru	Paid
1988 - 1998	$40	$50	$_____

- Inspired by the historic landmark in Boston, Christ Church, where sexton Robert Newman hung lanterns in its steeple to warn colonists in Charlestown that the British were on their way to Lexington and Concord.

CHERRY LANE SHOPS - Set of 3 59390

Dates	OSRP	GBTru	Paid
1988 - 1990	$80	$265	$_____

Ben's Barbershop 59390

Dates	OSRP	GBTru	Paid
1988 - 1990	$27	$95	$_____

Otis Hayes Butcher Shop			59390
Dates	OSRP	GBTru	Paid
1988 - 1990	**$27**	**$75**	$_____

- Do not handle by columns.

Anne Shaw Toys			59390
Dates	OSRP	GBTru	Paid
1988 - 1990	**$27**	**$115**	$_____

Ada's Bed And Boarding House   59404
(Version 1)

Dates	OSRP	GBTru	Paid
1988 - 1991	**$36**	**$175**	$_____

- Rear Steps: Part of the building's mold.
- 2nd Floor Windows: Alternating yellow panes.
- Color: Lemon yellow.
- Samples are pink/wine. **GBTru: $550** Paid: $_____

(Version 2)

		GBTru	Paid
		$110	$_____

- Rear Steps: Part of the building's mold.
- 2nd Floor Windows: Alternating yellow panes.
- Color: Pale yellow.

(Version 3)

		GBTru	Paid
		$80	$_____

- Rear Steps: Separate attachment.
- 2nd Floor Windows: Top halves solid, bottom halves cut out.
- Color: Pale yellow.
- This version also has less snow on the roof and at base.

Steeple Church (Version 3)			65390
Dates	OSRP	GBTru	Paid
1989 - 1990	**$30**	**$75**	$_____

- Front tree is attached with porcelain slip.
- Notice the different item number from original 1986 piece.

Berkshire House (Williamsburg Blue) — 59420

Dates	OSRP	GBTru	Paid
1989 - 1991	$40	$115	$_____

- This version has pale shutters and porch rail spindles.
- Be careful when removing this piece from the box as it is very easy to break off the porch railing.
- Samples are forest green. **GBTru: $105** Paid: $_____

(Teal Version)

GBTru	Paid
$75	$_____

- This version has yellow shutters and porch rail spindles.
- Be careful when removing this piece from the box as it is very easy to break off the porch railing.

Jannes Mullet Amish Farm House — 59439

Dates	OSRP	GBTru	Paid
1989 - 1992	$32	$75	$_____

Jannes Mullet Amish Barn — 59447

Dates	OSRP	GBTru	Paid
1989 - 1992	$48	$75	$_____

Shingle Creek House — 59463

Dates	OSRP	GBTru	Paid
1990 - 1994	$37.50	$35	$_____

- Early release to Showcase and NALED dealers.

Captain's Cottage — 59471

Dates	OSRP	GBTru	Paid
1990 - 1996	$40	$45	$_____

- Do not handle by columns.

SLEEPY HOLLOW - Set of 3 — 59544

Dates	OSRP	GBTru	Paid
1990 - 1993	**$96**	**$125**	$_____

- This set was inspired by Washington Irving's classic, *The Legend of Sleepy Hollow*. The story takes place along the Hudson River in North Tarrytown, NY.

Sleepy Hollow School — 59544

Dates	OSRP	GBTru	Paid
1990 - 1993	**$32**	**$75**	$_____

- A bell hangs in the tower.

Van Tassel Manor — 59544

Dates	OSRP	GBTru	Paid
1990 - 1993	**$32**	**$40**	$_____

Ichabod Crane's Cottage — 59544

Dates	OSRP	GBTru	Paid
1990 - 1993	**$32**	**$40**	$_____

Sleepy Hollow Church — 59552

Dates	OSRP	GBTru	Paid
1990 - 1993	**$36**	**$55**	$_____

McGrebe-Cutters & Sleighs — 56405

Dates	OSRP	GBTru	Paid
1991 - 1995	**$45**	**$50**	$_____

New England Village

Bluebird Seed And Bulb　　　　　　56421

Dates	OSRP	GBTru	Paid
1992 - 1996	$48	$45	$____

Yankee Jud Bell Casting　　　　　　56430

Dates	OSRP	GBTru	Paid
1992 - 1995	$44	$40	$____

Stoney Brook Town Hall　　　　　　56448

Dates	OSRP	GBTru	Paid
1992 - 1995	$42	$45	$____

A. BIELER FARM - Set of 2　　　　　56480

Dates	OSRP	GBTru	Paid
1993 - 1996	$92	$85	$____

Pennsylvania Dutch Farmhouse　　　56481

Dates	OSRP	GBTru	Paid
1993 - 1996	$42	$50	$____

Pennsylvania Dutch Barn　　　　　　56482

Dates	OSRP	GBTru	Paid
1993 - 1996	$50	$55	$____

Blue Star Ice Co. — 56472

Dates	OSRP	GBTru	Paid
1993 - 1997	$45	$55	$_____

• Acrylic ice blocks easily come unglued.

Arlington Falls Church — 56510

Dates	OSRP	GBTru	Paid
1994ᴹ - 1997	$40	$45	$_____

• Do not handle by columns.

Cape Keag Fish Cannery — 56529

Dates	OSRP	GBTru	Paid
1994 - 1998	$48	$50	$_____

Pigeonhead Lighthouse — 56537

Dates	OSRP	GBTru	Paid
1994 - 1998	$50	$55	$_____

• Posts near beacon and at front of building are extremely fragile.

BREWSTER BAY COTTAGES - Set of 2 — 56570

Dates	OSRP	GBTru	Paid
1995ᴹ - 1997	$90	$100	$_____

Jeremiah Brewster House — 56568

Dates	OSRP	GBTru	Paid
1995ᴹ - 1997	$45	$50	$_____

• Early pieces have sleeves that read "Thomas T. Julian House." Later ones have stickers with the correct name placed over the mistake.

Thomas T. Julian House — 56569

Dates	OSRP	GBTru	Paid
1995ᴹ - 1997	$45	$50	$____

- Early pieces have sleeves that read "Jeremiah Brewster House." Later ones have stickers with the correct name placed over the mistake.
- Do not handle by columns.

Chowder House — 56571

Dates	OSRP	GBTru	Paid
1995 - 1998	$40	$50	$____

- Sign is separate in box.

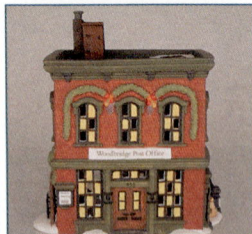

Woodbridge Post Office — 56572

Dates	OSRP	GBTru	Paid
1995 - 1998	$40	$50	$____

Pierce Boat Works — 56573

Dates	OSRP	GBTru	Paid
1995 - 2000	$55	$65	$____

Apple Valley School — 56172

Dates	OSRP	GBTru	Paid
1996ᴹ -	$35	-	$____

J. Hudson Stoveworks — 56574

Dates	OSRP	GBTru	Paid
1996 - 1998	$60	$65	$____

- Black metal kettle is separate in box.

Navigational Charts & Maps 56575

Dates	OSRP	GBTru	Paid
1996 - 1999	**$48**	**$65**	$_____

• Several attachments are very fragile.

Bobwhite Cottage 56576

Dates	OSRP	GBTru	Paid
1996 - 2001	**$50**	**$50**	$_____

• A bobwhite is a small quail native to North America.
• Spires are fragile.

Van Guilder's Ornamental Ironworks 56577

Dates	OSRP	GBTru	Paid
1997^M - 1999	**$50**	**$55**	$_____

• This is the first New England Village design with multiple weathervanes.

East Willet Pottery 56578

Dates	OSRP	GBTru	Paid
1997 - 1999	**$45**	**$50**	$_____

• Do not handle by columns.

Steen's Maple House 56579

Dates	OSRP	GBTru	Paid
1997 - 2001	**$60**	**$65**	$_____

• Uses Magic Smoke to create smoking effect rising from the chimney.
• Buckets are separate in box.

Semple's Smokehouse 56580

Dates	OSRP	GBTru	Paid
1997 - 1999	**$45**	**$50**	$_____

The Emily Louise 56581

Dates	OSRP	GBTru	Paid
1998ᴹ - 2000	$70	$75	$____

- The wreath is "free-floating" and is easily damaged.
- 2 flags are separate in box.
- Set of 2 includes the ship and a dock.

Franklin Hook & Ladder Co. 56601

Dates	OSRP	GBTru	Paid
1998 - 2000	$55	$60	$____

Moggin Falls General Store 56602

Dates	OSRP	GBTru	Paid
1998 - 2004	$60	$60	$____

- Picture on sleeve is reversed.
- Flag and 2 signs are separate in box.

Deacon's Way Chapel 56604

Dates	OSRP	GBTru	Paid
1998 - 2000	$68	$65	$____

Harper's Farm 56605

Dates	OSRP	GBTru	Paid
1998 - 2000	$65	$70	$____

- Weathervane and 2 spires are separate in box.

Little Women - The March Residence   56606

Dates	OSRP	GBTru	Paid
1999ᴹ - 2000	$90	$95	$_____

- Second in the Literary Classic Series. See this series in the Small Collection section.
- Louisa May Alcott based the March Residence on the Orchard House in Concord, MA where she grew up.
- Set of 4 plus book includes the Residence and the accessory "A Letter From Papa" which depicts Marmie, Jo, Amy, Beth, and Meg.
- The water pump's handle is very fragile.

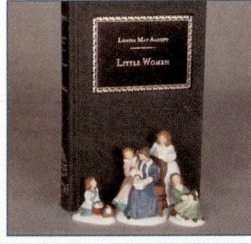

Hale & Hardy House   56610

Dates	OSRP	GBTru	Paid
1999 - 2001	$60	$65	$_____

- 2 signs are separate in box.

Trinity Ledge   56611

Dates	OSRP	GBTru	Paid
1999 - 2002	$85	$90	$_____

- The three pinafore flags attached signal U - S - A.
- Includes U.S. and Canadian flags.

Harper's Farmhouse   56612

Dates	OSRP	GBTru	Paid
1999 -	$57	-	$_____

- Dream House Sweepstakes Grand Prize winner assisted in the design.
- 3 lightning rods are separate in box.

P. L. Wheeler's Bicycle Shop   56613

Dates	OSRP	GBTru	Paid
1999 - 2002	$57	$65	$_____

- This is one of the first New England pieces not to have snow.
- Sign and weathervane are packaged separately.

Platt's Candles & Wax   56614

Dates	OSRP	GBTru	Paid
1999 - 2001	$60	$55	$_____

• Candelabra and weathervane are separate in box.

Susquehanna Station   56624

Dates	OSRP	GBTru	Paid
2000^M - 2002	$60	$60	$_____

• Set of 2 includes the Station and signal with coal car.

Mountain View Cabin   56625

Dates	OSRP	GBTru	Paid
2000 - 2001	$55	$285	$_____

• 25th Anniversary Limited Edition of 10,000.

Verna Mae's Boutique Gift Set   56626

Dates	OSRP	GBTru	Paid
2000 - 2001	$65	$75	$_____

• Discover Department 56 Spring Event Piece.
• Set of 3 includes building, "New Spring Finery" accessory, and flowering tree.
• Sign is separate in box.

New England Village

The Cranberry House — 56627

Dates	OSRP	GBTru	Paid
2000 - 2002	$60	$65	$_____

• Weathervane and 3 utensils are separate in the box.

Wm. Walton Fine Clocks & Pocket Pieces — 56628

Dates	OSRP	GBTru	Paid
2000 - 2002	$60	$60	$_____

• Clock and 2 lanterns are separate in the box.
• Hitching post is fragile.

Laurel Hill Church — 56629

Dates	OSRP	GBTru	Paid
2000 - 2003	$68	$70	$_____

• This is the first church to include a cemetery.
• Do not handle by fence when removing from box.
• Gravestones are fragile.

Revere Silver Works — 56632

Dates	OSRP	GBTru	Paid
2001^M - 2002	$60	$60	$_____

• Set of 2 includes shop and "Creating Silver Keepsakes."
• Pitcher ornament is included separately in the box.

Breakers Point Lighthouse — 56636

Dates	OSRP	GBTru	Paid
2001 -	$85	-	$_____

• Seaside Series.
• Weathervane is separate in the box.

Springfield Studio Gift Set   56634

Dates	OSRP	GBTru	Paid
2001 - 2002	$65	$75	$____

- First available during the Mother's Day Spring program.
- Set of 5 includes Studio, 2 piece accessory "Spring Portrait," sign, and tree.
- Hanging plant is separate in the box.
- 5% of proceeds goes to fight against breast cancer.

Captain Kensey's House   56651

Dates	OSRP	GBTru	Paid
2001 - 2003	$55	$55	$____

- Seaside Series.

Whale Tale Pub & Inn   56652

Dates	OSRP	GBTru	Paid
2001 - 2003	$62	$60	$____

- Seaside Series.
- Sign is separate in the box.

Otter Creek Sawmill   56653

Dates	OSRP	GBTru	Paid
2001 - 2003	$70	$70	$____

- Mountain Lake Lodge Series.

Whitehill Round Barn   56654

Dates	OSRP	GBTru	Paid
2001 -	$65	-	$____

- Four weathervanes are separate in the box.

Chapman's Cider House — 56655

Dates	OSRP	GBTru	Paid
2002ᴹ -	$65	-	$_____

- Named in honor of Johnny Appleseed.
- Sign is separate in the box.
- Do not handle by porch posts.

Salt Bay Lobster Co. — 56658

Dates	OSRP	GBTru	Paid
2002 -	$57	-	$_____

Warren Homestead And Walden Cottage — 56659

Dates	OSRP	GBTru	Paid
2002 -	$85	-	$_____

- Set of 2.
- Warren Homestead sign is separate in box. (But Walden Cottage sign is attached.)

Hutchison Grain Elevator — 56660

Dates	OSRP	GBTru	Paid
2002 - 2004	$55	$55	$_____

Castle Glassworks — 56661

Dates	OSRP	GBTru	Paid
2002 - 2003	$75	$85	$_____

- Limited to 15,000 numbered pieces.

Connacher's Nursery — 56662

Dates	OSRP	GBTru	Paid
2002 - 2004	$70	$70	$_____

Benjamin Bowman Violin Maker — 56663

Dates	OSRP	GBTru	Paid
2002 - 2004	$60	$60	$_____

Mt. Gibb Congregational Church — 56664

Dates	OSRP	GBTru	Paid
2003ᴹ -	$50	-	$_____

- Set of 2 includes "Announcements Sign" accessory and removable wedding trim.
- Can be personalized.

The Red Fox — 56665

Dates	OSRP	GBTru	Paid
2003 -	$55	-	$_____

Waterbury Button Company — 56666

Dates	OSRP	GBTru	Paid
2003 - 2004	$65	$65	$_____

- Limited to year of production.

Drummond Bank — 56667

Dates	OSRP	GBTru	Paid
2003 -	$55	-	$_____

- Can be personalized.

Woodbridge Town Hall — 56670

Dates	OSRP	GBTru	Paid
2004ᴹ -	$55	-	$____

Sawyer Family Tree Farm — 56671

Dates	OSRP	GBTru	Paid
2004ᴹ - 2004	$75	$75	$____

- Set of 5 includes house, "Taking The Tree Home" accessory, trees, and snow.
- Limited to year of production.

J. Noyes Mill — 56672

Dates	OSRP	GBTru	Paid
2004 -	$75	-	$____

- Windmill blades turn.
- Adapter included.

Woodbridge Gazette & Printing Office — 56673

Dates	OSRP	GBTru	Paid
2004 -	$55	-	$____

- Sign is separate in box.

Chas. Hoyt Blacksmith — 56674

Dates	OSRP	GBTru	Paid
2004 -	$60	-	$____

New England Village

Use the space(s) below to update your guide when the midyear introductions are announced.

	Dates	OSRP	GBTru	Paid
	___ - ___	$___	-	$___

	Dates	OSRP	GBTru	Paid
	___ - ___	$___	-	$___

	Dates	OSRP	GBTru	Paid
	___ - ___	$___	-	$___

	Dates	OSRP	GBTru	Paid
	___ - ___	$___	-	$___

	Dates	OSRP	GBTru	Paid
	___ - ___	$___	-	$___

Covered Wooden Bridge 65315 1986 - 1990 OSRP: $10 GBTru: $22 Paid: $_____ • The sleeve reads "Covered Bridge."	**New England Winter Set**  65323 - Set of 5 1986 - 1990 OSRP: $18 GBTru: $30 Paid: $_____ • Sleeves on early pieces read "Winter Village Accessories."
New England Village Sign 65706 1987 - 1993 OSRP: $6 GBTru: $10 Paid: $_____ • Bottomstamp reads "Handcrafted by Jiean Fung Porcelains, Taiwan." • Early signs have more detail and richer colors.	**Maple Sugaring Shed** 65897 - Set of 3 1987 - 1989 OSRP: $19 GBTru: $150 Paid: $_____ • Smokestack and pegs in trees are very fragile.
Village Harvest People  59412 - Set of 4 1988 - 1991 OSRP: $27.50 GBTru: $35 Paid: $_____ • The sleeves read "Harvest Time."	**Woodcutter And Son** 59862 - Set of 2 1988 - 1990 OSRP: $10 GBTru: $35 Paid: $_____
Red Covered Bridge  59870 1988 - 1994 OSRP: $15 GBTru: $18 Paid: $_____	**Farm Animals**  59455 - Set of 4 1989 - 1991 OSRP: $15 GBTru: $35 Paid: $_____ • Another item with the same name was produced in 1995.

Amish Family (With Mustache)   (Without Mustache)

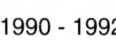

59480 - Set of 3
1990 - 1992
OSRP: $20
GBTru: $45
Paid: $_____

• Father has mustache which is against Amish customs.
• Early release: NALED and Showcase dealers.

GBTru: $30
Paid: $_____

• Re-issued with father without mustache.

Amish Buggy

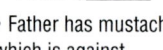

59498
1990 - 1992
OSRP: $22
GBTru: $45
Paid: $_____

Sleepy Hollow Characters

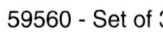

59560 - Set of 3
1990 - 1992
OSRP: $27.50
GBTru: $35
Paid: $_____

• From characters in Washington Irving's "Legend of Sleepy Hollow."

Skating Party

55239 - Set of 3
1991 - 2001
OSRP: $27.50
GBTru: $25
Paid: $_____

Market Day

56413 - Set of 3
1991 - 1993
OSRP: $35
GBTru: $35
Paid: $_____

Harvest Seed Cart

56456 - Set of 3
1992 - 1995
OSRP: $27.50
GBTru: $33
Paid: $_____

Town Tinker

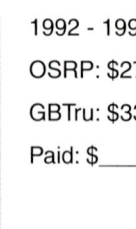

56464 - Set of 2
1992 - 1995
OSRP: $24
GBTru: $24
Paid: $_____

• Pots and pans are separate in box, and are easily lost.

Knife Grinder

56499 - Set of 2
1993 - 1996
OSRP: $22.50
GBTru: $25
Paid: $_____

• A pair of ice skates is separate in box.

Blue Star Ice Harvesters

56502 - Set of 2
1993 - 1997
OSRP: $27.50
GBTru: $30
Paid: $_____

• Porcelain and acrylic.
• Acrylic ice blocks easily come unglued.

Over The River And Through The Woods

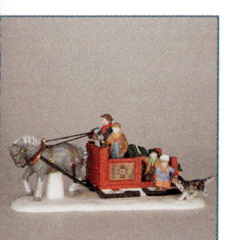

56545
1994 - 1998
OSRP: $35
GBTru: $33
Paid: $_____

The Old Man And The Sea

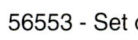

56553 - Set of 3
1994 - 1998
OSRP: $25
GBTru: $28
Paid: $_____

Two Rivers Bridge

56561
1994 - 1997
OSRP: $35
GBTru: $35
Paid: $_____

• Porcelain and resin.

Farm Animals

56588 - Set of 8
1995 -
OSRP: $32.50
GBTru: -
Paid: $_____

• Another item with the same name was produced in 1989.
• Also has 8 hay bales.

Lobster Trappers

56589 - Set of 4
1995 - 2000
OSRP: $35
GBTru: $35
Paid: $_____

• 3 "cooked" lobsters are separate in box.
• Lobster in man's hand often breaks off.

Lumberjacks

56590 - Set of 2
1995 - 1998
OSRP: $30
GBTru: $30
Paid: $_____

• Porcelain and wood.

New England Village Acc.

Harvest Pumpkin Wagon

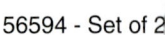

56591
1995 - 1999
OSRP: $45
GBTru: $65
Paid: $_____

• Similar designs were produced for Heinz and Bachman's. See the Special Design section.

Fresh Paint New England Village Sign

56592
1995 - 2001^M
OSRP: $20
GBTru: $22
Paid: $_____

A New Potbellied Stove For Christmas

56593 - Set of 2
1996 - 1998
OSRP: $35
GBTru: $35
Paid: $_____

Christmas Bazaar Handmade Quilts

56594 - Set of 2
1996 - 1999
OSRP: $25
GBTru: $30
Paid: $_____

Christmas Bazaar Woolens & Preserves

56595 - Set of 2
1996 - 1999
OSRP: $25
GBTru: $32
Paid: $_____

• Early shipments read "Jame & Jellies" on the sign.

Christmas Bazaar Flapjacks & Hot Cider

56596 - Set of 2
1997 - 1999
OSRP: $27.50
GBTru: $30
Paid: $_____

Christmas Bazaar Toy Vendor & Cart

56597 - Set of 2
1997 - 1999
OSRP: $27.50
GBTru: $28
Paid: $_____

Christmas Bazaar Sign

56598 - Set of
1997 - 1999
OSRP: $16
GBTru: $20
Paid: $_____

Tapping The Maples

56599 - Set of 7
1997 - 2001ᴹ
OSRP: $85
GBTru: $80
Paid: $_____

Sea Captain & His Mates

56587 - Set of 4
1998ᴹ - 2000
OSRP: $32.50
GBTru: $33
Paid: $_____

Load Up The Wagon

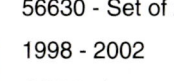

56630 - Set of 2
1998 - 2002
OSRP: $40
GBTru: $40
Paid: $_____

• Actual wood is used for the logs.

Under The Mistletoe

56631
1998 - 2001
OSRP: $16.50
GBTru: $20
Paid: $_____

Fly-casting In The Brook

56633
1998 - 2002
OSRP: $15
GBTru: $20
Paid: $_____

• Caution: Wire is very fragile.

Volunteer Firefighters

56635 - Set of 2
1998 - 2000
OSRP: $37.50
GBTru: $42
Paid: $_____

Farmer's Market

56637 - Set of 2
1998 - 2003
OSRP: $55
GBTru: $60
Paid: $_____

An Artist's Touch

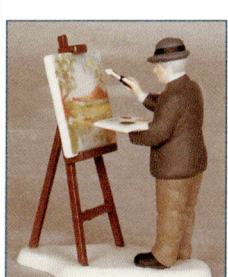

56638
1998 - 2001ᴹ
OSRP: $17
GBTru: $20
Paid: $_____

• "Canvas" is porcelain with a decal, and easel is metal.

A Letter From Papa

56606 - Set of 3
1999ᴹ - 2000
OSRP: *
GBTru: *

* Accessory contained in Little Women - The March Residence.

It's Almost Thanksgiving

56639 - Set of 4
1999ᴹ -
OSRP: $60
GBTru: -
Paid: $_____

• Porcelain and resin.

Pennyfarthing Pedaling

56615
1999 - 2003
OSRP: $13.50
GBTru: $15
Paid: $_____

Doctor's House Call

56616 - Set of 2
1999 - 2001
OSRP: $27.50
GBTru: $25
Paid: $_____

The Sailors' Knot

56617
1999 - 2003
OSRP: $27.50
GBTru: $28
Paid: $_____

The Woodworker

56619
1999 - 2003
OSRP: $35
GBTru: $35
Paid: $_____

• The Dream House Sweepstakes Deluxe Prize winner assisted in the design.

Making The Christmas Candles

56620 - Set of 2
1999 - 2002
OSRP: $25
GBTru: $28
Paid: $_____

Let's Go One More Time

56621 - Set of
1999 - 2001
OSRP: $30
GBTru: $30
Paid: $_____

Dairy Delivery Sleigh

56622
1999 -
OSRP: $37.50
GBTru: -
Paid: $_____

Mill Creek Crossing

56623
1999 - 2003
OSRP: $32.50
GBTru: $32
Paid: $_____

Postal Pick-up

56641
2000^M - 2001^M
OSRP: $14
GBTru: $20
Paid: $_____

New Spring Finery

56626
2000 - 2001
OSRP: *
GBTru: *

* Accessory contained in the Verna Mae's Boutique Gift Set.

A Day At The Cabin

56642 - Set of 2
2000 - 2003
OSRP: $25
GBTru: $28
Paid: $_____

Gathering Cranberries

56644
2000 - 2002
OSRP: $30
GBTru: $33
Paid: $_____

The Perfect Tree

56645
2000 -
OSRP: $20
GBTru: -
Paid: $_____

Here Comes Sinter Klaus

56646
2000 - 2002
OSRP: $17
GBTru: $18
Paid: $_____

Best Of The Harvest

56647 - Set of 2
2000 - 2002
OSRP: $25
GBTru: $28
Paid: $_____

Creating Silver Keepsakes

56632
2001^M - 2002
OSRP: *
GBTru: *

* Accessory contained in Revere Silver Works.

Silver For Sale

56650 - Set of 2
2001^M - 2002
OSRP: $20
GBTru: $24
Paid: $_____

Spring Portrait

56634
2001 - 2002
OSRP: *
GBTru: *

* The accessory contained in Springfield Studio Gift Set.

On The Boardwalk

56680 - Set of 3
2001 -
OSRP: $27.50
GBTru: -
Paid: $_____

• Seaside Series.

Boardwalk Sunday Stroll

56681 - Set of 2
2001 - 2004
OSRP: $20
GBTru: $20
Paid: $_____

• Seaside Series.

Lumberjack

56682
2001 -
OSRP: $27.50
GBTru: -
Paid: $_____

Milking The Cow

56683
2001 -
OSRP: $20
GBTru: -
Paid: $_____

Running The Apple Press  56684 2001 - OSRP: $24 GBTru: - Paid: $_____	**New England Raising The Flag**  56687 2001 - 2004 OSRP: $15 GBTru: $15 Paid: $_____
Loading The Grain  56688 - Set of 2 2002 - 2004 OSRP: $37.50 GBTru: $38 Paid: $_____	**Glassworks Craftsman**  56689 2002 - 2003 OSRP: $15 GBTru: $18 Paid: $_____
Admiring Nature's Beauty 56690 2002 - 2004 OSRP: $15 GBTru: $15 Paid: $_____	**Maestro And His Protégé**  56691 2002 - 2004 OSRP: $18 GBTru: $18 Paid: $_____
Salty's Live Bait Shack  56692 - Set of 2 2002 - OSRP: $35 GBTru: - Paid: $_____	**Today's Catch**  56693 2002 - OSRP: $17.50 GBTru: - Paid: $_____

Delivering The Christmas Spirit

56694
2002 -
OSRP: $20
GBTru: -
Paid: $_____

New England Town Tree

56695
2002 -
OSRP: $25
GBTru: -
Paid: $_____

Good Day, Reverend

56697 - Set of 2
2003^M -
OSRP: $18.50
GBTru: -
Paid: $_____

Masonry Bake Oven

56698
2003 -
OSRP: $16.50
GBTru: -
Paid: $_____

Dancing An Irish Jig

57102 - Set of 2
2003 -
OSRP: $20
GBTru: -
Paid: $_____

A Penny Saved Is A Penny Earned

57103
2003 -
OSRP: $12.50
GBTru: -
Paid: $_____

Family Sleigh Ride

57105
2003 -
OSRP: $30
GBTru: -
Paid: $_____

The Hitching Post

57106
2003 -
OSRP: $18
GBTru: -
Paid: $_____

Pitching Horseshoes 57107 2003 - OSRP: $15 GBTru: - Paid: $_____	**Taking The Tree Home**  56671 - Set of 2 2004^M - 2004 OSRP: * GBTru: * * The accessory contained in Sawyer Family Tree Farm.
Hear Ye Citizens  57108 2004^M - OSRP: $15 GBTru: - Paid: $_____	**Ambrose Adder's Tonics & Curatives**  57109 2004 - OSRP: $20 GBTru: - Paid: $_____
Not Too Fast, Please  57110 2004 - OSRP: $12.50 GBTru: - Paid: $_____	**Town Blacksmith**  57112 2004 - OSRP: $12.50 GBTru: - Paid: $_____
Use the following space(s) to update your guide when the midyear introductions are announced.	_____ _____ ____ - ____ OSRP: $_____ GBTru: - Paid: $_____

New England Village Acc.

_____		_____	
	_____		_____
	___ - ___		___ - ___
	OSRP: $_____		OSRP: $_____
	GBTru: -		GBTru: -
	Paid: $_____		Paid: $_____
_____		_____	
	_____		_____
	___ - ___		___ - ___
	OSRP: $_____		OSRP: $_____
	GBTru: -		GBTru: -
	Paid: $_____		Paid: $_____
_____		_____	
	_____		_____
	___ - ___		___ - ___
	OSRP: $_____		OSRP: $_____
	GBTru: -		GBTru: -
	Paid: $_____		Paid: $_____
_____		_____	
	_____		_____
	___ - ___		___ - ___
	OSRP: $_____		OSRP: $_____
	GBTru: -		
	Paid: $_____		

Alpine Village Series®

    The hills truly are "alive with the sounds of music" since Department 56 reached a licensing agreement with the parent organization of the famed musical. Since the von Trapp Villa and Wedding Church are larger than most early pieces, both the buildings and characters have added a new dimension to the mountainous European community. Collectors have also acquired their long-awaited castle, and displays have taken on a new look. Nor is this the first time that a change has occurred. After a decade of small, mostly pastel colors, buildings grew larger and brighter.

    For many years this was a quaint, intimate community. After its initial five buildings, it grew at a very slow pace; in fact, it is the only village that has ever gone an entire year (1989) without an addition. That intimacy is one of the appeals that have attracted many collectors to the village. It is composed primarily of rustic buildings that can be perched precariously on the sides of mountains or in secluded valleys.

    The musical sounds echoing through those valleys come not from one but two music boxes. "Something Good" accompanies the dancers in the musical gazebo. But the true classic is the "Silent Night" Music Box that plays the beloved classic that was composed at the Church of St. Nikolaus in Oberndorf, Austria, also depicted in the village.

    Many Alpine advocates base their love for the village on their personal heritage; others are attracted by the beauty and simplicity of the series. It is interesting that several of the names on buildings appear in German while others are printed in English. Regardless of the language, Alpine Village is wunderwschön…beautiful.

Alpine Village

ALPINE VILLAGE - Set of 5   65404

Dates	OSRP	GBTru	Paid
1986 - 1996/97	$125	$150	$____

- None of the buildings in this set have names on their bottoms or their sleeves.
- Early release to NALED dealers.

Besson Bierkeller   65405

Dates	OSRP	GBTru	Paid
1986 - 1996	$25	$35	$____

- English translation: Beer Cellar.
- Early release to NALED dealers.

Gasthof Eisl   65406

Dates	OSRP	GBTru	Paid
1986 - 1996	$25	$35	$____

- English translation: Guest House.
- Early release to NALED dealers.

Apotheke   65407

Dates	OSRP	GBTru	Paid
1986 - 1997	$25	$35	$____

- English translation: Apothecary.
- Early release to NALED dealers.

E. Staubr Backer   65408

Dates	OSRP	GBTru	Paid
1986 - 1997	$25	$35	$____

- English translation: Bakery.
- Early release to NALED dealers.

Milch-Kase   65409

Dates	OSRP	GBTru	Paid
1986 - 1996	$25	$35	$____

- English translation: Milk-Cheese.
- Early release to NALED dealers.

Josef Engel Farmhouse — 59528

Dates	OSRP	GBTru	Paid
1987 - 1989	$33	$780	$_____

Alpine Church (White Trim) — 65412

Dates	OSRP	GBTru	Paid
1987 - 1991	$32	$285	$_____

- This version was available in the early shipments and is the rarer of the two versions.

(Tan Trim)

GBTru	Paid
$165	$_____

- This version was available in later shipments.

Grist Mill — 59536

Dates	OSRP	GBTru	Paid
1988 - 1997	$42	$45	$_____

Bahnhof — 56154

Dates	OSRP	GBTru	Paid
1990 - 1993	$42	$65	$_____

- English translation: Train Station.
- The early pieces had gilded trim. The later ones had a yellow-mustard trim.

St. Nikolaus Kirche — 56170

Dates	OSRP	GBTru	Paid
1991 - 1999	$37.50	$40	$_____

- Designed after Church of St. Nikolaus in Oberndorf, Austria, the home of the Christmas hymn "Silent Night."

Alpine Village

ALPINE SHOPS - Set of 2 — 56189

Dates	OSRP	GBTru	Paid
1992 - 1997/98	$75	$75	$_____

Metterniche Wurst — 56190

Dates	OSRP	GBTru	Paid
1992 - 1997	$37.50	$40	$_____

• English translation: Sausage Shop.

Kukuck Uhren — 56191

Dates	OSRP	GBTru	Paid
1992 - 1998	$37.50	$40	$_____

• English translation: Clock Shop.

Sport Laden — 56120

Dates	OSRP	GBTru	Paid
1993 - 1998	$50	$45	$_____

• English translation: Sports Shop.

Konditorei Schokolade — 56146

Dates	OSRP	GBTru	Paid
1994 - 1998	$37.50	$40	$_____

• English translation: Bakery & Chocolate Shop.
• The bottomstamp and the sleeve read "Bakery & Chocolate Shop."

Kamm Haus — 5617

Dates	OSRP	GBTru	Paid
1995 - 1999	$42	$50	$_____

• English translation: House On The Crest.

Alpine Village

Danube Music Publisher   56173

Dates	OSRP	GBTru	Paid
1996 - 2000	**$55**	**$60**	**$_____**

- The German translation of the building's name, Donau Musik Verlag, is found above its front door.
- A sign is separate in the box.

Bernhardiner Hundchen   56174

Dates	OSRP	GBTru	Paid
1997ᴹ - 2000	**$50**	**$50**	**$_____**

- English translation: St. Bernard Kennel.

Spielzeug Laden   56192

Dates	OSRP	GBTru	Paid
1997 - 2000	**$65**	**$65**	**$_____**

- English translation: Toy Shop.
- Sign, doll, and 2 jack-in-the-boxes are separate in box.

Federbetten Und Steppdecken   56176

Dates	OSRP	GBTru	Paid
1998ᴹ - 2001	**$48**	**$50**	**$_____**

- English translation: Featherbeds And Quilts.
- A sign is separate in the box.

The Sound Of Music® von Trapp Villa   56178

Dates	OSRP	GBTru	Paid
1998 - 2002	**$130**	**$135**	**$_____**

- Inspired by the stately mansion where Maria, the Captain, and their children lived in the *Sound Of Music*®.
- 2 lanterns are separate in the box.
- Set of 5 includes Villa, the von Trapps, and a gate.
- Licensed by R&H Org., Argyle & Fox.

Alpine Village

Heidi's Grandfather's House — 56177

Dates	OSRP	GBTru	Paid
1998 - 2001	$64	$65	$____

• Inspired by Johanna Spyri's classic novel.
• Antlers are separate in the box.

Glockenspiel — 56210

Dates	OSRP	GBTru	Paid
1999 - 2003	$80	$85	$____

• Music box plays "Emperor Waltz."

The Sound Of Music® Wedding Church — 56211

Dates	OSRP	GBTru	Paid
1999 - 2002	$60	$65	$____

• Inspired by the church where Maria and the Captain got married in the *Sound Of Music*®.
• A star-shaped spire is separate in the box.
• Licensed by R&H Org., Argyle & Fox.

Hofburg Castle — 56216

Dates	OSRP	GBTru	Paid
2000ᴹ - 2002	$68	$70	$____

• 3 flags are separate in the box.

Nussknacker Werkstatt — 56217

Dates	OSRP	GBTru	Paid
2000 - 2001	$60	$325	$____

• English translation: Nutcracker Workshop.
• 25th Anniversary Limited Edition of 5,600.
• Sign and tin soldier are separate in the box.

Altstädter Bierstube — 56218

Dates	OSRP	GBTru	Paid
2000 -	$65	-	$____

• English translation: Altstadter Beerhouse.
• 2 signs are separate in the box.

Schwarzwalder Kuckucksuhren — 56220

Dates	OSRP	GBTru	Paid
2001ᴹ - 2003	$65	$60	$_____

- English translation: Cuckoo Clock Shop.

Alpine Village

Getreidemühle Zwettl — 56221

Dates	OSRP	GBTru	Paid
2001 - 2004	$85	$85	$_____

- English translation: Grain Mill.
- Animated.

Käsehändler Schmitt — 56222

Dates	OSRP	GBTru	Paid
2001 - 2003	$55	$55	$_____

- English translation: Cheese Shop.
- Sign is separate in the box.

Nikolausfiguren — 56223

Dates	OSRP	GBTru	Paid
2002ᴹ -	$65	-	$_____

- English translation: Nicholas Figurines.
- Sign and 3 hanging ornaments are separate in the box.

Bauernhof Drescher — 56229

Dates	OSRP	GBTru	Paid
2002 -	$95	-	$_____

- English translation: Barn and Farmhouse.
- Set of 2.

Alpine Village

Rathaus Neudorf — 56230

Dates	OSRP	GBTru	Paid
2002 -	$65	-	$____

• English translation: Town Hall.

Jägerutte - Hunting Cabin — 56231

Dates	OSRP	GBTru	Paid
2003ᴹ -	$65	-	$____

Alpen Akademie der Musik — 56232

Dates	OSRP	GBTru	Paid
2003 -	$65	-	$____

Bergermeister's House — 56233

Dates	OSRP	GBTru	Paid
2004 -	$65	-	$____

• English translation: Mayor's House.

Dates	OSRP	GBTru	Paid
____ - ____	$____	-	$____

Dates	OSRP	GBTru	Paid
____ - ____	$____	-	$____

Alpine Villagers

65420 - Set of 3
1986 - 1992
OSRP: $13
GBTru: $24
Paid: $_____

• Figures became thinner in later years of production.

Alpine Village Sign

65714
1987 - 1993
OSRP: $6
GBTru: $10
Paid: $_____

• Bottomstamp reads "Handcrafted by Jiean Fung Porcelains, Taiwan."
• Early signs have more detail and richer colors.

The Toy Peddler

56162 - Set of 3
1990 - 1998
OSRP: $22
GBTru: $22
Paid: $_____

Buying Bakers Bread

56197 - Set of 2
1992 - 1995
OSRP: $20
GBTru: $20
Paid: $_____

Climb Every Mountain

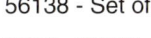
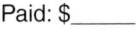

56138 - Set of 4
1993 - 2001ᴹ
OSRP: $27.50
GBTru: $30
Paid: $_____

Polka Fest

56073 - Set of 3
1994 - 1999
OSRP: $30
GBTru: $30
Paid: $_____

'Silent Night' Music Box

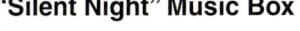

56180
1995 - 1999
OSRP: $32.50
GBTru: $35
Paid: $_____

• Based on the Silent Night Memorial Chapel in Oberndorf, Austria.
• First HV music box.

Alpenhorn Player Alpine Village Sign

56182
1995 - 2001ᴹ
OSRP: $20
GBTru: $18
Paid: $_____

Alpine Village Accessories

Alpine Village Accessories

Nutcracker Vendor & Cart

56183
1996 - 2002
OSRP: $20
GBTru: $25
Paid: $_____

A New Batch Of Christmas Friends

56175 - Set of 3
1997^M - 2000
OSRP: $27.50
GBTru: $30
Paid: $_____

Heidi & Her Goats

56201 - Set of 4
1997 - 2001^M
OSRP: $30
GBTru: $30
Paid: $_____

Trekking In The Snow

56202 - Set of 3
1998 - 2002
OSRP: $27.50
GBTru: $28
Paid: $_____

St. Nicholas

56203
1998 -
OSRP: $12
GBTru: -
Paid: $_____

The Sound Of Music® Gazebo

56212
1999 - 2002
OSRP: $40
GBTru: $40
Paid: $_____

• Plays "Something Good."
• R & H Org., Argyle & Fox.

Sisters Of The Abbey

56213 - Set of 2
1999 -
OSRP: $20
GBTru: -
Paid: $_____

Leading The Bavarian Cow

56214
1999 - 2002
OSRP: $20
GBTru: $25
Paid: $_____

Alpine Villagers

56215 - Set of 5
1999 -
OSRP: $32.50
GBTru: -
Paid: $_____

Here Comes The Bride

56300
2000^M - 2002
OSRP: $18
GBTru: $24
Paid: $_____

At The October Fest

56302 - Set of 3
2000 -
OSRP: $27.50
GBTru: -
Paid: $_____

Cuckoo Clock Vendor & Cart

56303 - Set of 2
2001^M - 2004
OSRP: $20
GBTru: $20
Paid: $_____

Home From The Mill

56304
2001 - 2003
OSRP: $20
GBTru: $20
Paid: $_____

A Head of Cheese

56305
2001 - 2003
OSRP: $12.50
GBTru: $15
Paid: $_____

The Finishing Touch

56306
2002^M - 2004
OSRP: $20
GBTru: $20
Paid: $_____

Back From The Fields

56309
2002 -
OSRP: $17.50
GBTru: -
Paid: $_____

Alpine Village Accessories

Alpine Village Accessories

Tap The First Barrel

56310
2002 -
OSRP: $17.50
GBTru: -
Paid: $_____

The Bierfest Judge

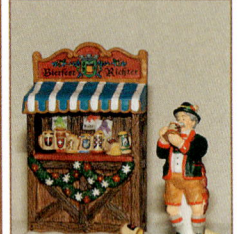

56311 - Set of 2
2002 -
OSRP: $25
GBTru: -
Paid: $_____

Going Hunting

56312
2003ᴹ -
OSRP: $15
GBTru: -
Paid: $_____

Mozart Monument

56313
2003 -
OSRP: $15
GBTru: -
Paid: $_____

Hear Ye, Citizens

56314
2004 -
OSRP: $15
GBTru: -
Paid: $_____

Use the following space(s) to update your guide when the midyear introductions are announced.

_____
_____
____ - ____
OSRP: $_____
GBTru: -
Paid: $_____

_____
_____
____ - ____
OSRP: $_____
GBTru: -
Paid: $_____

Christmas In The City® Series

Few places are as magical at the holiday season as a city with its bright lights, glittering decorations, and the sounds of Christmas. The normally hectic pace accelerates, but not in a frantic way. Many collectors recall this period vividly. Noses pressed against department store windows, we marveled at the trains, dolls, and stuffed animals that peered back at us. We looked in awe at the colorful town tree.

All of those memories are recaptured in miniature as Department 56 recalls scenes from the middle of the last century. Skaters in Rockefeller Center, trains carrying shoppers through Grand Central Station, the majesty of the Empire State Building, and celebrations of another new year under the Times Tower bring us back to an earlier age in New York. Or your City can be any urban area of that era. Boston, Chicago, and New York baseball stadiums may help you to define your metropolis. It features houses of worship, theaters, and restaurants. There are large stores and small shops. We have government buildings as well as hospital, police, and fire services. Culture can be found in the museum, art academy, and educational institutions. Recently a maritime portion has expanded the City's landscape.

Local neighborhoods with family businesses and ethnic shops contrast with the heart of "downtown." Townhouses and apartment buildings house local residents while hotels host tourists and businessmen. Merchants, shoppers, and visitors all add to the hustle and bustle on busy city streets. There are food vendors, school children, and street musicians on crowded corners. Vehicles fill city streets. It is a wonderful place to be at a wonderful time.

CHRISTMAS IN THE CITY - Set of 3   65129

Dates	OSRP	GBTru	Paid
1987 - 1990	$112	$415	$_____

- All 3 pieces have "Christmas In The City" inscribed on the bottoms. Individual names do not appear.

Bakery   65129

Dates	OSRP	GBTru	Paid
1987 - 1990	$37.50	$90	$_____

- Early pieces are light. Later ones are darker.
- Has 2 large and 2 small window grates.
- The chimneys are fragile.

Tower Restaurant   65129

Dates	OSRP	GBTru	Paid
1987 - 1990	$37.50	$175	$_____

- Sleeve reads "Tower Cafe." Bottom has no name.
- Early pieces are very dark. Later ones are lighter.
- Has 11 window grates.

Toy Shop And Pet Store   65129

Dates	OSRP	GBTru	Paid
1987 - 1990	$37.50	$175	$_____

- Early pieces are very dark. Later ones are lighter.
- Has 6 window grates.
- The chimneys are fragile.

Sutton Place Brownstones   5961?

Dates	OSRP	GBTru	Paid
1987 - 1989	$80	$700	$_____

- Bottom is inscribed with "Sutton Place Rowhouse."
- Earliest pieces have grates at attic windows.
- It's not unusual for this piece to have concave walls. On with straight walls is considered more valuable.

The Cathedral   5962?

Dates	OSRP	GBTru	Paid
1987 - 1990	$60	$245	$_____

- Early pieces are smaller (10½" high), darker, and hav snow on the steps. Later ones are larger (11½" high lighter, and have no snow on the steps.

Palace Theatre   59633

Dates	OSRP	GBTru	Paid
1987 - 1989	**$45**	**$535**	$_____

- Early pieces have gilded trim and more snow on roof. Later ones have yellow/mustard trim.
- It's not unusual for this piece to have concave walls. One with straight walls is considered more valuable.

Chocolate Shoppe   59684

Dates	OSRP	GBTru	Paid
1988 - 1991	**$40**	**$105**	$_____

- Early pieces are dark. Later ones are lighter.
- Has 2 window grates on second story.
- The roof of the attached bookstore is often not level.

City Hall   59692

Dates	OSRP	GBTru	Paid
1988 - 1991	**$65**	**$135**	$_____

- Do not handle by the tower.
- The City Hall "Proof" is smaller than the regular City Hall edition. It came in a box with no sleeve or lightcord.
  Proof GBTru = $100 $_____

Hank's Market   59706

Dates	OSRP	GBTru	Paid
1988 - 1992	**$40**	**$65**	$_____

- This is also referred to as the "Corner Grocer."
- Early samples have the vertical "Grocery" sign attached to the pillar to the right of the door and no 59¢ sign in the lettuce bin.

Variety Store And Barber Shop   59722

Dates	OSRP	GBTru	Paid
1988 - 1990	**$45**	**$135**	$_____

- The design was inspired by a store in Stillwater, MN.
- The mold was also used for the Bachman's Hometown Series Drugstore. See the Special Design section.
- Sleeve reads "Variety Store & Barbershop."

Ritz Hotel   59730

Dates	OSRP	GBTru	Paid
1989 - 1994	**$55**	**$65**	$_____

- Early pieces have yellow/mustard accents. Later ones have gilded accents and are smaller.
- Columns are easily broken.

Dorothy's Dress Shop — 59749

Dates	OSRP	GBTru	Paid
1989 - 1990	$70	$285	$_____

• Limited Edition of 12,500.

5607 Park Avenue Townhouse — 59773

Dates	OSRP	GBTru	Paid
1989 - 1992	$48	$75	$_____

• Early pieces have gilded trim at the top edge of the roof. Later ones have yellow/mustard trim.

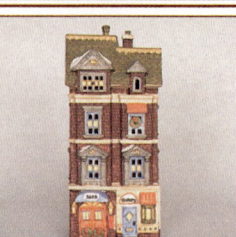

5609 Park Avenue Townhouse — 59781

Dates	OSRP	GBTru	Paid
1989 - 1992	$48	$75	$_____

• Early pieces have gilded trim at the top edge of the roof. Later ones have yellow/mustard trim.

Red Brick Fire Station — 55360

Dates	OSRP	GBTru	Paid
1990 - 1995	$55	$70	$_____

• Cornerstones vary from gray to light blue.

Wong's In Chinatown — 55379

Dates	OSRP	GBTru	Paid
1990 - 1994	$55	$75	$_____

• Early pieces have red top windows. Later ones have gilded windows.
• Includes fire escape and ladder packaged separately in the box.

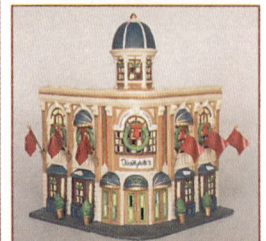

Hollydale's Department Store — 55344

Dates	OSRP	GBTru	Paid
1991 - 1997	$75	$90	$_____

• Early pieces are from Taiwan then China and have holly on first floor canopies only. Later ones are from China and then the Philippines and have holly on all canopies.
• Includes 4 porcelain topiaries and 6 metal flags in box.

Christmas In The City

"Little Italy" Ristorante — 55387

Dates	OSRP	GBTru	Paid
1991 - 1995	$50	$70	$_____

- Chimney on pizzeria oven can easily be broken when inserting in box.

All Saints Corner Church — 55425

Dates	OSRP	GBTru	Paid
1991 - 1998	$96	$100	$_____

- The spires and the steeple are very fragile.

Arts Academy — 55433

Dates	OSRP	GBTru	Paid
1991 - 1993	$45	$65	$_____

The Doctor's Office — 55441

Dates	OSRP	GBTru	Paid
1991 - 1994	$60	$70	$_____

- Includes fire escape and ladder separately in the box.

Cathedral Church Of St. Mark — 55492

Dates	OSRP	GBTru	Paid
1991 - 1992	$120	$1625	$_____

- Limited Edition of 3,024 instead of the intended 17,500 due to production problems.
- Commonly referred to as St. Mark's Church.
- Early release to GCC, the only dealers to receive them.
- This design was originally intended for Dickens' Village.
- This building is very susceptible to firing cracks and other flaws. When purchasing one, you should examine it very closely, being certain to insert a light in it while in a darkened room.

Christmas In The City

UPTOWN SHOPPES - Set of 3   55310

Dates	OSRP	GBTru	Paid
1992 - 1996	$150	$150	$____

Haberdashery   55311

Dates	OSRP	GBTru	Paid
1992 - 1996	$40	$45	$____

• Has 1 window grate.

Music Emporium   55312

Dates	OSRP	GBTru	Paid
1992 - 1996	$54	$65	$____

• Music on the side of the building was inspired by a similar idea on the side of a music store in Minneapolis, MN.

City Clockworks   55313

Dates	OSRP	GBTru	Paid
1992 - 1996	$56	$60	$____

• Clock is easily broken, especially when removing or inserting building in box.

Town Tree   55654

Dates	OSRP	GBTru	Paid
1993 -	$45	-	$____

• Set of 5 includes Tree and 4 porcelain benches.

WEST VILLAGE SHOPS - Set of 2   58807

Dates	OSRP	GBTru	Paid
1993 - 1996	$90	$90	$____

Potter's Tea Seller — 58808

Dates	OSRP	GBTru	Paid
1993 - 1996	**$45**	**$50**	**$_____**

Spring St. Coffee House — 58809

Dates	OSRP	GBTru	Paid
1993 - 1996	**$45**	**$50**	**$_____**

- Sign is separate in the box.

Brokerage House — 58815

Dates	OSRP	GBTru	Paid
1994 - 1997	**$48**	**$65**	**$_____**

- "18" is the price of Dept. 56's initial stock offering at $18.
- "Price & Price" is in honor of Judith Price—Dept. 56's Ms. Lit Town—and her husband.
- "1960" is in honor of the year they were married.

First Metropolitan Bank — 58823

Dates	OSRP	GBTru	Paid
1994 - 1997	**$60**	**$65**	**$_____**

- Do not handle by columns.

Heritage Museum Of Art — 58831

Dates	OSRP	GBTru	Paid
1994 - 1998	**$96**	**$100**	**$_____**

- Includes 2 red banners packaged separately in the box.
- Gold flags are easily broken when removing this piece from its box.
- Do not handle by columns.

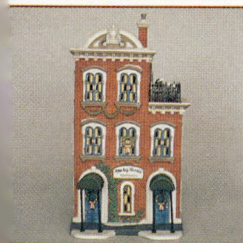

Ivy Terrace Apartments — 58874

Dates	OSRP	GBTru	Paid
1995^M - 1997	**$60**	**$60**	**$_____**

- Includes a sisal garden on the penthouse terrace.

Christmas In The City

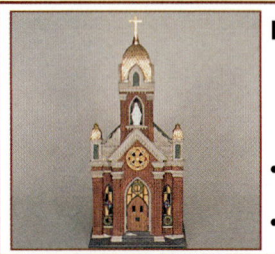

Holy Name Church — 58875

Dates	OSRP	GBTru	Paid
1995 - 2003	$96	$95	$____

- Inspired by the Cathedral of the Immaculate Conception in Kansas City, MO.
- Gold cross packaged separately in the box.

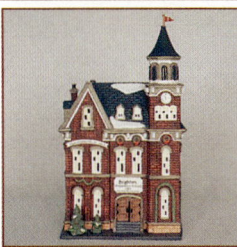

Brighton School — 58876

Dates	OSRP	GBTru	Paid
1995 - 1998	$52	$65	$____

- The flag on top of roof is easily broken, especially when removing the piece from its box.

BROWNSTONES ON THE SQUARE - Set of 2 — 58877

Dates	OSRP	GBTru	Paid
1995 - 1998/2000	$90	$90	$____

Beekman House — 58878

Dates	OSRP	GBTru	Paid
1995 - 2000	$45	$50	$____

- Has 1 window grate.
- Includes fire escape and ladder, as well as a lantern packaged separately in the box.

Pickford Place — 58879

Dates	OSRP	GBTru	Paid
1995 - 1998	$45	$50	$____

- Has 3 window grates.
- Includes lantern packaged separately in the box.

Washington Street Post Office — 58880

Dates	OSRP	GBTru	Paid
1996^M - 1998	$52	$65	$____

- Includes two mail boxes packaged separately in the box—one for local mail and one for air mail.

Grand Central Railway Station   58881

Dates	OSRP	GBTru	Paid
1996 - 1999	$90	$100	$_____

- Inspired by New York City's Grand Central Terminal.
- Includes 2 lanterns packaged separately in the box.
- The spires are easily broken, especially when removing the piece from its box.

Café Caprice French Restaurant   58882

Dates	OSRP	GBTru	Paid
1996 - 2001	$45	$55	$_____

- The sample pieces have a different color scheme, including striped awnings.

The City Globe   58883

Dates	OSRP	GBTru	Paid
1997^M - 2000	$65	$70	$_____

- The globe on the top of the building is very fragile and will easily break off.

Hi-De-Ho Nightclub   58884

Dates	OSRP	GBTru	Paid
1997^M - 1999	$52	$60	$_____

- The club name highlights a Cab Calloway jazz riff.

Johnson's Grocery & Deli   58886

Dates	OSRP	GBTru	Paid
1997 - 2002	$60	$65	$_____

- Includes sign packaged separately in the box.

The Capitol   58887

Dates	OSRP	GBTru	Paid
1997 - 1998	$110	$110	$_____

Christmas In The City

Christmas In The City

Riverside Row Shops — 58888

Dates	OSRP	GBTru	Paid
1997 - 1999	$52	$55	$_____

• Includes bank, barber shop, stationery store.

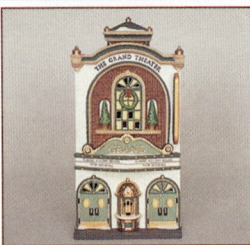

The Grand Movie Theater — 58870

Dates	OSRP	GBTru	Paid
1998ᴹ - 1999	$50	$60	$_____

Scottie's Toy Shop Exclusive Gift Set — 58871

Dates	OSRP	GBTru	Paid
1998ᴹ - 1998	$65	$90	$_____

• First available during the 1999 Homes for the Holidays event.
• This was the first Village design to include a three-dimensional scene in a building.
• Set of 10 includes the Toy Shop, the 3-piece accessory "5¢ Pony Rides," 4 sisal trees, Cobblestone Road, and a bag of Fresh Fallen Snow.

Old Trinity Church — 58940

Dates	OSRP	GBTru	Paid
1998 - 2000	$96	$100	$_____

Precinct 25 Police Station — 58941

Dates	OSRP	GBTru	Paid
1998 - 2003	$56	$65	$_____

• The globes on the front of the Station are fragile.

The Wedding Gallery 58943

Dates	OSRP	GBTru	Paid
1998 - 2002	$60	$65	$_____

- Includes a brass plaque that can be personalized and affixed to the building.

The University Club 58945

Dates	OSRP	GBTru	Paid
1998 - 2000	$60	$70	$_____

- Includes 3 green flags packaged separately in the box.

The Times Tower 55510

Dates	OSRP	GBTru	Paid
1999ᴹ - 1999	$185	$225	$_____

- Inspired by the Times Tower in Times Square.
- Includes numerals that can be substituted for those atop the building up to the year 2009.

- Set of 3 includes the Tower, the accessory "The New Year's Kiss," and confetti.
- There is also limited edition "party set" of 2000 numbered pieces.
  GBTru for LE: $295
- Licensed by Jamestown One Times Square, L.P.

Parkview Hospital 58947

Dates	OSRP	GBTru	Paid
1999ᴹ - 2000	$65	$70	$_____

Wintergarten Café 58948

Dates	OSRP	GBTru	Paid
1999ᴹ - 1999	$60	$65	$_____

- This piece is frequently adopted into Alpine Village by collectors.

5th Avenue Salon   58950

Dates	OSRP	GBTru	Paid
1999 - 2001	$68	$70	$_____

- The two lanterns on the back wall are easily damaged.

The Consulate   58951

Dates	OSRP	GBTru	Paid
1999 - 2000	$95	$95	$_____

- Limited to year of production.
- Main spire is packaged separately in the box.
- Spires are easily damaged when removing from box.
- Set of 2 includes Consulate, flag pole, and 25 flags.

Molly O'Brien's Irish Pub   58952

Dates	OSRP	GBTru	Paid
1999 -	$62	-	$_____

- Includes a lantern as well as a brass plaque that can be personalized. Both are packaged separately in the box.

Lafayette's Bakery   58953

Dates	OSRP	GBTru	Paid
1999 - 2002	$62	$65	$_____

Clark Street Automat   58954

Dates	OSRP	GBTru	Paid
1999 - 2000	$68	$65	$_____

- Includes special bulb that must be inserted on an angle.

Paramount Hotel   58911

Dates	OSRP	GBTru	Paid
2000^M - 2003	$85	$95	$_____

- Lighting includes traditional bulb at base plus flickering lights in ballroom and gold star on top of building.
- Includes separate cord for flickering lights.

Jenny's Corner Book Shop   58912

Dates	OSRP	GBTru	Paid
2000ᴹ - 2004	$65	$65	$_____

- Sign, bird cage, and weathervane are separate in the box.

The Majestic Theater   58913

Dates	OSRP	GBTru	Paid
2000 - 2001	$100	$150	$_____

- 25th Anniversary Limited Edition of 15,000.

42nd St. Fire Company   58914

Dates	OSRP	GBTru	Paid
2000 -	$80	-	$_____

- Includes lantern packaged separately in the box.
- Includes separate cord for flashing red lights above the overhead doors.
- The dog on the base is fragile.

Gardengate House   58915

Dates	OSRP	GBTru	Paid
2000 - 2002	$68	$70	$_____

Foster Pharmacy   58916

Dates	OSRP	GBTru	Paid
2000 - 2002	$85	$90	$_____

- Includes 3 lanterns packaged separately in the box.
- The separate sign is very easily broken when inserting or removing.

Mrs. Stover's Bungalow Candies   58917

Dates	OSRP	GBTru	Paid
2000 - 2003	$75	$75	$_____

- Includes sign packaged separately in the box.
- Licensed by Russell Stover Candies, Inc.

Christmas In The City

Department 56 Studio, 1200 Second Ave. 58918

Dates	OSRP	GBTru	Paid
2001ᴹ - 2001	$100	$315	$_____

- Replica of Architect's and Engineer's Building where Dept. 56 was once located in Minneapolis, MN.
- Special issue for Department 56's silver anniversary.
- Only available at that event. Lantern separate in box.

Baker Bros. Bagel Bakery 58920

Dates	OSRP	GBTru	Paid
2001ᴹ - 2002	$75	$75	$_____

- Includes table with umbrella packaged separately in the box.
- Several attachments can be easily broken when removing from box.

Paradise Travel Company 58921

Dates	OSRP	GBTru	Paid
2001ᴹ - 2002	$75	$80	$_____

- Includes sign packaged separately in the box.

Yankee Stadium 58923

Dates	OSRP	GBTru	Paid
2001ᴹ -	$85	-	$_____

- Legendary Ballparks Series.
- Replica of the facade of Yankee Stadium in New York.
- Includes two flags packaged separately in the box.
- Licensed by Major League Baseball Properties, Inc.

The Monte Carlo 58925

Dates	OSRP	GBTru	Paid
2001 - 2002	$85	$95	$_____

- Numbered limited edition of 15,000.
- Garland and 2 wreaths are separate in the box.

Sterling Jewelers 58926

Dates	OSRP	GBTru	Paid
2001 - 2003	$70	$80	$_____

Architectural Antiques 58927

Dates	OSRP	GBTru	Paid
2001 - 2003	$75	$80	$_____

- Set of 17 includes house and various antiques.

Tavern In The Park Restaurant 58928

Dates	OSRP	GBTru	Paid
2001 - 2004	$75	$75	$_____

- Christmas In The Park Series.
- Flag is separate in the box.

Nicholas & Co. Toys Starter Set 58929

Dates	OSRP	GBTru	Paid
2001 - 2003	$65	$70	$_____

- Set of 2 includes building and "Look At All The Toys" accessory.
- Sign is separate in the box.

Cathedral Of St. Paul 58930

Dates	OSRP	GBTru	Paid
2001 -	$150	-	$_____

- Re-issue of the Historical Landmark Series limited edition with copper colored roof. See that edition in the Small Collections section.

Fenway Park 58932

Dates	OSRP	GBTru	Paid
2001 -	$75	-	$_____

- Legendary Ballparks Series.
- Replica of the façade of Fenway Park in Boston.
- Includes flag and banners packaged separately in box.
- Licensed by Major League Baseball Properties, Inc.

Wrigley Field 58933

Dates	OSRP	GBTru	Paid
2001 -	$95	-	$_____

- Legendary Ballparks Series.
- Replica of the façade of Wrigley Field in Chicago.
- Includes three flags packaged separately in the box.
- Licensed by Major League Baseball Properties, Inc.

Radio City Music Hall 58924

Dates	OSRP	GBTru	Paid
2002^M -	$95	-	$_____

- Replica of Radio City Music Hall in New York City.
- A separate cord lights the marquee.
- Licensed by Radio City Trademarks L.L.C.

Parkside Holiday Brownstone 58937

Dates	OSRP	GBTru	Paid
2002^M - 2002	$75	$100	$_____

- Holiday 2002 Special Edition.
- A separate cord lights decorative Christmas lights.
- Set of 4 includes building and "Last String Of Lights" accessory, City Lit Bare Branch Tree with adapter, and snow.
- Lamp and rooftop tree separate in the box.

Chez Monet 58938

Dates	OSRP	GBTru	Paid
2002^M - 2003	$65	$70	$_____

- Intended to be used as a Valentine's Day design.

Hudson Public Library 58942

Dates	OSRP	GBTru	Paid
2002 - 2004	$80	$80	$_____

Midtown Barbershop 58944

Dates	OSRP	GBTru	Paid
2002 - 2004	$65	$65	$_____

• Sign is separate in the box.

East Harbor Fish Co. 58946

Dates	OSRP	GBTru	Paid
2002 -	$85	-	$_____

• Two signs and two "lamps" are separate in box.
• Special adapter is included to activate building's bulb and decorative Christmas lights.
• Do not handle by posts.

DeFazio's Pizzeria 58949

Dates	OSRP	GBTru	Paid
2002 - 2004	$65	$65	$_____

• Set of 2 includes the Pizzeria and "Pizza Pick-Up" accessory.

Seasons Department Store 59201

Dates	OSRP	GBTru	Paid
2002 - 2004	$70	$70	$_____

Harley-Davidson® City Dealership 59202

Dates	OSRP	GBTru	Paid
2002 -	$85	-	$_____

• Sign is separate in box.
• Licensed by Harley-Davidson®.

Christmas In The City

Ebbets Field — 59203

Dates	OSRP	GBTru	Paid
2002 - 2004	$75	$75	$____

- Legendary Ballparks Series.
- Replica of façade of Ebbets Field that stood in Brooklyn.
- Flag separate in box.
- Licensed by Major League Baseball Properties, Inc.

Central Synagogue — 59204

Dates	OSRP	GBTru	Paid
2002 - 2003	$110	$125	$____

- Limited to year of production.
- Historical Landmark Series.
- This is a replica of Central Synagogue in New York City.

1234 Four Seasons Parkway — 59205

Dates	OSRP	GBTru	Paid
2003ᴹ - 2004	$75	$75	$____

- Seasonal decorations and flowering trees are separate in box.
- First use of removable snow to winterize buildings.

Church Of The Holy Light — 59206

Dates	OSRP	GBTru	Paid
2003ᴹ - 2003	$75	$80	$____

- Holiday 2003 Special Edition.
- Set of 6 includes the Church, "Christmas Eve Visit" accessory, birch tree, frosted pine tree, and snow.
- Adapter included to light star atop nativity scene.

Katie McCabe's Restaurant & Books — 59208

Dates	OSRP	GBTru	Paid
2003ᴹ - 2004	$70	$70	$____

- Fire escape (4 pieces) and sign are separate in box.

Empire State Building 59207

Dates	OSRP	GBTru	Paid
2003ᴹ -	$185	-	$_____

- Historical Landmark Series.
- This is a replica of the Empire State Building in Manhattan.
- At 23 inches, this is the tallest building manufactured by Department 56.
- Features several holiday lighting effects, including different colors in detachable top section.
- Four American flags are separate in box.

Historic Chicago Water Tower 59209

Dates	OSRP	GBTru	Paid
2003 -	$65	-	$_____

- Historical Landmark Series.
- Set of 2 includes Tower and sign.
- This is a replica of the Chicago Water Tower, one of the few buildings to survive the great Chicago fire of 1871.

Blue Line Bus Depot 59210

Dates	OSRP	GBTru	Paid
2003 -	$75	-	$_____

Harrison House 59211

Dates	OSRP	GBTru	Paid
2003 -	$70	-	$_____

- Portions of the proceeds benefit ovarian cancer research.

5th Avenue Shoppes 59212

Dates	OSRP	GBTru	Paid
2003 -	$95	-	$_____

- Includes delicatessen, art gallery, wine cellar, and flower shop.
- Archway is separate in box.

Christmas In The City

East Harbor Ferry — 59213

Dates	OSRP	GBTru	Paid
2003 - 2004	$85	$85	$_____

- Numbered limited edtion of 10,000.
- Set of 3 includes Ferry and "Ferry Ticket Sales" 2 piece accessory.
- Can be personalized.
- American flag comes inserted in stern, and Canadian flags, separate in box, can be overlaid on it. Red flag for bow is separate in box.
- Lifeboats and supports are extremely fragile. Do not hold vessel by them when removing it from box or locating it in a display.

Harley-Davidson® Detailing, Parts & Service — 59214

Dates	OSRP	GBTru	Paid
2003 -	$85	-	$_____

- Lantern is separate in box.
- Licensed by Harley-Davidson®.

Old Comiskey Park — 59215

Dates	OSRP	GBTru	Paid
2003 -	$80	-	$_____

- Legendary Ballparks Series.
- Replica of the façade of Comiskey Park that once stood in Chicago.
- Licensed by Major League Baseball Properties, Inc.

Kelly's Irish Crafts — 59216

Dates	OSRP	GBTru	Paid
2003 -	$65	-	$_____

- Set of 2 includes building and "Tin Whistles - 25 Cents" accessory.
- Sign, Irish flag, lantern, and 2 baskets with hooks are all separate in box.

Christmas In The City

Crystal Gardens Conservatory 59219

Dates	OSRP	GBTru	Paid
2004ᴹ - 2004	$75	$75	$_____

- Limited to year of production.
- Set of 4 includes the building, "Christmas Topiaries" accessory, tree, and snow.

Royal Oil Company 59220

Dates	OSRP	GBTru	Paid
2004ᴹ -	$75	-	$_____

- Set of 2 includes the building and "Full Service Attendant" accessory.

Coca-Cola® Soda Fountain 59221

Dates	OSRP	GBTru	Paid
2004ᴹ -	$85	-	$_____

- Licensed by Coca-Cola®.

Art Institute Of Chicago 59222

Dates	OSRP	GBTru	Paid
2004ᴹ -	$85	-	$_____

- Lighted facade with historical facts on back.
- Licensed by Art Institute Of Chicago.

Souvenir Shops — See below

Dates	OSRP	GBTru	Paid
2004^M -	$45		See below

- The 4 Souvenir Shops are identical, other than the team names and colors.
- Legendary Ballparks Series.
- Licensed by Major League Baseball Properties, Inc.

Item #	Team	GBTru	Paid
59224	New York Yankees	-	$_____
59227	Chicago Cubs	-	$_____
59229	Boston Red Sox	-	$_____
59231	Chicago White Sox	-	$_____

Taverns — See below

Dates	OSRP	GBTru	Paid
2004^M -	$45		See below

- The 4 Taverns are identical, other than the team names and colors.
- Legendary Ballparks Series.
- Licensed by Major League Baseball Properties, Inc.

Item #	Team	GBTru	Paid
59225	New York Yankees	-	$_____
59228	Chicago Cubs	-	$_____
59230	Boston Red Sox	-	$_____
59232	Chicago White Sox	-	$_____

Christmas In The City

The Ed Sullivan Theater — 59233

Dates	OSRP	GBTru	Paid
2004 -	$70	-	$_____

- Licensed to year of production.
- Named for the theater on Broadway in New York City.
- Licensed by CBS, Inc.

Hensly Cadillac & Buick — 59235

Dates	OSRP	GBTru	Paid
2004 -	$80	-	$_____

- Licensed by General Motors.

Lowry Hill Apartments — 59236

Dates	OSRP	GBTru	Paid
2004 -	$75	-	$_____

Pier 56, East Harbor — 59237

Dates	OSRP	GBTru	Paid
2004 -	$85	-	$_____

- Includes adapter.

Milano Of Italy — 59238

Dates	OSRP	GBTru	Paid
2004 -	$65	-	$_____

Gardens Of Santorini — 59239

Dates	OSRP	GBTru	Paid
2004 -	$65	-	$_____

Christmas Treasures — 59240

Dates	OSRP	GBTru	Paid
2004 -	$75	-	$_____

- Decorating set of 4 includes building, tree, and 2 bushes.
- Long Life Cordless Lighting.

Golden Gate Bridge — 59241

Dates	OSRP	GBTru	Paid
2004 -	$120	-	$_____

- Historical Landmark Series.
- Replica of the famous bridge in California.

Use the space(s) below to update your guide when the midyear introductions are announced.

	_____ _____			
	Dates	OSRP	GBTru	Paid
	____ - ____	$____	-	$____

	_____ _____			
	Dates	OSRP	GBTru	Paid
	____ - ____	$____	-	$____

	_____ _____			
	Dates	OSRP	GBTru	Paid
	____ - ____	$____	-	$____

	_____ _____			
	Dates	OSRP	GBTru	Paid
	____ - ____	$____	-	$____

	_____ _____			
	Dates	OSRP	GBTru	Paid
	____ - ____	$____	-	$____

Christmas In The City

Lighted Tree W/Children & Ladder

65102 - Set of 3
1986 - 1989
OSRP: $35
GBTru: $140
Paid: $_____

• Sleeves from the early shipments read "Christmas In the City" even though the village didn't make its debut for another year.
• Battery operated.
• Many have been sold on the secondary market as defective, but it's usually just a matter of crossed wires. Once they are switched, the unit works nicely.
• The boy on the ladder is often damaged from falling off.

Christmas In The City Sign

59609
1987 - 1993
OSRP: $6
GBTru: $10
Paid: $_____

Automobiles

59641 - Set of 3
1987 - 1996
OSRP: $15
GBTru: $20
Paid: $_____

City People

59650 - Set of 5
1987 - 1990
OSRP: $27.50
GBTru: $40
Paid: $_____

City Newsstand

59714 - Set of 4
1988 - 1991
OSRP: $25
GBTru: $60
Paid: $_____

City Bus & Milk Truck

59838 - Set of 2
1988 - 1991
OSRP: $15
GBTru: $45
Paid: $_____

• Wording on sleeve reads "Transport."

Salvation Army Band

59854 - Set of 6
1988 - 1991
OSRP: $24
GBTru: $65
Paid: $_____

• Conductor's baton is easily damaged.

Boulevard

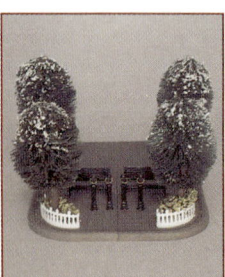

55166 - Set of 14

1989 - 1992

OSRP: $25

GBTru: $40

Paid: $_____

• Includes 4 sections (2 straight/ 2 curved), 4 trees, 4 hitching posts, and 2 benches.

Mailbox & Fire Hydrant

55174 - Set of 2

1989 - 1990

OSRP: $5

GBTru: $20

Paid: $_____

• Retired after one year due to unauthorized use of red and blue colors of U.S. Postal Service.

Organ Grinder

59579 - Set of 3

1989 - 1991

OSRP: $21

GBTru: $30

Paid: $_____

Popcorn Vendor

59587 - Set of 3

1989 - 1992

OSRP: $22

GBTru: $33

Paid: $_____

River Street Ice House Cart

59595

1989 - 1991

OSRP: $20

GBTru: $40

Paid: $_____

Central Park Carriage

59790

1989 -

OSRP: $30

GBTru: -

Paid: $_____

• Designated as Christmas In The Park Series in 2002.

Mailbox & Fire Hydrant

52140 - Set of 2

1990 - 1998

OSRP: $5

GBTru: $10

Paid: $_____

• Re-issue of Mailbox & Fire Hydrant (1989) after changing to red and green and putting "H.V. Mail" on front.

Busy Sidewalks

55352 - Set of

1990 - 1992

OSRP: $28

GBTru: $42

Paid: $_____

'Tis The Season

55395
1990 - 1994
OSRP: $12.50
GBTru: $12
Paid: $_____

• Separate metal kettle can easily be lost.

Rest Ye Merry Gentleman

55409
1990 - 2002
OSRP: $12.50
GBTru: $12
Paid: $_____

• Bench is metal.

Utility Accessories

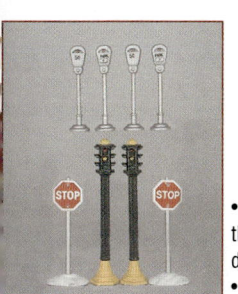

55123 - Set of 8
1991 - 1998
OSRP: $12.50
GBTru: $12
Paid: $_____

• It is not unusual for the stop signs to be discolored.
• Metal.

City Subway Entrance

55417
1991 - 1998
OSRP: $15
GBTru: $20
Paid: $_____

• Metal.

All Around The Town

55450 - Set of 2
1991 - 1993
OSRP: $18
GBTru: $24
Paid: $_____

The Fire Brigade

55468 - Set of 2
1991 - 1995
OSRP: $20
GBTru: $25
Paid: $_____

• Includes plastic fire ladder separate in box.

"City Fire Dept." Fire Truck

55476
1991 - 1995
OSRP: $18
GBTru: $28
Paid: $_____

• Includes plastic fire ladder separate in box.

Caroling Thru The City

55484 - Set of 3
1991 - 1998
OSRP: $27.50
GBTru: $30
Paid: $_____

Christmas In The City Acc.

Don't Drop The Presents!

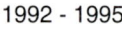

55328 - Set of 2
1992 - 1995
OSRP: $25
GBTru: $28
Paid: $_____

Welcome Home

55336 - Set of 3
1992 - 1995
OSRP: $27.50
GBTru: $25
Paid: $_____

Village Express Van

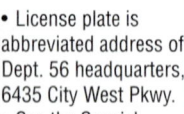

58653
1992 - 1996
OSRP: $25
GBTru: $26
Paid: $_____
• License plate is abbreviated address of Dept. 56 headquarters, 6435 City West Pkwy.
• See the Special Design section.

Playing In The Snow

55565 - Set of 3
1993 - 1996
OSRP: $25
GBTru: $26
Paid: $_____
• The branches are easily broken.

Street Musicians

55646 - Set of 3
1993 - 1997
OSRP: $25
GBTru: $28
Paid: $_____
• The violinist's bow is fragile.

Town Tree Trimmers

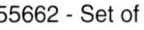

55662 - Set of 4
1993 - 2001
OSRP: $32.50
GBTru: $36
Paid: $_____

Christmas At The Park

58661 - Set of 3
1993 -
OSRP: $27.50
GBTru: -
Paid: $_____
• Intended for use with the Town Tree.

Chamber Orchestra

58840 - Set of 4
1994 - 1998
OSRP: $37.50
GBTru: $36
Paid: $_____
• The conductor's baton and the musicians' bows and flute are fragile.

Holiday Field Trip

58858 - Set of 3
1994 - 1998
OSRP: $27.50
GBTru: $30
Paid: $_____

Hot Dog Vendor

58866 - Set of 3
1994 - 1997
OSRP: $27.50
GBTru: $28
Paid: $_____

• Porcelain and metal.

"Yes, Virginia..."

58890 - Set of 2
1995 - 2000
OSRP: $12.50
GBTru: $14
Paid: $_____

One-Man Band & The Dancing Dog

58891 - Set of 2
1995 - 1998
OSRP: $17.50
GBTru: $22
Paid: $_____

Choirboys All-In-A-Row

58892
1995 - 1998
OSRP: $20
GBTru: $20
Paid: $_____

A Key To The City CIC Sign

58893
1995 - 2001ᴹ
OSRP: $20
GBTru: $20
Paid: $_____

• Porcelain and metal.

City Taxi

58894
1996 - 2001
OSRP: $12.50
GBTru: $20
Paid: $_____

• Similar designs were produced for several retailers. See the Special Design section.

The Family Tree

58895
1996 - 2003
OSRP: $18
GBTru: $22
Paid: $_____

Going Home For The Holidays

58896 - Set of 3
1996 - 1999
OSRP: $27.50
GBTru: $33
Paid: $_____

Steppin' Out On The Town

58885 - Set of 5
1997M - 1999
OSRP: $35
GBTru: $40
Paid: $_____

• The gentleman's walking stick is fragile.

Johnson's Grocery Holiday Deliveries

58897
1997 - 2001
OSRP: $18
GBTru: $24
Paid: $_____

• Similar designs were produced for retailers. See the Special Design section.

Spirit Of The Season

58898
1997 - 1999
OSRP: $20
GBTru: $22
Paid: $_____

Let's Go Shopping In The City

58899 - Set of 3
1997 - 1999
OSRP: $35
GBTru: $40
Paid: $_____

Big Smile For The Camera

58900 - Set of 2
1997 - 1999
OSRP: $27.50
GBTru: $30
Paid: $_____

5¢ Pony Rides

58871 - Set of 3
1998M - 1998
OSRP: *
GBTru: *

* Accessory contained in the Scottie's Toy Shop Gift Set.

Heritage Village Utility Accessories

52776 - Set of 1
1998 - 2001
OSRP: $15
GBTru: $18
Paid: $_____

• The sticker on the right side of the mailbox reads "S.V. Mail."

A Carriage Ride For The Bride

58901

1998 - 2004

OSRP: $40

GBTru: $40

Paid: $_____

• The front wheels can separate from the rest of the carriage and cause damage.

To Protect And To Serve

58902 - Set of 3

1998 -

OSRP: $32.50

GBTru: -

Paid: $_____

City Police Car

58903

1998 - 2001ᴹ

OSRP: $16.50

GBTru: $20

Paid: $_____

• Features a battery-operated beacon.

1919 Ford Model-T

58906

1998 - 2000

OSRP: $20

GBTru: $25

Paid: $_____

• Licensed by Ford Motor Co.

Ready For The Road

58907

1998 - 2000

OSRP: $20

GBTru: $24

Paid: $_____

• Licensed by Harley-Davidson.

The New Year's Kiss

55510

1999ᴹ - 1999

OSRP: *

GBTru: *

* Accessory contained in The Times Tower Gift Set.

Bringing Home The Baby

58909 - Set of 2

1999ᴹ - 2000

OSRP: $27.50

GBTru: $33

Paid: $_____

The City Ambulance

58910

1999ᴹ - 2000

OSRP: $15

GBTru: $24

Paid: $_____

Busy City Sidewalks

58955 - Set of 4
1999 -
OSRP: $32.50
GBTru: -
Paid: $_____

Visiting The Nativity

58956 - Set of 3
1999 -
OSRP: $37.50
GBTru: -
Paid: $_____

• Dream House Sweep-stakes Deluxe Prize winner assisted in the design. Also see Nativity Creche in GVA.

Fresh Flowers For Sale

58957 - Set of 2
1999 - 2001
OSRP: $30
GBTru: $35
Paid: $_____

• Dream House Sweep-stakes Deluxe Prize winner assisted in the design.

Excellent Taste

58958 - Set of 2
1999 - 2002
OSRP: $22
GBTru: $25
Paid: $_____

Picking Out The Christmas Tree

58959 - Set of 3
1999 -
OSRP: $37.50
GBTru: -
Paid: $_____

All In Together Girls

58960
1999 - 2001^M
OSRP: $23.50
GBTru: $25
Paid: $_____

Rockefeller Plaza Skating Rink

52504
2000^M - 2003
OSRP: $125
GBTru: $95
Paid: $_____

Hailing A Cab

58961 - Set of 2
2000^M - 2002
OSRP: $27.50
GBTru: $30
Paid: $_____

City Professions - Doctor & Nurse

58962 - Set of 2
2000^M - 2002
OSRP: $17.50
GBTru: $20
Paid: $_____

A Treasured Book

58963 - Set of 3
2000^M - 2003
OSRP: $35
GBTru: $35
Paid: $_____

1935 Duesenberg®

58964
2000^M - 2001
OSRP: $20
GBTru: $25
Paid: $_____

City Professions - Postman & Dairy Delivery Man

58965 - Set of 2
2000^M - 2001^M
OSRP: $17.50
GBTru: $20
Paid: $_____

City Professions - House Painter & Newspaper Boy

58966 - Set of 2
2000^M - 2001^M
OSRP: $17.50
GBTru: $22
Paid: $_____

On To The Show

58967
2000 - 2003
OSRP: $20
GBTru: $24
Paid: $_____

Fire Drill Practice

58968
2000 - 2004
OSRP: $25
GBTru: $25
Paid: $_____

1937 Pirsch Pumper Fire Truck

58969
2000 - 2003
OSRP: $25
GBTru: $28
Paid: $_____

The Life Of The Party

58970 - Set of 2
2000 - 2002
OSRP: $30
GBTru: $30
Paid: $_____

• Mask in woman's hand and man's cane are easily broken.

Hot Chocolate For Sale

58971
2000 - 2003
OSRP: $27.50
GBTru: $30
Paid: $_____

Russell Stover® Delivery Truck

58972
2000 - 2003
OSRP: $20
GBTru: $24
Paid: $_____

• Licensed by Russell Stover Candies, Inc.

Pretzel Cart

58973
2001ᴹ -
OSRP: $22
GBTru: -
Paid: $_____

Midtown News Stand

58974 - Set of 2
2001ᴹ -
OSRP: $32.50
GBTru: -
Paid: $_____

Planning A Winter Vacation

58975
2001ᴹ - 2002
OSRP: $12.50
GBTru: $16
Paid: $_____

Full Count

58977 - Set of 2
2001ᴹ -
OSRP: $25
GBTru: -
Paid: $_____

• Legendary Ballparks Series.
• Licensed by Major League Baseball Prop.

Look At All The Toys

58929
2001 - 2003
OSRP: *
GBTru: *

* The accessory contained in Nicholas & Co. Toys Starter Se[t]

City Zoological Garden

58978 - Set of 7
2001 - 2003
OSRP: $95
GBTru: $110
Paid: $_____

• Christmas In The Park Series.

Santa In The City

58979
2001 -
OSRP: $25
GBTru: -
Paid: $_____

• Christmas In The Park Series.
• Reindeer's antlers are very fragile.

City Shopping

58980
2001 - 2003
OSRP: $13
GBTru: $15
Paid: $_____

Architectural Treasure

58981
2001 - 2002
OSRP: $12.50
GBTru: $18
Paid: $_____

Hot Roasted Chestnuts

58983 - Set of 2
2001 -
OSRP: $18
GBTru: -
Paid: $_____

Raising The Flag In The City

58986
2001 - 2004
OSRP: $15
GBTru: $15
Paid: $_____

Last String Of Lights

58937
2002ᴹ - 2002
OSRP: *
GBTru: *

* The accessory contained in the Parkside Holiday Brownstone.

For Your Sweetheart

58987
2002ᴹ - 2004
OSRP: $22.50
GBTru: $24
Paid: $_____

Christmas In The City Acc.

Serving Irish Ale

58988
2002ᴹ -
OSRP: $20
GBTru: -
Paid: $_____

Peanuts, Pennants & Programs

58989
2002ᴹ -
OSRP: $15
GBTru: -
Paid: $_____

• Legendary Ballparks Series.

Choosing Rights

58990
2002ᴹ - 2003
OSRP: $15
GBTru: $20
Paid: $_____

• Legendary Ballparks Series.

The Radio City Rockettes

58991
2002ᴹ -
OSRP: $12.50
GBTru: -
Paid: $_____

• Originally designed with tall white hats.
• Licensed by Radio City Trademarks L.L.C.

Pizza Pick-Up

58949
2002 -
OSRP: *
GBTru: *

* The accessory contained in DeFazio's Pizzeria.

City Park Gateway

58992 - Set of 2
2002 - 2004
OSRP: $42.50
GBTru: $43
Paid: $_____

• Christmas In The Park Series.
• Working clock.

Asleep At The Bus Stop

58993
2002 -
OSRP: $12.50
GBTru: -
Paid: $_____

Presents For The Family

58994
2002 - 2004
OSRP: $12.50
GBTru: $13
Paid: $_____

Family Out For A Walk

58995 - Set of 2
2002 - 2004
OSRP: $20
GBTru: $20
Paid: $_____

Fresh Fish Today

58996 - Set of 2
2002 -
OSRP: $27.50
GBTru: -
Paid: $_____

America's Finest

58998
2002 -
OSRP: $20
GBTru: -
Paid: $_____

• Licensed by Harley-Davidson.

For The Love Of Books

58999
2002 - 2004
OSRP: $18
GBTru: $18
Paid: $_____

Keep America Beautiful

59400
2002 - 2004
OSRP: $13
GBTru: $13
Paid: $_____

Pumpkins In The Park

59402
2002 - 2004
OSRP: $40
GBTru: $40
Paid: $_____

Teaching The Torah

59403
2002 - 2003
OSRP: $15
GBTru: $18
Paid: $_____

Can I Have Your Autograph?

59405
2002 -
OSRP: $16.50
GBTru: -
Paid: $_____

• Legendary Ballparks Series.

Ebbets Field Scoreboard  59406 2002 - 2004 OSRP: $20 GBTru: $20 Paid: $_____ • Legendary Ballparks Series.	**How Tall Is It?**  59407 2003ᴹ - 2004 OSRP: $15 GBTru: $15 Paid: $_____
1930 Harley-Davidson® VL W/Sidecar  59409 2003ᴹ - OSRP: $22.50 GBTru: - Paid: $_____ • Licensed by Harley-Davidson.	**Milwaukee Or Bust** 59410 2003ᴹ - OSRP: $45 GBTru: - Paid: $_____ • Licensed by Harley-Davidson.
Christmas Eve Visit  59206 2003ᴹ - 2003 OSRP: * GBTru: * • Adapter included * The accessory contained in Church Of The Holy Light.	**Ferry Ticket Sales** 59213 2003 - OSRP: * GBTru: * * The accessory contained in East Harbor Ferry.
Tin Whistles - 25 Cents  59216 2003 - OSRP: * GBTru: * * The accessory contained in Kelly's Irish Crafts.	**Blue Line Bus**  59411 2003 - OSRP: $20 GBTru: - Paid: $_____ • Vintage Car Series.

Off To College!

59413
2003 -
OSRP: $17.50
GBTru: -
Paid: $_____

Harley-Davidson® Motorcycle Truck

59414
2003 -
OSRP: $20
GBTru: -
Paid: $_____

• Licensed by Harley-Davidson.

Hot Pretzels

59415
2003 -
OSRP: $25
GBTru: -
Paid: $_____

• Christmas In The Park Series.
• Includes adapter.

1940 V16 Cadillac® Coupe

59416
2003 -
OSRP: $20
GBTru: -
Paid: $_____

• Vintage Car Series.
• Licensed by General Motors.

Taxi

59417
2003 -
OSRP: $20
GBTru: -
Paid: $_____

• Vintage Car Series.

Pier 87 Bait & Tackle

59419 - Set of 2
2003 -
OSRP: $30
GBTru: -
Paid: $_____

• A simlar piece, "San Francisco Bait Shop" was sold at the D56 store in San Francisco.

Traffic Policeman

59421
2003 -
OSRP: $15
GBTru: -
Paid: $_____

Sidewalk Games

59422 - Set of 3
2003 -
OSRP: $20
GBTru: -
Paid: $_____

City Sledding

59423
2003 -
OSRP: $45
GBTru: -
Paid: $_____

• Includes adapter.

Warming Up

59425 - Set of 2
2003 -
OSRP: $16.50
GBTru: -
Paid: $_____

Christmas Topiaries

59219
2004ᴹ - 2004
OSRP: *
GBTru: *

* The accessory contained in Crystal Gardens Conservatory.

Full Service Attendant

59220
2004ᴹ -
OSRP: *
GBTru: *

* The accessory contained in Royal Oil Company.

Vintage Coca-Cola® Truck

59428
2004ᴹ -
OSRP: $20
GBTru: -
Paid: $_____

• Vintage Car Series.
• Licensed by Coca-Cola.

1939 Buick® Roadster

59429
2004ᴹ -
OSRP: $20
GBTru: -
Paid: $_____

• Vintage Car Series.
• Licensed by General Motors.

A Coke® For You And Me!

59430
2004ᴹ -
OSRP: $15
GBTru: -
Paid: $_____

• Licensed by Coca-Cola.

Ballpark Bleachers

59436
2004ᴹ -
OSRP: $45
GBTru: -
Paid: $_____

• Plays "Take Me Out To The Ballgame."

Refreshments Stands

	Dates	OSRP	GBTru	Paid
	2004ᴹ -	$17.50	See below	

Item #	Team	GBTru	Paid
59437	New York Yankees	-	$_____
59440	Chicago Cubs	-	$_____
59441	Chicago White Sox	-	$_____
59442	Boston Red Sox	-	$_____

- The 4 Stands are identical, other than the team names and colors.
- Legendary Ballpark Series.
- Licensed by Major League Baseball Properties, Inc.

A Day At The Ballpark

59443 - Set of 2
2004ᴹ -
OSRP: $18
GBTru: -
Paid: $_____

Baseball Diamond

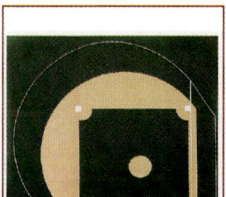

59444
2004ᴹ -
OSRP: $10
GBTru: -
Paid: $_____

A Shiny New Christmas Present

59445
2004 -
OSRP: $17.50
GBTru: -
Paid: $_____

- Licensed by General Motors.

Erin Go Bragh

59446
2004 -
OSRP: $15
GBTru: -
Paid: $_____

Luigi's Gelato Treats

59448
2004 -
OSRP: $20
GBTru: -
Paid: $_____

A Night On The Town

59452
2004 -
OSRP: $15
GBTru: -
Paid: $_____

- Limited to year of production.

Christmas In The City Acc.

Unloading Ice Blocks At The Dock

59453
2004 -
OSRP: $17.50
GBTru: -
Paid: $_____

Delivery Truck

59454
2004 -
OSRP: $20
GBTru: -
Paid: $_____

• Vintage Car Series.

Kid Gloves Moving

59456
2004 -
OSRP: $17.50
GBTru: -
Paid: $_____

Dressed For Success

59457
2004 -
OSRP: $10
GBTru: -
Paid: $_____

Today's Specials

59458
2004 -
OSRP: $12.50
GBTru: -
Paid: $_____

Use the following space(s) to update your guide when the midyear introductions are announced.

_____
_____
____ - ____
OSRP: $_____
GBTru: -
Paid: $_____

_____
_____
____ - ____
OSRP: $_____
GBTru: -
Paid: $_____

The Holy Land™ Collection

Formerly a separate collection, Little Town of Bethlehem is now one of the series within the Holy Land Collection. This umbrella collection also includes the Easter series and the Parables From The Holy Land. Furthermore, Department 56 has indicated that this collection will expand to include ancient Egypt, the Roman Empire, and caravan routes to the Far East.

Department 56 originally created its version of the Nativity story in 1987. A self-contained set of 12, including three buildings and the primary characters, was released in porcelain and remained unchanged for a dozen years. In keeping with the tale and life of the time, the buildings were simple stone and brick structures.

In 1999 the set was retired, but within weeks new releases were announced. Collectors could purchase individual buildings and accessories that would complement the original set, or begin their Nativity scene using just the new pieces. The new accessories were crafted in resin, rather than porcelain, enabling the designs to be more detailed.

The new pieces have not only augmented the original series with historical pieces such as Herod's Temple but have also added brilliantly crafted buildings like the Rug Merchant's Colonnade and accessories featuring people and animals in a desert camp and oasis, as well in routine daily activities.

The establishment of different series within the Holy Land will enable collectors to create a vast geographical display, develop seasonal approaches, or form vignettes using only a single series from the entire collection.

Little Town Of Bethlehem Series

Little Town Of Bethlehem   59757

Dates	OSRP	GBTru	Paid
1987 - 1999	$150	$220	$____

- The early pieces have a small amount of snow on the manger's right wall. The later ones do not.
- Set of 12 includes manger with Jesus, inn, marketplace, Joseph, Mary, 3 wise men, shepherd with sheep, camel, cow and sheep, a donkey, and cypress trees.
- For the first 4 years of production, a sheep stood next to the cow. From 1991 through 1999, the sheep was not included.

Innkeeper's Caravansary   59795

Dates	OSRP	GBTru	Paid
1999 - 2003	$70	$75	$____

Gatekeeper's Dwelling   59797

Dates	OSRP	GBTru	Paid
1999 - 2001	$55	$60	$____

The Holy Land

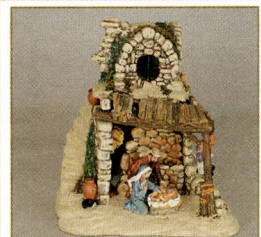

Nativity 59796

Dates	OSRP	GBTru	Paid
1999 -	**$55**	-	$_____

- Set of 2 includes the building and Joseph, Mary, and Jesus accessory.
- This set is also included as part of the Gift Set, Holy Night Nativity, in 2002.

Herod's Temple 59799

Dates	OSRP	GBTru	Paid
2000 - 2001	**$150**	**$155**	$_____

- 25th Anniversary Limited Edition of 5,600.
- Set of 5 includes Temple, 2 piece accessory "High Priests," gate, and vinyl ancient stone courtyard.

Carpenter's Shop 59801

Dates	OSRP	GBTru	Paid
2000 - 2002	**$72**	**$75**	$_____

- Set of 3 includes Shop and 2 piece accessory "Carpenter & Son."

The Holy Land

Rug Merchant's Colonnade 59802

Dates	OSRP	GBTru	Paid
2000 -	$110	-	$____

• Set of 4 includes Colonnade, 2 piece accessory "Rug Merchant & Wool Spinner," and ladder.

Caravansary Corner 59806

Dates	OSRP	GBTru	Paid
2001 - 2003	$75	$80	$____

• Set of 2 includes building and man.

Caravansary Rooms at the Inn 59807

Dates	OSRP	GBTru	Paid
2001 - 2003	$110	$115	$____

• Set of 3 includes building and two figurines.

Holy Night Nativity   05837

Dates	OSRP	GBTru	Paid
2002ᴹ - 2002	$85	$95	$_____

- Department store exclusive.
- Limited to year of production.
- Set of 6 is the combination of Nativity, "Wise Men From The East" accessory, and "Palm Trees."

Potter's Shop   59812

Dates	OSRP	GBTru	Paid
2002 -	$65	-	$_____

- Set of 2 includes building and "Pottery Craftsman" accessory.

The Birth Of Christ Nativity Set   59816

Dates	OSRP	GBTru	Paid
2003 -	$75	-	$_____

- Set of 11 includes the manger, the Holy Family, the wise men, and animals.

Use the spaces on the next page to update your guide when the midyear introductions are announced.

	_____	_____
	Dates OSRP GBTru Paid	
	____ - ____ $_____ - $_____	

	_____	_____
	Dates OSRP GBTru Paid	
	____ - ____ $_____ - $_____	

	_____	_____
	Dates OSRP GBTru Paid	
	____ - ____ $_____ - $_____	

	_____	_____
	Dates OSRP GBTru Paid	
	____ - ____ $_____ - $_____	

	_____	_____
	Dates OSRP GBTru Paid	
	____ - ____ $_____ - $_____	

The Holy Land

The Easter Story Series

House Of The Last Supper Gift Set   59809

Dates	OSRP	GBTru	Paid
2001 - 2004	$65	$65	$____

- First available during the 2002 Spring Discover Dept. 56 event.
- Set of 2 includes building and "Palm Sunday" accessory.

Tower Of David   59810

Dates	OSRP	GBTru	Paid
2002ᴹ - 2004	$75	$75	$____

- Set of 3 includes Tower and 2 piece accessory, "Tower Guard & Garden Archway" and scroll.

Church Of The Holy Sepulcher   59814

Dates	OSRP	GBTru	Paid
2003ᴹ - 2004	$85	$85	$____

- Two crosses separate in box.

Notes:

Heralding Angels

59759 - Set of 3
1999 -
OSRP: $20
GBTru: -
Paid: $_____

Good Shepherd & His Animals

59791 - Set of 6
1999 -
OSRP: $25
GBTru: -
Paid: $_____

Wise Men From The East

59792 - Set of 2
1999 -
OSRP: $25
GBTru: -
Paid: $_____

• Also included as part of Holy Night Nativity Gift Set.

Town Well & Palm Trees

59793 - Set of 3
1999 -
OSRP: $46
GBTru: -
Paid: $_____

Town Gate

59794 - Set of 2
1999 - 2001
OSRP: $25
GBTru: $26
Paid: $_____

Palm Trees

52820 - Set of 2
1999 -
OSRP: $45
GBTru: -
Paid: $_____

• Also included as part of Holy Night Nativity Gift Set.

Desert Oasis

59901 - Set of 5
2000 - 2003
OSRP: $60
GBTru: $65
Paid: $_____

High Priests

59799 - Set of 2
2000 - 2001
OSRP: *
GBTru: *

* Accessory contained in Herod's Temple.

Carpenter & Son

59801 - Set of 2
2000 - 2002
OSRP: *
GBTru: *

* Accessory contained in Carpenter's Shop.

Rug Merchant & Wool Spinner

59802 - Set of 2
2000 -
OSRP: *
GBTru: *

* Accessory contained in Rug Merchant's Colonnade.

Merchant Cart

59902 - Set of 2
2000 - 2003
OSRP: $30
GBTru: $34
Paid: $_____

Stonemason At Work

59903 - Set of 3
2000 - 2003
OSRP: $45
GBTru: $40
Paid: $_____

Desert Camp

59904 - Set of 4
2000 - 2003
OSRP: $52
GBTru: $60
Paid: $_____

Oil Lamps

59905 - Set of 2
2000 - 2002
OSRP: $25
GBTru: $30
Paid: $_____

• Battery operated.

Star Of Wonder

59906
2000 - 2003
OSRP: $20
GBTru: $28
Paid: $_____

• Battery/adapter operated.

Cypress Trees

59907 - Set of 3
2000 -
OSRP: $20
GBTru: -
Paid: $_____

• Originally released as "Cyprus" trees.

Town Wall Sections

59908 - Set of 2
2000 -
OSRP: $16.50
GBTru: -
Paid: $_____

• Coordinates with Town Gate.

Desert Road

59909 - Set of 4
2000 -
OSRP: $22.50
GBTru: -
Paid: $_____

Desert Rocks

59910 - Set of 5
2000 - 2003
OSRP: $25
GBTru: $24
Paid: $_____

Limestone Outcropping

59911
2000 - 2003
OSRP: $40
GBTru: $45
Paid: $_____

Olive Harvest

59912 - Set of 3
2000 - 2003
OSRP: $40
GBTru: $45
Paid: $_____

The Holy Land Backdrop

52965
2001 - 2003
OSRP: $45
GBTru: $45
Paid: $_____

Palm Sunday

59809
2001 -
OSRP: *
GBTru: *

* The accessory contained in House Of The Last Supper.

Spice & Copper Vendors' Colonnade

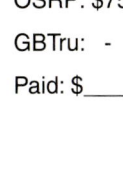

59913 - Set of 3
2001 -
OSRP: $75
GBTru: -
Paid: $_____

The Holy Land Accessories

Desert Caravan

59914 - Set of 5
2001 -
OSRP: $48
GBTru: -
Paid: $_____

Caravansary Drinking Well

59915
2001 - 2003
OSRP: $27.50
GBTru: $30
Paid: $_____

Caravansary Gate & Guard

59916 - Set of 2
2001 - 2003
OSRP: $42
GBTru: $45
Paid: $_____

Caravansary Wall

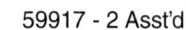

59917 - 2 Asst'd
2001 - 2003
OSRP: $30
GBTru: $33
Paid: $_____

Waterfall In The Wilderness

59918 - Set of 2
2001 - 2003
OSRP: $85
GBTru: $85
Paid: $_____

- Working fountain.
- Includes accessory "Man Drawing Water."

Tower Guard & Garden Archway

59810
2002ᴹ -
OSRP: *
GBTru: *

* The accessory contained in the Tower Of David.

Sand Road

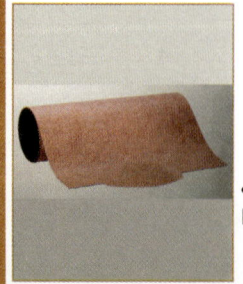

59921 - Set of 2
2002ᴹ -
OSRP: $15
GBTru: -
Paid: $_____

- Includes road and bag of sand.

Pottery Craftsman

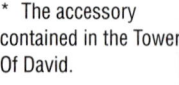

59812
2002 -
OSRP: *
GBTru: *

* The accessory contained in Potter's Shop.

Revolving Nativity Scene

59813
2002 - 2004
OSRP: $130
GBTru: $130
Paid: $_____

• Animated.

Holy Land Animals

59922 - Set of 3
2002 -
OSRP: $35
GBTru: -
Paid: $_____

The Prodigal Son

59923 - Set of 3
2002 - 2004
OSRP: $35
GBTru: $35
Paid: $_____

• Parables Series.

The Good Samaritan

59924 - Set of 3
2002 - 2004
OSRP: $35
GBTru: $35
Paid: $_____

• Parables Series.

The Sower And The Seed

59925 - Set of 2
2002 - 2004
OSRP: $35
GBTru: $35
Paid: $_____

• Parables Series.

Holy Night Fiber Optic Backdrop

59815
2003 -
OSRP: $150
GBTru: -
Paid: $_____

• Includes adapter.
• Both town and sky light up.

Use the following space(s) to update your guide when the midyear introductions are announced.

_____
_____
____ - ____
OSRP: $_____
GBTru: -
Paid: $_____

National Council of 56 Clubs

NCC
22 Samoset Road
Orleans, MA 02653
(540) 659-6804
www.ncc56.com

NCC pins

Why Join an NCC Club?

- Make friends with nice people who understand your addiction.
- Learn the latest news about D56 products and your villages.
- Obtain the NCC exclusive pieces, when available, such as "Jack's Umbrella Shop" (set of 2) and the "Under the NCC Umbrella" accessories.
- Discuss the many techniques for making mountains or water.
- Discover the subtle nuances of lighting methods.
- Find out about special deals, closeouts and sales.
- Win door, game and contest prizes.

- Take excursions to yard sales, gatherings, house tours.
- Learn more about your village and display techniques from seasoned collectors.
- Contribute to a good cause (most NCC clubs support local charities.)
- Glean information and ideas from other clubs and collectors in the US and Canada through the NCC Bulletin.
- Have others help you search for missing pieces.
- Meet new collector friends from outside your area in the NCC hospitality rooms at gatherings.

Produced as an NCC exclusive lighted house and 2002 lapel pin

How to Find a Club

- Ask your local dealer
- Visit the National Council of 56 Clubs' Web site at www.ncc56.com
- Inquire at Internet chat sites (AOL, Yahoo, etc.)
- Watch for special feature articles on collectors and check the events column in your local newspaper
- Introduce yourself to fellow shoppers
- Attend village gatherings and collectable shows (The NCC often staffs information tables.)
- Start your own club. (Contact the NCC for the "Handbook for Clubs," better known as the "Start A Club" guide.)

The National Council of 56 Clubs is an independent umbrella organization for Department 56 collector clubs in the United States and Canada. The NCC is operated by volunteers dedicate to the goal of "clubs helping clubs help collectors."

North Pole Series™

From the time we first saw a Christmas tree, we each developed our own vivid images of Santa Claus, elves, flying reindeer, and a secret land called the North Pole. It seems safe to say that none of us—in our wildest imaginations—ever matched the Department 56 version of that fantasy place. When the village was introduced, there were the three buildings that we expected—Santa's Workshop, the Reindeer Barn, and the Elf Bunkhouse. The designs may have been different from the way we visualized them, but those were the buildings we all knew were there.

And then it grew. And grew. And grew. Over 70 buildings later, the North Pole is a very busy place. The famed "pitter patter of little feet" belongs not to children rushing downstairs on Christmas morning but to hundreds of little elves. In fact, the Pole has gotten so crowded that there is even a housing subdivision—Elf Land™ that is intended as a spot for the busy elves to relax.

Seven buildings have monogrammed letters on them that spell out North Pole. There are shops of every kind, places where everything is produced from dolls and cars to lights and ornaments. Even a few commercial vendors have moved in due to licensing agreements that have brought LEGO® blocks, Barbie®, Warner Bros® characters, and the familiar Coca-Cola® polar bears to the frosty north. The famed Post Office is included, as is a Weather and Time Station to be certain that Santa reaches every home in one night. Elves make and test toys, bake, deliver mail and toys, sing, chart the night's course, skate and ski, and even use their tiny fingers to untangle lights and tinsel.

North Pole

Santa's Workshop — 56006

Dates	OSRP	GBTru	Paid
1990 - 1993	$72	$260	$_____

• The original samples had a green roof.

NORTH POLE - Set of 2 — 56014

Dates	OSRP	GBTru	Paid
1990 - 1996/2000	$70	$75	$_____

Reindeer Barn ✓ — 56015

Dates	OSRP	GBTru	Paid
1990 - 2000	$35	$50	$_____

• Variations exist with reindeer names duplicated and others omitted. The duplicated names vary.

Elf Bunkhouse — 56016

Dates	OSRP	GBTru	Paid
1990 - 1996	$35	$40	$_____

• The box and the bottomstamp both read "Elf Bunkhouse" while the sign above the door reads "Elves Bunkhouse."

NeeNee's Dolls And Toys — 56200

Dates	OSRP	GBTru	Paid
1991 - 1995	$36	$40	$_____

• The wreath on the front of the building contains the first letter spelling out "NORTH POLE."
• Early release to Showcase and GCC dealers.

NORTH POLE SHOPS - Set of 2 — 56219

Dates	OSRP	GBTru	Paid
1991 - 1995	$75	$95	$_____

Orly's Bell & Harness Supply — 56219

Dates	OSRP	GBTru	Paid
1991 - 1995	$37.50	$45	$_____

- The wreath on the front of the building contains the second letter spelling out "NORTH POLE."

Rimpy's Bakery — 56219

Dates	OSRP	GBTru	Paid
1991 - 1995	$37.50	$60	$_____

- The wreath on the front of the building contains the third letter spelling out "NORTH POLE."

Tassy's Mittens & Hassel's Woolies — 56227

Dates	OSRP	GBTru	Paid
1991 - 1995	$50	$65	$_____

- The wreaths on the front of the building contain the fourth and fifth letters spelling out "NORTH POLE."

Post Office — 56235

Dates	OSRP	GBTru	Paid
1992 - 1999	$45	$50	$_____

- The wreath on the front of the building contains the sixth letter spelling out "NORTH POLE."
- Early release to Showcase Dealers.

Obbie's Books & Letrinka's Candy — 56243

Dates	OSRP	GBTru	Paid
1992 - 1996	$70	$70	$_____

- The wreaths on the front of the building contain the seventh and eighth letters spelling out "NORTH POLE."
- The flag is fragile.

Elfie's Sleds & Skates — 56251

Dates	OSRP	GBTru	Paid
1992 - 1996	$48	$50	$_____

- The wreath on the front of the building contains the last letter spelling out "NORTH POLE."

North Pole

North Pole Chapel ✓   56260

Dates	OSRP	GBTru	Paid
1993 - 2000	$45	$50	$_____

• Early release to Showcase Dealers and select buying groups.
• There is a bell in the tower.

North Pole Express Depot ✓   56278

Dates	OSRP	GBTru	Paid
1993 - 1998	$48	$50	$_____

• The flags are fragile.

Santa's Woodworks ✓   56286

Dates	OSRP	GBTru	Paid
1993 - 1996	$42	$35	$_____

Santa's Lookout Tower ✓   56294

Dates	OSRP	GBTru	Paid
1993 - 2000	$45	$50	$_____

• Early samples have a completely red tower.
• Flags are easily damaged when removing from box.

Elfin Snow Cone Works ✓   56332

Dates	OSRP	GBTru	Paid
1994 - 1997	$40	$40	$_____

Beard Barber Shop   56340

Dates	OSRP	GBTru	Paid
1994 - 1997	$27.50	$30	$_____

• A sign is separate in the box.

North Pole Dolls & Santa's Bear Works

56359

Dates	OSRP	GBTru	Paid
1994 - 1997	$96	$95	$_____

- Set of 3 includes two lit towers and a non-lit center piece.

Tin Soldier Shop

56383

Dates	OSRP	GBTru	Paid
1995ᴹ - 1997	$42	$50	$_____

- Metal sign attached to the front is easily broken.

Elfin Forge & Assembly Shop

56384

Dates	OSRP	GBTru	Paid
1995 - 1998	$65	$65	$_____

Weather & Time Observatory

56385

Dates	OSRP	GBTru	Paid
1995 - 1999	$50	$55	$_____

Santa's Rooming House

56386

Dates	OSRP	GBTru	Paid
1995 - 1999	$50	$55	$_____

Elves' Trade School

56387

Dates	OSRP	GBTru	Paid
1995 - 1998	$50	$55	$_____

- Early pieces have signs that read "E**vl**es Trade School."

Popcorn & Cranberry House 56388

Dates	OSRP	GBTru	Paid
1996ᴹ - 1997	$45	$90	$____

- A lantern is separate in the box.

Santa's Bell Repair 56389

Dates	OSRP	GBTru	Paid
1996ᴹ - 1998	$45	$45	$____

North Pole Start A Tradition Set 56390

Dates	OSRP	GBTru	Paid
1996ᴹ - 1996	$85	$85	$____

- First available during the November 1996 Homes for the Holidays event. The price was reduced to $65 during the event.
- Set of 12 includes Candy Cane Lane set of 2 **Candy Cane & Peppermint Shop** (top) and **Gift Wrap & Ribbons** (bottom), a 2 piece accessory "Candy Cane Elves," 6 trees, Brick Road, and a bag of snow.

Route 1, North Pole, Home Of Mr. & Mrs. Claus 56391

Dates	OSRP	GBTru	Paid
1996 -	$110	-	$____

- Earliest shipments had the two green gates included in the box. Later ones have the gates already inserted into the fence. 3 flags are separate in the box.

Hall Of Records 56392

Dates	OSRP	GBTru	Paid
1996 - 1999	$50	$55	$____

North Pole

Christmas Bread Bakers — 56393

Dates	OSRP	GBTru	Paid
1996 - 2000	$55	$60	$_____

• A directional sign is separate in the box.

The Glacier Gazette — 56394

Dates	OSRP	GBTru	Paid
1997ᴹ - 1999	$48	$50	$_____

Mrs. Claus' Greenhouse — 56395 ✓

Dates	OSRP	GBTru	Paid
1997 - 2001	$68	$75	$_____

• A sign is separate in the box.

Glass Ornament Works — 56396

Dates	OSRP	GBTru	Paid
1997 - 2003	$60	$60	$_____

• Glass ornaments and stands are extremely fragile.

Santa's Light Shop — 56397

Dates	OSRP	GBTru	Paid
1997 - 2000	$52	$55	$_____

Elsie's Gingerbread — 56398

Dates	OSRP	GBTru	Paid
1997 - 1998	$65	$75	$_____

• Limited to year of production.
• Uses Magic Smoke to create smoking effect rising from the chimney.

Custom Stitchers 56400

Dates	OSRP	GBTru	Paid
1998 - 2000	$37.50	$40	$_____

- Elf Land.
- 3 pieces of clothing and a bell are separate in the box.

Tillie's Tiny Cup Café 56401

Dates	OSRP	GBTru	Paid
1998 - 2000	$37.50	$40	$_____

- Elf Land.
- A bell is separate in the box.
- The sign on top of the building is easily snapped off.

The Elf Spa 56402

Dates	OSRP	GBTru	Paid
1998 - 2001	$40	$40	$_____

- Elf Land.
- A flag is separate in the box.

Real Plastic Snow Factory 56403

Dates	OSRP	GBTru	Paid
1998 - 2001	$80	$85	$_____

- A bell is separate in the box.

Reindeer Flight School 56404

Dates	OSRP	GBTru	Paid
1998 - 2002	$55	$65	$_____

- A weathervane and windsock are separate in the box.

Marie's Doll Museum 56405

Dates	OSRP	GBTru	Paid
1999^M - 1999	$55	$70	$_____

- Inspired by Marie Osmond, the entertainer and avid do designer and North Pole collector

Santa's Visiting Center — 56407

Dates	OSRP	GBTru	Paid
1999ᴹ - 1999	$65	$75	$____

- First available at the 1999 Discover Dept. 56 event.
- Set of 6 includes the Visiting Center, girl with dog, fence, tree, walkway, and bag of snow.
- Several national flags are separate in the box.

Elf Mountain Ski Resort — 56700

Dates	OSRP	GBTru	Paid
1999 - 2002	$70	$70	$____

- 2 flags are separate in the box.

The Peanut Brittle Factory — 56701

Dates	OSRP	GBTru	Paid
1999 - 2002	$80	$85	$____

- A sign is separate in the box.

Mini-Donut Shop — 56702

Dates	OSRP	GBTru	Paid
1999 - 2001	$42	$50	$____

- Elf Land.
- The umbrella is very fragile.

Cold Care Clinic — 56703

Dates	OSRP	GBTru	Paid
1999 - 2000	$42	$50	$____

- Elf Land.
- A sign and a bell are separate in the box.

North Pole

Northern Lights Tinsel Mill — 56704

Dates	OSRP	GBTru	Paid
1999 - 2002	$55	$60	$_____

Jack In The Box Plant No. 2 — 56705

Dates	OSRP	GBTru	Paid
1999 - 2000	$65	$65	$_____

- Limited to year of production.
- The smokestack is fragile.

Sweet Rock Candy Co. Gift Set — 56725

Dates	OSRP	GBTru	Paid
2000^M - 2000	$75	$110	$_____

- First available during the 2000 Discover Dept. 56 event.
- The silver bell honors Dept. 56's 25th anniversary.
- Set of 9 includes the building with silver bell, "Candy Mining" accessory, 3 Peppermint Trees, cobblestone walkway, 2 Candy Cane Fences, and a bag of snow.
- The sign is easily broken.

Crayola® Polar Palette Art Center — 56726

Dates	OSRP	GBTru	Paid
2000^M - 2002	$65	$75	$_____

- 2 signs are separate in the box.
- Licensed by Binney & Smith.

Toot's Model Train Mfg. — 5672

Dates	OSRP	GBTru	Paid
2000 - 2001	$110	$225	$_____

- 25th Anniversary Limited Edition of 25,000.
- Includes animated model train that circles the smok stack.

ACME Toy Factory ✓ 56729

Dates	OSRP	GBTru	Paid
2000 - 2002	$80	$95	$_____

- Set of 5 includes Factory and 4 Looney Tunes characters—Bugs Bunny, Daffy Duck, Sylvester, and Taz.
- Pennant is packaged separately in the box.
- Licensed by Warner Bros.

Northern Lights Fire Station 56730

Dates	OSRP	GBTru	Paid
2000 -	$64	-	$_____

- Do not handle by candy cane pole.

Wedding Bells Chapel 56731

Dates	OSRP	GBTru	Paid
2000 - 2001	$45	$60	$_____

- Elf Land.

Ginny's Cookie Treats (Regular Issue) 56732

Dates	OSRP	GBTru	Paid
2000 - 2004	$50	$50	$_____

- Elf Land.
- This version includes only the building and 2 piece accessory "Gingerbread Corner."
- Sign is packaged separately in the box.

(Early Release) 56727

Dates	OSRP	GBTru	Paid
2000ᴹ - 2002	$50	$85	$_____

- This was an early release to the various May Co. department stores. It includes the building, accessory, 3 trees, and snow.

North Pole Beauty Shoppe ✓ 05733

Dates	OSRP	GBTru	Paid
2001ᴹ - 2001	$40	$80	$_____

- Elf Land.
- Was available only through the Avon cosmetics catalog.
- Includes 2 trees and a bag of snow.

Design Works North Pole — 56733

Dates	OSRP	GBTru	Paid
2001ᴹ - 2001	$75	$595	$_____

- Each of the building's four sides depicts an aspect of the creative process.
- Only available at Dept. 56's silver anniversary event.
- Pennant and 4 signs separate in box.

Santa's Sleigh Launch — 56734

Dates	OSRP	GBTru	Paid
2001ᴹ - 2001	$75	$85	$_____

- First available during the 2001 Holiday Discover Department 56 event.
- Though box shows straight trees, this set includes curved trees.
- Set of 5 includes building, "All Clear For Take Off" accessory, 2 green glitter sisal trees, and a bag of snow.

LEGO® Building Creation Station — 56735

Dates	OSRP	GBTru	Paid
2001ᴹ - 2003	$90	$100	$_____

- Licensed by The LEGO® Group.

Caribou Coffee® Shop — 56736

Dates	OSRP	GBTru	Paid
2001ᴹ - 2003	$62	$65	$_____

- Set of 3 includes the Shop, a sign, and a reindeer.
- Licensed by Caribou Coffee® Co.

The Egg Nog Pub — 56737

Dates	OSRP	GBTru	Paid
2001ᴹ - 2003	$40	$45	$_____

- Elf Land.
- Sign is separate in the box.

Twinkle Brite Glitter Factory   56738

Dates	OSRP	GBTru	Paid
2001 - 2003	$70	$75	$____

Barbie™ Boutique   56739

Dates	OSRP	GBTru	Paid
2001 - 2004	$80	$80	$____

- Sign and flag are separate in the box.
- Licensed by Mattel, Inc®.

Beard Bros. Sleigh Wash   56740

Dates	OSRP	GBTru	Paid
2001 - 2003	$70	$70	$____

Polar Palace Theater   56741

Dates	OSRP	GBTru	Paid
2001 - 2003	$40	$50	$____

- Elf Land.
- Bell is separate in the box.

Starlight Dance Hall   56742

Dates	OSRP	GBTru	Paid
2001 - 2002	$75	$80	$____

- Numbered limited edition of 25,000.
- Sign is separate in the box.

Grandma's Bakery   05841

Dates	OSRP	GBTru	Paid
2002ᴹ - 2002	$40	$95	$____

- Elf Land.
- Was available only through the Avon cosmetics catalog.
- Set of 3 includes the Bakery and 2 sisal trees.
- Sign is separate in the box.

The Antler Inn — 56744

Dates	OSRP	GBTru	Paid
2002ᴹ - 2004	$75	$75	$_____

- Two signs are separate in the box.

Glacier Park Pavilion — 56745

Dates	OSRP	GBTru	Paid
2002ᴹ - 2002	$110	$110	$_____

- Holiday 2002 Special Edition.
- Limited to year of production.
- Animated.
- Set of 9 includes Pavilion with skating rink, "Skating With Santa" accessory, 2 elf skaters, 2 winter birch trees, 2 frosted topiaries, and snow.
- Four flags and sign are separate in the box.

Play-Doh® Sculpting Studio — 56746

Dates	OSRP	GBTru	Paid
2002ᴹ - 2003	$80	$85	$_____

- Licensed by Hasbro Consumer Products.

Santa's Reindeer Rides — 56748

Dates	OSRP	GBTru	Paid
2002ᴹ - 2002	$50	$55	$_____

- Holiday 2002 Special Edition.
- Limited to year of production.
- Animated.
- Set of 6 includes the building, "Look At Him Go!" accessory, frosted topiary tree, 2 frosted topiary bushes, and snow.

Polar Power Company   56749

Dates	OSRP	GBTru	Paid
2002 - 2003	$95	$115	$_____

- Limited to year of production.
- Animated with lighting effects.

Kringle Elfementary School   56750

Dates	OSRP	GBTru	Paid
2002 - 2004	$45	$45	$_____

- Elf Land.

Northwind Knitters   56751

Dates	OSRP	GBTru	Paid
2002 - 2004	$65	$65	$_____

- Set of 2 includes building and "Drying The Wool" accessory.

Frosty Pines Outfitters   56752

Dates	OSRP	GBTru	Paid
2002 - 2003	$60	$65	$_____

Hand Carved Nutcracker Factory   56753

Dates	OSRP	GBTru	Paid
2002 -	$65	-	$_____

North Pole

Coca-Cola® Fizz Factory　　　　　　　　56754

Dates	OSRP	GBTru	Paid
2002 -	$85	-	$_____

- Animated.
- If the bottle does not fizz, Dept. 56 suggests turning it over for 3 seconds, then upright before turning it on.
- Licensed by Coca-Cola®.

McElfin's Irish Restaurant & Gifts　　　　　56755

Dates	OSRP	GBTru	Paid
2002 - 2004	$55	$55	$_____

Mitten Manor　　　　　　　　　　　　　56756

Dates	OSRP	GBTru	Paid
2002 - 2004	$45	$45	$_____

- Elf Land.
- Set of 2 includes Manor and "Newt & Emma" accessory.

Checking It Twice Wind-Up Toys　　　　　56757

Dates	OSRP	GBTru	Paid
2003ᴹ - 2003	$75	$80	$_____

- Holiday 2003 Special Edition.
- Limited to year of production.
- Animated. Includes adapter.
- Set of 5 includes the building, "Everything Looks A Okay" accessory, walkway, sparkle glitter birch tree, and snow.

Naughty Or Nice Detective Agency — 56758

Dates	OSRP	GBTru	Paid
2003ᴹ - 2003	$50	$65	$_____

- Holiday 2003 Special Edition.
- Limited to year of production.
- Animated. Includes adapter.
- Set of 6 includes the building, "Lots Of Good Children This Year" accessory, frosted pine tree, frosted pine shrubs, and snow.

Mickey's North Pole Holiday House — 56759

Dates	OSRP	GBTru	Paid
2003ᴹ -	$85	-	$_____

- Disney Showcase Collection.
- Licensed by Disney Theme Parks.

KOLD Radio — 56761

Dates	OSRP	GBTru	Paid
2003ᴹ - 2004	$60	$60	$_____

The Christmas Candy Mill — 56762

Dates	OSRP	GBTru	Paid
2003 -	$75	-	$_____

- Animated.

Flurry's Snowglobe Maker — 56763

Dates	OSRP	GBTru	Paid
2003 -	$68	-	$_____

North Pole

North Pole

Polar Roller Rink — 56764

Dates	OSRP	GBTru	Paid
2003 -	$65	-	$_____

- Animated.
- Includes "Elves On Wheels" accessory.

Red's Elf Land Diner — 56765

Dates	OSRP	GBTru	Paid
2003 -	$50	-	$_____

- Elf Land.

Pointy Toed Shoemaker — 56766

Dates	OSRP	GBTru	Paid
2003 -	$35	-	$_____

- Elf Land.
- Plays "Jingle Bells."

North Pole Town Hall — 56767

Dates	OSRP	GBTru	Paid
2003 -	$65	-	$_____

Santa's Castle — 56768

Dates	OSRP	GBTru	Paid
2003 - 2004	$95	$95	$_____

- Limited to year of production.
- Inspired by the Castle in the cartoon "Rudolph The Red-Nosed Reindeer."
- Licensed by Good-Times Merchandising & Licensing.

Rudolph's Misfit Headquarters — 56769

Dates	OSRP	GBTru	Paid
2003 - 2004	$70	$70	$_____

- Limited to year of production.
- Inspired by the location in the cartoon "Rudolph The Red-Nosed Reindeer."
- Licensed by Good-Times Merchandising & Licensing.

Yummy Gummy Gumdrop Factory — 56771

Dates	OSRP	GBTru	Paid
2004ᴹ -	$75	-	$_____

• Animated.

Christmas Critters Pet Store — 56772

Dates	OSRP	GBTru	Paid
2004ᴹ -	$45	-	$_____

• Elf Land.

North Pole M&M's® Candy Factory — 56773

Dates	OSRP	GBTru	Paid
2004ᴹ -	$95	-	$_____

• Animated.
• Licensed by Mars, Inc.

Teddy Bear Training Center — 56774

Dates	OSRP	GBTru	Paid
2004ᴹ - 2004	$75	$75	$_____

• Limited to year of production.
• Set of 6 includes the building, a plush bear, flagpole, trees, and snow.

Bjorn Turoc Rocking Horse Maker — 56775

Dates	OSRP	GBTru	Paid
2004ᴹ -	$70	-	$_____

• Animated.

Lucky's Pony Rides — 56776

Dates	OSRP	GBTru	Paid
2004ᴹ - 2004	$65	$85	$_____

• Club 56 dealer exclusive. Limited edition of 5,000.

North Pole

Santa's Toy Company (Early Release) — 56892

Dates	OSRP	GBTru	Paid
2004ᴹ - 2004	$75	$100	$_____

- 15th Anniversary Series; first of 5 buildings that spell Santa.
- Limited to 10,000 pieces.
- Early release, available through select Department 56 retailers.

Alfie's Toy School For Elves (Early Release) — 56894

Dates	OSRP	GBTru	Paid
2004ᴹ - 2004	$65	$75	$_____

- 15th Anniversary Series; second of 5 buildings that spell Santa.
- Limited to year of production.
- Available only on Department 56's web site.

Mrs. Claus' Hand Knit Christmas Stockings — 56778

Dates	OSRP	GBTru	Paid
2004 -	$70	-	$_____

- Includes trees.

Arctic Game Station — 56779

Dates	OSRP	GBTru	Paid
2004 -	$50	-	$_____

- Elf Land.

Krinkles Christmas Ornament Design Studio — 56780

Dates	OSRP	GBTru	Paid
2004 -	$75	-	$_____

- Includes tree.

Alfie's Toy School For Elves (Second Release) — 56781

Dates	OSRP	GBTru	Paid
2004 -	$65	-	$_____

- 15th Anniversary Series; second of 5 buildings that spell Santa.
- Limited to year of production.
- Has different color scheme from early release version.

Santa's Toy Company (Second Release)   56893

Dates	OSRP	GBTru	Paid
2004 -	$75	-	$_____

- 15th Anniversary Series; first of 5 buildings that spell Santa.
- Limited to year of production.
- Has different color scheme from early release version.

Nettie's Mistletoe Manor   56895

Dates	OSRP	GBTru	Paid
2004 -	$55	-	$_____

- 15th Anniversary Series; third of 5 buildings that spell Santa.
- Limited to year of production.

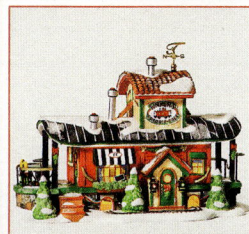

Tinker's Caboose Cafe   56896

Dates	OSRP	GBTru	Paid
2004 -	$65	-	$_____

- 15th Anniversary Series; fourth of 5 buildings that spell Santa.
- Limited to year of production.

Art's Hobbies & Crafts   56897

Dates	OSRP	GBTru	Paid
2004 -	$60	-	$_____

- 15th Anniversary Series; fifth of 5 buildings that spell Santa.
- Limited to year of production.

Scrooge McDuck & Marley's Counting House   56900

Dates	OSRP	GBTru	Paid
2004 -	$75	-	$_____

- Licensed by Disney.

Mickey's Cratchit's Cottage   56901

Dates	OSRP	GBTru	Paid
2004 -	$65	-	$_____

- Licensed by Disney.

North Pole

North Pole

Use the space(s) below to update your guide when the midyear introductions are announced.

North Star Commuter Station _____

Dates   OSRP   GBTru   Paid
___ - ___ $___   - $___

Hot Wheels _____

Dates   OSRP   GBTru   Paid
___ - ___ $___   - $___

_____ _____

Dates   OSRP   GBTru   Paid
___ - ___ $___   - $___

_____ _____

Dates   OSRP   GBTru   Paid
___ - ___ $___   - $___

_____ _____

Dates   OSRP   GBTru   Paid
___ - ___ $___   - $___

Trimming The North Pole

56081
1990 - 1993
OSRP: $10
GBTru: $30
Paid: $_____

Santa & Mrs. Claus

56090 - Set of 2
1990 -
OSRP: $15
GBTru: -
Paid: $_____

• Early samples had books that read "Good Boys" instead of "Good Kids."

Santa's Little Helpers

56103 - Set of 3
1990 - 1993
OSRP: $28
GBTru: $40
Paid: $_____

• The reindeer's antlers are very fragile.

Sleigh & Eight Tiny Reindeer

56111 - Set of 5
1990 -
OSRP: $40
GBTru: -
Paid: $_____

• The reindeer's antlers are very fragile.

Toymaker Elves

56022 - Set of 3
1991 - 1995
OSRP: $27.50
GBTru: $28
Paid: $_____

Baker Elves

56030 - Set of 3
1991 - 1995
OSRP: $27.50
GBTru: $25
Paid: $_____

Letters For Santa

56049 - Set of 3
1992 - 1994
OSRP: $30
GBTru: $55
Paid: $_____

• The reindeer's antlers are very fragile.

Testing The Toys

56057 - Set of 2
1992 - 1999
OSRP: $16.50
GBTru: $18
Paid: $_____

North Pole Accessories

Woodsmen Elves

56308 - Set of 3
1993 - 1995
OSRP: $30
GBTru: $42
Paid: $_____

Sing A Song For Santa

56316 - Set of 3
1993 - 1998
OSRP: $28
GBTru: $28
Paid: $_____

North Pole Gate

56324
1993 - 1998
OSRP: $32.50
GBTru: $32
Paid: $_____

• The flags are fragile.

Last Minute Delivery

56367
1994 - 1998
OSRP: $35
GBTru: $36
Paid: $_____

• Though introduced in 1994, shipments were delayed due to production problems.

Snow Cone Elves

56375 - Set of 4
1994 - 1997
OSRP: $30
GBTru: $28
Paid: $_____

• Features the first "elfette" in North Pole.
• Porcelain and metal.

Charting Santa's Course

56364 - Set of 2
1995 - 1997
OSRP: $25
GBTru: $30
Paid: $_____

I'll Need More Toys

56365 - Set of 2
1995 - 1998
OSRP: $25
GBTru: $24
Paid: $_____

• Porcelain and acrylic.

A Busy Elf North Pole Sign

56366
1995 - 1999
OSRP: $20
GBTru: $22
Paid: $_____

• Porcelain and acrylic.

North Pole Express

56368 - Set of 3
1996 - 1999
OSRP: $37.50
GBTru: $40
Paid: $_____

• Some samples read "N.E. Express" on the side of the tender.

Early Rising Elves

56369 - Set of 5
1996 - 1999
OSRP: $32.50
GBTru: $33
Paid: $_____

End Of The Line

56370 - Set of 2
1996 - 1999
OSRP: $28
GBTru: $32
Paid: $_____

• Includes sign and signal packaged separately in the box.

Holiday Deliveries

56371
1996 - 2001ᴹ
OSRP: $16.50
GBTru: $18
Paid: $_____

Candy Cane Elves

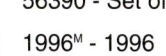

56390 - Set of 2
1996ᴹ - 1996
OSRP: *
GBTru: *

* Accessory contained in the North Pole Start A Tradition Set.

Don't Break The Ornaments

56372 - Set of 2
1997 - 2001
OSRP: $27.50
GBTru: $26
Paid: $_____

• Ornaments are very fragile.

Delivering The Christmas Greens

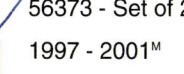

56373 - Set of 2
1997 - 2001ᴹ
OSRP: $27.50
GBTru: $28
Paid: $_____

Untangle The Christmas Lights

56374
1997 - 2000
OSRP: $35
GBTru: $40
Paid: $_____

• Lit by battery/adapter.

North Pole Accessories

North Pole Accessories

Peppermint Skating Party
56363 - Set of 6
1998ᴹ - 2000
OSRP: $64
GBTru: $65
Paid: $_____

Welcome To Elf Land Gateway Entrance
56431
1998 -
OSRP: $35
GBTru: -
Paid: $_____

Loading The Sleigh
52732 - Set of 6
1998 -
OSRP: $125
GBTru: -
Paid: $_____

• Animated—handcar runs back and forth along track. Lights on building flash.

Christmas Fun Run
56434 - Set of 6
1998 - 2000
OSRP: $35
GBTru: $35
Paid: $_____

Delivering Real Plastic Snow
56435
1998 - 2001ᴹ
OSRP: $17
GBTru: $20
Paid: $_____

Reindeer Training Camp
56436 - Set of 2
1998 - 2002
OSRP: $27.50
GBTru: $28
Paid: $_____

• The reindeer's antlers are very fragile.

Have A Seat Elves
56437 - Set of
1998 -
OSRP: $30
GBTru: -
Paid: $_____

Dash Away Delivery

56438
1998 - 2001^M
OSRP: $40
GBTru: $45
Paid: $_____

- The basket often comes unglued.
- Similar design made for Lord & Taylor. See Special Design section.

Tee Time Elves

56442 - Set of 2
1999^M - 2001^M
OSRP: $27.50
GBTru: $30
Paid: $_____

Happy New Year!

56443
1999^M - 2000
OSRP: $17.50
GBTru: $18
Paid: $_____

A Happy Harley Day

56706
1999 - 2001
OSRP: $17
GBTru: $20
Paid: $_____

- Licensed by Harley-Davidson Motor Co.

Downhill Daredevils

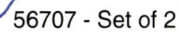

56707 - Set of 2
1999 - 2001
OSRP: $16.50
GBTru: $20
Paid: $_____

Tangled In Tinsel

56708
1999 -
OSRP: $25
GBTru: -
Paid: $_____

Canine Courier

56709 - Set of 3
1999 - 2002
OSRP: $32.50
GBTru: $35
Paid: $_____

Ski Bums

56710
1999 - 2001
OSRP: $22.50
GBTru: $25
Paid: $_____

North Pole Accessories

North Pole Accessories

Check This Out
56711
1999 - 2001
OSRP: $13.50
GBTru: $18
Paid: $_____

Marshmallows Around The Campfire
56712 - Set of 3
1999 - 2002
OSRP: $30
GBTru: $35
Paid: $_____

• The campfire is battery/adapter operated.

Open Wide!
56713
1999 - 2000
OSRP: $13
GBTru: $15
Paid: $_____

Elf Tree House
56446
1999 - 2000
OSRP: $42
GBTru: $45
Paid: $_____

Candy Mining
56725
2000^M - 2000
OSRP: *
GBTru: *

* Accessory contained in the Sweet Rock Candy Co. Gift Set.

Cruisin' Crayola® Elves
56800 - Set of 2
2000^M - 2002
OSRP: $16.50
GBTru: $20
Paid: $_____

• Licensed by Binney & Smith.

Leonardo & Vincent
56801
2000^M - 2002
OSRP: $16.50
GBTru: $20
Paid: $_____

Party In The Hot Tub!
56802 - Set of 2
2000^M - 2001
OSRP: $30
GBTru: $33
Paid: $_____

North Pole Accessories

Gingerbread Corner

56732 - Set of 2
2000 -
OSRP: *
GBTru: *

* Accessory contained in the Ginny's Cookie Treats Set.

All Aboard!

56803 - Set of 2
2000 - 2003
OSRP: $16.50
GBTru: $22
Paid: $_____

Rescue Ready

56804
2000 - 2004
OSRP: $16.50
GBTru: $17
Paid: $_____

Little Newlyweds

56805
2000 - 2001
OSRP: $13
GBTru: $20
Paid: $_____

Cutting The Trail

56806
2000 - 2003
OSRP: $14
GBTru: $18
Paid: $_____

Catch The Wind

56807
2000 - 2002
OSRP: $17.50
GBTru: $20
Paid: $_____

Icy Delights

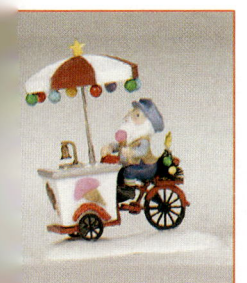

56808
2000 - 2003
OSRP: $17.50
GBTru: $22
Paid: $_____

All Clear For Take Off

56734
2001ᴹ - 2001
OSRP: *
GBTru: *

* Accessory contained in the Santa's Sleigh Launch Gift Set.

North Pole Accessories

Brick Lift

56809
2001ᴹ - 2003
OSRP: $17.50
GBTru: $20
Paid: $_____

• Licensed by the LEGO® Group.

Little Builders

56810
2001ᴹ - 2003
OSRP: $16
GBTru: $20
Paid: $_____

• Licensed by the LEGO® Group.

Just A Cup Of Joe

56811
2001ᴹ - 2003
OSRP: $22.50
GBTru: $24
Paid: $_____

• This was originally shipped in North Pole Woods sleeves.

Glitter Detail

56812 - Set of 2
2001 - 2004
OSRP: $20
GBTru: $22
Paid: $_____

Car Wash Cadets

56813
2001 - 2003
OSRP: $16.50
GBTru: $22
Paid: $_____

Two For The Show

56814
2001 - 2003
OSRP: $16.50
GBTru: $20
Paid: $_____

Kick Up Your Heels

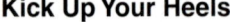

56815
2001 - 2002
OSRP: $13.50
GBTru: $15
Paid: $_____

Peppermint Front Yard

56817
2001 - 2004
OSRP: $42.50
GBTru: $43
Paid: $_____

North Pole Accessories

Wrap And Roll

56818
2001 - 2003
OSRP: $20
GBTru: $30
Paid: $_____

Raising The Flag At The North Pole

56820
2001 - 2004
OSRP: $15.00
GBTru: $15
Paid: $_____

LEGO® Warehouse Forklift

56819 - Set of 5
2001 - 2003
OSRP: $140.00
GBTru: $135
Paid: $_____

• Animated—forklift runs back and forth along track.
• Licensed by the LEGO® Group.

Skating With Santa

56745
2002ᴹ - 2002
OSRP: *
GBTru: *

* The accessory contained in Glacier Park Pavilion.

Look At Him Go!

56748
2002ᴹ - 2002
OSRP: *
GBTru: *

* The accessory contained in the Santa's Reindeer Rides.

More Play-Doh®, Please!

56822 - Set of 2
2002ᴹ - 2003
OSRP: $20
GBTru: $24
Paid: $_____

• Licensed by Hasbro Consumer Products.

North Pole Petting Zoo

56823
2002ᴹ - 2004
OSRP: $35
GBTru: $35
Paid: $_____

North Pole Accessories

This Looks Like A Good Spot

56831 - Set of 2
2002ᴹ - 2004
OSRP: $16.50
GBTru: $17
Paid: $_____

Kringle Street Snowman

56833
2002ᴹ - 2002
OSRP: $32.50
GBTru: $35
Paid: $_____

• Limited to year of production.
• Available only at Gold Key dealers.

Drying The Wool

56751
2002 -
OSRP: *
GBTru: *

* The accessory contained in the Northwind Knitters.

Newt & Emma

56756
2002 - 2004
OSRP: *
GBTru: *

• Elf Land.
* The accessory contained in Mitten Manor.

S'mores & Hot Chocolate Stand

56835
2002 -
OSRP: $32.50
GBTru: -
Paid: $_____

• Elf Land.

Sparky The Plant Manager

56836
2002 - 2003
OSRP: $15
GBTru: $20
Paid: $_____

School Sleigh Express

56837
2002 -
OSRP: $25
GBTru: -
Paid: $_____

• Elf Land.

Running The Loom

56838
2002 - 2004
OSRP: $12.50
GBTru: $13
Paid: $_____

Ready For Adventure

56839
2002 - 2003
OSRP: $17.50
GBTru: $20
Paid: $_____

Frozen Veggies

56840
2002 - 2004
OSRP: $15
GBTru: $15
Paid: $_____

Coca-Cola® Taste Test

56841
2002 -
OSRP: $17.50
GBTru: -
Paid: $_____

• Licensed by Coca-Cola.

Nutcracker Delivery

56842 - Set of 2
2002 -
OSRP: $25
GBTru: -
Paid: $_____

Chimney Sweep For Hire!

56843
2002 - 2004
OSRP: $13.50
GBTru: $13
Paid: $_____

Frostbite Tree House Day Care

56844
2002 -
OSRP: $40
GBTru: -
Paid: $_____

• Elf Land.

Frosty Playground

56846
2002 -
OSRP: $32.50
GBTru: -
Paid: $_____

• Elf Land.
• Animated.

Everything Looks A-Okay

56757
2003ᴹ - 2003
OSRP: *
GBTru: *

* The accessory contained in Checking It Twice Wind-Up Toys.

North Pole Accessories

North Pole Accessories

Lots Of Good Children This Year

56758
2003^M - 2003
OSRP: *
GBTru: *

* The accessory contained in Naughty Or Nice Detective Agency.

Kringle Street Town Tree

56847
2003^M - 2003
OSRP: $35
GBTru: $40
Paid: $_____

• Includes adapter.
• Limited to year of production.

An Irish Cheer For Santa

56848 - Set of 2
2003^M - 2004
OSRP: $20
GBTru: $20
Paid: $_____

Mickey Builds A Snowman

56849
2003^M -
OSRP: $22.50
GBTru: -
Paid: $_____

• Licensed by Disney Theme Parks.

Bustin' A Move

56850 - Set of 2
2003^M - 2004
OSRP: $15
GBTru: $15
Paid: $_____

Coca-Cola® Sliding Hill

56851
2003^M -
OSRP: $60
GBTru: -
Paid: $_____

• Licensed by Coca-Cola.
• Includes adapter.

Reindeer Games

56853
2003 - 2004
OSRP: $45
GBTru: $45
Paid: $_____

• Limited to year of production.
• Licensed by Good-Times M & L.

Don't Let Go!

56854
2003 -
OSRP: $10
GBTru: -
Paid: $_____

Fillers & Flakers

56855
2003 -
OSRP: $20
GBTru: -
Paid: $_____

A Perfect Fit

56856
2003 -
OSRP: $16.50
GBTru: -
Paid: $_____

• Elf Land

The Key To The North Pole

56857
2003 -
OSRP: $15
GBTru: -
Paid: $_____

Fly Through Elf

56858
2003 -
OSRP: $15
GBTru: -
Paid: $_____

• Elf Land

Candy Cane Shack

56859
2003 -
OSRP: $40
GBTru: -
Paid: $_____

• Working bubble lights.
• includes adapter.

The Misfits

56860
2003 - 2004
OSRP: $35
GBTru: $35
Paid: $_____

• Limited to year of production.
• Licensed by Good-Times M & L.

Mrs. Claus' Cookies & Milk

56861
2003 -
OSRP: $25
GBTru: -
Paid: $_____

Proud Papa & Mama

56862
2003 -
OSRP: $13.50
GBTru: -
Paid: $_____

• Elf Land

North Pole Accessories

New Year's At The North Pole
56863
2003 -
OSRP: $20
GBTru: -
Paid: $_____

Ice & Snow Skating Pond

56867
2003 -
OSRP: $50
GBTru: -
Paid: $_____
• Animated.
• Includes adapter.

Can I Keep Them
56864
2004ᴹ -
OSRP: $10
GBTru: -
Paid: $_____
• Elf Land.

M&M's® Stamp Of Approval

56865
2004ᴹ -
OSRP: $18
GBTru: -
Paid: $_____
• Licensed by Mars, Inc.

Swinging Disney Fab 5

56866
2004ᴹ -
OSRP: $65
GBTru: -
Paid: $_____
• Animated, includes adapter.
• Licensed by Disney Theme Parks.

Do I Have A Deal For You!

56868 - Set of 2
2004ᴹ -
OSRP: $20
GBTru: -
Paid: $_____

Kringle Street Town Santa

56869
2004ᴹ - 2004
OSRP: $32.50
GBTru: $33
Paid: $_____
• Limited to year of production.

Gumdrop Taste Test

56870
2004ᴹ -
OSRP: $10
GBTru: -
Paid: $_____

Christmas Around The World - Feliz Navidad

56871
2004 -
OSRP: $30
GBTru: -
Paid: $_____

• Christmas Around The World Series.

Hot Chocolate Tower

56872
2004 -
OSRP: $30
GBTru: -
Paid: $_____

Ice Cold Coca-Cola®

56873
2004 -
OSRP: $20
GBTru: -
Paid: $_____

• Ice sculpture is lighted.
• Licensed by Coca-Cola®.

More Yarn For Your Stockings, Mrs. Claus!

56874
2004 -
OSRP: $17.50
GBTru: -
Paid: $_____

Testing Video Games Is The Perfect Job!

56875
2004 -
OSRP: $12.50
GBTru: -
Paid: $_____

• Elf Land.

Krinkles For Sale

56876
2004 -
OSRP: $18.50
GBTru: -
Paid: $_____

Welcome To Nettie's B&B

56877
2004 -
OSRP: $17.50
GBTru: -
Paid: $_____

• 15th Anniversary Series.

One Choo-Choo Burger Coming Up!

56889
2004 -
OSRP: $10
GBTru: -
Paid: $_____

• 15th Anniversary Series.

North Pole Accessories

North Pole Accessories

Everybody's Been Good This Year!
56891
2004 -
OSRP: $25
GBTru: -
Paid: $_____
• 15th Anniversary Series.

Passing Inspection With Flying Colors
56898
2004 -
OSRP: $17.50
GBTru: -
Paid: $_____
• 15th Anniversary Series.

We Don't Need Instructions!
56899
2004 -
OSRP: $15
GBTru: -
Paid: $_____
• 15th Anniversary Series.

Scrooge McDuck & The Ghosts Of Christmas
56940
2004 -
OSRP: $50
GBTru: -
Paid: $_____
• Adapter included.
• Licensed by Disney.

A Merry Mickey Christmas, Cratchits!
56941 - Set of 2
2004 -
OSRP: $18.50
GBTru: -
Paid: $_____
• Licensed by Disney.

Use the space(s) on the following page to update your guide when the midyear introductions are announced.

Gulf _____
_____
____ - ____
OSRP: $_____
GBTru: -
Paid: $_____

_____
_____
____ - ____
OSRP: $_____
GBTru: -
Paid: $_____

North Pole Accessories

_____
_____
___ - ___
OSRP: $_____
GBTru: -
Paid: $_____

_____
_____
___ - ___
OSRP: $_____
GBTru: -
Paid: $_____

_____
_____
___ - ___
OSRP: $_____
GBTru: -
Paid: $_____

_____
_____
___ - ___
OSRP: $_____
GBTru: -
Paid: $_____

_____
_____
___ - ___
OSRP: $_____
GBTru: -
Paid: $_____

_____
_____
___ - ___
OSRP: $_____
GBTru: -
Paid: $_____

_____
_____
___ - ___
OSRP: $_____
GBTru: -
Paid: $_____

_____
_____
___ - ___
OSRP: $_____
GBTru: -
Paid: $_____

Enjoy collecting the villages more than ever. Visit

The Marketplace

on pages 462 thru 464

For copies of the photos of the 2005 midyear introductions, send $3 and a self-addressed stamped envelope to:

> Greenbook
> 56 Freeway Drive
> Cranston RI 02920

The pages will be mailed in June or as orders are received after June.

Small Collections

While most village collections seem to almost grow by leaps and bounds, there
(ar)e a few that have followed a very different pattern. These small series were over
(al)most as soon as they began, while two continuing collections are growing slowly.
Meadowland is a series of ceramic pieces that debuted—and retired—three years
(af)ter Snow Village first appeared. It is the first instance of a village intended to be
(di)splayed other than during the winter.

Introduced in 1994, Disney Parks Village™ Series excited both village collectors
(an)d Disney fans with its reproductions of buildings from Orlando's Disney World
(an)d Anaheim's Disneyland. But within two years the relationship between the two
(co)mpanies abruptly ended.

Seasons Bay debuted in 1998 with six special first edition buildings and a series
(of) seasonal accessories. The smaller pewter figures were created in scale to the
(bu)ildings, a first for Department 56. A number of general accessories rounded out
(thi)s Victorian village that retired after four years.

North Pole Woods™ began in 2000 and was produced for less than three years. It
(wa)s treated by both Department 56 and collectors as a stepchild to the more popular
(No)rth Pole Series™ and never seemed to acquire its own identity.

(T)he two continuing series are the Historical Landmark® and Literary Classics®
(pie)ces. Each had its roots within other Heritage Villages. The Literary Calssics®
(pie)ces all include a building, accessory, and a copy of the book. Historical Landmarks®
(inc)lude several London structures as well as familiar American buildings.

THE HISTORICAL LANDMARK SERIES™

Initial Pieces were originally classified as part of Dickens' Village Series®. This varied series depicts some of the most well-known buildings in the world.

Tower Of London   58500

Dates	OSRP	GBTru	Paid
1997ᴹ - 1997	$165	$225	$_____

- Limited to year of production.
- This, the White Tower, is one of the many towers that comprise the Tower of London, famous for housing a prison as well as the Crown Jewels. Legend says six ravens must be at the tower to preserve the monarchy.
- The actual Tower of London is located along the Thames River in London.
- Set of 5 includes the Tower, a gate with tower, the raven master, a sign, and a wall with ravens.

The Old Globe Theatre   58501

Dates	OSRP	GBTru	Paid
1997 - 1998	$175	$165	$_____

- Limited to year of production.
- First samples of the building were made as two pieces. For production, it is one piece.
- Some early shipments have "The City Globe" stamped on the bottom.
- The Globe Theatre, located along the Thames River in London, was demolished in 1644 and was rebuilt in 1996 near the original site.
- Set of 4 includes the Theatre, two trumpeters, and a sign.

Independence Hall   5550●

Dates	OSRP	GBTru	Paid
1998 - 2000ᴹ	$110	$125	$_____

- This replica of Philadelphia's Independence Hall was first Historical Landmark not associated with England.
- First available during the 1999 July event.
- Set of 2 includes Hall and sign.

Big Ben — 58341

Dates	OSRP	GBTru	Paid
1998 - 2003	$95	$115	$_____

- It features a working clock on one of its faces. The other three read "5 of 6."
- It is a replica of London's Big Ben along the Thames River.
- Set of 2 includes Big Ben and sign.

The Old Royal Observatory Gold Dome Edition — 58451

Dates	OSRP	GBTru	Paid
1999 - 2000	Promo	$365	$_____

- Limited to 5,500, Department 56 sent one to its valued retailers as a thank you for their support.

The Old Royal Observatory — 58453

Dates	OSRP	GBTru	Paid
1999 - 2000	$95	$105	$_____

- Limited to 35,000.
- This is a replica of the Old Royal Observatory in Greenwich, England which keeps the world's time.
- Set of 2 includes Observatory and sign.

Cathedral Of St. Paul — 58919

Dates	OSRP	GBTru	Paid
2001^M - 2001	$150	$470	$_____

- Replica of Cathedral of St. Paul in St. Paul, MN.
- Copper-colored roof.
- Only available at Dept. 56 25th Anniversary celebration.
- Christmas In The City bottomstamp. DV logo on box.

Cathedral Of St. Paul — 58930

Dates	OSRP	GBTru	Paid
2001 -	$150	-	$_____

- Re-issue of the copper colored roof version that was available at the Dept. 56 25th Anniversary celebration.
- Also designated as a Christmas In The City design.

Temple Bar — 58564

Dates	OSRP	GBTru	Paid
2002 - 2003	$60	$65	$_____

- This is a replica of a gate that once stood in London and is now on private property.
- Also designated as a Dickens' Village accessory.

Small Collections

Central Synagogue — 59204

Dates	OSRP	GBTru	Paid
2002 - 2003	$110	$125	$_____

- Limited to year of production.
- This is a replica of Central Synagogue in New York City.
- Also designated as a Christmas In The City design.

Empire State Building — 59207

Dates	OSRP	GBTru	Paid
2003ᴹ -	$185	-	$_____

- This is a replica of the Empire State Building in Manhattan.
- At 23 inches, this is the tallest building manufactured by Department 56.
- Features several holiday lighting effects, including different colors in detachable top section.
- Four American flags are separate in box.
- Also designated as a Christmas In The City design.

Tower Bridge Of London — 58705

Dates	OSRP	GBTru	Paid
2003 - 2004	$165	$225	$_____

- Numbered limited edition of 20,000.
- Dickens' Village 20th Anniversary Series. Includes pin.
- It is a replica of London's Tower Bridge.
- Set of 4.

Historic Chicago Water Tower — 59209

Dates	OSRP	GBTru	Paid
2003 -	$65	-	$_____

- Set of 2 includes Tower and sign.
- This is a replica of the Chicago Water Tower, one of the few buildings to survive the great Chicago fire of 1871.
- Also designated as a Christmas In The City design.

Windsor Castle — 58720

Dates	OSRP	GBTru	Paid
2004 -	$95	-	$_____

- This lighted facade is a replica of the world's largest occupied castle.
- Also designated as a Dickens' Village design.

Small Collections

Tower Bridge Of London   58721

Dates	OSRP	GBTru	Paid
2004 -	**$135**	-	$____

- Re-issue of the limited edition that was issued in 2003.
- Also designated as a Dickens' Village design.

Guarding The Castle   58594

Dates	OSRP	GBTru	Paid
2004 -	**$17.50**	-	$____

- Also designated as a Dickens' Village design.

Golden Gate Bridge   59241

Dates	OSRP	GBTru	Paid
2004 -	**$120**	-	$____

- Also designated as a Christmas In The City design.
- Replica of the famous bridge in California.

LITERARY CLASSICS® COLLECTION

These designs are Department 56's interpretation of the buildings and characters that come to life in some of the literary world's most cherished works. Each set includes a specially printed copy of the classic in addition to a lit building and accessories which help to bring the stories to life. Other literary works have also been recognized in several of the villages, but none have been as comprehensive or detailed as these versions. Notice that none of the buildings have snow on them.

Great Expectations Satis Manor — 58310

Dates	OSRP	GBTru	Paid
1998 - 2001	$110	$110	$_____

- Charles Dickens used Restoration House in Rochester, England as the model for his Satis Manor.
- Set of 4 plus book includes the Manor and a 3 piece accessory "Miss Havisham, Estella, and Pip."

Little Women - The March Residence — 56606

Dates	OSRP	GBTru	Paid
1999ᴹ - 2000	$90	$95	$_____

- Louisa May Alcott based the March Residence on the Orchard House in Concord, MA. where she grew up.
- Set of 4 plus book includes the Residence and a 3 piece accessory "A Letter From Papa" which includes Marmie, Jo, Amy, Beth, and Meg.
- The water pump's handle is very fragile.

The Great Gatsby West Egg Mansion — 58939

Dates	OSRP	GBTru	Paid
1999 - 2001	$135	$145	$_____

- This is Department 56's interpretation of the Long Island mansion that F. Scott Fitzgerald depicted in his novel.
- Some pieces were shipped with extra statues in anticipation of breakage.
- Set of 4 plus book includes the Mansion, Jay Gatsby, Daisy Buchanan, and the infamous car.
- Licensed through the Fitzgerald Estate, LTD.

The Adventures Of Tom Sawyer, Aunt Polly's House — 58600

Dates	OSRP	GBTru	Paid
2000ᴹ - 2001	$90	$100	$_____

- Inspired by Mark Twain's first book, this is a depiction of the home and characters made famous in the book.
- Set of 5 plus book includes the House, and a 4 piece accessory "Painting The White Picket Fence" which includes Tom Sawyer, two friends, and the fence.

Sherlock Holmes - 221B Baker Street — 58601

Dates	OSRP	GBTru	Paid
2000 - 2003	$90	$100	$_____

- Inspired by Arthur Conan Doyle's famous works, this is Department 56's interpretation of the home of England's greatest fictional detective.
- Set of 3 plus book includes the house and 2 piece accessory "Elementary My Dear Watson."

Small Collections

DISNEY PARKS VILLAGE™ SERIES

Available for less than two years, this series reproduced familiar buildings at the Disney theme parks. First year releases were more plentiful, while scarcity of later buildings resulted in higher aftermarket values.

Mickey's Christmas Carol (10 Points)   53503

Dates	OSRP	GBTru	Paid
1994 - 1996	$144	$175	$_____

- This version has gold spires at the lower corners and peaks of the dormers.
- Replica of Disney World building.
- Set of 2 includes main building and outbuilding.
- Holiday Collection stamped piece (#07420) sold by Disney Parks has   **GBTru: $235** $_____

(6 Points)   53503

		GBTru	Paid
		$110	$_____

- Has no spires at the lower corners of the dormers.
- Holiday Collection has   **GBTru: $195** $_____

OLDE WORLD ANTIQUES SHOPS - Set of 2   53511

Dates	OSRP	GBTru	Paid
1994 - 1996	$90	$80	$_____

- Holiday Collection stamped piece (#07429) sold by Disney Parks has   **GBTru: $150** $_____

Olde World Antiques I   5351*

Dates	OSRP	GBTru	Paid
1994 - 1996	$45	$45	$_____

- A similar building is in Disney World's Liberty Square.
- Holiday Collection stamped piece (#07429) sold by Disney Parks has   **GBTru: $85** $_____

Olde World Antiques II   5351

Dates	OSRP	GBTru	Paid
1994 - 1996	$45	$45	$_____

- A similar building is in Disney World's Liberty Square.
- Holiday Collection stamped piece (#07429) sold by Disney Parks has   **GBTru: $85** $_____

Disneyland Fire Department #105 — 53520

Dates	OSRP	GBTru	Paid
1994 - 1996	$45	$60	$_____

- Inspired by fire station on Main Street in Disneyland.
- Holiday Collection stamped piece (#07439) sold by Disney Parks has **GBTru: $105** $_____

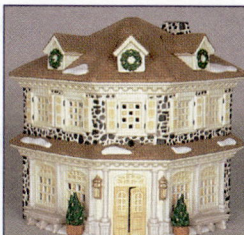

Silversmith — 53521

Dates	OSRP	GBTru	Paid
1995 - 1996	$50	$175	$_____

- Holiday Collection stamped piece (#07448) sold by Disney Parks has **GBTru: $225** $_____

Tinker Bell's Treasures — 53522

Dates	OSRP	GBTru	Paid
1995 - 1996	$60	$175	$_____

- Holiday Collection stamped piece (#07449) sold by Disney Parks has **GBTru: $225** $_____

Small Collections

Mickey & Minnie

53538 - Set of 2
1994 - 1996
OSRP: $22.50
GBTru: $30
Paid: $_____

Disney Parks Family

53546 - Set of 3
1994 - 1996
OSRP: $32.50
GBTru: $30
Paid: $_____

Olde World Antiques Gate

53554
1994 - 1996
OSRP: $15
GBTru: $18
Paid: $_____

Balloon Seller

53539 - Set of 2
1995 - 1996
OSRP: $25
GBTru: $35
Paid: $_____

NORTH POLE WOODS™ SERIES

Available for only three years, these life-in-a-forest pieces were incorporated by many collectors into their North Pole villages, while others treated it as a separate area. The accessories were more readily placed within the North Pole Series™ than the lighted trees.

Town Meeting Hall — 56880

Dates	OSRP	GBTru	Paid
2000ᴹ - 2002	$73	$60	$_____

• Adapter included.

Oakwood Post Office Branch — 56881

Dates	OSRP	GBTru	Paid
2000ᴹ - 2002	$70	$60	$_____

• Adapter included.
• Set of 2 includes Post Office and elf.

Reindeer Care & Repair — 56882

Dates	OSRP	GBTru	Paid
2000ᴹ - 2002	$65	$55	$_____

• Adapter included.

Trim-A-Tree Factory — 56884

Dates	OSRP	GBTru	Paid
2000ᴹ - 2001	$55	$55	$_____

• Adapter included.
• Set of 2 includes Factory and elf.

Santa's Retreat — 56883

Dates	OSRP	GBTru	Paid
2000 - 2002	$70	$55	$_____

• Early release to Parade of Gifts stores.
• Adapter included.
• Set of 2 includes tree and Mrs. Claus.

Rudolph's Condo 56885

Dates	OSRP	GBTru	Paid
2000 - 2002	**$50**	**$50**	$___

• Licensed by GTM&L.

Reindeer Condo 56886

Dates	OSRP	GBTru	Paid
2000 - 2001	**$70**	**$60**	$___

• Adapter included.
• Windsock separate in the box.

Chisel McTimber Art Studio 56887

Dates	OSRP	GBTru	Paid
2001 - 2002	**$65**	**$65**	$___

• Adapter included.
• Set of 2 includes tree and "Elf Sculpting" accessory.

Welcome To North Pole Woods
Gateway Entrance

56920
2000^M - 2002
OSRP: $25
GBTru: $18
Paid: $_____

Tailored For You

56921 - Set of 2
2000^M - 2001
OSRP: $22.50
GBTru: $18
Paid: $_____

• The snowman's arms are fragile.

Elves

56922 - Set of 4
2000^M - 2002
OSRP: $30
GBTru: $22
Paid: $_____

Scissors Wizards

56923 - Set of 2
2000^M - 2001
OSRP: $25
GBTru: $20
Paid: $_____

• The reindeer's antlers are very fragile.

Nuts About Broomball

56926
2000^M - 2001^M
OSRP: $20
GBTru: $24
Paid: $_____

Birch Bench & Table

56927 - Set of 2
2000^M - 2001^M
OSRP: $9
GBTru: $10
Paid: $_____

Pinecone Path

52874 - Set of 6
2000 - 2002
OSRP: $15
GBTru: $12
Paid: $_____

• Straight and curved.

Acorn Street Lamps

52875 - Set of 4
2000 - 2002
OSRP: $15
GBTru: $12
Paid: $_____

• Battery/adapter operated.

Birch Bridge

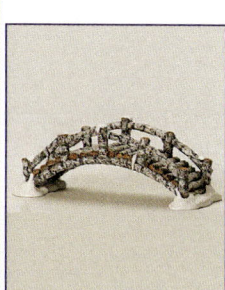

52876
2000 - 2002
OSRP: $13.50
GBTru: $12
Paid: $_____

Birch Gazebo

52877
2000 - 2002
OSRP: $20
GBTru: $18
Paid: $_____

• Weathervane is very fragile.

Birch Fence

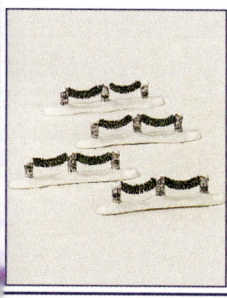

52878 - Set of 4
2000 - 2002
OSRP: $12
GBTru: $12
Paid: $_____

Star Of The Show

56928
2000 - 2002
OSRP: $25
GBTru: $20
Paid: $_____

• Licensed by Good-Times Merchandising & Licensing.

Polar Plowing Service

56929
2000 - 2002
OSRP: $30
GBTru: $24
Paid: $_____

Gone Fishing

56930
2000 - 2002
OSRP: $35
GBTru: $30
Paid: $_____

Ring Toss

56931 - Set of 2
2000 - 2002
OSRP: $17.50
GBTru: $18
Paid: $_____

• Licensed by Good-Times Merchandising & Licensing.

Balancing Act

56932 - Set of 3
2000 - 2002
OSRP: $25
GBTru: $15
Paid: $_____

• The reindeer's antlers are very fragile.

Small Collections

SEASONS BAY® SERIES

For many years Department 56 was famed for creating winter villages. But many collectors wanted to display their pieces for more than just a few months each year, and Seasons Bay met that need. The buildings were exceptionally crafted, but what made them different was the fact that they all lacked snow.

It was not the buildings, though, that made this a truly unique village. It was the accessories. Set in the Victorian era, the collection featured people engaged in year-round activities. A variety of plants and trees reinforced the seasonal designs. Another unique feature was the diminutive size of the people. Accessories were created in pewter in order to present them in proportion to their residences. This is the only village in which this is true.

Grandview Shores Hotel (First Edition)   53300

Dates	OSRP	GBTru	Paid
1998 - 1999	$150	$175	$_____

• This version is identified by its gold flags, weathervane, and First Edition decal on its bottom.

(Open Edition)   53400

Dates	OSRP	GBTru	Paid
1998 - 2000	$150	$125	$_____

Bay Street Shops (First Edition)   53301

Dates	OSRP	GBTru	Paid
1998 - 1999	$135	$150	$_____

• This version is identified by its gold flags and First Edition decal on its bottom.
• Set of 2 includes two buildings—Maggie's Millinery and Bayside Clothiers/Book Nook—that fit together.

(Open Edition)   53401

Dates	OSRP	GBTru	Paid
1998 - 2002	$135	$120	$_____

• Set of 2 includes two buildings—Maggie's Millinery and Bayside Clothiers/Book Nook—that fit together.

Chapel On The Hill (First Edition) — 53302

Dates	OSRP	GBTru	Paid
1998 - 1999	$72	$80	$____

• This version is identified by its gold cross and First Edition decal on its bottom.

(Open Edition) — 53402

Dates	OSRP	GBTru	Paid
1998 - 2001	$72	$60	$____

Side Porch Café (First Edition) — 53303

Dates	OSRP	GBTru	Paid
1998 - 1999	$50	$65	$____

• This version is identified by the First Edition decal on its bottom.

(Open Edition) — 53403

Dates	OSRP	GBTru	Paid
1998 - 2002	$50	$50	$____

Inglenook Cottage #5 (First Edition) — 53304

Dates	OSRP	GBTru	Paid
1998 - 1999	$60	$70	$____

• This version is identified by the First Edition decal on its bottom.

(Open Edition) — 53404

Dates	OSRP	GBTru	Paid
1998 - 2000	$60	$50	$____

Small Collections

The Grand Creamery (First Edition)   53305

Dates	OSRP	GBTru	Paid
1998 - 1999	$60	$60	$____

- This version is identified by its gold flag and First Edition decal on its bottom.

(Open Edition)   53405

Dates	OSRP	GBTru	Paid
1998 - 2001	$60	$50	$____

Parkside Pavilion   53411

Dates	OSRP	GBTru	Paid
1999 - 2002	$65	$60	$____

- Set of 2 includes the Pavilion and fountain.

Parkside Pavilion Gift Set   53412

Dates	OSRP	GBTru	Paid
1999 - 2000	$75	$85	$____

- Available during the 2000 Spring Discover Department 56 event.
- Set of 9 includes the Pavilion, a 4 piece accessory "Art Classes At Morning's Light," and stick-on floral arrangements.

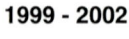

Springlake Station   53413

Dates	OSRP	GBTru	Paid
1999 - 2002	$90	$90	$____

- Early shipments had "filled-in" windows. Later shipments had the bottom half of the windows cut-out.
- Clock and 4 potted plants are separate in box.

Stillwaters Boathouse   53414

Dates	OSRP	GBTru	Paid
1999 - 2002	$70	$80	$____

• Weathervane separate in box.

Mystic Ledge Lighthouse   53445

Dates	OSRP	GBTru	Paid
2000ᴹ - 2000	$96	$235	$____

• Limited Edition - 5,600 pieces.

Garden Valley Vineyards   53446

Dates	OSRP	GBTru	Paid
2000 - 2001	$125	$165	$____

• 25th Anniversary Limited Edition of 5,600.

Breezy Hill Stables   53447

Dates	OSRP	GBTru	Paid
2000 - 2002	$68	$80	$____

• Weathervane and potted plant are separate in box.

East Cape Cottages   53448

Dates	OSRP	GBTru	Paid
2000 - 2002	$95	$125	$____

• Set of 2.
• Do not handle by railings or columns.
• Ladders are very fragile.
• Boats are easily damaged.

Small Collections

Seaside Inn 53449

Dates	OSRP	GBTru	Paid
2001ᴹ - 2002	$68	$65	$_____

• Weathervane and potted plant are separate in box.

Bayport Souvenir And Kite Shop 53450

Dates	OSRP	GBTru	Paid
2001 - 2002	$60	$60	$_____

• Pilings and fence are fragile.

SEASONS BAY ACCESSORIES

Relaxing In A Garden

53307 - Set of 3
1998 - 2001
OSRP: $25
GBTru: $22
Paid: $_____
• Spring

A Stroll In The Park

53308 - Set of 5
1998 - 2002
OSRP: $25
GBTru: $22
Paid: $_____
• Spring

I'm Wishing

53309
1998 - 2001ᴹ
OSRP: $13
GBTru: $12
Paid: $_____
• Spring

Sunday Morning At The Chapel

53311 - Set of 2
1998 - 2001
OSRP: $17
GBTru: $15
Paid: $_____
• Spring

Fishing In The Bay

53313
1998 - 2002
OSRP: $13
GBTru: $12
Paid: $_____

• Summer

Here Comes The Ice Cream Man

53314 - Set of 4
1998 - 2002
OSRP: $35
GBTru: $32
Paid: $_____

• Summer

4th Of July Parade

53317 - Set of 5
1998 - 2002
OSRP: $32.50
GBTru: $30
Paid: $_____

• Summer

Trick Or Treat

53319 - Set of 4
1998 - 2002
OSRP: $25
GBTru: $24
Paid: $_____

• Fall

Back From The Orchard

53320
1998 - 2001
OSRP: $27.50
GBTru: $25
Paid: $_____

• Fall

Afternoon Sleigh Ride

53322
1998 - 2001ᴹ
OSRP: $27.50
GBTru: $24
Paid: $_____

• Winter

Fun In The Snow

53323 - Set of 2
1998- 2001ᴹ
OSRP: $15
GBTru: $12
Paid: $_____

• Winter

Skating On The Pond

53324 - Set of 2
1998 - 2002
OSRP: $20
GBTru: $18
Paid: $_____

• Winter

Small Collections

A Day At The Waterfront

53326 - Set of 2
1998 - 2002
OSRP: $20
GBTru: $22
Paid: $_____

• Summer

The Garden Cart

53327
1998 - 2002
OSRP: $27.50
GBTru: $25
Paid: $_____

• Spring

Art Classes At Morning's Light

53412 - Set of 4
1999 - 2000
OSRP: *
GBTru: *

* Accessory contained in the 1999 Parkside Pavilion Gift Set.

The Garden Swing

53415
1999 - 2002
OSRP: $13
GBTru: $10
Paid: $_____

• Spring

Arriving At The Station

53416 - Set of 5
1999 - 2002
OSRP: $32.50
GBTru: $28
Paid: $_____

• Spring

The Perfect Wedding

53417 - Set of 7
1999 - 2002
OSRP: $25
GBTru: $24
Paid: $_____

• Summer
• Includes the book "Wedding Customs And Keepsakes."

Gently Down The Stream

53418
1999 - 2002
OSRP: $25
GBTru: $22
Paid: $_____

• Summer

A Grand Day Of Fishing

53419
1999 - 2002
OSRP: $25
GBTru: $24
Paid: $_____

• Summer

An Afternoon Picnic 53420 - Set of 3 1999 - 2002 OSRP: $18 GBTru: $15 Paid: $_____ • Fall	**A Bicycle Built For Two** 53421 1999 - 2002 OSRP: $17.50 GBTru: $15 Paid: $_____ • Fall
Rocking Chair Readers 53422 - Set of 2 1999 - 2002 OSRP: $15 GBTru: $14 Paid: $_____ • Fall	**Lifeguard On Duty** 53423 1999 - 2002 OSRP: $20 GBTru: $20 Paid: $_____ • Summer
A Day Of Holiday Shopping 53425 - Set of 3 1999 - 2002 OSRP: $25 GBTru: $20 Paid: $_____ • Winter	**The First Snow** 53426 1999 - 2002 OSRP: $15 GBTru: $15 Paid: $_____ • Winter
Singing Carols In Town 53427 1999 - 2002 OSRP: $22.50 GBTru: $20 Paid: $_____ • Winter	**Pull Together** 53600 2000 - 2002 OSRP: $35 GBTru: $28 Paid: $_____ • Summer

Small Collections

Evening Of Horseback Riding

53601 - Set of 2
2000 - 2002
OSRP: $30
GBTru: $25
Paid: $_____
• Summer

Gathering Grapes

53602 - Set of 2
2000 - 2001
OSRP: $25
GBTru: $24
Paid: $_____
• Fall

A Sleigh Ride With Santa

53603 - Set of 2
2000 - 2002
OSRP: $35
GBTru: $28
Paid: $_____
• Winter

Fresh Seafood By The Shore

53604
2000 - 2002
OSRP: $27.50
GBTru: $25
Paid: $_____
• Summer

The Kite of Spring

53608
2001 - 2002
OSRP: $12
GBTru: $10
Paid: $_____
• Spring

Seasons Bay Flag Raising

53611
2001 - 2002
OSRP: $12.50
GBTru: $14
Paid: $_____
• Spring

Small Collections

SEASONS BAY GENERAL VILLAGE ACCESSORIES

Mini Sisal Evergreens
Set of 12
$13   52763
1998 - 2002

Garden Fountain
Set of 9
$40   53330
1998 - 2001

Potted Flowers
8 Assorted
$12.50   53331
1998 - 2001ᴹ

Flowering Potted
Tree - 2 Assorted
$20   53332
1998 - 2001

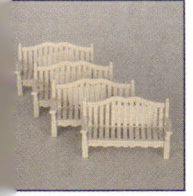

Garden Park Bench
Set of 4
$12   53333
1998 - 2001ᴹ

Planter Box
Topiaries - Set of 4
$15   53334
1998 - 2001ᴹ

Garden Gazebo
$15   53338
1998 - 2002

Seasons Bay Sign
$10   53343
1998 - 2001

Flowering Vine
Assorted
$10   53344
1998 - 2001

Geranium Window
Box
$12   53345
1998 - 2001

Beach Front
Set of 3
$15   53355
1998 - 2001

Park Street Lights
Set of 4
$15   53366
1998 - 2002

Potted Topiaries
Set of 4
$15   53370
1998 - 2001ᴹ

Beach Front
Extensions - Set of 4
$15   53374
1998 - 2001

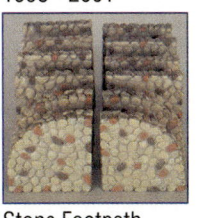

Stone Footpath
Sections - Set of 12
$15   53375
1998 - 2002

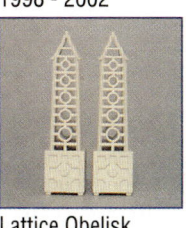

Lattice Obelisk
Set of 2
$8.50   53376
1998 - 2001ᴹ

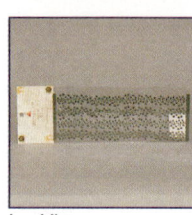
Ivy Vine
Set of 4
$7.50   53377
1998 - 2001ᴹ

Spring/Summer
Trees - Set of 4
$24   53382
1998 - 2001

Autumn Trees
Set of 4
$24   53383
1998 - 2001

Winter Trees
Set of 4
$24   53384
1998 - 2001

Amusement Park
Carousel
$75   53410
1999 - 2002

Seasons Bay Park
Set of 8
$70   53428
1999 - 2002

Christmas Garlands
& Wreaths - Set of 14
$10   53429
1999 - 2002

Sandy Beach
$7.50   53431
1999 - 2001

Adirondack Chairs
Set of 4
$10   53436
1999 - 2002

Harvest Decorations
Set of 12
$22.50   53431
2000ᴹ - 2002

Patriotic Decorations
Set of 7
$12   53605
2000 - 2002

MEADOWLAND

This "non-winter" series was short-lived. Made of ceramic, it is considered by many collectors to be a companion series to the Original Snow Village®.

Thatched Cottage   50500

Dates	OSRP	GBTru	Paid
1979 - 1980	$30	$445	$_____

Countryside Church   50518

Dates	OSRP	GBTru	Paid
1979 - 1980	$25	$460	$_____

• This is a snowless version of the Snow Village 1979 Countryside Church.

Aspen Trees   50526

Dates	OSRP	GBTru	Paid
1979 - 1980	$16	$125	$_____

Sheep   50534

Dates	OSRP	GBTru	Paid
1979 - 1980	$12	$60	$_____

• Set of 12 includes 9 white and 3 black sheep.

Small Collections

Notes:

Heritage Village® Collection

The term Heritage Village Collection® has sometimes confused collectors. It is not a separate village but an umbrella term that encompasses six porcelain villages—Dickens' Village Series®, New England Village® Series, Alpine Village Series®, Christmas in the City® Series, North Pole Series™, and Little Town of Bethlehem™ Series, as well as smaller series such as Disney Parks Village™ Series, Historical Landmark Series®, and Literary Classics® Collection.

Most of these pieces clearly belong to a specific village, and often can only be displayed in that series. This is true for most buildings and accessories. There is not too much flexibility when it comes to placing elves, taxicabs, or the angels and wise men. But there are some (usually) porcelain pieces that are more versatile and can equally well be placed in two or more of the villages. Many of those pieces are from the earlier years of the collection. Today Department 56 "assigns" most pieces to a specific village or considers them as General Village Accessories. That was not always the case, as some accessories were seemingly designed with the intention of crossing village lines. Even today an occasional piece is actually designated for this category. Recently a number of the ubiquitous Village Vans have begun appearing to celebrate holidays. The Crystal Ice Palace is the only lit building in this category. The items in this section are more versatile than those in the individual village sections. That does not mean that each of them can go in every village, but none are restricted to a single location. Among the most versatile are a number of porcelain trees, porcelain fences, and several Event Pieces.

Sleighride (Version 1)

65110

1986 - 1990

OSRP: $19.50

GBTru: $40

Paid: $_____

• Early pieces have sleeves that read "Dickens' Sleighride," and the man has a narrow white scarf with red polka dots.

(Version 2)

GBTru: $35

Paid: $_____

• Later pieces have a man with red polka dots on his scarf and lapels.

Porcelain Trees

65374 - Set of 2

1986 - 1992

OSRP: $14

GBTru: $18

Paid: $_____

Skating Pond

65455

1987 - 1990

OSRP: $24

GBTru: $45

Paid: $_____

• Early shipments were made in Taiwan and had blue-streaked ice. Later shipments were made in the Philippines and had all blue ice.

Stone Bridge

65463

1987 - 1990

OSRP: $12

GBTru: $45

Paid: $_____

• Varies from light to dark color.

Snow Children

59382 - Set of 3

1988 - 1994

OSRP: $15

GBTru: $18

Paid: $_____

Village Train Trestle

59811

1988 - 1990

OSRP: $17

GBTru: $40

Paid: $_____

• Sleeves read "Stone Train Trestle."

One Horse Open Sleigh

59820

1988 - 1993

OSRP: $20

GBTru: $30

Paid: $_____

Village Sign With Snowman

55727
1989 - 1994
OSRP: $10
GBTru: $12
Paid: $_____

Heritage Village Promotional Sign

99538
1989 - 1990
OSRP: $5
GBTru: $10
Paid: $_____

• Variation features green lettering on green facade.

Porcelain Pine, Large

52183
1992 - 1997
OSRP: $12.50
GBTru: $18
Paid: $_____

Porcelain Pine, Small

52191
1992 - 1997
OSRP: $10
GBTru: $15
Paid: $_____

Churchyard Fence & Gate

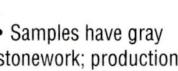

55638 - Set of 3
1992 - 1992
OSRP: $15
GBTru: $35
Paid: $_____

• Samples have gray stonework; production pieces have brown.
• Early release to GCC.

Churchyard Gate And Fence

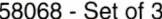

58068 - Set of 3
1992 - 1997
OSRP: $15
GBTru: $24
Paid: $_____

Churchyard Fence Extensions

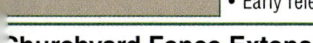
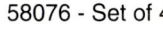
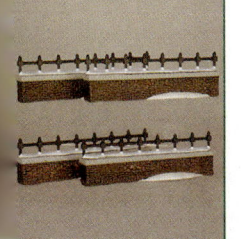

58076 - Set of 4
1992 - 1997
OSRP: $16
GBTru: $22
Paid: $_____

Porcelain Pine Trees

52515 - Set of 2
1994 - 1997
OSRP: $15
GBTru: $20
Paid: $_____

Christmas Bells

98711
1996ᴹ - 1996
OSRP: $35
GBTru: $35
Paid: $_____

• 1996 Homes for the Holidays event piece.

Village Square Clock Tower

52591
1996 - 2000
OSRP: $32.50
GBTru: $25
Paid: $_____

• Battery-operated.

The Holly & The Ivy

56100 - Set of 2
1997ᴹ - 1997
OSRP: $17.50
GBTru: $15
Paid: $_____

• 1997 Homes for the Holidays event piece.

Poinsettia Delivery Truck

59000
1997 - 1999
OSRP: $32.50
GBTru: $38
Paid: $_____

• Similar designs were produced for retailers. See the Special Design section.

Porcelain Pines

59001 - Set of 4
1997 -
OSRP: $17.50
GBTru: -
Paid: $_____

Our Own Village Park Bench

02211
1997 - 1999
OSRP: $10
GBTru: $10
Paid: $_____

• Sold plain or with retailer name on the back of the bench as a promotional piece.

Painting Our Own Village Sign

55501
1998 - 2000
OSRP: $12.50
GBTru: $12
Paid: $_____

• Sold plain or with retailer name on the sign as a promotional piece.

Stars And Stripes Forever

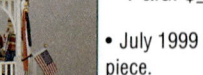

55502
1998 - 1999
OSRP: $50
GBTru: $55
Paid: $_____

• July 1999 event piece.
• Plays "Stars and Stripes Forever."
• Includes 3 flags.

Dorothy's Skate Rental

55515
1999 - 2002
OSRP: $35
GBTru: $40
Paid: $_____

- Named after Olympic Gold Medal winner, Dorothy Hamill.
- Early release to only two stores.
- Lighted. Includes skates.

Hear Ye, Hear Ye

55523
1999 - 2001ᴹ
OSRP: $13.50
GBTru: $10
Paid: $_____

- Includes stickers so the scroll can be personalized.

Village Monuments

55524 - Set of 3
1999 - 2001ᴹ
OSRP: $25
GBTru: $22
Paid: $_____

Christmas Carolers

58631 - Set of 3
2000 -
OSRP: $27.50
GBTru: -
Paid: $_____

Crystal Ice Palace

58922 - Set of 9
2001ᴹ - 2001
OSRP: $165
GBTru: $175
Paid: $_____

- Set of 9 includes Palace, 2 piece accessory "Palace Bears," 4 trees, snow crystals, and ice path. Pennant separate in box.
- Although this design is considered a Heritage village design, it was shipped with an Original Snow Village Collection hang tag.
- This was a 25th Anniversary celebration design and, therefore, should have been stamped as such. When Department 56 became aware that it had not been stamped, it supplied decals to retailers who in turn could provide them to collectors.

Crystal Ice King & Queen

58976 - Set of 2
2001^M - 2001
OSRP: $20
GBTru: $28
Paid: $_____

• Limited edition of 25,000.
• 25th Anniversary celebration design.

Mountie

58632
2001 - 2003
OSRP: $24
GBTru: $32
Paid: $_____

• Available only in Canada.

Village Memorial

53028
2002^M - 2003
OSRP: $35
GBTru: $30
Paid: $_____

• Be careful removing from box; the globe is separate.

Halloween Village Express

58634
2002^M - 2002
OSRP: $25
GBTru: $40
Paid: $_____

• Club 56 and Gold Key dealer exclusive.

Christmas Village Express

58635
2002^M - 2002
OSRP: $25
GBTru: $26
Paid: $_____

• Club 56 and Gold Key dealer exclusive.

Village Square Snowman

58638
2002^M - 2002
OSRP: $32.50
GBTru: $33
Paid: $_____

• Limited to year of production.
• Available only at Gold Key dealers.

Valentine Village Express

58639
2002 - 2003
OSRP: $25
GBTru: $25
Paid: $_____

St. Patrick's Village Express

58640
2002 - 2003
OSRP: $25
GBTru: $25
Paid: $_____

Easter Village Express 58641 2002 - 2003 OSRP: $25 GBTru: $30 Paid: $____	**Happy Birthday Village Express**  58642 2002 - 2003 OSRP: $25 GBTru: $28 Paid: $____
Walter's Hot Dog Stand No Photo Available 58643 2002 - N/A OSRP: $45 GBTru: N/A Paid: $____ • This design was never produced.	**Village Square Town Tree** 58644 2002ᴹ - 2003 OSRP: $35 GBTru: $35 Paid: $____ • Limited to year of production.

Use the following space(s) to update your guide when the midyear introductions are announced.

____ - ____
OSRP: $____
GBTru: -
Paid: $____

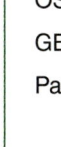

____ - ____
OSRP: $____
GBTru: -
Paid: $____

____ - ____
OSRP: $____
GBTru: -
Paid: $____

Heritage Village

Notes:

Special Designs

It could be argued that all designs are special…and they are. In this case, the reference is to individual pieces or small groupings designed for specific organizations, businesses, or retailers. They are not available to collectors through traditional resources but must be acquired directly from a single source. Although they may be difficult to obtain, virtually every item in this section has been adopted into one or more villages by enthusiastic displayers.

The earliest pieces—the Bachman's Hometown Series—were produced for only a year. They have traits similar to Heritage Village® Collection pieces; in fact one piece served as the mold for a building in the Christmas In The City® Series.

The Profiles Department 56® pieces are manufactured by Department 56 for other corporations to distribute through their own marketing approaches, to stockholders, employees, or the general public.

The National Council of Clubs, an umbrella organization for collectors clubs, has released a number of pieces that have only been available at special events or through local collecting clubs that are affiliated with the national organization.

The largest grouping involves contract arrangements with retailers or companies who have specially designed variations of regular village pieces. At times a single piece has been adapted for a number of retailers; other times only one variation has been created. These unique yet familiar pieces have often found their way into village displays where sometimes they are more appreciated than those they imitated. After all, something different always draws the attention of fellow collectors.

BACHMAN'S HOMETOWN SERIES

This short-lived series was produced for Bachman's of Minneapolis, MN, the original parent company of Department 56. Three buildings were manufactured and distributed, but a fourth, a bookstore, never made it past the drawing board.

Boarding House — 06700

Dates	OSRP	GBTru	Paid
1987 - 1988	$34	$275	$_____

• Inspired by the Sprague House in Red Wing, MN.

Church — 06718

Dates	OSRP	GBTru	Paid
1987 - 1988	$40	$295	$_____

• Designed after a St. Paul, MN church.

Drugstore — 06726

Dates	OSRP	GBTru	Paid
1988 - 1989	$40	$685	$_____

• Same mold as the Christmas In The City 1988 Variety Store And Barber Shop. See the CIC section.
• Inspired by a store in Stillwater, MN.

NATIONAL COUNCIL OF CLUBS (NCC)

The National Council of Clubs is an umbrella organization that dispenses information and advice to local Department 56 collectors' clubs.

Collectors Club House — 54800

Dates	OSRP	GBTru	Paid
1998 - 1998	$56	$135	$_____

- An exclusive for members of National Council of Clubs related collectors clubs, this set was available directly to clubs from Department 56.
- Collectors who purchased the Club House could have decals of their clubs' logos affixed to the signs.
- Set of 2 includes House and man & woman accessory.

Under The NCC Umbrella — See below

Dates	OSRP	GBTru	Paid
2000 - 2001	$20	$65	$_____

- Based on Dickens' Village Under The Bumbershoot, this accessory was sold by the NCC at Dept 56 events.
- Available in 5 colors—yellow (02100), green (02101), red (02102), blue (02103), and silver (02104).

Jack's Umbrella Shop — 05826

Dates	OSRP	GBTru	Paid
2001 - 2002	$56	$140	$_____

- An exclusive for members of National Council of Clubs related collectors clubs, this set was available through member clubs.
- Named after Jack Skeels who envisioned the National Council of Clubs, an organization that would assist and support local clubs.
- Set of 2 includes Shop, "Is It Raining?" accessory, and pin.
- The umbrella stand is very fragile.

PROFILES DEPARTMENT 56®

This is a series produced by Department 56 for use as promotional pieces by other companies. Many collectors, however, have adapted them into some of the Heritage Village Collections®.

Heinz® House — 07826

Dates	OSRP	GBTru	Paid
1996ᴹ - 1996	$28	$70	$_____

- A replica of the home and first Heinz production building, this was given as a gift to Heinz vendors in late 1996 and sold by direct mail to its stockholders in 1997.

State Farm® - Main Street Memories — 56000

Dates	OSRP	GBTru	Paid
1997 - 1997	$35.50	$105	$_____

- Made available to State Farm employees, this building depicts one similar to a Randy Souder painting.
- The gumball machine, broom, and awnings are fragile.
- Spire and sign are separate in box.

Heinz® Grocery Store — 05600

Dates	OSRP	GBTru	Paid
1998 - 1998	$34	$85	$_____

- This corner grocery store was used by Heinz as a gift to Heinz vendors in late 1998 and sold by direct mail to its stockholders in 1999.
- Pickle sign is separate in the box.

Heinz® Hitch — 02291

Dates	OSRP	GBTru	Paid
1999 - 1999	$31	$65	$_____

- Based on The Pumpkin Wagon, this was used by Heinz as a gift to Heinz vendors in late 1999 and sold by direct mail to its stockholders in 2000.

Heinz® Evaporated Horse Radish Factory — 02291

Dates	OSRP	GBTru	Paid
2000 - 2000	$40	$75	$_____

- This design was used by Heinz as a gift to Heinz vendors in late 2000 and sold by direct mail to its stockholders in 2001.

State Farm® - Main Street Fire Station No. 1   05709

Dates	OSRP	GBTru	Paid
2000 - 2000	$37	$100	$_____

- Made available to its employees, this building depicts a similar one in Randy Souder's painting Main Street Memories that was commissioned by State Farm.
- Spire and lamppost are separate in the box.

Heinz® Town Clock   05834

Dates	OSRP	GBTru	Paid
2001ᴹ - 2001	$15	$35	$_____

- This working Clock was used by Heinz as a gift to Heinz vendors in late 2001 and sold by direct mail to its stockholders in 2002.

Wells Fargo® Historic Office   05930

Dates	OSRP	GBTru	Paid
2002ᴹ - 2002	$42.50	$75	$_____

- This building was used by Wells Fargo as a promotional item to celebrate its 150th anniversary.

Spam® Museum   06956

Dates	OSRP	GBTru	Paid
2003ᴹ - 2003	$63.25	$95	$_____

- This building was used by Hormel's Spam division as a promotional item.
- It is a replica of the Spam Museum in Austin, MN.
- Licensed by Hormel Foods Corporation.

Applebee's® Neighborhood Grill & Bar   06230

Dates	OSRP	GBTru	Paid
2004ᴹ - 2004	$25	$200	$_____

- This building was produced exclusively for Applebee's in honor of its 25th anniversary.
- Limited to 4,000 pieces.

MISCELLANEOUS

Designs in this category include those that were made for one retailer or company or a select group of retailers. In almost all instances, they were based on existing pieces.

John Deere® Water Tower 25104

Dates	OSRP	GBTru	Paid
1988 - 1988	$24	$655	$_____

- Produced exclusively for the John Deere catalog.
- The tower reads "Moline Home of John Deere."
- Licensed by Deere & Co.

Bachman's For Sale Sign 05398

Dates	OSRP	GBTru	Paid
1989 - 1989	$4.50	$14	$_____

- This version of the For Sale Sign was produced exclusively for Bachman's of Minneapolis, MN. to sell during its 1990 Village Gathering.

To date 27 versions of the **VILLAGE EXPRESS VAN** have been produced. A green edition in Christmas in the City was one of the regular releases in 1992. That same year a black promotional edition was created, followed by the rarest, a gold version. Seventeen retailers' versions were produced in 1994 and 1995. A silver edition was created in 2001 to celebrate Department 56's 25th anniversary. Several holiday versions are recent additions.

Village Express Van - Black 9951

Dates	OSRP	GBTru	Paid
1992 - 1992	Promotional	$50	$_____

- This van was originally given to Department 56 sales representatives as a gift at their National Sales conference in 1992. It was later used as a special event piece at the 1993 Bachman's Village Gathering.

Village Express Van - Gold 9977

Dates	OSRP	GBTru	Paid
1993 - 1993	Promotional	$475	$_____

- Packed in a special gold box, this promotional "Road Show" edition was presented to potential investors before the company's initial public offering.

Village Express Van - Gatherings   See below

Dates	OSRP	GBTru	Paid
1994 - 1994	$25	See below	

- The right side of each van features the Department 56 logo. The left side has the specific retailer's logo. 14 vans were produced—13 for Department 56 sponsored Village Gatherings and one for The Lemon Tree which sold it to its Collector's Club members.

Item #	Van	GBTru	Paid
07293	Bachman's	**$40**	$____
07374	Bronner's	**$35**	$____
07307	Christmas Dove	**$40**	$____
07390	European Imports	**$40**	$____
07358	Fortunoff	**$60**	$____
07323	Incredible Christmas	**$40**	$____
07218	Lemon Tree	**$35**	$____
07331	Limited Edition	**$40**	$____
07315	Lock, Stock & Barrel	**$40**	$____
07366	North Pole City	**$35**	$____
07340	Robert's	**$38**	$____
07412	Stat's	**$30**	$____
07382	William Glen	**$35**	$____
07404	Windsor Shoppe	**$35**	$____

Village Express Van   See below

Dates	OSRP	GBTru	Paid
1995 - 1995	See below	See below	

- The Parkwest van was a gift to retailers who were members of the Parkwest catalog group. It features the Department 56 logo on the right side, and Parkwest's logo on the left side.
- St. Nick's van features the Department 56 logo on the right side and its logo on the left.
- The Canadian van was produced for retailers in Canada. It features the Department 56 logo on the right side, and a red maple leaf on the left side.

Item #	Van	OSRP	GBTru	Paid
07522	Parkwest	**Promo**	$325	$____
07560	St. Nick's	$25	$38	$____
21637	Canadian	$40	$40	$____

Squash Cart   07536

Dates	OSRP	GBTru	Paid
1995ᴹ - 1995	$50	$80	$____

- Produced exclusively for Bachman's of Minneapolis, MN, this commemorated the company's 110th anniversary and notes this with a bottomstamp. It was first sold at the 1995 Bachman's Village Gathering.

A Visit With Santa

See below

Dates	OSRP	GBTru	Paid
1995 - 1995	$25	See below	

- Eight stores had this piece personalized with their names and choice of colors for the packages.

Item #	Store	GBTru	Paid
07544	Bachman's	$40	$_____
07676	Fortunoff	$40	$_____
07684	Lemon Tree	$30	$_____
07641	Limited Edition	$40	$_____
07730	Pine Cone Christmas	$35	$_____
07650	Stat's	$30	$_____
07668	William Glen	$35	$_____
07692	Young's Ltd.	$30	$_____

Here Comes Santa

See below

Dates	OSRP	GBTru	Paid
1996 - 1996	$25	See below	

- 24 stores had this piece personalized with their names on the banner. One store, Bachman's, had "Joy to the World" on the banner.

Item #	Store	GBTru	Paid
07744	Bachman's	$40	$_____
07745	Bronner's	$40	$_____
07748	Broughton Christmas	$30	$_____
07752	Cabbage Rose	$35	$_____
07753	Calabash Nautical Gifts	$40	$_____
07751	Calico Butterfly	$35	$_____
07763	Carson Pirie Scott	$35	$_____
07755	Christmas Loft	$35	$_____
07750	Dickens' Gift Shoppe	$40	$_____
07762	European Imports	$40	$_____
07747	Fibber Magee's	$35	$_____
07741	Fortunoff	$45	$_____
07759	Gustaf's	$35	$_____
07754	Ingle's Nook	$40	$_____
07746	Limited Edition	$40	$_____
07742	North Pole City	$40	$_____
07740	Pine Cone Christmas	$35	$_____
07760	Royal Dutch Collectibles	$30	$_____
07756	Russ Country Gardens	$30	$_____
07757	St. Nick's	$40	$_____
07758	Seventh Avenue	$35	$_____
07749	Stat's	$30	$_____
07743	William Glen	$40	$_____
07761	Young's Ltd.	$35	$_____

St. Nick's Pick-up And Delivery   07821

Dates	OSRP	GBTru	Paid
1996^M - 1996	$10	$20	$_____

- Limited to 1,080 pieces, this personalized version of the Snow Village piece was produced exclusively for St. Nick's of Littleton, Co.

Bachman's Flower Shop   08802

Dates	OSRP	GBTru	Paid
1997^M - 1997	$50	$85	$_____

- A personalized version of the Snow Village Secret Garden Florist, this was produced exclusively for Bachman's of Minneapolis, MN and was first sold at its 1997 Village Gathering.

Bachman's Wilcox Truck   08803

Dates	OSRP	GBTru	Paid
1997^M - 1997	$30	$40	$_____

- A personalized version of the Heritage Village Poinsettia Truck, this replica of a Bachman's 1919 Wilcox was produced exclusively for Bachman's of Minneapolis, MN and was sold at its 1997 Gathering.

Lionel® Electric Train Shop   02202

Dates	OSRP	GBTru	Paid
1998^M - 1998	$55	$180	$_____

- Limited to 5,000, this personalized Snow Village design was produced exclusively for Allied Model Trains of Culver City, CA. 1946 is the year Allied opened, and 4411 is its actual street number. Licensed by Lionel.

Bachman's Greenhouse   02203

Dates	OSRP	GBTru	Paid
1998^M - 1998	$60	$70	$_____

- A personalized version of the Snow Village Secret Garden Greenhouse, this was produced exclusively for Bachman's of Minneapolis, MN and was first sold at its 1998 Village Gathering.

Say It With Flowers   02204

Dates	OSRP	GBTru	Paid
1998^M - 1998	$30	$45	$_____

- A personalized version of the Snow Village Christmas Visit To The Florist, this set was produced exclusively for Bachman's of Minneapolis, MN and was first sold at its 1998 Village Gathering.

Special Designs

Bachman's Tending The Cold Frame — 02208

Dates	OSRP	GBTru	Paid
1998^M - 1998	$35	$45	$____

• This personalized version of the Dickens' Village Tending The Cold Frame was produced exclusively for Bachman's of Minneapolis, MN and was first sold at its 1998 Village Gathering.

North Pole City's Father Christmas's Journey — 02244

Dates	OSRP	GBTru	Paid
1998^M - 1998	$30	$40	$____

• This personalized version of the Dickens' Village design was produced exclusively for North Pole City of Oklahoma City, OK to honor its 10th anniversary.

William Glen Delivery Truck — 02300

Dates	OSRP	GBTru	Paid
1998^M - 1998	$37.50	$40	$____

• This personalized version of the Heritage Village Poinsettia Delivery Truck was produced exclusively for William Glen of Sacramento, CA and was first sold at its 1998 Village Gathering.

Lord & Taylor Delivery Wagon — 07880

Dates	OSRP	GBTru	Paid
1998^M - 1998	$32.50	$45	$____

• This personalized version of the Dickens' Village Fezziwig Delivery Wagon was produced exclusively for Lord & Taylor department stores.

Lord & Taylor Flower Cart — 02250

Dates	OSRP	GBTru	Paid
1999^M - 1999	$27.50	$40	$____

• This personalized version of the Dickens' Village Chelsea Market Flower Monger & Cart was produced exclusively for Lord & Taylor department stores.

William Glen Grocery Delivery — 02413

Dates	OSRP	GBTru	Paid
1999 - 1999	$18	$35	$____

• This personalized version of the Christmas In The City Johnson's Delivery Wagon was produced exclusively for William Glen of Sacramento, CA and was first sold at its 1999 Village Gathering.

Bachman's Original Homestead, 1885 — 02255

Dates	OSRP	GBTru	Paid
1999^M - 1999	$75	$105	$_____

- Limited to 7,500, it is the first numbered limited edition Snow Village design. Inspired by a Bachman family home, it was sold as a commemorative piece during the 1999 Bachman's Village Gathering.

Lilac City Water Tower — 02423

Dates	OSRP	GBTru	Paid
1999 - 2000	$40	$65	$_____

- Limited to 500 pieces. Produced exclusively for Lock, Stock And Barrel of Rochester, NY.
- The tower reads "Lilac City… Rochester, New York, Incorporated 1834."

William Glen Taxi — 02270

Dates	OSRP	GBTru	Paid
2000^M - 2000	$12.50	$20	$_____

- This personalized version of the Christmas In The City City Taxi was produced exclusively for William Glen of Sacramento, CA and was first sold at its 2000 Village Gathering.

Feeney's Delivery Of Dreams — 02272

Dates	OSRP	GBTru	Paid
2000^M - 2000	$12.50	$20	$_____

- This personalized version of the Christmas In The City City Taxi was produced exclusively for Feeney's of Feasterville, PA.

Lord & Taylor Hot Air Balloon 2000 — 02440

Dates	OSRP	GBTru	Paid
2000^M - 2000	$40	$45	$_____

- This personalized version of North Pole Dash Away Delivery was produced exclusively for Lord & Taylor department stores.
- The basket often comes unglued from the base.

Town Tree Carolers — 05702

Dates	OSRP	GBTru	Paid
2000^M - 2000	$65	$105	$_____

- Produced exclusively for NALED/Parkwest dealers.
- Set of 6 includes tree, set of 3 carolers, lampposts, and bench.
- Battery/adapter operated.

Special Designs

Village Express Van - Silver 52911

Dates	OSRP	GBTru	Paid
2001ᴹ - 2001	$25	$60	$_____

- Special issue for Department 56's silver anniversary.
- Only available at that event.

25th Anniversary Village Footbridge 52910

Dates	OSRP	GBTru	Paid
2001ᴹ - 2001	$15	$30	$_____

- Special issue for Department 56's silver anniversary.
- Only available at that event.

Toys For Tots 05746

Dates	OSRP	GBTru	Paid
2001ᴹ - 2001	$50	$80	$_____

- Produced exclusively for the Carson Pirie Scott department stores.

Feeney's Our Sign For All Seasons 05832

Dates	OSRP	GBTru	Paid
2001ᴹ - 2001	$15	$18	$_____

- This personalized version of the Village Sign And Bench was produced exclusively for Feeney's of Feasterville, PA.

Wegmans Delivery Wagon 05838

Dates	OSRP	GBTru	Paid
2001ᴹ - 2001	$22.50	$35	$_____

- Based on Christmas In The City Johnson's Delivery Wagon, this piece was produced exclusively for Lock, Stock And Barrel of Rochester, NY. It features the name of a well known regional grocery chain.

Feeney's Anniversary Lamppost 06001

Dates	OSRP	GBTru	Paid
2002ᴹ - 2002	$5	$12	$_____

- This personalized Lamppost was produced exclusively for Feeney's of Feasterville, PA.

Bronner's Custom Building

Dates	OSRP	GBTru	Paid
2004ᴹ - 2004	$80	$80	$_____

• This personalized building was produced exclusively for Bronner's Christmas Wonderland in Frankenmuth, MI.

Frango Chocolate Shop — 06300

Dates	OSRP	GBTru	Paid
2004ᴹ - 2004	$65	$75	$_____

• This building was produced exclusively for the Marshall Field's stores in honor of the chocolates that are sold only in its stores.

Frangos For You And I — 06301

Dates	OSRP	GBTru	Paid
2004ᴹ - 2004	$15	$20	$_____

• This accessory was produced exclusively for the Marshall Field's stores in honor of the chocolates that are sold only in its stores.

Special Designs

ALLIED MODEL TRAINS DEPARTMENT 56 TRAINS

Allied Model Trains, one of the largest model train stores in the world, has produced a unique train set that has become highly collectible. Manufactured by Lionel Trains, each car features village-related artwork.

Snow Village Box Car

Dates	OSRP	GBTru	Paid
1995 - 1995	$45	$85	$_____

• Limited Edition of 5,000.
• Produced by Lionel Trains.
• Licensed by Department 56.

Special Designs

Heritage Village Box Car

Dates	OSRP	GBTru	Paid
1996 - 1996	$50	$75	$_____

- Limited Edition of 5,000.
- Produced by Lionel Trains.
- Licensed by Department 56.

Department 56 Caboose

Dates	OSRP	GBTru	Paid
1997 - 1997	$60	$95	$_____

- Limited Edition of 3,000.
- Produced by Lionel Trains.
- Licensed by Department 56.

Holly Bros. Tank Car

Dates	OSRP	GBTru	Paid
1998 - 1998	$60	$80	$_____

- Limited Edition of 3,000.
- Produced by Lionel Trains.
- Licensed by Department 56.

Department 56 Locomotive

Dates	OSRP	GBTru	Paid
1999 - 1999	$380	$610	$_____

- Limited Edition of 1,717.
- Includes tender.
- Produced by Lionel Trains.
- Licensed by Department 56.

Real Plastic Snow Hopper

Dates	OSRP	GBTru	Paid
2000 - 2000	$60	$75	$_____

- Limited Edition of 3,000.
- Produced by Lionel Trains.
- Licensed by Department 56.

Happy Holidays Gondola

Dates	OSRP	GBTru	Paid
2001 - 2001	$50	$65	$_____

- Limited Edition of 3,000.
- Produced by Lionel Trains.
- Licensed by Department 56.

General Village Accessories

Items in this category are designed to accompany virtually any village. They are the final decorating touches that add character to a scene, or help to bring it to life. In this guide these accessories have been divided into five categories:

TREES: You can never have too many trees, and virtually all of them are here. A few, like Bethlehem's palm trees and the porcelain pieces can be found elsewhere, but all the other trees, shrubs, and hedges are in this section. If it's a tree—even if it lights—it's found in this category, not under the "Electrical" section.

ELECTRICAL: Both the pieces on display and the cords, bulbs, adapters, and multiple plugs that activate them are found under "Electrical." This includes all animated pieces, trains, Brite Lites, streetlights, and colored lights. The sole exception is trees with lights, which may be found in the "Trees" category.

FENCES, GATES, AND WALLS: With the exception of a few porcelain pieces, all the boundary markers and their entrances are located in this section.

SNOW AND ICE: The final finishing touches to every winter village are located in this frosty area.

MISCELLANEOUS: If it didn't appear in any of the above sections—and it's not made of porcelain or ceramic, this is the catchall category where you'll find roads, mountains, trim pieces, bridges, resin animals, and Mill Creek pieces.

Those General Village Accessories that have unique application to North Pole or Halloween displays are listed in separate color-coded pages at the conclusion of this section.

TREES
TREES
TREES
TREES
TREES
TREES
TREES
TREES

Photo Not Available

Spruce Forest
$90   65943
1987 - 1990

Spruce Tree With Wooden Base, Sm
$3.50   65951
1987 - 1995

Spruce Tree With Wooden Base, Med
$5   65978
1987 - 1995

Spruce Tree With Wooden Base, Lg
$7   65986
1987 - 1995

Christmas Wreaths
$5   51110
1988 - 1991

Frosted Topiary Village Garden
$16   51152
1988 - 1990

Sisal Topiary Garden
$50   51853
1988 - 1992

Frosted Cone Tree w/Wood Base, Lg
$10   51934
1988 - 1989

Frosted Norway Pines
$12   51756
1989 - 1998

Winter Oak Tree With 2 Red Birds
$16   51845
1989 - 1990

Photo Not Available

Sisal Topiary, Lg
N/A   51861
1989 - 1989

Photo Not Available

Sisal Topiary, Med
N/A   51870
1989 - 1989

Photo Not Available

Sisal Topiary, Sm
N/A   51888
1989 - 1989

Photo Not Available

Sisal Topiary, Mini
N/A   51896
1989 - 1989

Potted Topiary Pair
$5   51922
1989 - 1994

Frosted Topiary Trees, S/2
$12   52000
1989 - 1999

Frosted Topiary, s/4
$10   52019
1989 - 1999

Frosted Topiary, s/8, Lg
$12   52027
1989 - 1999

Frosted Topiary, s/8 Sm
$7.50   52035
1989 - 1999

Mini Spruce Forest
$50   65790
1989 - 1990

Winter Oak, Sm
$4.50   51810
1990 - 1994

Winter Oak, Lg
$8   51829
1990 - 1994

Sisal Trees, s/7
$16   51837
1990 - 1990

Frosted Evergreen
Papier-Maché, s/3
$16   65820
1990 - 1996

Evergreen Trees
$13   52051
1991 - 1997

Sisal Wreaths
$4   54194
1991 - 1998

Winter Birch Tree
$12.50   52167
1993 - 1996

Pine Cone Trees
$15   52213
1993 - 1995

Frosted Spruce Tree
15"
$12.50   52310
1994 - 1996

Frosted Spruce Tree
22"
$27.50   52329
1994 - 1996

Bare Branch Tree
With 25 Lights
$13.50   52434
1994 - 2001

Pencil Pines
$15   52469
1994 - 1998

Autumn Maple Tree
$15   52540
1994 - 1997

Frosted Bare Branch
Tree, Sm
$6.50   52418
1995 - 1996

Frosted Bare Branch
Tree, Lg
$12.50   52426
1995 - 1996

Spruce Tree Forest
$25   52485
1995 - 1996

Frosted Zig–Zag
Tree, White
$15   52493
1995 - 1996

Frosted Zig–Zag
Tree, Green
$15   52507
1995 - 1996

Snowy White Pine
Tree, Sm
$15   52558
1995 - 1996

General Village Accessories

Snowy White Pine Tree, Lg
$20   52566
1995 - 1996

Landscape
$16.50   52590
1995 -

Flexible Sisal Hedge
$7.50   52596
1995 - 2001ᴹ

Hybrid Landscape
$35   52600
1995 -

Lighted Snowcapped Revolving Tree
$35   52603
1995 - 1997

Lighted Snowcapped Trees
$45   52604
1995 - 1997

Frosted Fir Trees
$15   52605
1995 - 1998

Cedar Pine Forest
$15   52606
1995 - 1998

Ponderosa Pines
$13   52607
1995 - 1998

Arctic Pines
$12   52608
1995 - 1998

Fallen Leaves
$5   52610
1995 -

Snowy Evergreen Trees, Sm
$8.50   52612
1995 - 2000

Snowy Evergreen Trees, Med
$25   52613
1995 -

Snowy Evergreen Trees, Lg
$32.50   52614
1995 - 2001

Snowy Scotch Pines
$15   52615
1995 -

Autumn Trees
$13.50   52616
1995 - 1998

Wagon Wheel Pine Grove
$22.50   52617
1995 - 1998

Pine Point Pond
$37.50   52618
1995 - 1999

Double Pine Trees
$13.50   52619
1995 - 1998

Jack Pines
$18   52620
1996 -

Bare Branch Trees
$22.50 52623
1996 -

Holly Tree
$10 52630
1996 - 2000

Birch Tree Cluster
$20 52631
1996 - 2001

Towering Pines
$13.50 52632
1996 - 1999

Winter Birch
$22.50 52636
1996 -

Frosted Spruce
$25 52637
1996 -

Frosted Hemlock Trees
$32.50 52638
1996 - 1998

Town Tree
$35 52639
1996 -

Autumn Birch/Maple Trees
$27.50 52655
1997 -

Wintergreen Pines, s/3
$7.50 52660
1997 -

Wintergreen Pines, s/2
$15 52661
1997 - 2003

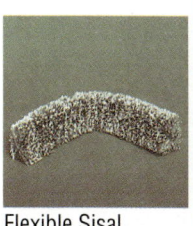
Flexible Sisal Hedge, Lg
$10 52662
1997 -

Lighted Snowy Tree
$27.50 52683
1997 - 2000

Lighted Christmas Tree
$48 52690
1997 - 1998

Flexible Autumn Hedges
$10 52703
1998 - 2000

Decorated Sisal Trees
$12.50 52714
1998 - 2001

Craggy Oak Tree
$12.50 52748
1998 - 2001

Swinging Under The Old Oak Tree
$30 52769
1998 - 2001ᴹ

Pine Trees With Pine Cones
$15 52771
1998 - 2001

Winter Pine Trees With Pine Cones
$15 52772
1998 - 2001

General Village Accessories

General Village Accessories

Flocked Pine Trees.
s/3
$15   53367
1998 - 2000

Twinkling Tip Tree
$17.50   52781
1999 - 2001

Pequot Pines
$50   52818
1999 -

Pequot Pine, XLg
$32.50   52819
1999 -

Twinkling Lit Town Tree
$35   52837
1999 - 2001

Frosted Topiaries
$40   52842
1999 - 2001

Frosted Shrubbery
$20   52843
1999 - 2001

Frosty Light Trees
$20   52844
1999 - 2001

Up In The Apple Tree
$27.50   56640
1999 - 2000

Flocked Pine Trees, s/2
$16   56715
1999 - 2001

Icicle Trees
$27.50   56722
1999 - 2001

Twinkling Lit Trees, White
$32.50   56723
1999 - 2001[M]

Twinkling Lit Shrubs, White
$15   56724
1999 - 2001[M]

Twinkling Lit Trees, Green
$32.50   52823
1999 -

Twinkling Lit Shrubs, Green
$15   52824
1999 -

Celebration Tree 2000
$30   52856
2000[M] -

Pinewood Trees, Lg
$17   56924
2000[M] - 2002

Pinewood Trees, Sm
$13.50   56925
2000[M] - 2002

Natural Evergreens, s/8
$24   52885
2000 -

Natural Evergreens s/16
$45   52886
2000 - 2003

Fiber Optic Trees
$17.50   52888
2000 - 2002

Icy Trees, Sm
$17.50   52889
2000 - 2003

Icy Trees, Med
$25   52890
2000 - 2003

Icy Tree, Lg
$27.50   52891
2000 - 2002

Winter Green Spruce
$17   52892
2000 - 2001

Landscape Starter Set
$6.50   52898
2000 -

Holly Topiaries
$12.50   52899
2000 - 2002

Holly Hedges
$15   52900
2000 - 2003

Holly Tree & Bush
$10   52901
2000 - 2001

Metal Bare Branch Trees
$25   52931
2001ᴹ - 2002

Village Twinkle Brite Tree, Lg
$22.50   52301
2001 -

City Lit Bare Branch Tree
$12.50   52973
2001 -

Village Spring/Summer Trees, s/4
$22.50   52974
2001 -

Village Autumn Trees, s/4
$22.50   52975
2001 -

Village Winter Trees, s/4
$22.50   52976
2001 -

Village Twinkle Brite Tree, Sm
$17.50   52983
2001 -

Fiber Optic Woods, Green Trees
$48   52985
2001 - 2004

Fiber Optic Woods, White Trees
$48   52986
2001 - 2003

Bag-O-Frosted Topiaries, s/10
$8.50   52996
2001 -

Fiber Optic Woods Grn Trees/Multi-lights
$48   53001
2001 - 2003

General Village Accessories

Tinsel Trees, s/4
$15   53012
2001 -

Bag-O-Frosted Topiaries, s/2
$6.50   53018
2001 -

Acrylic Green Glitter Trees, s/3
$25   53032
2002ᴹ -

Lighted Acrylic Trees, s/2
$25   5303
2002ᴹ - 2003

Ice Crystal Pines, s/3
$50   53081
2002 -

Lighted Crystal Pines, s/3
$75   53083
2002 - 2004

Spring Oaks, s/2
$17.50   53084
2002 -

Village Frosted Spruce, Small, s/3
$20   5308
2002 -

Fall Oaks, s/2
$17.50   53086
2002 -

Willow Trees, s/2
$17.50   53134
2003 -

Lighted Street Boulevard
$17.50   53137
2003 -

Twisty Glitter Pine
$22.50   531
2004 -

Christmas In The Forest
$25   53178
2004 -

Classic Tinsel Trees - Red, Green, Silver
$10   53192
2004 -

Lighted Christmas Bare Branch Tree
$15   53193
2004 -

Lighted Peppermi Tree
$30   531
2004 -

Urban Landscape Set
$35   53197
2004 -

Classic Tinsel Trees - White
$10   53207
2004 -

ELECTRICAL
ELECTRICAL
ELECTRICAL
ELECTRICAL
ELECTRICAL
ELECTRICAL
ELECTRICAL
ELECTRICAL
ELECTRICAL

Multi Color 10 Light Set
N/A   36323
1987 - 1989

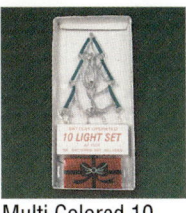
Multi Colored 10 Light Set
N/A   36331
1987 - 1989

Amber 10 Light Set
N/A   36358
1987 - 1989

Street Lamps
10   36366
1987 - 2000

Village Express Train - Black
$90   59978
1987 - 1988

Village Express Train - Red, Green
$95   59803
1988 - 1996

Streetlamp Wrapped In Garland
$10   59935
1988 - 1988

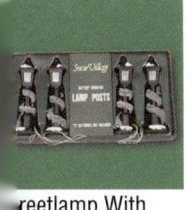
Streetlamp With Garland
$8   59943
1988 - 1988

Replacement Light Bulb
$2.50   99002
1988 - 1990

Single Cord Set
$3.50   99028
1988 -

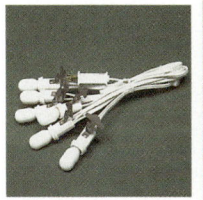
6 Socket Lite Set
$13   99279
1988 -

Traffic Light
$10   55000
1989 - 2001

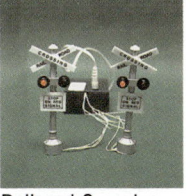
Railroad Crossing Sign
$10   55018
1989 - 2000

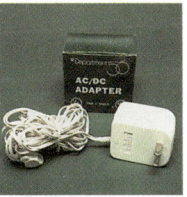
AC/DC Adapter
$10   55026
1989 -

Old World Streetlamp
$22   55034
1989 - 1991

Turn Of The Century Lamppost
$ 55042
1989 -

Turn Of The Century Lamppost
$22   55050
1989 - 1991

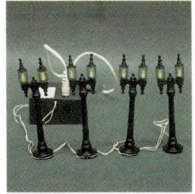
Double Street Lamps
$13   59960
1989 -

Candles By The Doorstep
$7   52060
1990 - 1994

General Village Accessories

General Village Accessories

Battery Operated Light
$2.50   99260
1990 - 1991

Lights Out Remote Control
$25   52132
1991 - 1994

Mini Lights
$12.50   52159
1991 - 2000

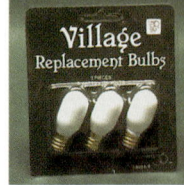
Replacement Light Bulbs
$2.50   9924
1991 -

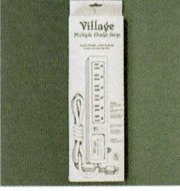
Multi-Outlet Plug Strip, 6 Outlets
$10   99333
1991 -

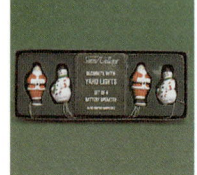
Yard Lights
$13   54160
1992 - 1994

I Love My Village Brite Lites
$15   52221
1993 - 1997

Merry Christmas Brite Lites
$13.50   5222
1993 - 2000

Reindeer Brite Lites
$10   52248
1993 - 1999

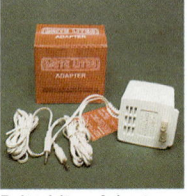
Brite Lites Adapter
$10   52256
1993 -

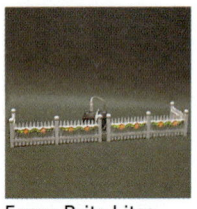
Fence Brite Lites
$19   52361
1993 - 1999

Snowman Brite Lites
$15   523
1993 - 1999

Tree Brite Lites
$10   52388
1993 - 1999

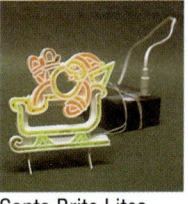
Santa Brite Lites
$15   52396
1993 - 1999

Department 56 Brite Lites
$10   98469
1993 - 1997

Animated Skating Pond
$60   522
1994 -

Streetcar
$65   52400
1994 - 1998

Waving Flag Brite Lites
$15   52442
1994 - 1997

Set of 20 Red Lights Brite Lites
$9   52450
1994 - 1997

Animated All Around The Park
$95   52
1994 - 1996

Coca-Cola Neon Sign
$16.50   54828
1994 - 1998

Let It Snow Machine
$85   52592
1995 - 1997

Up, Up & Away
$40   52593
1996 - 2001

Spotlight
$7   52611
1996 - 2000

Mini Lights
10   52626
1996 - 1998

Boulevard
Lampposts
$15   52627
1996 -

Country Road
Lampposts, s/2
$12   52628
1996 - 1997

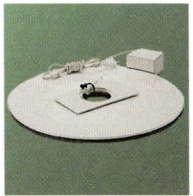
Revolving Turntable
$50   52640
1996 - 1999

Animated Ski
Mountain
75   52641
1996 - 1998

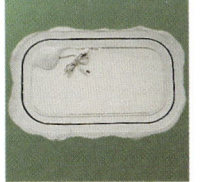
Animated
Accessory Track
$65   52642
1996 - 1999

Waterfall W/Electric
Pump
$65   52644
1996 - 1999

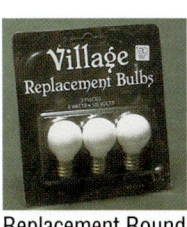
Replacement Round
Light Bulbs
$2   99245
1996 -

ED Light Bulb
.50   99247
96 - 2000

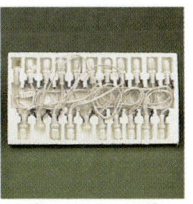
20 Socket Light Set
With Bulbs
$25   99278
1996 -

Animated Sledding
Hill
$65   52645
1997 -

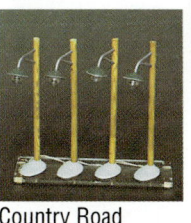
Country Road
Lampposts, s/4
$15   52663
1997 - 2001

ndy Canes Brite
es
              52670
7 - 1999

Angel Brite Lites
$15   52671
1997 - 1999

Snow Dragon Brite
Lites
$20   52672
1997 - 1999

Santa In Chimney
Brite Lites
$15   52673
1997 - 1999

General Village Accessories

General Village Accessories

Candles Brite Lites
$17 52674
1997 - 1999

Holly Archway Brite Lites
$25 52675
1997 - 1999

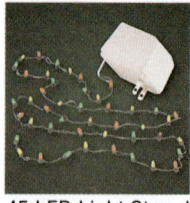
45 LED Light Strand
$22.50 52678
1997 -

Lighted Christmas Pole
$32.50 52679
1997 - 2000

Road Construction Sign
$12 52680
1997 - 2001ᴹ

Walkway Lights
$12 52681
1997 - 2000

Frosty Light Sprays
$12 52682
1997 - 1999

String Of Starry Lights
$12.50 5268
1997 - 2000

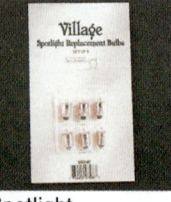
Spotlight Replacement Bulbs
$2.50 99246
1997 - 2000

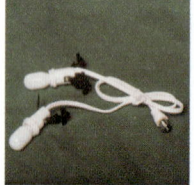
Double Light Socket Adapter
$4 99280
1997 -

Camden Park Fountain
$84 52705
1998 - 2000

Carnival Carousel LED Light Set
$20 5270
1998 - 2001

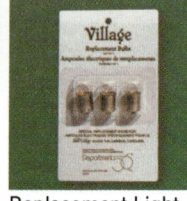
Replacement Light Bulb, Clear
$3 52707
1998 -

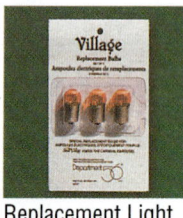
Replacement Light Bulb, Yellow
$3 52708
1998 -

Village Express Electric Train Set
$270 52710
1998 -

Christmas Luminaries
$15 527
1998 - 2002

Fireworks
$25 52727
1998 - 2004

String Of 25 Mini LED Lights
$10 52728
1998 -

Biplane Up In The Sky
$50 52731
1998 - 2000

Ski Slope
$75 527
1998 -

Railroad Lamps
$15   52760
1998 - 2001ᴹ

String Of Spotlights
$15   52779
1998 - 2002

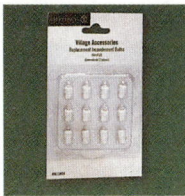
Replacement Incandescent Bulbs
$4   13638
1999 -

Animated Photo With Santa
$90   52790
1999 - 2001ᴹ

Through The Woods Mountain Trail
$75   52791
1999 - 2003

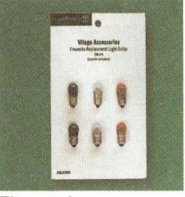
Fireworks Replacement Bulbs
$3.50   52800
1999 - 2004

Remote Switches, Right & Left
$20   52807
1999 -

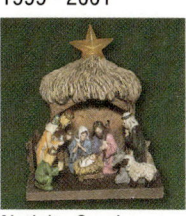
Nativity Creche
$20   52822
1999 -

Fieldstone Footbridge
$40   52827
1999 -

Frosted Fountain
$20   52831
1999 -

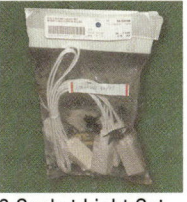
3 Socket Light Set
$7.50   52835
1999 -

Stadium Lights
$22.50   52845
1999 -

Bumper Fun Ride
$78   52500
2000ᴹ - 2002

Look, It's The Goodyear Blimp
$45   52501
2000ᴹ - 2001

Santa's On His Way
$65   52502
2000ᴹ -

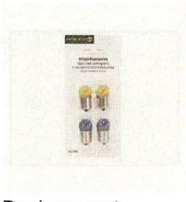
Replacement Lightning Bulbs
$3   52846
2000ᴹ -

Electric Foam Cutter
$25   52847
2000ᴹ -

Light Adapter for NPW
$5   52852
2000ᴹ - 2000

Light Adapter With 3 Jacks for NPW
$6   52853
2000ᴹ - 2002

Mill Falls Working Waterfall
$75   52503
2000 -2001

General Village Accessories

General Village Accessories

Holiday Singers
$75   52505
2000 -

Festive Front Yard
$75   52506
2000 -

Perfect Putt
$65   52508
2000 - 2001

Woodland Carousel
$75   52509
2000 - 2001

Village Junkyard
$85   52861
2000 - 2004

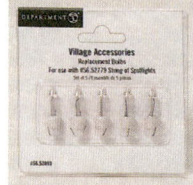
Repl Bulbs For 52779 String Of Spotlights
$15   52893
2000 - 2002

Repl Flickering Bulb For Creepy Creek Hs
$5   52904
2000 -

Santa's Sleigh
$68   58630
2000 -

Gondola Animated Scene
$85   52511
2001[M] -

Santa By The Light of The Moon
$37.50   52984
2001 - 2003

Hockey Practice, s/3
$37.50   52512
2001 -

Valentine's Decorating Set, s/5
$22.50   53020
2002[M] - 2004

Easter Decorating Set, s/5
$22.50   53021
2002[M] - 2004

St. Patrick's Day Decorating Set, s/5
$22.50   53022
2002[M] - 2004

4th Of July Decorating Set, s/5
$22.50   53024
2002[M] - 2004

Sounds Of The North Woods
$85   53013
2002[M] -

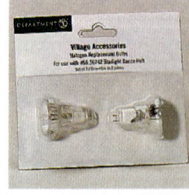
Repl. Halogen Bulb Starlight Dance Hall
$4   53027
2002[M] -

Packages Delivery
$50   53038
2002 - 2004

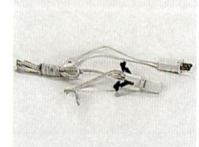
Replacement Aux. Cord With Light
$4.50   53039
2002 -

Snowflake Light Poles, s/4
$17.50   53039
2002 -

String Of 12
Snowman Lights
$10   53053
2002 - 2004

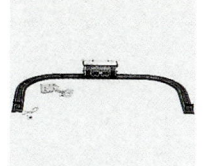
City Trolley, s/6
$75   53054
2002 - 2004

Lighted Tiered
Platform
$250   53089
2002 - 2004

Sounds Of The City
$65   53111
2003 -

Replacement 3 Volt
Light Bulb, s/2
$4   53121
2003 -

String Of 12
Snowflake Lights
$10   53122
2003 -

String Of 12 Santa
Lights
$10   53123
2003 -

Year Round Lighted
Lawn Orns , s/6
$20   53125
2003 -

Village Twinkling
Snow Tree Skirt
$30   53152
2003 - 2004

Village Twinkling
Blanket Of Snow
$30   53153
2003 -

Let's Swing!
$30   53154
2004ᴹ -

Replacement 12
Volt Light Bulbs
$4   53161
2004 -

Clearing The
Driveway Again!
$ 53184
2004 -

Figure Skater On Ice
$35   53185
2004 -

Winter Sled Ride
$40   53186
2004 -

String Of 12 Christmas
Candy Lights
$10   53187
2004 -

String of 12 Christmas
Ornaments Lights
$ 53188
2004 -

Snowman Street
Lights
$17   53189
2004 -

Christmas Star
Street Lights
$15   53190
2004 -

Vintage Christmas
Lights Street Lights
$15   53191
2004 -

General Village Accessories

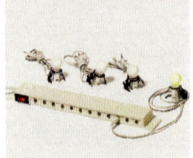

Multi-Building
Lighting System
$35   53204
2004 -

WALLS
FENCES
GATES
WALLS
FENCES
GATES
WALLS
FENCES
GATES

White Picket Fence
$3   51004
1987 - 2000

White Picket Fence s/4
$12   51012
1987 - 1997

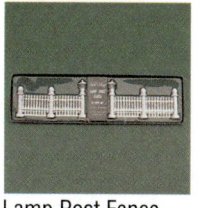
Lamp Post Fence
$13   55069
1989 - 1991

Lamp Post Fence
$13   55077
1989 - 1989

Lamp Post Fence Extension
$10   55085
1989 - 1991

Lamp Post Extension
$10   55093
1989 - 1989

Wrought Iron Fence
$2.50 each   59986
1989 - 1998

General Village Accessories

ow Fence
52043
91 - 1998

Frosty Tree-Lined Picket Fence
$6.50   52078
1991 - 1997

Tree-Lined Courtyard Fence
$4   52124
1990 - 1998

Wrought Iron Gate And Fence
$15   55140
1991 - 1998

ught Iron Fence nsions
.50   55158
1 - 1998

Wrought Iron Fence
$10   59994
1991 - 1999

Courtyard Fence With Steps
$4   52205
1992 - 1998

Chain Link Fence With Gate
$12   52345
1993 - 1998

in Link Fence nsions
52353
3 - 1998

Victorian Wrought Iron Fence w/Gate
$15   52523
1994 - 2001^M

Victorian Wrought Iron Fence Extension
$15   52531
1994 - 2001^M

Split Rail Fence, With Mailbox
$12.50   52597
1995 - 1997

Twig Snow Fence,
Wood
$6   52598
1995 - 2000

White Picket Fence
With Gate
$10   52624
1996 - 1998

White Picket Fence
Extensions
$10   52625
1996 - 1998

Stone Wall
$2.50   52629
1996 -

Stone Curved
Wall/Bench
$15   52650
1997 - 2001

Snow Fence
$7   52657
1997 -

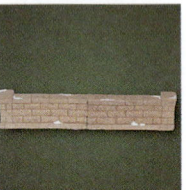

Camden Park
Square Stone Wall
$2.50   52689
1997 - 2000

Fieldstone Wall
$3.50   52717
1998 -

Fieldstone Entry
Gate
$10   52718
1998 - 2001 M

Holly Split Rail
Fence
$18   52722
1998 - 2001

Holly Split Rail Fence
w/Seated Children
$13.50   52723
1998 - 2001

Stone Wall With
Sisal Hedge
$5   52724
1998 - 2001

Corral Fence
$32   52746
1998 - 2001

Fieldstone Wall
With Apple Tree
$25   52768
1998 - 2001 M

Ice Crystal Gate &
Walls
$32.50   56716
1999 - 2002

Ice Crystal Walls
$15   56717
1999 - 2001

Tall Stone Walls
$20   52825
1999 -

Fieldstone Curved
Wall/Bench, s/4
$15   53009
2001 -

SNOW & ICE
SNOW & ICE
SNOW & ICE
SNOW & ICE
SNOW & ICE
SNOW & ICE
SNOW & ICE
SNOW & ICE
SNOW & ICE

Real Plastic Snow
7 oz. Bag
$3   49981
1977 -

Real Plastic Snow
2 lb. Box
$10   49999
1977 - 2000

Acrylic Icicles
$4.50   52116
1990 - 2000

Blanket Of New
Fallen Snow
$7.50   49956
1991 -

Let It Snow
Crystals, 8 oz. Box
$6.50   49964
1991 - 1992

Fresh Fallen Snow
7 oz. Bag
$3.20   49979
1995 -

Fresh Fallen Snow
2 lb. Box
$12   49980
1995 - 2000

Clear Ice
$6.50   52729
1998 - 2001^M

Glistening Snow
$10   53362
1998 - 2001

Ice Crystal Blanket
Of Snow
$6   52841
1999 -

Pine Scented Fresh
Fallen Snow
$4.30   52848
2000 - 2004

First Frost Snow
Crystals
$4.50   52906
2000 -

Crushed Ice
$5   52908
2000 - 2003

Acrylic Ice Block
Display Piece
$20   53088
2002 - 2004

Real Acrylic Ice,
mini, bag of 12
$10   44476
2003^M -

Real Acylic Ice,
small, bag of 6
$10   44477
2003^M -

Real Acylic Ice,
medium, bag of 4
$12.50   44478
2003^M -

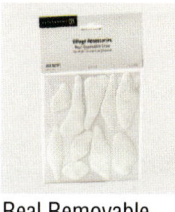
Real Removable
Snow, s/10
$5   53101
2003 -

Village Real Acrylic
Ice, s/22
$10   53141
2003 -

General Village Accessories

405

Real Acrylic Icicles
$5 53151
2003 -

MISCELLANEOUS

Park Bench
$3.20   51098
1987 - 1993

Town Clock
$3   51101
1988 - 1998

SV Garland Trim
$4.50   51128
1988 - 1991

Up On A Roof Top
$6.50   51390
1988 - 1999

Birds
$3.50   51802
1989 - 1994

Christmas Eave Trim
$3.50   55115
1989 -

Town Square Gazebo
$19   55131
1989 - 1997

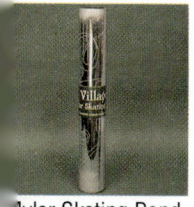
Mylar Skating Pond
$6   52086
1991 - 2000

Brick Road
$10   52108
1991 -

"It's A Grand Old Flag"
$4   54178
1991 - 1997

Greetings
$5   54186
1991 - 1994

Cobblestone Road
$10   59846
1991 -

Tacky Wax
$2.50   52175
1992 -

"Village Sounds" Tape With Speakers
$25   55247
1992 - 1994

"Village Sounds" Tape
$8   55255
1992 - 1994

Mountain, Sm
$2.50   52264
1992 - 2000

Mountain, Med
$65   52272
1992 - 2000

Mountain, Lg
$150   52280
1992 - 2004

Heritage Banners
$6   55263
1992 - 1995

General Village Accessories

General Village Accessories

Heritage Village Promotional Banner
$0   09482
1992 - 1992

Wrought Iron Park Bench
$5   52302
1993 -

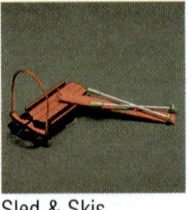
Sled & Skis
$6   52337
1993 - 2000

Mountain Backdrop
$65   52574
1994 -

Mountain Tunnel
$37.50   52582
1994 - 2000

Let It Snow Snowman Sign
$12.50   52594
1995 - 1998

Pink Flamingos
$7.50   52595
1995 -

Election Yard Signs
$10   52599
1995 - 1997

Brick Town Square
$15   52601
1995 -

Cobblestone Town Square
$15   52602
1995 -

Magic Smoke
$2.50   52620
1996 - 2000

Mill Creek (Straight Section)
$12.50   5263
1996 - 2001

Mill Creek (Curved Section)
$12.50   52634
1996 - 2001

Mill Creek Bridge
$35   52635
1996 - 2000

Mountain Centerpiece
$45   52643
1996 - 2000

Stone Footbridge
$16   5264
1997 -

Stone Trestle Bridge
$37.50   52647
1997 - 2001ᴹ

Stone Holly Corner Posts And Archway
$20   52648
1997 -

Stone Holly Tree Corner Posts
$8.50   52649
1997 - 2000

Mill Creek Pond
$55   526
1997 - 2002

Village Gazebo
$22.50   52652
1997 - 2000

Mill Creek Wooden Bridge
$32.50   52653
1997 - 2002

Mill Creek Park Bench
$14   52654
1997 - 1999

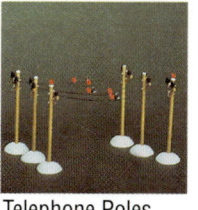
Telephone Poles
$15   52656
1997 - 2001

Television Antenna
$5   52658
1997 - 1999

Weather Vane
$6.50   52659
1997 - 1999

Log Pile
$3   52665
1997 -

Two Lane Paved Road
$15   52668
1997 -

Blue Skies Backdrop
$7.50   52685
1997 - 2000

Starry Night Sky Backdrop
$7.50   52686
1997 - 2000

Camden Park Square
$75   52687
1997 - 2000

Camden Park Cobblestone Road
$10   52691
1997 - 2001

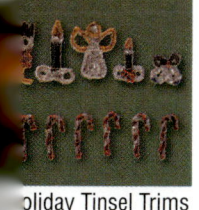
Holiday Tinsel Trims
$8   52712
1998 - 2000

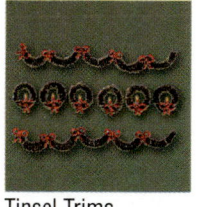
Tinsel Trims
$8   52713
1998 -

Slate Stone Path Straight
$3   52719
1998 -

Woodland Animals At Mill Creek
$32.50   52720
1998 - 2001

Stone Stairway
$6.50   52725
1998 -

Green
$12.50   52739
1998 -

Putting Green
$22.50   52740
1998 - 2002

Moose In The Marsh
$25   52742
1998 - 1999

General Village Accessories

General Village Accessories

Bears In The Birch
$25 52743
1998 - 2003

Foxes In The Forest
$22.50 52744
1998 - 2000

Thoroughbreds
$45 52747
1998 - 2001

Gray Cobblestone Section
$7.50 52751
1998 - 2000

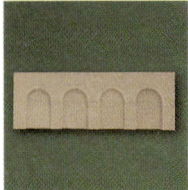
Gray Cobblestone Archway
$10 52752
1998 - 2000

Gray Cobblestone Tunnel
$6.50 52753
1998 - 2000

Real Gray Gravel
$5 52754
1998 - 2000

Gray Cobblestone Capstones
$6 52755
1998 - 2000

Gravel Road
$10 52756
1998 - 2000

Wolves In The Woods
$25 52765
1998 - 2001

Wooden Pier
$32.50 52766
1998 -

Slate Stone Path Curved
$3 5276_
1998 -

Grassy Ground Cover
$7.50 53347
1998 -

Nativity Sand
$6.50 41430
1999 - 2001ᴹ

Craggy Cliff Platform
$65 52794
1999 - 2003

Craggy Cliff Extensions
$25 5279_
1999 - 2003

Wooden Rowboats
$20 52797
1999 - 2002

Autumn Moss
$7.50 52802
1999 - 2001

Spring/Summer Moss
$7.50 52803
1999 - 2001

9" Straight Track
$12.50 528_
1999 -

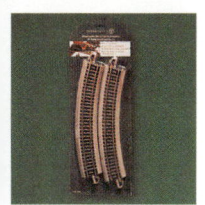
18" Radius Curved Track
$12.50   52809
1999 -

Personalize Your Village Accessories
$16.50   52811
1999 - 2001

Woodland Wildlife Animals, Lg
$32.50   52813
1999 -

Majestic Woodland Birds
$25   52814
1999 - 2002

Woodland Animals At Cliff's Edge
$75   52816
1999 -2001

Fieldstone Stairway
$10   52826
1999 - 2001

Cats & Dogs
$15   52828
1999 -

Lookout Tower
$32.50   52829
1999 - 2001

Wooden Canoes
$20   52830
1999 - 2003

The Trout Stream
$50   52834
1999 -

Real Gravel
$5   52839
1999 - 2001 M

Ground Cover
$12.50 ea.   52840
1999 -

Family Winter Outing
$10   55033
1999 - 2001

Woodland Wildlife Animals, Sm
$27.50   55525
1999 -

North Pole Photo With Santa
$7.50   56444
1999 - 2000

Red Wrought Iron Park Bench
$5   56445
1999 -

Park Bench
$7.50   52851
2000 - 2001

The Dockhouse
$40   52863
2000 -

Mountain Lion's Den
$22.50   52864
2000 - 2001

Buffalo On The Prairie
$22.50   52865
2000 - 2001

General Village Accessories

General Village Accessories

Birds Out Back
$30   52866
2000 - 2003

Smokehouse
Incense Burner
$15   52880
2000 - 2001

Balsam Fir Incense
$5   52881
2000 - 2001

Village Sign and Bench
$8.50   52882
2000 - 2001

Fabric Cobblestone Road
$10   52884
2000 -

Light Hole Protectors
$7.50   52887
2000 - 2004

Mill Creek Campsite
$55   52894
2000 -

The Woodshed & Chopping Block
$40   52895
2000 - 2003

Personalize Pen
$5   52897
2000 - 2003

Mountain Stream
$150   52909
2000 - 2004

Good Fishing
$35   56643
2000 -

Winter Scene Backdrop
$45   5293
2001 - 2003

Here Fishy Fishy Ice House
$37.50   52937
2001 - 2004

Watching For Ducks, s/2
$30   52938
2001 - 2004

Turkeys/Geese In The Field, s/2
$27.50   52939
2001 - 2004

Village Lamppost And Sign
$7.50   5294
2001 - 2002

American Flags, s/7
$12.50   52943
2001 - 2004

Village Flea Market, s/38
$65   52945
2001 - 2003

Mountain Creek Y Shape
$42.50   52946
2001 -

Dog And Puppies, Cat And Kittens, s
$20   529
2001 - 2004

Village Bicycle And Tricycle, s/2
$12.50   52950
2001 - 2004

Deer In The Woods
$22.50   52953
2001 -

Bald Eagle Nesting
$18.50   52972
2001 - 2003

Village Mountain High
$75   52977
2001 -

Village Moss 4 Asst'd Colors
$7.50   52979
2001 -

Woodland Landscape Set, s/9
$35   52989
2001 - 2003

Snowy Landscape Set, s/5
$35   52990
2001 - 2002

City Landscape Set, s/13
$35   52993
2001 - 2004

Mallard And Wood Duck, s/2
$12.50   53002
2001 - 2003

Mountain Creek Waterfall
$42.50   53003
2001 -

Mountain Creek Curved Section
$17.50   53005
2001 -

Mountain Creek Straight Section, s/2
$25   53006
2001 -

Fieldstone Fireplace
$12.50   53010
2001 - 2003

Mountain Creek Bear/Moose, s/2
$22.50   53017
2001 - 2003

A Christmas Eve Flight Backdrop
$45   53037
2002 - 2004

Holiday Trimmings, s/14
$10   53042
2002 -

Village Boats, s/2
$20   53043
2002 -

A Harvest Feast
$35   53045
2002 -

Rocky Mt. Wildlife- Bears/Bobcat, s/2
$30   53047
2002 -

Seasonal Lampposts, s/4
$17.50   53048
2002 - 2004

General Village Accessories

General Village Accessories

Village Santa Sign
$7.50   53051
2002 - 2003

Village Roll Of Moss
$20   53052
2002 -

Spring/Summer Landscape Set, s/10
$35   53076
2002 - 2004

Create A Scene Village Platform
$25   53093
2003ᴹ - 2004

Snowy Platform, s/3
$20   53094
2003ᴹ -

Summer Platform, s/3
$20   53095
2003ᴹ -

Fall Platform, s/3
$20   53096
2003ᴹ -

Potted Poinsettias, s/4
$7.50   53105
2003 -

Fresh Flower Cart
$20   53106
2003 -

Winter Trimmings
$45   53107
2003 -

Harvest Bounty
$45   53108
2003 -

Spring Is Everywhere!
$45   53109
2003 -

Fishing At Trout Lake
$35   53110
2003 -

Brick Path, s/6
$15   53136
2003 -

Autumn Landscape Set, s/27
$35   53138
2003 -

Winter Wonderland Landscape Set, s/1
$35   53140
2003 -

Holiday Streetlights, s/2
$10   59427
2003 -

Wiener Roast
$18.50   53179
2004 -

The Ice Man Waiteth, s/2
$25   53181
2004 -

Village Santa's Sleigh Sign
$7.50   53180
2004 -

Winter Display
Platforms
$15   53202
2004 -

Several buildings and accessories have been produced within the North Pole Series.

These General Village pieces can be used by themselves or in combination with those items.

NORTH POLE
NORTH POLE
NORTH POLE
NORTH POLE
NORTH POLE
NORTH POLE
NORTH POLE
NORTH POLE
NORTH POLE

North Pole General Village Acc.

Pole Pine Forest
$48   55271
1991 - 1998

Pole Pine Tree, Sm
$10   55280
1991 - 1998

Pole Pine Tree, Lg
$12.50   55298
1991 - 1998

Elves On Ice
$9   52298
1996 - 2000

North Pole Candy Cane Lampposts
$13   52621
1996 - 2001ᴹ

Candy Cane Fence
$8.50   52664
1997 -

Peppermint Road (Straight Section)
$5   52666
1997 -

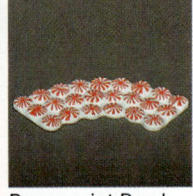
Peppermint Road (Curved Section)
$5   52667
1997 -

Candy Cane Bench
$5   52669
1997 -

Downhill Elves
$9   56439
1998 - 2000

Holiday Cobblestone Road
$10   5644
1999 - 2001

Peppermint Trees
$17.50   56721
1999 - 2003

Elves On Track
$10   56714
1999 - 2001

Bridge Over The Icy Pond
$40   56720
1999 - 2002

Gumdrop Street Lamps
$20   5287
2000 - 2001

Green Glitter Sisal Trees
$17.50   52902
2000 - 2001

North Pole Backdrop
$45   52962
2001 - 2002

Gumdrop Street Lamp, s/4
$18   52966
2001 -

Gumdrop Tree w/LED Lights, 9 inch
$25   52967
2001 -

Gumdrop Tree Non-Lit, 9"
$12   52968
2001 - 2004

Gumdrop Tree Non-Lit, 12"
$15   52969
2001 - 2003

Tinsel Ball Trees, s/5
$15   52971
2001 - 2004

Village Gumdrop Road, s/4
$10   52978
2001 -

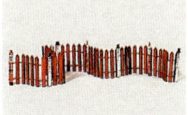

Peppermint Landscape Set, s/7
$35   52991
2001 - 2003

Peppermint Trees s/2
$15   53011
2001 - 2003

Faces Of The Season Picket Fence
$42.50   53029
2002ᴹ -2004

North Pole Animated Train With Track, s/7
$42.50   53030
2002ᴹ - 2003

Village Peppermint Sign
$7.50   53114
2003 -

Curved Village Gumdrop Road, s/4
$10   53135
2003 -

Gumdrop Topiaries
$12.50   53195
2004 -

M&M'S Tree
$15   53196
2004 -

M&M'S Road
$12.50   53199
2004 -

North Pole General Village Acc.

Several Halloween buildings and accessories have been produced within the Original Snow Village Collection.

These General Village pieces can be used by themselves or in combination with those items.

Halloween General Village Acc.

String Of 12 Pumpkin Lights
$13   52700
1998 - 2001

Jack-O' Lanterns
$10   52701
1998 - 2002

Up, Up & Away Witch - Animated
$50   52711
1998 - 2003

Halloween Luminaries
$15   52738
1998 - 2002

Halloween Fence
$12.50   52702
1998 - 2004

Halloween Accessories
$50   52704
1998 - 2001

Halloween Spooky Tree
$15   52770
1998 - 2002

Witch By The Light Of The Moon
$30   52879
2000 - 2004

Lit Spooky Tree
$30   52896
2000 -

Haunted Front Yard
$65   52924
2001ᴹ -

Halloween Scene
$45   52929
2001ᴹ - 2004

Haunted Graveyard
$36   52513
2001 - 2004

Village Swinging Skeleton - Animated
$36   52514
2001 - 2003

Hocus Pocus Witch - Animated
$30   52516
2001 -

Halloween Pumpkin Stand
$35   52929
2001 - 2004

Halloween Village
Set, s/24
$35   52957
2001 - 2003

Halloween Full Moon
$30   52960
2001 - 2003

Gothic Street Lamp,
s/2
$17.50   52961
2001 - 2004

Spooky Black Bare
Branch Trees, s/3
$12.50   52964
2001 - 2002

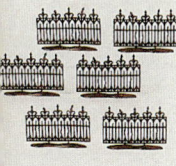
Spooky Wrought
Iron Fence, s/6
$15   52982
2001 -

Autumn/Halloween
Landscape Set, s/6
$35   52992
2001 - 2002

Jack-O'-Lantern
String of 12 Lights
$7.50   53000
2001 - 2004

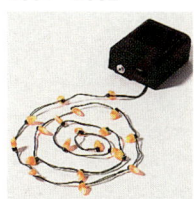
Candy Corn String
of 20 Lights
$10   53013
2001 - 2003

Halloween Village
Sign
$7.50   53044
2002 - 2003

Witch Crash
$36   53056
2002 - 2004

Haunted Hearse
$42.50   53057
2002 -

Skeleton Fence
$12.50   53059
2002 -

Gravely Landscape
Set, s/8
$35   53060
2002 -

Lighted Halloween
Scarecrows, s/2
$25   53061
2002 - 2004

Halloween
Topiaries, s/3
$17.50   53062
2002 - 2003

Spooky Totem
$12.50   53063
2002 - 2003

Tombstones, s/6
$10   53065
2002 -

Spooky Black Glitter
Tree, s/3
$17.50   53067
2002 -

Haunted Outhouse
$25   53068
2002 -

Creepy Creek Bridge
$35   53071
2002 -

Halloween General Village Acc.

Over The Hill Tombstone
$12 53072
2002 - 2004

Haunted Fiber Optic Backdrop
$65 53075
2002 - 2004

Jack-O-Lantern Pumpkins, s/12
$7.50 53077
2002 - 2004

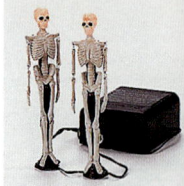
Skull Street Lamps, s/4
$17.50 53079
2002 -

Glowing String of Scary Lights, 2 Astd
$12.50 53080
2002 - 2004

Spooky Willows, s/2
$17.50 53087
2002 - 2004

Ghostly Landscape Set, s/12 (Exclusive)
$35 04771
2003 -

Eerie Rocks & Road, s/8
$35 5311
2003 -

Phantom Of The Organ
$65 53126
2003 -

Rock-A-Bye Vampire
$36 53128
2003 -

Lit Graveyard Tree
$17.50 53129
2003 -

Halloween Yard Decorations, s/22
$12.50 5313
2003 -

Scary Twisted Trees, s/2
$20 53131
2003 -

Scaredy Bat
$45 53132
2003 -

Swinging Ghoulies
$55 53133
2003 -

Ghostly Landscape Set, s/12
$35 531
2003 -

Spooky Village Sign
$7.50 53144
2003 - 2004

Harvest Gourds, s/10
$7.50 53145
2003 -

Resting My Bones
$25 53146
2003 -

Mummy Mischief
$30 531
2003 -

Bubble Light Ghosts s/2
$25   53149
2003 - 2004

Pumpkin Street Lamps, s/2
$12.50   53150
2003 -

Halloween Parade
$32.50   53157
2004 -

Honest, This Tree Came Out Of Nowhere!
$17.50   53158
2004 -

Taking Bones For A Walk
$55   53159
2004 -

Escape From The Crypt
$55   53160
2004 -

Shaking Graveyard
$45   53162
2004 -

Killing Time
$25   53164
2004 -

Halloween Scenery, s/9
$12.50   53165
2004 -

Monster Park Statues
$20   53166
2004 -

Bat Lights, s/2
$17.50   53167
2004 -

Halloween Twinkle Brite Tree
$20   53168
2004 -

Harvest Mailbox
$12.50   53169
2004 -

Creepy Village Sign
$7.50   53170
2004 -

Spinning Pumpkins
$75   53173
2004 -

Bats & Spooks Tree
$17.50   53176
2004 -

Spooky Yard Scene
$7.50   53177
2004 -

Candy Corn Trees
$15   53205
2004 -

Halloween General Village Acc.

These Carnival General Village pieces can be used by themselves or in combination with the villages.

The Red Ruby Carousel
$85   53801
2004 -

The Golden Vine Ferris Wheel
$85   53802
2004 -

Twirling Tea Cups
$75   53803
2004 -

Ball Toss At The Carnival
$20   53804
2004 -

Family Day At The Carnival
$18.50   53805
2004 -

ITEM NUMBER INDEX

HOW DESIGNS ARE LISTED:

For years Department 56 used hyphens in its item numbers. For instance, a design's item number may have been 1234-5. However, several years ago, the company stopped using the hyphens. Therefore, we have omitted all hyphens in both the index as well as in the content of the book. That same design's number would now appear as 12345.

Item	Page	Item	Page	Item	Page	Item	Page
02100	375	07293	379	07759	380	50096	7
02101	375	07307	379	07760	380	50105	18
02102	375	07315	379	07761	380	50112	7
02103	375	07323	379	07762	380	50120	8
02104	375	07331	379	07763	380	50121	18
02202	381	07340	379	07821	381	50130	24
02203	381	07358	379	07826	376	50138	8
02204	381	07366	379	07880	382	50146	8
02208	382	07374	379	08802	381	50153	8
2210	44	07382	379	08803	381	50156	19
2211	368	07390	379	08960	42	50161	9
2244	382	07404	379	09482	408	50172	14
2250	382	07412	379	13638	399	50180	69
2255	383	07420	346	21637	379	50199	14, 24
2270	383	07429	346	25104	378	50202	14
2272	383	07439	347	34050	113	50210	14
2291	376	07448	347	36323	395	50229	14
2300	382	07449	347	36331	395	50237	15
2413	382	07522	379	36358	395	50245	15, 24
2423	383	07536	379	36366	395	50253	16
2440	383	07544	380	41430	410	50261	16
2973	166, 194	07560	379	44476	405	50270	24
4771	420	07641	380	44477	405	50288	17
5398	378	07650	380	44478	405	50296	17
5600	376	07668	380	49956	405	50300	25
5700	154, 185	07676	380	49964	405	50318	17
5702	383	07684	380	49979	405	50326	17
5709	377	07692	380	49980	405	50334	17
5733	309	07730	380	49981	405	50342	19
5746	384	07740	380	49999	405	50350	19
5826	375	07741	380	50008	15	50369	19
5832	384	07742	380	50013	6	50377	19
5834	377	07743	380	50016	16	50385	69
5837	289	07744	380	50021	6	50393	19
5838	384	07745	380	50024	16	50407	69
5841	311	07746	380	50032	16	50415	21
5923	57, 100	07747	380	50039	6	50423	21
5925	160, 190	07748	380	50040	16	50431	21
5930	377	07749	380	50047	6	50440	26
6001	384	07750	380	50054	6	50458	20
6230	377	07751	380	50059	18	50466	20
6300	385	07752	380	50062	6	50474	20
6301	385	07753	380	50067	24	50482	20
6700	374	07754	380	50070	7	50490	20
6718	374	07755	380	50075	18	50500	363
6726	374	07756	380	50083	18	50504	20
6956	377	07757	380	50088	7	50512	21
7218	379	07758	380	50091	18	50518	363

Item	Page	Item	Page	Item	Page	Item	Page
50520	21	51039	71	51624	76	52272	407
50526	363	51047	71	51632	76	52280	407
50534	363	51055	71	51640	76	52298	416
50539	69	51063	71	51659	76	52299	396
50542	9	51071	71	51667	74	52301	393
50547	26	51080	71	51675	74	52302	408
50555	70	51098	407	51683	74	52310	389
50559	9	51101	407	51691	74	52329	389
50563	70	51110	388	51705	74	52337	408
50567	10	51128	407	51713	74	52345	403
50571	70	51136	71	51721	74	52353	403
50575	10	51144	28	51730	75	52361	396
50583	10	51152	388	51748	75	52370	396
50591	10	51160	72	51756	388	52388	396
50598	70	51179	72	51764	75	52396	396
50601	22	51187	72	51772	75	52400	396
50609	10	51195	28	51780	75	52418	389
50617	10	51209	28	51799	75	52426	389
50625	11	51217	26	51802	407	52434	389
50628	22	51225	26	51810	389	52442	390
50633	11	51233	26	51829	389	52450	390
50636	22	51241	27	51837	389	52469	381
50641	69	51250	27	51845	388	52477	39
50652	22	51268	27	51853	388	52485	38
50658	11	51276	27	51861	388	52493	38
50660	22	51284	27	51870	388	52500	39
50666	11	51292	72	51888	388	52501	39
50674	11	51306	72	51896	388	52502	39
50679	22	51314	72	51926	388	52503	39
50682	11	51322	72	51934	388	52504	27
50687	23	51330	73	51977	77	52505	40
50690	69	51349	75	51985	77	52506	40
50709	12, 23	51357	73	52000	388	52507	38
50717	12, 23	51365	73	52019	388	52508	40
50725	13	51373	73	52027	388	52509	40
50733	13, 23	51381	73	52035	388	52511	40
50741	13	51390	407	52043	403	52512	40
50768	13, 23	51403	28	52051	389	52513	41
50776	13, 23	51411	28	52060	395	52514	41
50784	13, 24	51420	28	52078	403	52515	3
50792	69	51438	29	52086	407	52516	4
50806	14	51446	29	52094	77	52523	4
50814	15, 25	51454	29	52108	407	52531	4
50822	15, 25	51462	73	52116	405	52540	3
50830	15	51470	73	52124	403	52558	3
50849	17	51489	74	52132	396	52566	3
50856	12	51497	29	52140	268	52574	4
50865	12	51500	29	52159	396	52582	4
50873	12	51519	29	52167	389	52590	3
50890	25	51527	30	52175	407	52592	3
50911	25	51535	30	52183	367	52593	3
50920	25	51543	30	52191	367	52594	4
50946	70	51551	30	52205	403	52595	4
50954	70	51560	30	52213	389	52596	3
50962	70	51578	30	52221	396	52597	4
50970	31	51586	76	52230	396	52598	4
51004	403	51594	76	52248	396	52599	4
51012	403	51608	76	52256	396	52600	
51020	71	51616	76	52264	407	52601	

Item	Page	Item	Page	Item	Page	Item	Page
52602	408	52662	391	52742	409	52839	411
52603	390	52663	397	52743	410	52840	411
52604	390	52664	416	52744	410	52841	405
52605	390	52665	409	52746	404	52842	392
52606	390	52666	416	52747	410	52843	392
52607	390	52667	416	52748	391	52844	392
52608	390	52668	409	52751	410	52845	399
52610	390	52669	416	52752	410	52846	399
52611	397	52670	397	52753	410	52847	399
52612	390	52671	397	52754	410	52848	405
52613	390	52672	397	52755	410	52850	392
52614	390	52673	397	52756	410	52851	411
52615	390	52674	398	52760	399	52852	399
52616	390	52675	398	52763	361	52853	399
52617	390	52678	398	52765	410	52861	400
52618	390	52679	398	52766	410	52863	411
52619	390	52680	398	52767	410	52864	411
52620	408	52681	398	52768	404	52865	411
52621	416	52682	398	52769	391	52866	412
52622	390	52683	391	52770	418	52867	93
52623	391	52684	398	52771	391	52868	93
52624	404	52685	409	52772	391	52869	93
52625	404	52686	409	52775	87	52871	416
52626	397	52687	409	52776	272	52874	350
52627	397	52689	404	52779	399	52875	350
52628	397	52690	391	52780	88	52876	351
52629	404	52691	409	52781	392	52877	351
52630	391	52700	418	52790	399	52878	351
52631	391	52701	418	52791	399	52879	418
52632	391	52702	418	52794	410	52880	412
52633	408	52703	391	52795	410	52881	412
52634	408	52704	418	52797	410	52882	412
52635	408	52705	398	52800	399	52884	412
52636	391	52706	398	52802	410	52885	392
52637	391	52707	398	52803	410	52886	392
52638	391	52708	398	52807	399	52887	412
52639	391	52710	398	52808	410	52888	393
52640	397	52711	418	52809	411	52889	393
52641	397	52712	409	52811	411	52890	393
52642	397	52713	409	52813	411	52891	393
52643	408	52714	391	52814	411	52892	393
52644	397	52715	398	52816	411	52893	400
52645	397	52717	404	52818	392	52894	412
52646	408	52718	404	52819	392	52895	412
52647	408	52719	409	52820	293	52896	418
52648	408	52720	409	52822	399	52897	412
52649	408	52722	404	52823	392	52898	393
52650	404	52723	404	52824	392	52899	393
52651	408	52724	404	52825	404	52900	393
52652	409	52725	409	52826	411	52901	393
52653	409	52727	398	52827	399	52902	417
52654	409	52728	398	52828	411	52904	400
52655	391	52729	405	52829	411	52906	405
52656	409	52731	398	52830	411	52908	405
52657	404	52732	324	52831	399	52909	412
52658	409	52733	398	52834	411	52910	384
52659	409	52738	418	52835	399	52911	384
52660	391	52739	409	52836	90	52924	418
52661	391	52740	409	52837	392	52930	412

Item	Page	Item	Page	Item	Page	Item	Page
52931	393	53024	400	53114	417	53190	401
52933	418	53025	400	53119	420	53191	401
52937	412	53027	400	53121	401	53192	394
52938	412	53028	370	53122	401	53193	394
52939	412	53029	417	53123	401	53194	394
52940	412	53030	417	53125	401	53195	417
52943	412	53032	394	53126	420	53196	417
52945	412	53033	394	53128	420	53197	394
52946	412	53037	413	53129	420	53199	417
52948	412	53038	400	53130	420	53202	415
52950	413	53039	400	53131	420	53204	402
52953	413	53042	413	53132	420	53205	421
52956	418	53043	413	53133	420	53207	394
52957	419	53044	419	53134	394	53300	352
52960	419	53045	413	53135	417	53301	352
52961	419	53047	413	53136	414	53302	353
52962	417	53048	413	53137	394	53303	353
52964	419	53049	400	53138	414	53304	353
52965	295	53051	414	53140	414	53305	354
52966	417	53052	414	53141	405	53307	354
52967	417	53053	401	53143	420	53308	354
52968	417	53054	401	53144	420	53309	354
52969	417	53056	419	53145	420	53311	35
52971	417	53057	419	53146	420	53313	35
52972	413	53059	419	53148	420	53314	35
52973	393	53060	419	53149	421	53317	35
52974	393	53061	419	53150	421	53319	35
52975	393	53062	419	53151	406	53320	35
52976	393	53063	419	53152	401	53322	35
52977	413	53065	419	53153	401	53323	35
52978	417	53067	419	53154	401	53324	35
52979	413	53068	419	53156	122, 421	53326	35
52982	419	53071	419	53157	421	53327	35
52983	393	53072	420	53158	421	53330	36
52984	400	53075	420	53159	421	53331	36
52985	393	53076	414	53160	421	53332	36
52986	393	53077	420	53161	401	53333	36
52989	413	53079	420	53162	421	53334	36
52990	413	53080	420	53164	421	53338	36
52991	417	53081	394	53165	421	53343	36
52992	419	53083	394	53166	421	53344	36
52993	413	53084	394	53167	421	53345	36
52996	393	53085	394	53168	421	53347	4
53000	419	53086	394	53169	421	53355	36
53001	393	53087	420	53170	421	53362	4
53002	413	53088	405	53172	394	53366	3
53003	413	53089	401	53173	421	53367	3
53005	413	53093	414	53176	421	53370	3
53006	413	53094	414	53177	421	53374	3
53009	404	53095	414	53178	394	53375	3
53010	413	53096	414	53179	414	53376	3
53011	417	53101	405	53181	414	53377	3
53012	394	53105	414	53183	414	53382	3
53013	419	53106	414	53184	401	53383	3
53017	413	53107	414	53185	401	53384	3
53018	394	53108	414	53186	401	53400	
53020	400	53109	414	53187	401	53401	3
53021	400	53110	414	53188	401	53402	
53022	400	53111	401	53189	401	53403	

Item	Page	Item	Page	Item	Page	Item	Page
53404	353	54070	32	54666	36	54894	84
53405	354	54089	77	54674	37	54895	84
53410	362	54097	77	54682	37	54896	85
53411	354	54100	77	54690	37	54897	85
53412	354, 358	54119	77	54704	37	54898	85
53413	354	54127	77	54712	81	54899	85
53414	355	54135	78	54720	81	54900	85
53415	358	54143	78	54739	81	54901	85
53416	358	54151	78	54747	81	54902	41, 85
53417	358	54160	396	54755	81	54903	42
53418	358	54178	407	54763	81	54904	42
53419	358	54186	407	54771	81	54905	85
53420	359	54194	389	54780	82	54910	42
53421	359	54208	32	54798	82	54911	42
53422	359	54216	32	54800	375	54912	42
53423	359	54224	32	54801	82	54913	43
53425	359	54232	33	54810	82	54914	43
53426	359	54240	33	54828	397	54915	43
53427	359	54259	33	54836	37	54916	43
53428	362	54267	33	54844	37	54917	43
53429	362	54275	33	54850	38	54918	43
53431	362	54283	78	54851	38	54920	87
53433	362	54291	78	54852	38	54921	86
53436	362	54305	78	54853	38	54922	86
53445	355	54313	78	54854	38	54923	86
53446	355	54321	78	54855	38	54924	86
53447	355	54330	79	54856	39	54925	86
53448	355	54348	79	54857	39	54926	86
53449	356	54356	79	54858	39	54927	86
53450	356	54364	79	54859	39	54928	86
53503	346	54372	33	54860	82	54929	87
53511	346	54380	34	54861	82	54930	87
53520	347	54399	34	54862	82	54931	87
53521	347	54402	79	54863	83	54932	44
53522	347	54410	34	54864	83	54933	44
53538	347	54429	34	54865	83	54934	44, 87
53539	347	54437	34	54866	83	54935	113
53546	347	54445	34	54867	83	54936	87
53554	347	54453	35	54868	83	54937	119
53600	359	54461	35	54869	83	54938	87
53601	360	54470	35	54870	83	54939	88
53602	360	54488	35	54871	39	54940	44
53603	360	54496	79	54872	39	54941	45
53604	360	54500	79	54873	40	54942	45
53605	362	54518	79	54874	40	54943	45
53608	360	54526	80	54875	84	54944	45
53611	360	54534	80	54879	84	54945	45
53801	422	54542	80	54880	40	54946	46
53802	422	54550	80	54881	40	54947	46
53803	422	54569	80	54882	40	54948	46
53804	422	54577	80	54883	40	54949	46
53805	422	54585	80	54884	41	54950	88
54003	31	54593	80	54885	41	54951	88
54011	31	54607	36	54886	41	54952	88
54020	31	54615	35	54887	41	54953	88
54038	31	54623	36, 82	54890	84	54954	88
54046	31	54631	81	54891	84	54955	88
54054	32	54640	36	54892	84	54956	89
54062	32	54658	36	54893	84	54957	89

Item	Page	Item	Page	Item	Page	Item	Page
54958	89	55053	51	55131	407	55207	105
54959	89	55054	51	55132	97	55208	105
54970	89	55055	113	55133	98	55209	105
54971	89	55056	51	55134	98	55215	105
54972	89	55058	113	55135	98	55217	106
54973	119	55059	51	55136	98	55218	106
54974	89	55060	114, 119	55137	98	55222	106
54975	90	55061	52, 96	55139	98	55224	106
54976	90	55062	52	55140	403	55225	106
54977	46	55063	52	55141	98	55227	10
54978	47	55064	52	55142	98	55228	107
54979	47, 90	55065	52	55143	99	55229	107
54982	119	55066	53	55144	99	55230	107
54983	90	55067	53, 96	55148	119	55231	10
55000	395	55068	53, 96	55149	119	55232	10
55001	47	55069	403	55150	120	55233	10
55002	47	55070	53	55152	99	55235	10
55003	48	55071	54	55153	99	55238	12
55004	113	55072	54, 97	55154	99	55239	22
55006	48	55074	55	55155	99	55240	12
55008	48	55077	403	55156	100	55241	12
55009	48	55078	54	55157	100	55244	12
55010	48	55080	54, 97	55158	403	55245	12
55011	48	55081	55	55159	101	55246	12
55012	49	55085	403	55160	101	55247	40
55013	90	55087	114	55161	101	55248	12
55014	90	55088	114	55164	101	55251	10
55015	90	55090	55, 97	55165	101	55252	10
55016	119	55091	55, 100	55166	268	55253	10
55017	91	55093	403	55168	101	55254	10
55018	395	55094	114, 120	55169	102	55255	40
55019	91	55095	56, 100	55170	102	55256	10
55020	91	55096	56	55171	102	55257	12
55021	91	55097	56, 100	55172	102	55258	10
55022	91	55100	92	55173	102	55260	1
55023	91	55103	93	55174	268	55261	1
55024	91	55104	93	55175	102	55262	1
55025	91	55105	93	55176	102	55263	4
55026	395	55106	93	55177	102	55264	1
55030	92	55108	93	55178	103	55265	1
55031	92	55109	94	55179	103	55266	1
55032	92	55110	94	55180	103	55267	1
55033	411	55111	94	55181	103	55268	1
55034	395	55112	94	55183	103	55269	1
55035	92	55115	407	55185	120	55270	1
55036	92	55116	94	55186	120	55271	4
55040	49, 92	55117	119	55189	120	55272	1
55041	49, 92	55118	94	55192	120	55273	1
55042	395	55119	94	55194	103	55274	1
55043	49	55120	94	55195	103	55275	1
55044	50	55121	95	55196	103	55276	1
55045	50	55122	97	55197	104	55277	1
55046	50	55123	269	55198	120	55280	4
55047	50	55124	96	55199	104	55281	
55048	50	55125	96	55200	120	55282	
55049	50	55126	96	55201	121	55283	
55050	395	55127	97	55202	104	55284	
55051	51	55128	97	55203	121	55285	
55052	51	55129	97	55205	105	55286	

Item Number Index

Item	Page	Item	Page	Item	Page	Item	Page
55287	95	55348	63	55565	270	56174	235
55288	96	55349	63	55573	138	56175	240
55289	96	55350	63, 109	55581	175	56176	235
55291	368	55351	64	55590	175	56177	236
55292	99	55352	268	55603	175	56178	235
55293	99	55353	64	55611	175	56180	239
55294	100	55354	64, 109	55620	138	56182	239
55295	100	55355	64, 109	55638	367	56183	240
55296	101	55358	65, 111	55646	270	56189	234
55297	101	55359	65	55654	248	56190	234
55298	416	55360	246	55662	270	56191	234
55299	104	55361	65	55670	137	56192	235
55300	57	55362	65	55689	137	56197	239
55301	175	55363	65	55690	137	56200	300
55302	57, 104	55364	66	55691	137	56201	240
55303	56	55365	66	55697	174	56202	240
55304	58	55366	66	55700	174	56203	240
55305	57, 104	55367	66	55719	174	56210	236
55306	58	55368	66	55727	367	56211	236
55307	58	55369	66	55735	174	56212	240
55308	58	55370	67	55743	134	56213	240
55309	58	55374	117	55751	175	56214	240
55310	248	55375	116	55778	173	56215	241
55311	248	55376	117	55786	173	56216	236
55312	248	55377	117	55794	173	56217	236
55313	248	55379	246	55808	174	56218	236
55314	59, 104	55387	247	55816	174	56219	300
55315	115	55395	269	55824	134	56220	237
55316	115	55409	269	55832	135	56221	237
55317	115	55417	269	55840	136	56222	237
55318	58	55425	247	55859	136	56223	237
55319	115, 121	55433	247	55867	136	56227	301
55320	59, 105	55441	247	55875	136	56229	237
55321	59	55450	269	55883	174	56230	238
55322	59	55468	269	55891	174	56231	238
55323	60	55476	269	56000	376	56232	238
55324	60	55484	269	56006	300	56233	238
55325	60, 105	55492	247	56014	300	56235	301
55326	105	55500	340	56015	300	56243	301
55327	106	55501	368	56016	300	56251	301
55328	270	55502	368	56022	321	56260	302
55330	60	55506	135	56030	321	56278	302
55331	60	55510	253, 273	56049	321	56286	302
55332	61	55514	173	56057	321	56294	302
55333	61, 108	55515	369	56073	239	56300	241
55334	61	55522	137	56081	321	56302	241
55335	61	55523	369	56090	321	56303	241
55336	270	55524	369	56100	368	56304	241
55337	61	55525	411	56103	321	56305	241
55338	62, 108	55530	138	56111	321	56306	241
55339	62	55532	104	56120	234	56308	322
55340	62	55533	106	56138	239	56309	241
55341	63	55534	106	56146	234	56310	242
55342	62, 108	55535	108	56154	233	56311	242
55343	116, 122	55536	108	56162	239	56312	242
55344	246	55537	109	56170	233	56313	242
55345	115	55538	111	56171	234	56314	242
55346	116	55549	175	56172	208	56316	322
55347	116, 122, 123	55557	137	56173	235	56324	322

Item Number	Page	Item Number	Page	Item Number	Page	Item Number	Page
56332	302	56472	207	56626	212, 225	56700	307
56340	302	56480	206	56627	213	56701	307
56359	303	56481	206	56628	213	56702	307
56363	324	56482	206	56629	213	56703	307
56364	322	56499	221	56630	223	56704	308
56365	322	56502	221	56631	223	56705	308
56366	322	56510	207	56632	213, 226	56706	325
56367	322	56529	207	56633	223	56707	325
56368	323	56537	207	56634	214, 226	56708	325
56369	323	56545	221	56635	223	56709	325
56370	323	56553	221	56636	213	56710	325
56371	323	56561	221	56637	223	56711	326
56372	323	56568	207	56638	223	56712	326
56373	323	56569	208	56639	224	56713	326
56374	323	56570	207	56640	392	56714	41
56375	322	56571	208	56641	225	56715	39
56383	303	56572	208	56642	225	56716	40
56384	303	56573	208	56643	412	56717	40
56385	303	56574	208	56644	225	56720	41
56386	303	56575	209	56645	225	56721	41
56387	303	56576	209	56646	225	56722	39
56388	304	56577	209	56647	226	56723	39
56389	304	56578	209	56650	226	56724	39
56390	304, 323	56579	209	56651	214	56725	308, 32
56391	304	56580	209	56652	214	56726	30
56392	304	56581	210	56653	214	56727	30
56393	305	56587	223	56654	214	56728	30
56394	305	56588	221	56655	215	56729	30
56395	305	56589	221	56658	215	56730	30
56396	305	56590	221	56659	215	56731	30
56397	305	56591	222	56660	215	56732	309, 32
56398	305	56592	222	56661	215	56733	31
56400	306	56593	222	56662	216	56734	310, 32
56401	306	56594	222	56663	216	56735	31
56402	306	56595	222	56664	216	56736	31
56403	306	56596	222	56665	216	56737	31
56404	306	56597	222	56666	216	56738	31
56405	205	56598	222	56667	216	56739	31
56407	307	56599	223	56670	217	56740	3
56408	306	56601	210	56671	217, 229	56741	3
56413	220	56602	210	56672	217	56742	3
56421	206	56604	210	56673	217	56744	3
56430	206	56605	210	56674	217	56745	312, 3
56431	324	56606	211, 224, 344	56680	226	56746	3
56434	324	56610	211	56681	226	56748	312, 3
56435	324	56611	211	56682	226	56749	3
56436	324	56612	211	56683	226	56750	3
56437	324	56613	211	56684	227	56751	313, 3
56438	325	56614	212	56687	227	56752	3
56439	416	56615	224	56688	227	56753	3
56442	325	56616	224	56689	227	56754	3
56443	325	56617	224	56690	227	56755	3
56444	411	56619	224	56691	227	56756	314, 3
56445	411	56620	224	56692	227	56757	314, 3
56446	326	56621	224	56693	227	56758	315, 3
56447	416	56622	225	56694	228	56759	3
56448	206	56623	225	56695	228	56761	
56456	220	56624	212	56697	228	56762	
56464	220	56625	212	56698	228	56763	

Item	Page	Item	Page	Item	Page	Item	Page
56764	316	56856	333	57105	228	58310	150, 182, 344
56765	316	56857	333	57106	228	58311	149
56766	316	56858	333	57107	229	58313	149
56767	316	56859	333	57108	229	58314	150
56768	316	56860	333	57109	229	58315	150
56769	316	56861	333	57110	229	58316	150
56771	317	56862	333	57112	229	58319	178
56772	317	56863	334	57509	138	58322	146, 182
56773	317	56864	334	57517	139	58323	146
56774	317	56865	334	57525	139	58324	147
56775	317	56866	334	57533	142	58326	181
56776	317	56867	334	57534	143	58327	142, 180
56778	318	56868	334	57535	145	58328	143
56779	318	56869	334	58009	139	58329	143
56780	318	56870	334	58017	139	58330	143
56781	318	56871	335	58025	175	58331	143
56800	326	56872	335	58033	176	58332	143
56801	326	56873	335	58041	176	58333	144
56802	326	56874	335	58050	176	58334	144
56803	327	56875	335	58068	367	58335	142
56804	327	56876	335	58076	367	58336	144, 180
56805	327	56877	335	58084	140	58337	144
56806	327	56880	348	58085	140	58338	144
56807	327	56881	348	58086	140	58339	145
56808	327	56882	348	58087	140	58340	150
56809	328	56883	348	58092	139	58341	151, 341
56810	328	56884	348	58106	141	58343	142
56811	328	56885	349	58114	139	58344	145
56812	328	56886	349	58122	140	58345	145
56813	328	56887	349	58130	176	58346	145
56814	328	56889	335	58149	176	58347	145
56815	328	56891	336	58157	176	58348	146
56817	328	56892	318	58165	176	58351	178
56818	329	56893	319	58173	177	58352	151
56819	329	56894	318	58181	177	58353	151
56820	329	56895	319	58190	177	58360	178
56822	329	56896	319	58203	177	58378	178
56823	329	56897	319	58211	140	58379	179
56831	330	56898	336	58220	141	58381	179
56833	330	56899	336	58238	142	58382	179
56835	330	56900	319	58246	141	58383	180
56836	330	56901	319	58247	141	58384	180
56837	330	56920	350	58248	141	58385	181
56838	330	56921	350	58249	141	58386	181
56839	331	56922	350	58254	177	58387	183
56840	331	56923	350	58262	177	58390	179
56841	331	56924	392	58270	177	58391	179
56842	331	56925	392	58289	177	58392	179
56843	331	56926	350	58297	178	58393	179
56844	331	56927	350	58300	178	58394	179
56846	331	56928	351	58301	147, 182	58395	180
56847	332	56929	351	58302	147	58396	180
56848	332	56930	351	58303	148	58397	180
56849	332	56931	351	58304	148	58400	180
56850	332	56932	351	58305	148	58401	181
56851	332	56940	336	58306	147	58402	181
56853	332	56941	336	58307	148	58403	181
56854	332	57102	228	58308	149, 182	58404	181
56855	333	57103	228	58309	149	58405	181

Item	Page	Item	Page	Item	Page	Item	Page
58406	182	58492	159	58564	192, 341	58710	165
58407	182	58493	159	58565	192	58711	166
58408	182	58494	159, 188	58566	192	58712	166
58409	195	58495	159	58567	192	58713	166
58410	182	58496	159	58568	192	58714	166
58411	183	58498	160	58569	192	58715	167
58412	195	58500	146, 340	58571	193	58716	167
58413	183	58501	148, 340	58572	193	58717	167, 195
58414	183	58502	160	58573	193	58719	167, 195
58415	183	58506	160, 190	58574	193	58720	168, 342
58416	183	58507	161	58575	193	58721	168, 343
58417	183	58508	161	58576	193	58722	168
58420	183	58509	161	58577	193	58723	168
58440	152	58510	162	58578	194	58724	168
58441	152	58511	162	58579	194	58725	168
58442	152, 184	58512	162	58580	194	58726	169
58443	151	58513	162, 191	58581	194	58727	169
58444	152	58514	163, 191	58583	194	58728	169
58445	152	58515	163, 191	58584	194	58729	169
58446	153	58517	162	58585	195	58730	169
58447	153	58518	163, 191	58587	195	58731	169
58448	153	58520	185	58588	195	58807	248
58449	153	58521	186	58589	195	58808	249
58451	153, 341	58522	186	58590	196	58809	249
58453	153, 341	58523	186	58591	196	58815	249
58454	184	58524	186	58593	196	58823	249
58455	184	58525	186	58594	196, 343	58831	249
58456	184	58526	186	58595	196	58840	27
58457	184	58527	186	58596	196	58858	27
58458	184	58528	187	58597	196	58866	27
58460	184	58529	187	58598	196	58870	25
58461	184	58530	187	58599	197	58871	252, 27
58462	185	58531	187	58600	345	58874	24
58464	185	58532	187	58601	157, 188, 345	58875	25
58465	185	58533	187	58630	400	58876	25
58466	185	58534	187	58631	369	58877	25
58467	185	58535	187	58632	370	58878	25
58470	154, 185	58536	188	58633	161, 190	58879	25
58471	154	58537	188	58634	370	58880	25
58472	154	58538	188	58635	370	58881	25
58473	155	58539	189	58638	370	58882	25
58474	155	58540	189	58639	370	58883	25
58475	155, 186	58541	189	58640	370	58884	25
58476	155	58542	189	58641	371	58885	27
58477	155	58545	189	58642	371	58886	25
58478	156	58546	189	58643	371	58887	25
58479	156	58547	189	58644	371	58888	25
58480	156	58548	189	58645	176	58890	27
58481	156	58549	190	58653	270	58891	27
58482	156	58550	190	58661	270	58892	27
58483	156	58551	190	58700	164, 193	58893	27
58484	157	58552	190	58702	164	58894	27
58485	157, 188	58555	190	58703	164	58895	27
58486	157	58557	191	58704	164, 194	58896	27
58487	158, 188	58559	191	58705	165, 342	58897	27
58488	158, 188	58560	191	58706	165	58898	27
58489	158	58561	191	58707	165	58899	2
58490	158	58562	192	58708	165	58900	2
58491	161	58563	192	58709	165	58901	2

Item	Page
58902	273
58903	273
58906	273
58907	273
58909	273
58910	273
58911	254
58912	255
58913	255
58914	255
58915	255
58916	255
58917	255
58918	256
58919	341
58920	256
58921	256
58922	369
58923	256
58924	258
58925	256
58926	256
58927	257
58928	257
58929	257, 276
58930	257, 341
58932	257
58933	258
58937	258, 277
58938	258
58939	345
58940	252
58941	252
58942	258
58943	253
58944	259
58945	253
58946	259
58947	253
58948	253
58949	259, 278
58950	254
58951	254
58952	254
58953	254
58954	254
58955	274
58956	274
58957	274
58958	274
58959	274
58960	274
58961	274
58962	275
58963	275
58964	275
58965	275
58966	275
58967	275
58968	275
58969	275
58970	276
58971	276
58972	276
58973	276
58974	276
58975	276
58976	370
58977	276
58978	277
58979	277
58980	277
58981	277
58983	277
58986	277
58987	277
58988	278
58989	278
58990	278
58991	278
58992	278
58993	278
58994	278
58995	279
58996	279
58998	279
58999	279
59000	368
59001	368
59005	131
59013	171
59021	132
59030	173
59048	132
59056	131
59161	131
59201	259
59202	259
59203	260
59204	260, 342
59205	260
59206	260, 280
59207	261, 342
59208	260
59209	261, 342
59210	261
59211	261
59212	261
59213	262, 280
59214	262
59215	262
59216	262, 280
59219	263, 282
59220	263, 282
59221	263
59222	263
59224	264
59225	264
59227	264
59228	264
59229	264
59230	264
59231	264
59232	264
59233	264
59235	264
59236	265
59237	265
59238	265
59239	265
59240	265
59241	265, 343
59242	132
59250	134
59269	133
59277	134
59285	173
59293	173
59307	201
59315	202
59323	202
59340	171
59382	366
59390	202, 203
59400	279
59402	279
59403	279
59404	203
59405	279
59406	280
59407	280
59409	280
59410	280
59411	280
59412	219
59413	281
59414	281
59415	281
59416	281
59417	281
59419	281
59420	204
59421	281
59422	281
59423	282
59425	282
59427	414
59428	282
59429	282
59430	282
59436	282
59437	283
59439	204
59440	283
59441	283
59442	283
59443	283
59444	283
59445	283
59446	283
59447	204
59448	283
59452	283
59453	284
59454	284
59455	219
59456	284
59457	284
59458	284
59463	204
59471	204
59480	220
59498	220
59501	171
59510	172
59528	233
59536	233
59544	205
59552	205
59560	220
59579	268
59587	268
59595	268
59609	267
59617	244
59625	244
59633	245
59641	267
59650	267
59668	172
59676	172
59684	245
59692	245
59706	245
59714	267
59722	245
59730	245
59749	246
59757	286
59759	293
59773	246
59781	246
59790	268
59791	293
59792	293
59793	293
59794	293
59795	286
59796	287
59797	286
59799	287, 293
59801	287, 294
59802	288, 294
59803	395
59806	288
59807	288

Item #	Page
59809	291, 295
59810	291, 296
59811	366
59812	289, 296
59813	297
59814	291
59815	297
59816	289
59820	366
59838	267
59846	407
59854	267
59862	219
59870	219
59901	293
59902	294
59903	294
59904	294
59905	294
59906	294
59907	294
59908	295
59909	295
59910	295
59911	295
59912	295
59913	295
59914	296
59915	296
59916	296
59917	296
59918	296
59921	296
59922	297
59923	297
59924	297
59925	297
59935	395
59943	395
59960	395
59978	395
59986	403
59994	403
64599	69
65005	129
65013	171
65021	128
65072	130
65080	129
65102	267
65110	366
65129	244
65153	126
65161	127
65188	128
65196	127
65269	171
65277	171
65285	130
65307	200, 201
65315	219
65323	219
65374	366
65382	201
65390	203
65404	232
65405	232
65406	232
65407	232
65408	232
65409	232
65412	233
65420	239
65439	202
65447	202
65455	366
65463	366
65471	173
65498	131
65684	131
65692	171
65706	219
65714	239
65790	389
65820	389
65897	219
65900	172
65943	388
65951	388
65978	388
65986	388
81833	73
98469	396
98710	178
98711	368
99002	395
99028	395
99244	396
99245	397
99246	398
99247	397
99260	396
99278	397
99279	395
99280	398
99333	396
99481	75
99511	378
99538	367
99775	378

ALPHABETICAL INDEX

HOW DESIGNS ARE LISTED:

A, An, or The: A design with a name beginning with "A," "An," or "The" is listed by the second word in its name. For instance, "The Emily Louise" is listed as "Emily Louise, The."

Nicknames: Some designs are often referred to by more than one name. For instance, "C. Fletcher Public House" is also called "Public House." In order to make this index easier to use, the designs' common references are listed in addition to their proper names.

Royal Tree Court 160	1957 Cadillac Eldorado Brougham 108
Nuns With Songbooks 71	1957 Chevrolet Bel Air 95
Socket Light Set 399	1958 Corvette Roadster 95
Train Cars 12	1958 John Deere 730 Diesel Tractor 95
th of July Celebration 98	1959 Cadillac Eldorado 100
th Of July Decorating Set 400	1959 Chevrolet Impala Convertible 96
th Of July Parade 357	1961 Ford Ranchero 104
th Avenue Salon 254	1964-1/2 Ford Mustang 88
th Avenue Shoppes 261	1965 Ford Mustang 2+2 Fastback 109
Pony Rides 252, 272	2000 Holly Lane 46
Socket Lite Set 395	2001 Space Oddity 94
Straight Track 410	2101 Maple 21
Days Of Dickens' Village Sign 185	5607 Park Avenue Townhouse 246
Radius Curved Track 411	5609 Park Avenue Townhouse 246
Socket Light Set With Bulbs 397	A. Bieler Farm - Set 206
th Anniversary Village Footbridge 384	Abandoned Gas Pump, The 95
nd St. Fire Company 255	Abel Beesley Butcher 127
LED Light Strand 398	Abington Bridge 188
s Hot Rod 95	Abington Canal 187
Flavors Ice Cream Parlor 29	Abington Canal Boat 186
Gasoline Pump And Sign 57, 104	Abington Lockkeeper's Residence 155
B Baker Street 157, 345	Abington Locks 186
1 Trick-Or-Treat Drive 116	Abington Lockside Inn 155
0 Second Ave. 256	Abner's Implement Co. 51
4 Kissing Claus Lane 55	AC/DC Adapter 395
4 Four Seasons Parkway 260	ACME Toy Factory 309
9 Ford Model-T 273	Acorn Street Lamps 350
0 Harley-Davidson VL With Sidecar ... 280	Acrylic Green Glitter Trees 394
5 Duesenberg 275	Acrylic Ice Block Display Piece 405
7 Pirsch Pumper Fire Truck 275	Acrylic Icicles 405
9 Buick Roadster 282	Ada's Bed And Boarding House 203
0 V16 Cadillac Coupe 281	Adirondack Chairs 362
9 Ford Woody Wagon 96	Admiring Nature's Beauty 227
0 Ford F-1 Pickup 95	Adobe House 11
0 Studebaker 99	Adventures Of Tom Sawyer, Aunt Polly's
1 Custom Mercury 100	House, The 345
4 Willy's CJ3 Jeep 95	Afternoon Picnic, An 359
5 Ford Thunderbird 108	Afternoon Sleigh Ride 357
5 Ford Automobiles 88	Airport 34
5 Pink Cadillac Fleetwood 49, 92	Al's TV Shop 33
5 Hook & Ladder 101	Aldeburgh Music Box Shop 152
5 Mainline Police Sedan 101	Aldeburgh Music Box Shop Gift Set ... 152
5 Pumper 106	Ale Mates 183
5 Ambulance 104	Alfie's Toy School For Elves 318

Entry	Page
All Aboard!	327
All Around The Town	269
All Clear For Take Off	310, 327
All In Together Girls	274
All Saints Church	23, 165
All Saints Corner Church	247
All The World's A Stage	163
All The World's AStage	191
Allied Model Train Set	385
Alpen Akademie der Musik	238
Alpenhorn Player Alpine Village Sign	239
Alpine Church	233
Alpine Shops - Set	234
Alpine Village - Set	232
Alpine Village Sign	239
Alpine Villagers (1986)	239
Alpine Villagers (1999)	241
Altstädter Bierstube	236
Amber 10 Light Set	395
Ambrose Adder's Tonics & Curatives	229
America's Finest	279
American Bandstand	64
American Flags	412
American Hero Comics	59
Amish Buggy	220
Amish Family	220
Amusement Park Carousel	362
Angel Brite Lites	397
Angels In The Snow	91
Animals On The Farm	104
Animated Accessory Track	397
Animated All Around The Park	396
Animated Photo With Santa	399
Animated Skating Pond	396
Animated Ski Mountain	397
Animated Sledding Hill	397
Anne Shaw Toys	203
Another Man's Treasure Accessories	90
Another Man's Treasure Garage	45
Antiquarian Bookseller	161
Antler Inn, The	312
Apothecary (NEV)	200
Apothecary (SV)	23
Apotheke	232
Apple Girl/Newspaper Boy	72
Apple Valley School	208
Applebee's Neighborhood Grill & Bar	377
Architectural Antiques	257
Architectural Treasure	277
Arctic Game Station	318
Arctic Pines	390
Arlington Falls Church	207
Armed Forces Recruiting Station	55
Arriving At The Station	358
Art Classes At Morning's Light	354, 358
Art Institute Of Chicago	263
Art's Hobbies & Crafts	319
Artist's Touch, An	223
Arts Academy	247
Ashbury Inn	137
Ashley Pond Skating Party	181
Ashwick Lane Gift Set	154
Ashwick Lane Hose & Ladder	148
Asleep At The Bus Stop	278
Aspen Trees	363
At The Barn Dance, It's Allemande Left	87
At The Fire House	154, 185
At The October Fest	24
At Your Service	10
Aunt Polly's House	343
Auto With Tree	7
Automobiles	26
Autumn Birch/ Maple Trees	39
Autumn Landscape Set	41
Autumn Maple Tree	38
Autumn Moss	41
Autumn Trees (GVA)	39
Autumn Trees (SB)	36
Autumn/Halloween Landscape Set	41
Bachman's Flower Shop	38
Bachman's For Sale Sign	37
Bachman's Greenhouse	38
Bachman's Hometown Series	37
Bachman's Original Homestead, 1885	38
Bachman's Squash Cart	37
Bachman's Tending The Cold Frame	38
Bachman's Wilcox Truck	38
Back From The Fields	24
Back From The Orchard	35
Backwoods Outhouse	
Backyard Patio, The	
Bag-O-Frosted Topiaries, s/10	3
Bag-O-Frosted Topiaries, s/2	3
Bahnhof	2
Baker Bros. Bagel Bakery	2
Baker Elves	3
Bakery (CIC)	2
Bakery (SV-1981)	
Bakery (SV-1986)	
Balancing Act	3
Bald Eagle Nesting	4
Ball Toss At The Carnival	4
Balloon Seller	3
Ballpark Bleachers	2
Balsam Fir Incense	4
Bank	
Barbie Boutique	3
Bare Branch Tree With 25 Lights	
Bare Branch Trees	
Barley Bree Farmhouse and Barn	
Barleycorn Manor	
Barmby Moor Cottage	
Barn	
Baseball Diamond	
Basket Full Of Blooms, A	
Bass Cabin	
Bat Lights, s/2	
Bats & Spooks Tree	

Entry	Page
Battery Operated Light	396
Bauernhof Drescher	237
Bay Street Shops	352
Bayly's Blacksmith	159
Bayport	19
Bayport Souvenir And Kite Shop	356
Beach Front	361
Beach Front Extensions	361
Beacon Hill House	22
Beacon Hill Victorian	39
Bean And Son Smithy Shop	126
Beard Barber Shop	302
Beard Bros. Sleigh Wash	311
Bearing Gifts	160, 190
Bears In The Birch	410
Beauty Shoppe	309
Beekman House	250
Before The Big Game	91
Begging For Soul Cakes	195
Belle's House	162
Belle's House - Special Edition	166
Ben & Buddy's Lemonade Stand	99
Ben's Barbershop	202
Benjamin Bowman Violin Maker	216
Bergermeister's House	238
Berkshire House	204
Bernhardiner Hundchen	235
Besson Bierkeller	232
Best Friends	102
Best Of The Harvest	226
Best Part Of Easter, The	64, 109
Betsy Trotwood's Cottage	135
Bicycle Built For Two, A	359
Bidwell Windmill #2	158
Bierfest Judge, The	242
Big Ben	151, 341
Big Bill's Service Station	27
Big Prize Turkey, The	189
Big Smile For The Camera	272
Billboard Surprise	107
Biplane Up In The Sky	398
Birch Bench & Table	350
Birch Bridge	351
Birch Fence	351
Birch Gazebo	351
Birch Run Ski Chalet	40
Birch Tree Cluster	391
Bird Seller, The	176
Birds	407
Birds Out Back	412
Birth Of Christ Nativity Set, The	289
Bishops Oast House	137
Bjorn Turoc Rocking Horse Maker	317
Black Cat Diner	115
Black Kittens For Sale	123
Blacksmith	171
Blacksmith To The Rescue	189
Blanket Of New Fallen Snow	405
Blenham Street Bank	143
Blue Line Bus	280
Blue Line Bus Depot	261
Blue Skies Backdrop	409
Blue Star Ice Co.	207
Blue Star Ice Harvesters	221
Bluebird Seed And Bulb	206
Blythe Pond Mill House	129
Boarding & Lodging School - #18	139
Boarding & Lodging School - #43	141
Boarding House	374
Boardwalk Sunday Stroll	226
Bob Cratchit And Tiny Tim	188
Bobbing For Apples	120
Bobwhite Cottage	209
Booter And Cobbler	132
Boston Red Sox Refreshment Stand	283
Boston Red Sox Souvenir Stand	264
Boston Red Sox Tavern	264
Boulder Springs House	40
Boulevard	268
Boulevard Lampposts	397
Bowling Alley	39
Boxing Day Tradition, A	196
Brand New Recruit	99
Brand New Shoes!	106
Brandon Bungalow, The	43
Breakers Point Lighthouse	213
Breezy Hill Stables	355
Brew Ha-Ha	123
Brewster Bay Cottages - Set	207
Brick Abbey	131
Brick Lift	328
Brick Path	414
Brick Road	407
Brick Town Hall	200
Brick Town Square	408
Bridge Over The Icy Pond	416
Brighton School	250
Brighton Train	171
Brightsmith & Sons, Queens Jewellers	157
Bringing Christmas Cheer, Queens Port	194
Bringing Fleeces To The Mill	177
Bringing Home The Baby	273
Bringing Home The Holly	163, 191
Bringing Home The Tree	74
Bringing Home The Yule Log	175
Bringing The Irish Cheer	97
Brite Lites Adapter	396
Brixton Road Watchman	179
Brokerage House	249
Bronner's Custom Building	385
Browning Cottage	141
Brownlow House	138
Brownstone	10
Brownstones	244
Brownstones On The Square - Set	250
Bubble Light Ghosts	421
Buck's County Farmhouse	51
Buck's County Horse Barn	50

Buck's County Horse Trailer	95
Buck's County Stables	94
Buck's County Water Tower	94
Budweiser Brewery	65
Budweiser Clydesdales	109
Buffalo On The Prairie	411
Building The Scarecrow	121
Bumper Fun Ride	399
Bumpstead Nye Cloaks & Canes	140
Bungalow	58
Burwickglen Golf Clubhouse	155
Buster Helps Out	63, 109
Bustin' A Move	332
Busy City Sidewalks	274
Busy Day In Town, A	194
Busy Elf North Pole Sign, A	322
Busy Railway Station	185
Busy Sidewalks	268
Butter Tub Barn	144
Butter Tub Farmhouse	144
Buying Bakers Bread	239
By The Pond	129
C. Bradford, Wheelwright & Son	177
C. Fletcher Public House	132
C. H. Watt Physician	137
Café Caprice French Restaurant	251
Calling All Cars	75
Camden Park Cobblestone Road	409
Camden Park Fountain	398
Camden Park Square	409
Camden Park Square Stone Wall	404
Campbell's Soup Counter	58
Campbell's Trick-Or-Treat	120
Can I Have Your Autograph?	279
Can I Keep Them	334
Can I Open One Now?	110
Can't Wait For Halloween!	123
Canadian Pub	167
Canadian Trading Co.	147
Candle Shop	126
Candlerock Lighthouse Restaurant	50
Candles Brite Lites	398
Candles By The Doorstep	395
Candy Cane & Peppermint Shop	304
Candy Cane Bench	416
Candy Cane Elves	304, 323
Candy Cane Fence	416
Candy Cane Lane - Set	304
Candy Cane Shack	333
Candy Canes Brite Lites	397
Candy Corn String of 20 Lights	419
Candy Corn Trees	421
Candy Mining	308, 326
Canine Courier	325
Canine Trick-Or-Treaters	121
Cannon And Flag	54, 97
Cape Cod	8
Cape Keag Fish Cannery	207
Capitol, The	251

Captain Black Bart's Ghost	119
Captain Kensey's House	214
Captain's Cottage	204
Car Hop	53, 96
Car Wash Cadets	328
Car Wash Fundraiser	102
Caramel Apple Stand	123
Caravansary Corner	288
Caravansary Drinking Well	296
Caravansary Gate & Guard	296
Caravansary Rooms at the Inn	288
Caravansary Wall	296
Caribou Coffee Shop	310
Carmel Cottage	36
Carnival Carousel	44
Carnival Carousel LED Light Set	398
Carnival Tickets & Cotton Candy	87
Carolers (DVA)	17
Carolers (SVA)	69
Carolers On The Doorstep	17
Caroling At The Farm	8
Caroling Family	7
Caroling Through The Snow	8
Caroling Thru The City	26
Caroling We Shall Go, A	19
Caroling With The Cratchit Family	18
Carpenter & Son	287, 29
Carpenter Gothic Bed & Breakfast	4
Carpenter's Shop	26
Carriage House (1982)	1
Carriage House (1986)	2
Carriage Ride For The Bride, A	27
Carry Out Boy	10
Cascades Marina	6
Castle	1
Castle Blackstone	1
Castle Glassworks	2
Catch Of The Day, The	8
Catch The Wind	32
Cathedral Church (1980)	
Cathedral Church (1987)	
Cathedral Church Of St. Mark	2
Cathedral Of St. Paul	257, 3
Cathedral, The	2
Cats & Dogs	4
Cedar Pine Forest	3
Cedar Point Cabin	
Cedar Ridge School	
Celebration Tree 2000	3
Centennial House	
Center For The Arts	
Central Park Carriage	2
Central Synagogue	260, 3
Ceramic Car	
Ceramic Sleigh	
Chadbury Station And Train	1
Chain Link Fence Extensions	4
Chain Link Fence With Gate	4
Chamber Orchestra	2

Champsfield Stadium 47	Christmas Bells 368
Chancery Corner 151	Christmas Bread Bakers 305
Chapel Of Love 64	Christmas Cadillac 78
Chapel On The Hill 353	Christmas Candy Mill, The 315
Chapman's Cider House 215	Christmas Carol Christmas
Charitable Vicar, The 192	Morning Figures 174
Charting Santa's Course 322	Christmas Carol Christmas
Chas. Hoyt Blacksmith 217	Spirits Figures 174
Chateau 17	Christmas Carol Cottage, The 145
Check It Out Bookmobile 79	Christmas Carol Cottages - Set 129
Check This Out 326	Christmas Carol Figures 171
Checking It Twice Wind-Up Toys 314	Christmas Carol Holiday Trimming Set 178
Checking The Ship's Manifest 197	Christmas Carol Reading
Chelsea Lane Shoppers 176	By Charles Dickens 181
Chelsea Market Curiosities Monger & Cart .. 177	Christmas Carol Visit, A 189
Chelsea Market Fish Monger & Cart 176	Christmas Carolers 369
Chelsea Market Flower Monger & Cart ... 176	Christmas Children 71
Chelsea Market Fruit Monger & Cart 176	Christmas Cove Lighthouse 37
Chelsea Market Hat Monger & Cart 179	Christmas Critters Pet Store 317
Chelsea Market Mistletoe Monger & Cart .. 177	Christmas Eave Trim 407
Cherry Lane Shops - Set 202	Christmas Eve Celebration 157, 188
Chesterton Manor House 131	Christmas Eve Delivery 55, 100
Chestnut Vendor 191	Christmas Eve Flight Backdrop, A 413
Chez Monet 258	Christmas Eve Visit 260, 280
Chicago Cubs Refreshment Stand 283	Christmas Fun Run 324
Chicago Cubs Souvenir Shop 264	Christmas Garlands & Wreaths 362
Chicago Cubs Tavern 264	Christmas In The City - Set 244
Chicago Water Tower 342	Christmas In The City Sign 267
Chicago White Sox Refreshment Stand ... 283	Christmas In The Forest 394
Chicago White Sox Souvenir Stand 264	Christmas Is Coming 107
Chicago White Sox Tavern 264	Christmas Kids 86
Child's Play 183	Christmas Lake Chalet 52
Childe Pond And Skaters 173	Christmas Lake High School 40
Children In Band 71	Christmas Lights Tour 110
Chimney Sweep & Son 189	Christmas Luminaries 398
Chimney Sweep For Hire! 331	Christmas Morning Parade 193
China Trader, The 153	Christmas Pudding Costermonger 182
Chisel McTimber Art Studio 349	Christmas Puppies 78
Chocolate Bunny Factory 64	Christmas Shop, The 31
Chocolate Shoppe 245	Christmas Star Street Lights 401
Choir Kids 73	Christmas Time Post Office 66
Choirboys All-In-A-Row 271	Christmas Topiaries 263, 282
Choosing Rights 278	Christmas Trash Cans 77
Chop Shop, The 144	Christmas Treasures 265
Chopping Firewood 83	Christmas Village Express 370
Chowder House 208	Christmas Visit To The Florist 89
Christmas Apples 149, 182	Christmas Wreaths 388
Christmas Around The World -	Christmastime Trimming 94
Feliz Navidad 335	Church 374
Christmas At Codington Cottage 160	Church Of The Holy Light 260
Christmas At The Farm 79	Church Of The Holy Sepulcher 291
Christmas At The Park 270	Church Of The Open Door 20
Christmas Barn Dance 42	Churchyard Fence & Gate 367
Christmas Bazaar Flapjacks & Hot Cider ... 222	Churchyard Fence Extensions 367
Christmas Bazaar Handmade Quilts 222	Churchyard Gate And Fence 367
Christmas Bazaar Sign 222	Cinema 56 47
Christmas Bazaar Toy Vendor & Cart 222	City Ambulance 273
Christmas Bazaar Woolens & Preserves .. 222	City Bus & Milk Truck 267
Christmas Beginning, A 192	City Clockworks 248

Entry	Page
City Fire Dept. Fire Truck	269
City Globe, The	251
City Hall	245
City Landscape Set	413
City Lights Christmas Trimmings	63
City Lit Bare Branch Tree	393
City Newsstand	267
City Park Gateway	278
City People	267
City Police Car	273
City Professions - Doctor & Nurse	275
City Professions - House Painter & Newspaper Boy	275
City Professions - Postman & Dairy Delivery Man	275
City Shopping	277
City Sledding	282
City Subway Entrance	269
City Taxi	271
City Trolley	401
City Workers	172
City Zoological Garden	277
Clark Street Automat	254
Classic Cars	80
Classic Tinsel Trees - Red, Green, Silver	394
Classic Tinsel Trees - White	394
Clear Ice	405
Clearing The Driveway Again!	401
Climb Every Mountain	239
Cobb Cottage	141
Cobbler & Clock Peddler	179
Cobbler's Corner Stand	189
Cobblestone Antique Shop	26
Cobblestone Road	407
Cobblestone Shops - Set	132
Cobblestone Town Square	408
Cobles Police Station	135
Coca-Cola Fizz Factory	314
Coca-Cola Neon Sign	397
Coca-Cola Sliding Hill	332
Coca-Cola Soda Fountain	263
Coca-Cola Taste Test	331
Coca–Cola brand Billboard	82
Coca–Cola brand Bottling Plant	37
Coca–Cola brand Corner Drugstore	37
Coca–Cola brand Delivery Men	82
Coca–Cola brand Delivery Truck	82
Cocoa Stop, The	56
Codington Cottage	163
Coffee-Stall, The	193
Coke For You And Me!, A	282
Cold Care Clinic	307
Cold Weather Sports	77
Collectors Club House	375
College Kids At Krispy Kreme	98
Collyweston Post Office	162
Colonial Church	28
Colonial Farm House	12
Come Into The Inn	175
Come Join The Parade	77
Congratulations…Recruit!	99
Congregational Church	19
Connacher's Nursery	216
Constables	173
Consulate, The	254
Corner Cafe	27
Corner Grocer	245
Corner Store	13
Corral Fence	404
Costume Parade	121
Costumes For Sale	119
Cottage of Bob Cratchit & Tiny Tim, The	129
Cottage Toy Shop	130
Couldn't Wait Until Christmas	89
Counting House	132
Counting House & Silas Thimbleton Barrister	132
Country Church	6
Country Harvest	78
Country Quilts And Pies	54
Country Road Lampposts, s/2	397
Country Road Lampposts, s/4	397
Countryside Church	363
Countryside Church (SV)	10
Courthouse	29
Courtyard Fence With Steps	403
Covered Bridge	219
Covered Bridge At The Manor	192
Covered Wooden Bridge	219
Crack The Whip	74
Craftsman Cottage	33
Craggy Cliff Extensions	410
Craggy Cliff Platform	410
Craggy Cove Lighthouse	201
Craggy Oak Tree	39
Cranberry House, The	213
Cratchit's Corner	157
Crayola Polar Palette Art Center	308
Create AScene Village Platform	414
Creating Silver Keepsakes	213, 22
Creative Carvings	12
Creepy Creek Bridge	41
Creepy Creek Carriage House	11
Creepy Village Sign	42
Crooked Fence Cottage	14
Crosby House	5
Crown & Cricket Inn	13
Crowntree Freckleton Windmill	15
Crowntree Inn	12
Cruisin' Crayola Elves	32
Crushed Ice	40
Crystal Gardens Conservatory	26
Crystal Ice King & Queen	37
Crystal Ice Palace	36
Cuckoo Clock Vendor &Cart	24
Cumberland House	2
Curved Village Gumdrop Road	4
Custom House	1

Custom Stitchers	306
Customs House, Queens Port	169
Cutting The Trail	327
Cypress Trees	294
Daily News, The	162
Dairy Barn	35
Dairy Delivery Sleigh	225
Dairy Land Creamery	58
Dancing An Irish Jig	228
Danube Music Publisher	235
Dash Away Delivery	325
Dashing Through The Snow	177
David Copperfield - Set	135
David Copperfield Characters	173
Day At The Ballpark, A	283
Day At The Beach, A	107
Day At The Cabin, A	225
Day At The Waterfront, A	358
Day Of Holiday Shopping, A	359
Deacon's Way Chapel	210
Dead End Motel	117
Decorate The Tree	44, 87
Decorated Sisal Trees	391
Decorating With Holiday Greenery	194
Dedlock Arms	139
Deer In The Woods	413
DeFazio's Pizzeria	259
Delivering Coal For The Hearth	181
Delivering Real Plastic Snow	324
Delivering The Christmas Greens	323
Delivering The Christmas Spirit	228
Delivery Truck	284
Delta House	18
Department 56 Brite Lites	396
Department 56 Caboose	386
Department 56 Locomotive	386
Department 56 Studio, 1200 Second Ave.	256
Depot And Train With 2 Train Cars	21
Desert Camp	294
Desert Caravan	296
Desert Oasis	293
Desert Road	295
Desert Rocks	295
Design Works North Pole	310
Dickens Learns To Read	193
Dickens Writing	158, 188
Dickens' Birthplace	165
Dickens' Cottages - Set	128
Dickens' Gad's Hill Chalet	158
Dickens' Lane Shops	130
Dickens' Raising The Flag	190
Dickens' Sleighride	366
Dickens' Village Church	127
Dickens' Village Mill	127
Dickens' Village Sign	171
Dickens' Village Start A Tradition Set (1995)	142
Dickens' Village Start A Tradition Set (1997)	146
Dinah's Drive-In	35
Diner	24
Dinner Guests	65, 111
Disney Parks Family	347
Disney Parks Village Series	346
Disneyland Fire Department #105	347
Do I Have A Deal For You!	334
Dockhouse, The	411
Doctor & Nurse	275
Doctor's House	29
Doctor's House Call	224
Doctor's Office, The	247
Dog And Puppies, Cat And Kittens	412
Doghouse/Cat In Garbage Can	72
Don't Break The Ornaments	323
Don't Drop The Presents!	270
Don't Let Go!	332
Door-To-Door Sales	98
Doorman	159, 188
Dorothy's Dress Shop	246
Dorothy's Skate Rental	369
Double Bungalow	32
Double Light Socket Adapter	398
Double Pine Trees	390
Double Street Lamps	395
Dover Coach	172
Down The Chimney He Goes	76
Downhill Daredevils	325
Downhill Elves	416
Dragon Parade, The	92
Dressed For Success	284
Dressed In Our Easter Best	106
Dressed Up For Fun	114, 120
Drugstore	374
Drummond Bank	216
Drying The Wool	313, 330
Duck Pond	8
Dudden Cross Church	142
Dudley Docker	151
Duplex	20
Dursley Manor	143
Dutch Colonial	39
E. Staubr Backer	232
E. Tipler, Agent For Wines & Spirits	168
Early Morning Delivery	78
Early Rising Elves	323
East Cape Cottages	355
East Harbor Ferry	262
East Harbor Fish Co.	259
East Indies Trading Co.	147
East Willet Pottery	209
Easter Decorating Set	400
Easter Egg Hunt	105
Easter Village Express	371
Ebbets Field	260
Ebbets Field Scoreboard	280
Ebenezer Scrooge's House	158
Ed Sullivan Theater, The	264
Eerie Rocks &Road	420
Egg Hunt	55, 97

Egg Nog Pub, The	310
Eight Maids A-Milking - #VIII	180
Election Yard Signs	408
Electric Foam Cutter	399
Elegant Ride, An	190
Elementary My Dear Watson	157, 188, 345
Eleven Lords A-Leaping - #XI	183
Elf Bunkhouse	300
Elf Mountain Ski Resort	307
Elf Sculpting	349
Elf Spa, The	306
Elf Tree House	326
Elfie's Sleds & Skates	301
Elfin Forge & Assembly Shop	303
Elfin Snow Cone Works	302
Elsie's Gingerbread	305
Elves	350
Elves On Ice	416
Elves On Track	416
Elves On Wheels	316
Elves' Trade School	303
Elvis Presley's Autograph	93
Elvis Presley's Graceland Gift Set	49
Emily Louise, The	210
Empire State Building	261, 342
End Of The Line	323
English Church	13
English Cottage	13
English Post Box	176
English Tudor	17
Erin Go Bragh	283
Escape From The Crypt	421
Evening Of Horseback Riding	360
Evergreen Trees	389
Everybody Goes Skating At Rollerama	86
Everybody's Been Good This Year!	336
Everything Looks A-Okay	314, 331
Excellent Taste	274
Fabric Cobblestone Road	412
Faces Of The Season Picket Fence	417
Fagin's Hide-A-Way	137
Fall Oaks	394
Fall Platform	414
Fallen Leaves	390
Family Canoe Trip	94
Family Day At The Carnival	422
Family Mom/Kids, Goose/Girl	70
Family Out For A Walk	279
Family Sleigh Ride	228
Family Tradition, A	189
Family Tree, The	271
Family Winter Outing	411
Farm Accessory Set	87
Farm Animals (1989)	219
Farm Animals (1995)	221
Farm House (1987)	25
Farm House (1997)	42
Farm People & Animals	171
Farmer's Co-Op Granary, The	46
Farmer's Flatbed	88
Farmer's Market	223
Father Christmas's Journey	182
Faversham Lamps & Oil	142
Federal House	36
Federbetten Und Steppdecken	235
Feeding The Birds	81
Feeding The Ducks	97
Feeney's Anniversary Lamppost	384
Feeney's Delivery Of Dreams	383
Feeney's Our Sign For All Seasons	384
Fence Brite Lites	396
Fenway Park	257
Ferry Ticket Sales	262, 280
Festive Front Yard	400
Fezziwig And Friends	173
Fezziwig Delivery Wagon, The	180
Fezziwig's Ballroom Animated Gift Set	154
Fezziwig's Warehouse	129
Fiber Optic Trees	393
Fiber Optic Woods Green Trees/Multi-lights	393
Fiber Optic Woods, Green Trees	393
Fiber Optic Woods, White Trees	393
Fieldstone Curved Wall/Bench	40
Fieldstone Entry Gate	40
Fieldstone Fireplace	41
Fieldstone Footbridge	39
Fieldstone Stairway	41
Fieldstone Wall	40
Fieldstone Wall With Apple Tree	40
Figure Skater On Ice	40
Fillers &Flakers	33
Final Touch, The	52, 9
Finding The Bird's Song	9
Fine Asian Antiques	18
Finishing Touch, The	24
Finklea's Finery: Costume Shop	3
Fire Brigade Of London Town, The	18
Fire Brigade, The	26
Fire Drill Practice	27
Fire Hydrant & Mailbox	7
Fire Station	1
Fire Station #3	4
Fire Station No. 2	
Fireman To The Rescue	
Firewood Delivery Truck	8
Fireworks	39
Fireworks Replacement Bulbs	39
First Deposit	
First Edition, The	162, 1
First Frost Snow Crystals	4
First Metropolitan Bank	2
First Round Of The Year	
First Snow, The	3
Fisherman's Nook Cabins	
Fisherman's Nook Resort	
Fishing At Trout Lake	4
Fishing In The Bay	3

Entry	Page
Five Golden Rings - #V	179
Flag Pole	75
Flat Of Ebenezer Scrooge, The	136
Flexible Autumn Hedges	391
Flexible Sisal Hedge	390
Flexible Sisal Hedge, Lg	391
Flocked Pine Trees, s/2	392
Flocked Pine Trees. s/3	392
Flower Shop	15
Flowering Potted Tree	361
Flowering Vine	361
Flurry's Snowglobe Maker	315
Fly Through Elf	333
Fly-casting in The Brook	223
Flying Scot Train, The	174
Following The Leader	186
For Sale Sign	74
For The Love Of Books	279
For You, My Lady	164, 194
For Your Sweetheart	277
Forever On Guard	122
Formal Gardens	190
Foster Pharmacy	255
Four Calling Birds - #IV	179
Foxes In The Forest	410
Frango Chocolate Shop	385
Frangos For You And I	385
Franklin Hook & Ladder Co.	210
Fred Holiwell's House	159
Freight Truck	111
Fresh Dairy Delivery	103
Fresh Fallen Snow 2 lb. Box	405
Fresh Fallen Snow 7 oz. Bag	405
Fresh Fish Today	279
Fresh Flower Cart	414
Fresh Flowers For Sale	274
Fresh Frozen Fish	76
Fresh Paint New England Village Sign	222
Fresh Seafood By The Shore	360
Friendly Used Car Sales	62
Frogmore Chemist	147
Frost And Sons 5 & Dime	50
Frostbite Tree House Day Care	331
Frosted Bare Branch Tree, Lg	389
Frosted Bare Branch Tree, Sm	389
Frosted Cone Tree w/Wood Base, Lg	388
Frosted Evergreen Papier-Maché, s/3	389
Frosted Fir Trees	390
Frosted Fountain	399
Frosted Hemlock Trees	391
Frosted Norway Pines	388
Frosted Shrubbery	392
Frosted Spruce	391
Frosted Spruce Tree 15"	389
Frosted Spruce Tree 22"	389
Frosted Topiaries	392
Frosted Topiary Trees, S/2	388
Frosted Topiary Village Garden	388
Frosted Topiary, s/4	388
Frosted Topiary, s/8, Lg	388
Frosted Topiary, s/8, Sm	388
Frosted Zig–Zag Tree, Green	389
Frosted Zig–Zag Tree, White	389
Frosty Light Sprays	398
Frosty Light Trees	392
Frosty Pines Outfitters	313
Frosty Playground	331
Frosty Playtime	82
Frosty Tree-Lined Picket Fence	403
Frozen Swirl, The	58
Frozen Veggies	331
Full Count	276
Full Service Attendant	263, 282
Fun At The Firehouse	88
Fun In The Snow	357
Fun In The Snow (SVA)	96
Future Hockey Stars	110
G. Choir's Weights &Scales	147
Gabled Cottage	6
Gabled House	15
Gad's Hill Place	145
Galena House	18
Garden Cart, The	358
Garden Fountain	361
Garden Gazebo	361
Garden Park Bench	361
Garden Swing, The	358
Garden Valley Vineyards	355
Gardengate House	255
Gardens Of Santorini	265
Gasthof Eisl	232
Gate House	175
Gatekeeper's Dwelling	286
Gathering Cranberries	225
Gathering Grapes	360
Gathering Pumpkins	120
General Store (NEV)	200
General Store (SV)	8
Gentleman and Lady, A	191
Gently Down The Stream	358
Geo. Weeton Watchmaker	133
Geranium Window Box	361
Get Your Spices 'Ere!	196
Getreidemühle Zwettl	237
Ghost Of Christmas Present Visits Scrooge	188
Ghostly Carousel	115
Ghostly Landscape Set	420
Giant Trees	11
Gift Wrap & Ribbons	304
Gifts for Easter	56, 100
Gifts On The Go	92
Giggelswick Mutton & Ham	141
Gingerbread Chalet	6
Gingerbread Corner	309, 327
Gingerbread House	16
Gingerbread Vendor	181
Ginny's Cookie Treats	309

Entry	Page
Girl/Snowman, Boy	70
Glacier Gazette, The	305
Glacier Park Pavilion	312
Glass Ornament Works	305
Glassworks Craftsman	227
Glendun Cocoa Works	156
Glenhaven House	37
Glistening Snow	405
Glitter Detail	328
Glockenspiel	236
Glowing String of Scary Lights	420
Going Home For The Holidays	272
Going Hunting	242
Going To The Chapel	81
Golden Dragon Restaurant	48
Golden Gate Bridge	265, 343
Golden Swan Baker	126
Golden Vine Ferris Wheel, The	422
Gondola Animated Scene	400
Gone Fishing	110, 351
Good Day's Catch, A	183
Good Day, Reverend	228
Good Fishing	412
Good Samaritan, The	297
Good Shepherd & His Animals	293
Good Shepherd Chapel & Church School	33
Gothic Church	17
Gothic Farmhouse	31
Gothic Street Lamp	419
Gourmet Chocolates Delivery Wagon	186
Governor's Mansion	16
Graceland	49
Gracie's Dry Goods & General Store	43
Grand Central Railway Station	251
Grand Creamery, The	354
Grand Day Of Fishing, A	358
Grand Movie Theater, The	252
Grand Ole Opry Carolers	83
Grandma's Bakery	311
Grandma's Cottage	32
Grandpap's Cabin	66
Grandview Shores Hotel	352
Grapes Inn, The	143
Grassy Ground Cover	410
Gravel Road	410
Gravely Haunting - 2004, A	121
Gravely Haunting - 2005, A	122
Gravely Landscape Set	419
Gray Cobblestone Archway	410
Gray Cobblestone Capstones	410
Gray Cobblestone Section	410
Gray Cobblestone Tunnel	410
Great Denton Mill	140
Great Expectations Satis Manor	150, 344
Great Gatsby West Egg Mansion, The	345
Green	409
Green Gate Cottage	136
Green Glitter Sisal Trees	417
Green Grocer	126
Green's Park Nosegays	164
Greetings	407
Grimsly Manor	113
Grist Mill	233
Grocery	16
Ground Cover	411
Guarding The Castle	196, 343
Gumdrop Street Lamp	417
Gumdrop Street Lamps	416
Gumdrop Taste Test	334
Gumdrop Topiaries	417
Gumdrop Tree Non-Lit, 12"	417
Gumdrop Tree Non-Lit, 9"	417
Gumdrop Tree w/LED Lights	417
Gunnersbury Park Folly	164
Gus's Drive-In	53
Haberdashery	248
Hailing A Cab	274
Hale & Hardy House	211
Halfpenny Showman, The	193
Hall Of Records	304
Halloween Accessories	418
Halloween Dance	120
Halloween Fence	418
Halloween Full Moon	419
Halloween Hayride	119
Halloween Hot Rod	123
Halloween Kids	120
Halloween Luminaries	418
Halloween Parade	421
Halloween Pumpkin Stand	418
Halloween Scene	418
Halloween Scenery, s/9	421
Halloween Spooky Tree	418
Halloween Topiaries	419
Halloween Twinkle Brite Tree	421
Halloween Village Express	370
Halloween Village Set	419
Halloween Village Sign	419
Halloween Yard Decorations	420
Hand Carved Nutcracker Factory	313
Handmade Quilts For Sale	54, 97
Hank's Market	24
Happy Birthday Village Express	37
Happy Couple, The	64, 10
Happy Easter Church	6
Happy Easter House	5
Happy Harley Day, A	32
Happy Haunting	12
Happy Holidays Gondola	38
Happy New Year (SVA)	9
Happy New Year! (NP)	32
Hard Rock Café Snow Village	6
Harley-Davidson City Dealership	25
Harley-Davidson Fat Boy & Softail	8
Harley-Davidson Holiday, A	8
Harley-Davidson Motorcycle Truck	28
Harley-Davidson Sign	8
Harley-Davidson Water Tower	9

Entry	Page
Harley-Davidson Detailing, Parts & Service	262
Harley-Davidson Manufacturing	46
Harley-Davidson Motorcycle Shop	41
Harmony House	57
Harper's Farm	210
Harper's Farmhouse	211
Harrison House	261
Hartford House	33
Harvest Bounty	414
Harvest Decorations	362
Harvest Feast, A	413
Harvest Gourds	420
Harvest Mailbox	421
Harvest Pumpkin Wagon	222
Harvest Seed Cart	220
Harvest Time	219
Harvest Yard Fun	109
Hather Harness	142
Haunted Barn	114
Haunted Coal Car	122, 421
Haunted Fiber Optic Backdrop	420
Haunted Front Yard	418
Haunted Fun House Gift Set	114
Haunted Graveyard	418
Haunted Harvest	121
Haunted Hearse	419
Haunted Mansion	113
Haunted Outhouse	419
Haunted Tower Tours	122
Haunted Tree House	120
Haunted Windmill	115
Hauntsburg House	113
Have A Seat Elves	324
Haversham House	18
Hayride	72
He Led Them Down The Streets Of Town	86
Head of Cheese, A	241
Heading For The Hills	85
Hear Ye Citizens (NEV)	229
Hear Ye, Citizens (AV)	242
Hear Ye, Hear Ye	369
Hearts & Blooms Cottage	56
Heathmoor Castle	149
Heavy Snowfall, A	79
Hedgerow Dovecote	186
Hedgerow Garden Cottage	155
Heidi & Her Goats	240
Heidi's Grandfather's House	236
Heinz Evaporated Horse Radish Factory	376
Heinz Grocery Store	376
Heinz Hitch	376
Heinz House	376
Heinz Town Clock	377
Helga's House Of Fortunes	115
Hembleton Pewterer	139
Hensly Cadillac & Buick	264
Heralding Angels	293
Herd Of Holiday Heifers, A	80
Here Comes Santa	380
Here Comes Sinter Klaus	225
Here Comes The Birdie!	107
Here Comes The Bride	241
Here Comes The Ice Cream Man	357
Here Fishy Fishy Ice House	412
Here We Come A Caroling	76
Here We Come A-Wassailing	182
Heritage Banners	407
Heritage Museum Of Art	249
Heritage Village Box Car	386
Heritage Village Farm Set	171
Heritage Village Promotional Banner	408
Heritage Village Promotional Sign	367
Heritage Village Utility Accessories	272
Herod's Temple	287
Hershey's Chocolate Shop	43
Hi-De-Ho Nightclub	251
Hidden Ponds House	45
High Priests	287, 293
High Roller Riverboat Casino	60
High Tea	158, 188
Highland Park House	22
Hiking In The North Woods	98
Historic Chicago Water Tower	261, 342
Historical Landmark Series, The	340
Hitch-Up The Buckboard	87
Hitching Post, The	228
HMS Britannia	196
Hockey Practice	400
Hocus Pocus Witch	418
Hofburg Castle	236
Holiday Coach	175
Holiday Cobblestone Road	416
Holiday Deliveries	323
Holiday Field Trip	271
Holiday Fun Run	96
Holiday Hoops	84
Holiday House, The	50
Holiday Joy	190
Holiday Quintet	185
Holiday Reindeer Run	96
Holiday Singers	400
Holiday Sleigh Ride Together, A	86
Holiday Streetlights, s/2	414
Holiday Tinsel Trims	409
Holiday Travelers	174
Holiday Trimmings	413
Holly & The Ivy, The	368
Holly Archway Brite Lites	398
Holly Bros. Tank Car	386
Holly Brothers Garage	38
Holly Hedges	393
Holly Split Rail Fence	404
Holly Split Rail Fence w/Seated Children	404
Holly Topiaries	393
Holly Tree	391
Holly Tree & Bush	393
Hollyberry Cottage	169

Hollydale's Department Store 246	Icicle Trees 392
Holy Land Animals 297	Icy Delights 327
Holy Land Backdrop, The 295	Icy Tree, Lg 393
Holy Name Church 250	Icy Trees, Med 393
Holy Night Fiber Optic Backdrop 297	Icy Trees, Sm 393
Holy Night Nativity 289	Independence Hall 340
Holy Spirit Baptistery 91	Inglenook Cottage #5 353
Holy Spirit Church 48	Inn, The 6
Home Away From Home 102	Innkeeper's Caravansary 286
Home Delivery 76	Irish Cheer For Santa, An 332
Home For The Holidays Caboose 63	Is It Raining? 375
Home For The Holidays Express 59	Is That Frosty? 92
Home For The Holidays, A 76	It's A Grand Old Flag 407
Home From The Mill 241	It's Almost Thanksgiving 224
Home In The Making Accessories, A 47, 90	It's The Easter Bunny! 101
Home In The Making, A 47	It's Time For An Icy Treat 90
Home Sweet Home 27	Italianate Villa 42
Homestead 7	Ivy Glen Church 134
Honest, This Tree Came Out Of Nowhere! .. 421	Ivy Terrace Apartments 249
Honeymooner Motel, The 31	Ivy Vine 362
Hop Castle Folly 161	J. D. Nichols Toy Shop 143
Hope Chest Consignment Shop 66	J. Horsley Christmas Cards 168
Horse And Hounds Pub, The 150	J. Hudson Stoveworks 208
Horse Drawn Hearse 193	J. Lytes Coal Merchant 146
Horse With Coach 172	J. Noyes Mill 217
Horses At The Lampguard 187	J. Young's Granary 29
Hospital For Sick Children	Jack In The Box Plant No. 2 308
At Ormond Street 166	Jack Pines 390
Hot Chocolate For Sale 276	Jack's Corner Barber Shop 32
Hot Chocolate Tower 335	Jack's Umbrella Shop 375
Hot Dog Vendor 271	Jack-O' Lanterns 418
Hot Pretzels 281	Jack-O'-Lantern String of 12 Lights 419
Hot Roasted Chestnuts 277	Jack-O-Lantern Pumpkins 420
House For Sale Sign 71	Jack-Of-The-Lantern 191
House Of The Last Supper Gift Set 291	Jacob Adams Farmhouse & Barn 201
House Painter & Newspaper Boy 275	Jägerutte - Hunting Cabin 238
How Tall Is It? 280	Jannes Mullet Amish Barn 204
How The Grinch Stole Christmas -	Jannes Mullet Amish Farm House 204
Movie Premiere 93	Jefferson School 25
Howard Street Row Houses 169	Jenny's Corner Book Shop 255
Hudson Public Library 258	Jeremiah Brewster House 207
Hunting Lodge 35	Jingle Belle Houseboat 28
Hurry - The Movie's About To Start! 117	John Deere Water Tower 378
Hurry The Movie's About To Start! 123	Johnson's Grocery & Deli 251
Hutchison Grain Elevator 215	Johnson's Grocery Holiday Deliveries ... 272
Hybrid Landscape 390	Jonathan The Bear Man 104
I Love My Village Brite Lites 396	Jonathan The Bear Man's Carving Studio ... 58
I'll Need More Toys 322	Jones & Co. Brush & Basket Shop 127
I'm Home! 105	Josef Engel Farmhouse 233
I'm Wishing 356	Joyful Greetings 60, 105
Ice &Snow Skating Pond 334	Juliette's School Of French Cuisine 52
Ice Cold Coca-Cola 335	Just A Cup Of Joe 328
Ice Cream For Everyone 103	Just Married 84
Ice Crystal Blanket Of Snow 405	Just Treats, No Tricks, Please 116, 122
Ice Crystal Gate & Walls 404	Kamm Haus 234
Ice Crystal Pines 394	Käsehändler Schmitt 231
Ice Crystal Walls 404	Katie McCabe's Restaurant & Books 264
Ice Man Waiteth, The s/2 414	KBRR TV 6
Ichabod Crane's Cottage 205	Keep America Beautiful 27

Keeping The Streets Clean	187
Kelly's Irish Crafts	262
Kenilworth Castle	131
Kensington Palace	149
Kenwood House	26
Key To The City CIC Sign, A	271
Key To The North Pole, The	333
Kick Up Your Heels	328
Kid Gloves Moving	284
Kiddie Parade	103
Kids Around The Tree	70
Kids Decorating The Village Sign	75
Kids Love Hershey's!	86
Kids Tree House	74
Kids, Candy Canes…& Ronald McDonald	86
Killing Time	421
King's Road - Set	137
King's Road Cab	174
King's Road Market Cross	184
King's Road Post Office	139
Kingsford's Brew House	139
Kisses - 25 Cents	105
Kissing Under The Mistletoe	167, 195
Kite of Spring, The	360
Knife Grinder	221
Knob Hill	9
Knottinghill Church	134
KOLD Radio	315
Konditorei Schokolade	234
Kringle Elfementary School	313
Kringle Street Snowman	330
Kringle Street Town Santa	334
Kringle Street Town Tree	332
Kringles Toy Shop	41
Krinkles Christmas Ornament Design Studio	318
Krinkles For Sale	335
Krispy Kreme Doughnut Deliveries	101
Krispy Kreme Doughnut Shop	54
Kukuck Uhren	234
Lafayette's Bakery	254
LaGhosti Movie Theater	117
Lamp Post Extension	403
Lamp Post Fence	403
Lamp Post Fence Extension	403
Lamplighter With Lamp	173
Landscape	390
Landscape Starter Set	393
Large Single Tree	14
Last Mail Call Of The Day	192
Last Minute Delivery	322
Last Stop Gas Station	49
Last String Of Lights	258, 277
Lattice Obelisk	361
Laundry Day	91
Laurel Hill Church	213
Leacock Poulterer	148
Leading The Bavarian Cow	240
Leather Bottle, The	162
LED Light Bulb	397
Leed's Oyster House	153
LEGO Warehouse Forklift	329
LEGO Building Creation Station	310
Leonardo & Vincent	326
Let It Snow Crystals, 8 oz. Box	405
Let It Snow Machine	397
Let It Snow Snowman Sign	408
Let It Snow, Let It Snow	86
Let's Get A New Bike	59, 104
Let's Go One More Time	224
Let's Go Shopping In The City	272
Let's Play House	102
Let's Swing!	401
Letter From Papa, A	211, 224, 344
Letters For Santa	321
Life Of The Party, The	276
Lifeguard On Duty	359
Light Adapter	399
Light Adapter With 3 Jacks	399
Light Hole Protectors	412
Lighted Acrylic Trees	394
Lighted Christmas Bare Branch Tree	394
Lighted Christmas Pole	398
Lighted Christmas Tree	391
Lighted Crystal Pines	394
Lighted Halloween Scarecrows	419
Lighted Peppermint Tree	394
Lighted Snowcapped Revolving Tree	390
Lighted Snowcapped Trees	390
Lighted Snowy Tree	391
Lighted Street Boulevard	394
Lighted Tiered Platform	401
Lighted Tree W/Children & Ladder	267
Lighthouse	25
Lighthouse, Queens Port	166
Lighting The Jack-O'-Lanterns	119
Lighting Up Halloween	121
Lights Out Remote Control	396
Lilac City Water Tower	383
Lily's Nursery & Gifts	56
Lilycott Garden Conservatory	155
Limestone Outcropping	295
Lincoln Park Duplex	22
Linden Hills Country Club	43
Lionel Electric Train Shop (SD)	381
Lionel Electric Train Shop (SV)	46
Lionhead Bridge	176
Listening To A Summer Concert	107
Lit Graveyard Tree	420
Lit Spooky Tree	418
Literary Classics Collection	344
Little Builders	328
Little Italy Ristorante	247
Little Newlyweds	327
Little Town Of Bethlehem	286
Little Women - The March Residence	211, 344
Livery Stable & Boot Shop	200

Load Up The Wagon	223
Loading The Grain	227
Loading The Sleigh	324
Lobster Trappers	221
Lock Keeper	189
Locomotive Shed & Water Tower	185
Log Cabin	10
Log Pile	409
Lomas Ltd. Molasses	140
London Gas Worker	193
London Newspaper Stand	191
London Skating Club	164
Long Haul Truck Stop	66
Look At All The Toys	257, 276
Look At Him Go!	312, 329
Look, It's The Goodyear Blimp	399
Lookout Tower	411
Looney Tunes Film Festival	90
Lord & Taylor Delivery Wagon	382
Lord & Taylor Flower Cart	382
Lord & Taylor Hot Air Balloon 2000	383
Lord Of The Follies	161, 190
Lot 56, Christmas Court	61
Lots Of Good Children This Year	315, 332
Love or Money?	192
Lowell Inn	51
Lowry Hill Apartments	265
Lucky Dragon Restaurant	48
Lucky's Irish Souvenirs	100
Lucky's Pony Rides	317
Luigi's Gelato Treats	283
Lumberjack	226
Lumberjacks	221
Lydby Trunk &Satchel Shop	147
Lynton Point Tower	150
M&M'S Road	417
M&M's Stamp Of Approval	334
M&M'S Tree	417
Maestro And His Protégé	227
Magic Smoke	408
Mailbox	75
Mailbox & Fire Hydrant	268
Main Street Christmas Tree	105
Main Street House	18
Main Street Medical	58
Main Street Office Building	65
Main Street Town Santa	109
Main Street Villagers	98
Mainstreet Gift Shop	41
Mainstreet Hardware Store	30
Mainstreet Snowman	101
Majestic Theater, The	255
Majestic Woodland Birds	411
Making A House Call	102
Making The Christmas Candles	224
Mallard And Wood Duck	413
Maltings, The	142
Man On Ladder Hanging Garland	72
Manchester Square	147
Manchester Square Accessory Set	147, 182
Manor	131
Mansion	7
Maple Ridge Inn	26
Maple Sugaring Shed	219
March Residence, The	211, 344
Margrove Orangery	152
Marie's Doll Museum	306
Market Day	220
Marshmallow Roast	82
Marshmallows Around The Campfire	326
Marvel's Beauty Salon	37
Masonry Bake Oven	228
Master Gardeners	184
Master Potter	186
Maylie Cottage	138
McDonald's	43
McDonald's…Lights Up The Night	86
McElfin's Irish Restaurant & Gifts	314
McGrebe-Cutters & Sleighs	205
McGuire's Irish Pub	53
McShane Cottage	152
Meadowbrook Church	63
Meeting Family At The Railroad Station	184
Melancholy Tavern (2003)	164
Melancholy Tavern, The (1996)	145
Members Of Parliament	184
Men At Work	84
Merchant Cart	294
Merchant Shops - Set	133
Mermaid Fish Shoppe, The	133
Merrily Round We Go	103
Merry Christmas Brite Lites	396
Merry Go Roundabout	187
Merry Mickey Christmas, Cratchits!, A	336
Metal Bare Branch Trees	393
Metterniche Wurst	234
Mickey & Minnie	347
Mickey Builds A Snowman	332
Mickey's Christmas Carol	340
Mickey's Cratchit's Cottage	313
Mickey's Diner	2
Mickey's Haunted House	11
Mickey's North Pole Holiday House	315
Midtown Barbershop	25
Midtown News Stand	27
Midtown Shops	6
Milano Of Italy	26
Milch-Kase	23
Milking The Cow	22
Mill Creek (Curved)	40
Mill Creek (Straight)	40
Mill Creek Bridge	40
Mill Creek Campsite	41
Mill Creek Crossing	22
Mill Creek Park Bench	40
Mill Creek Pond	40
Mill Creek Wooden Bridge	40
Mill Falls Working Waterfall	39

Entry	Page
Milwaukee Or Bust	280
Mini Lights (1991)	396
Mini Lights (1996)	397
Mini Sisal Evergreens	361
Mini Spruce Forest	389
Mini-Donut Shop	307
Misfits, The	333
Miss Havisham, Estella, and Pip	150, 182, 344
Mission Church	11
Mission Style House	61
Mitten Manor	314
Mm! Mm! Good!	103
Mobile Home	11
Moggin Falls General Store	210
Molly O'Brien's Irish Pub	254
Monks-A-Caroling	69
Monster Park Statues	421
Monte Carlo, The	256
Moonlight Bay Bunk And Breakfast	55
Moose In The Marsh	409
Mordecai Mould Undertaker	161
More Decorations?	107
More Play-Doh, Please!	329
More Yarn For Your Stockings, Mrs. Claus!	335
Morningside House	30
Morston Steak And Kidney Pie	142
Mother's Gift, The	152, 184
Mount Olivet Church	34
Mountain Backdrop	408
Mountain Centerpiece	408
Mountain Creek Bear/Moose	413
Mountain Creek Curved Section	413
Mountain Creek Straight Section	413
Mountain Creek Waterfall	413
Mountain Creek Y Shape	412
Mountain Lion's Den	411
Mountain Lodge	6
Mountain Stream	412
Mountain Tunnel	408
Mountain View Cabin	212
Mountain, Lg	407
Mountain, Med	407
Mountain, Sm	407
Mountie	370
Moving Day	84
Mozart Monument	242
Mr. & Mrs. Pickle	141
Mr. Wickfield Solicitor	135
Mrs. Brimm's Tea Room Gift Set	158
Mrs. Claus' Cookies & Milk	333
Mrs. Claus' Greenhouse	305
Mrs. Claus' Hand Knit Christmas Stockings	318
Mrs. Stover's Bungalow Candies	255
Mt. Gibb Congregational Church	216
Mulberrie Court Brownstones	145
Multi Color 10 Light Set	395
Multi Colored 10 Light Set	395
Multi-Building Lighting System	402
Multi-Outlet Plug Strip, 6 Outlets	396
Mummy Mischief	420
Mush!	81
Music Emporium	248
Mylar Skating Pond	407
Mystic Ledge Lighthouse	355
Nanny And The Preschoolers	78
Nantucket	8
Nantucket Renovation	34
Nathaniel Bingham Fabrics	200
National Council Of Clubs	375
Nativity	289
Nativity (HL)	287
Nativity (SVA)	73
Nativity Creche	399
Nativity Sand	410
Natural Evergreens, s/16	392
Natural Evergreens, s/8	392
Nature Walk	100
Naughty Or Nice Detective Agency	315
Naval Academy, Queens Port	166
Navigational Charts & Maps	209
NeeNee's Dolls And Toys	300
Neighborhood Christmas Scene	108
Neighborhood Poinsettia Salesman	107
Nephew Fred's Flat	138
Nettie Quinn Puppets & Marionettes	145
Nettie's Mistletoe Manor	319
New Batch Of Christmas Friends, A	240
New England Raising The Flag	227
New England Town Tree	228
New England Village - Set	200
New England Village Farm	201
New England Village Sign	219
New England Winter Set	219
New Hope Church	42
New Potbellied Stove For Christmas, A	222
New School House	19
New Spring Finery	212, 225
New Stone Church	15
New Year's At The North Pole	334
New Year's Kiss, The	253, 273
New York Yankees Refreshment Stand	283
New York Yankees Souvenir Shop	264
New York Yankees Tavern	264
News Flash!	106
Newt & Emma	314, 330
Nicholas & Co. Toys Starter Set	257
Nicholas Nickleby - Set	134
Nicholas Nickleby Characters	173
Nicholas Nickleby Cottage	134
Nick's Tree Farm	39
Nickolas Nickleby	134
Night On The Town, A	283
Nikki's Cocoa Shop	41
Nikolausfiguren	237
Nine Ladies Dancing - #IX	181
No Girls Allowed	106

Noel House, The	63
Norfolk Biffins Bakery	161
Norman Church	128
North Creek Cottage	28
North Eastern Sea Fisheries Ltd.	150
North Pole - Set	300
North Pole Animated Train With Track	417
North Pole Backdrop	417
North Pole Beauty Shoppe	309
North Pole Candy Cane Lampposts	416
North Pole Chapel	302
North Pole City's Father Christmas's Journey	382
North Pole Dolls & Santa's Bear Works	303
North Pole Express	323
North Pole Express Depot	302
North Pole Gate	322
North Pole M&M's Candy Factory	317
North Pole Petting Zoo	329
North Pole Photo With Santa	411
North Pole Shops - Set	300
North Pole Start A Tradition Set	304
North Pole Town Hall	316
North Pole Woods Series	348
Northern Lights Fire Station	309
Northern Lights Tinsel Mill	308
Northwind Knitters	313
Not Too Fast, Please	229
Notting Hill Water Tower	165
Now Showing - Elvis Presley Sign	93
Nussknacker Werkstatt	236
Nutcracker Delivery	331
Nutcracker Vendor & Cart	240
Nuts About Broomball	350
Oak Grove Tudor	31
Oakwood Post Office Branch	348
Obbie's Books & Letrinka's Candy	301
Off To College!	281
Oh, Brother!	98
Oh, Christmas Tree	49, 92
Oil Lamps	294
Old Chelsea Mansion	42
Old Comiskey Park	262
Old Curiosity Shop, The (1987)	131
Old Curiosity Shop, The (2000)	156
Old East Rectory	146
Old Globe Theatre, The	148, 340
Old Man And The Sea, The	221
Old Michaelchurch	138
Old North Church	202
Old Pickup Truck, The	93
Old Puppeteer, The	175
Old Queensbridge Station	151
Old Royal Observatory Gold Dome Edition, The	153, 341
Old Royal Observatory, The	153, 341
Old Trinity Church	252
Old World Streetlamp	395
Olde Camden Town Church, The	145
Olde World Antiques Gate	347
Olde World Antiques I	346
Olde World Antiques II	346
Olde World Antiques Shops - Set	346
Olive Harvest	295
Oliver Twist	138
Oliver Twist Characters	175
Omnibus	192
On Our Wedding Day	53, 96
On The Beat	94
On The Boardwalk	226
On The Road Again	84
On The Way To Ballet Class	92
On Time Delivery	196
On To The Show	275
One Choo-Choo Burger Coming Up!	335
One Hop Walk	101
One Horse Open Sleigh	366
One More Christmas Card To Post, Please	196
One-Man Band & The Dancing Dog	271
Open Wide!	326
Organ Grinder	268
Original Shops Of Dickens' Village - Set	126
Orly's Bell & Harness Supply	301
Otis Hayes Butcher Shop	203
Otter Creek Sawmill	214
Our Best Vintage, Sir	196
Our Own Village Park Bench	368
Over The Hill Tombstone	420
Over The River And Through The Woods	221
Ox Sled	172
P. L. Wheeler's Bicycle Shop	211
Pacific Heights House	22
Packages Delivery	400
Painting Our Own Village Sign	368
Painting The White Picket Fence	345
Palace Bears	369
Palace Guards	144, 180
Palace Theatre	245
Palm Lounge Supper Club	50
Palm Sunday	291, 295
Palm Trees	289, 295
Palos Verdes	28
Par For The Course	186
Paradise Travel Company	250
Paramount Hotel	254
Paramount Theater	28
Parish Church	19
Park Bench (1987)	40
Park Bench (2000)	41
Park Street Lights	36
Parkside Holiday Brownstone	25
Parkside Pavilion	35
Parkside Pavilion Gift Set	35
Parkview Hospital	25
Parsonage	1
Partridge In A Pear Tree - #I, A	17
Party In The Hot Tub!	32

Entry	Page
Passing Inspection With Flying Colors	336
Patriotic Decorations	362
Patrolling The Road	89
Peaceful Glow On Christmas Eve, A	178
Peanut Brittle Factory, The	307
Peanuts, Pennants & Programs	278
Pedal Cars For Christmas	93
Peggotty's Seaside Cottage	135
Pencil Pines	389
Pennsylvania Dutch Barn	206
Pennsylvania Dutch Farmhouse	206
Penny Saved Is A Penny Earned, A	228
Pennyfarthing Pedaling	224
Peppermint Front Yard	328
Peppermint House, The	63
Peppermint Landscape Set	417
Peppermint Porch Day Care	38
Peppermint Road (Curved Section)	416
Peppermint Road (Straight Section)	416
Peppermint Skating Party	324
Peppermint Trees (1999)	416
Peppermint Trees (2001)	417
Pequot Pine, XLg	392
Pequot Pines	392
Perfect Fit, A	333
Perfect Putt	400
Perfect Tree, The	225
Perfect Wedding, The	358
Personalize Pen	412
Personalize Your Village Accessories	411
Personalized School Bus	106
Pets On Parade	81
Phantom Of The Organ	420
Piccadilly Gallery	160
Pick Your Own Pumpkin	121
Pick-up And Delivery	80
Pickford Place	250
Picking Out The Christmas Tree	274
Pied Bull Inn, The	139
Pier 56, East Harbor	265
Pier 87 Bait &Tackle	281
Pierce Boat Works	208
Pigeonhead Lighthouse	207
Pillsbury Doughboy	62
Pillsbury Doughboy Bake Shop	62
Pillsbury Doughboy, The	108
Pine Cone Trees	389
Pine Point Pond	390
Pine Scented Fresh Fallen Snow	405
Pine Trees With Pine Cones	391
Pinecone Path	350
Pinewood Log Cabin	29
Pinewood Trees, Lg	392
Pinewood Trees, Sm	392
Pink Flamingos	408
Pint-Size Pony Rides	80
Pioneer Church	14
Pisa Pizza	38
Pitching Horseshoes	229
Pizza Delivery	83
Pizza Pick-Up	259, 278
Planning A Winter Vacation	276
Plantation House	20
Planter Box Topiaries	361
Platt's Candles & Wax	212
Play-Doh Sculpting Studio	312
Playing In The Snow	270
Pleasing The Palate!	107
Poinsettia Delivery Truck	368
Poinsettias For Sale	82
Pointy Toed Shoemaker	316
Polar Palace Theater	311
Polar Plowing Service	351
Polar Power Company	313
Polar Roller Rink	316
Polaris Snowmobile Dealership	54
Pole Pine Forest	416
Pole Pine Tree, Lg	416
Pole Pine Tree, Sm	416
Polka Fest	239
Polo Players	187
Ponderosa Pines	390
Popcorn & Cranberry House	304
Popcorn Vendor	268
Popping The Cracker	167, 195
Porcelain Pine Trees	367
Porcelain Pine, Large	367
Porcelain Pine, Small	367
Porcelain Pines	368
Porcelain Trees	366
Portobello Road Peddlers	177
Portobello Road Thatched Cottages	141
Post Office	301
Postal Pick-up	225
Postern	178
Postman & Dairy Delivery Man	275
Potted Flowers	361
Potted Poinsettias	414
Potted Topiaries	361
Potted Topiary Pair	388
Potter's Shop	289
Potter's Tea Seller	249
Pottery Craftsman	289, 296
Poulterer	133
Poultry Market	175
Practice Makes Perfect	116, 122
Prairie House	30
Praying Monks	71
Precinct 25 Police Station	252
Preparing For Halloween	119
Presents For The Family	278
Pretzel Cart	276
Print Shop & Village News	33
Prodigal Son, The	297
Profiles Series	376
Proud Papa & Mama	333
Public House	132
Pull Together	359

Pump Lane Shoppes - Set	140
Pumpkin Street Lamps	421
Pumpkins In The Park	279
Putting Green	409
Quality Service At Ford	89
Queen Anne Victorian	30
Queen's Parliamentary Coach, The	184
Queensbridge Railroad Yard Accessories	185
Quilly's Antiques	146
Radio City Music Hall	258
Radio City Rockettes, The	278
Railroad Crossing Sign	395
Railroad Lamps	399
Raising The Flag At The North Pole	329
Raising The Flag In The City	277
Ramsey Hill House	22
Ramsford Palace	144
Rare Find, A	192
Rathaus Neudorf	238
Ready For Adventure	331
Ready For Duty, Queens Port	194
Ready For The Road	273
Real Acrylic Icicles	406
Real Acrylic Ice, medium, bag of 4	405
Real Acrylic Ice, mini, bag of 12	405
Real Acrylic Ice, small, bag of 6	405
Real Gravel	411
Real Gray Gravel	410
Real Plastic Snow Factory	306
Real Plastic Snow Hopper	386
Real Plastic Snow, 2 lb. Box	405
Real Plastic Snow, 7 oz. Bag	405
Real Removable Snow	405
Red Barn	25
Red Brick Fire Station	246
Red Christmas Sulky	181
Red Covered Bridge	219
Red Fox, The	216
Red Lion Pub, The	167
Red Owl Grocery Store	56
Red Ruby Carousel, The	422
Red Schoolhouse	201
Red Wrought Iron Park Bench	411
Red's Elf Land Diner	316
Redeemer Church	27
Regent Street Coffeehouse	161
Reindeer Barn	300
Reindeer Brite Lites	396
Reindeer Bus Depot	40
Reindeer Care &Repair	348
Reindeer Condo	349
Reindeer Flight School	306
Reindeer Games	332
Reindeer Training Camp	324
Relaxing In A Garden	356
Remote Switches, Right & Left	399
Replacement Bulbs For 52779 String Of Spotlights	400
Replacement Flickering Bulb For Creepy Creek House	400
Replacement Halogen Bulb Starlight Dance Hall	400
Replacement 12 Volt Light Bulbs	401
Replacement 3 Volt Light Bulb	401
Replacement Aux. Cord With Light	400
Replacement Incandescent Bulbs	399
Replacement Light Bulb	395
Replacement Light Bulb, Clear	398
Replacement Light Bulb, Yellow	398
Replacement Light Bulbs	396
Replacement Lightning Bulbs	399
Replacement Round Light Bulbs	397
Rescue Ready	327
Resort Lodge	25
Rest Stop?	98
Rest Ye Merry Gentleman	269
Resting My Bones	420
Revere Silver Works	213
Revolving Nativity Scene	297
Revolving Turntable	397
Richardsonian Romanesque House	65
Ride On The Reindeer Lines, A	84
Ridgewood	21
Rimpy's Bakery	301
Ring Toss	351
Ritz Hotel	245
River Road House	18
River Street Ice House Cart	263
Riverside Row Shops	253
Road Construction Sign	395
Roadside Billboards	94
Rock Creek Mill House	4
Rock-A-Bye Vampire	421
Rockabilly Records	4
Rockefeller Plaza Skating Rink	274
Rocking Chair Readers	357
Rockingham School	15
Rocky Mountain Wildlife-Bears/Bobcat	41
Rocky's 56 Filling Station	5
Rollerama Roller Rink	4
Ronald McDonald House (The House That ♥ Built, 1998)	4
Ronald McDonald House (The House That ♥ Built, 1997)	4
Roosevelt Park Band Shell	6
Rose Garden Beauty	163, 19
Rosita's Cantina	4
Round & Round We Go!	7
Route 1, North Pole, Home Of Mr. & Mrs. Claus	30
Royal Coach	17
Royal Oil Company	26
Royal Staffordshire Porcelains	15
Royal Stock Exchange	15
Rudolph's Condo	34
Rudolph's Misfit Headquarters	3
Rug Merchant & Wool Spinner	288, 2

Rug Merchant's Colonnade 288	School Children 72
Running The Apple Press 227	School House 10
Running The Loom 330	School Sleigh Express 330
Russell Stover Delivery Truck 276	School's Out! 97
Ruth Marion Scotch Woolens 136	Schwarzwalder Kuckucksuhren 237
Ryman Auditorium 38	Scissors Wizards 350
S'mores & Hot Chocolate Stand 330	Scotland Yard Station 169
Safety Patrol 79	Scottie With Tree 69
Sailors' Knot, The 224	Scottie's Toy Shop Exclusive Gift Set 252
Saint James Church 23	Scrooge 166, 194
Salt Bay Lobster Co. 215	Scrooge & Marley Counting House (1986) 129
Salty's Live Bait Shack 227	Scrooge & Marley Counting House (2000) 156
Salvation Army Band 267	Scrooge At Fezziwig's Ball 154, 185
Sampling The Treats 57, 100	Scrooge McDuck &
Sand Road 296	Marley's Counting House 319
Sandy Beach 362	Scrooge McDuck &
Santa & Mrs. Claus 321	The Ghosts Of Christmas 336
Santa Brite Lites 396	Scrooge's Flat 136
Santa By The Light of The Moon 400	Sea Captain & His Mates 223
Santa Comes to Town - 2005 110	Seaside Inn 356
Santa Comes To Town, 1995 81	Seasonal Lampposts 413
Santa Comes To Town, 1996 82	Seasons Bay Flag Raising 360
Santa Comes To Town, 1997 85	Seasons Bay Park 362
Santa Comes To Town, 1998 87	Seasons Bay Series 352
Santa Comes To Town, 1999 89	Seasons Bay Sign 361
Santa Comes To Town, 2000 90	Seasons Department Store 259
Santa Comes To Town, 2001 94	Secret Garden Florist, The 41
Santa Comes To Town, 2002 97	Secret Garden Greenhouse, The 46
Santa Comes To Town, 2003 103	Semple's Smokehouse 209
Santa Comes To Town, 2004 106	Send In The Clown! 91
Santa In Chimney Brite Lites 397	Service Station 27
Santa In The City 277	Service With A Smile 83
Santa's Bell Repair 304	Serving Irish Ale 278
Santa's Castle 316	Set of 20 Red Lights Brite Lites 396
Santa's Light Shop 305	Seton Morris Spice Merchant Gift Set 149
Santa's Little Helpers (NPA) 321	Seven Swans A-Swimming - #VII 180
Santa's Little Helpers (SVA) 91	Shady Oak Church 36
Santa's Lookout Tower 302	Shakespeare's Birthplace 163
Santa's On His Way 399	Shaking Graveyard 421
Santa's Reindeer Rides 312	Sheep 363
Santa's Retreat 348	Sheffield Manor 159
Santa's Rooming House 303	Shelly's Diner 48
Santa's Sleigh 400	Sherlock Holmes - 221B Baker St .. 157, 345
Santa's Sleigh Launch 310	Sherlock Holmes - The Hansom Cab 187
Santa's Toy Company 318	Shingle Creek House 204
Santa's Visiting Center 307	Shingle Victorian 41
Santa's Wonderland House 65	Shiny New Christmas Present, A 283
Santa's Woodworks 302	Shipwreck Lighthouse 114
Santa's Workshop 300	Shoeing The Horse 189
Santa/Mailbox 70	Shopkeepers 172
Satis Manor 150, 344	Shopping Girls With Packages 70
Saturday Morning Downtown 41, 85	Side Porch Café 353
Sawyer Family Tree Farm 217	Sidewalk Games 281
Say It With Flowers 381	Silas Thimbleton Barrister 132
Scarecrow Jack 114, 119	Silent Night Music Box 239
Scaredy Bat 420	Silo & Hay Shed 171
Scary Twisted Trees 420	Silver Bells Christmas Shop Gift Set 49
School Bus 99, 106	Silver For Sale 226
School Bus, Snow Plow 73	Silversmith 347

Sing A Song For Santa	322
Singing Carols In Town	359
Singing Nuns	69
Single Car Garage	27
Single Cord Set	395
Sir John Falstaff Inn	142
Sisal Topiary Garden	388
Sisal Topiary, Lg	388
Sisal Topiary, Med	388
Sisal Topiary, Mini	388
Sisal Topiary, Sm	388
Sisal Tree Lot	73
Sisal Trees, s/7	389
Sisal Wreaths	389
Sisters Of The Abbey	240
Sitting In Camden Park	183
Sitting In The Park	92
Sitting In The Village	104
Six Geese A-Laying - #VI	179
Skate & Ski Shop	37
Skate Faster Mom	74
Skaters & Skiers	81
Skating On The Pond	357
Skating Party	220
Skating Pond (HV)	366
Skating Pond (SV)	14
Skating Rink	8
Skating Rink/Duck Pond Set	8
Skating With Santa	312, 329
Skeleton Fence	419
Ski Bums	325
Ski Slope	398
Skull Street Lamps	420
Slate Stone Path	409
Slate Stone Path Curved	410
Sled & Skis	408
Sleepy Hollow - Set	205
Sleepy Hollow Characters	220
Sleepy Hollow Church	205
Sleepy Hollow School	205
Sleigh & Eight Tiny Reindeer	321
Sleigh Ride With Santa, A	360
Sleighride (HV)	366
Sleighride (SVA)	76
Sliding Down Cornhill With Bob Cratchit	187
Slone Hotel, The	159
Small Chalet	6
Small Double Trees	9
Smokehouse Incense Burner	412
Smokey Mountain Retreat	39
Smythe Woolen Mill	202
Sno-Jet Snowmobile	76
Snow Carnival Ice Palace	38
Snow Carnival Ice Sculptures	83
Snow Carnival King & Queen	83
Snow Children	366
Snow Cone Elves	322
Snow Dragon Brite Lites	397
Snow Fence (1991)	403
Snow Fence (1997)	404
Snow Kids	71
Snow Kids Sled, Skis	70
Snow Village Box Car	385
Snow Village Factory	24
Snow Village House For Sale Sign	72
Snow Village Promotional Sign	75
Snow Village Raising The Flag	99
Snow Village Resort Lodge	25
Snow Village Start A Tradition Set	41
Snow Village Starter Set	36
Snow Village Utility Accessories	87
Snowball Fort	78
Snowflake Light Poles	400
Snowman Brite Lites	396
Snowman Sonata And Fence	57, 104
Snowman Street Lights	401
Snowman With Broom	69
Snowmobile Racers	98
Snowy Evergreen Trees, Lg	390
Snowy Evergreen Trees, Med	390
Snowy Evergreen Trees, Sm	390
Snowy Hills Hospital	35
Snowy Landscape	413
Snowy Pines Inn Exclusive Gift Set	44
Snowy Platform	414
Snowy Scotch Pines	390
Snowy White Pine Tree, Lg	390
Snowy White Pine Tree, Sm	389
Somerset Valley Church	157
Something For Me?	110
Sonoma House	22
Sound Of Music Gazebo, The	240
Sound Of Music von Trapp Villa, The	235
Sound Of Music Wedding Church, The	236
Sounds Of The City	40
Sounds Of The North Woods	40
Southern Colonial	3
Sower And The Seed, The	29
Spam Museum	37
Spanish Mission Church	3
Sparky The Plant Manager	33
Special Delivery (1989)	7
Special Delivery (1990)	7
Spice & Copper Vendors' Colonnade	29
Spider Box Locks, The	15
Spielzeug Laden	23
Spinning Pumpkins	42
Spirit Of Giving, The	146, 18
Spirit Of Snow Village Airplane (1992)	7
Spirit Of Snow Village Airplane (1993)	8
Spirit Of The Season	27
Split Rail Fence, With Mailbox	40
Spooky Black Bare Branch Trees	41
Spooky Black Glitter Tree	41
Spooky Farmhouse	1
Spooky Schooner, The	1
Spooky Totem	4
Spooky Village Sign	4

Entry	Page
Spooky Willows	420
Spooky Wrought Iron Fence	419
Spooky Yard Scene	421
Sport Laden	234
Spotlight	397
Spotlight Replacement Bulbs	398
Spring Is Everywhere!	414
Spring Oaks	394
Spring Portrait	214, 226
Spring St. Coffee House	249
Spring/Summer Landscape Set	414
Spring/Summer Moss	410
Spring/Summer Trees	362
Springfield House	24
Springfield Studio Gift Set	214
Springlake Station	354
Spruce Forest	388
Spruce Place	20
Spruce Tree Forest	389
Spruce Tree With Wooden Base, Lg	388
Spruce Tree With Wooden Base, Med	388
Spruce Tree With Wooden Base, Sm	388
Squash Cart	379
St. Anthony Hotel &Post Office	24
St. Ives Lock House	159
St. Luke's Church	32
St. Mark's Church	247
St. Martin-In-The-Fields Church	154
St. Nicholas	240
St. Nick's Pick-up And Delivery	381
St. Nick's Toy Land	66
St. Nikolaus Kirche	233
St. Patrick's Day Decorating Set	400
St. Patrick's Day Parade	105
St. Patrick's Village Express	370
St. Stephen's Church	168
Stadium Lights	399
Staghorn Lodge	152
Star Of The Show	351
Star Of Wonder	294
Starbucks Coffee	39
Starbucks Coffee Cart	83
Stardust Drive-In Theater	52
Stardust Refreshment Stand	52
Starlight Dance Hall	311
Starry Night Sky Backdrop	409
Stars And Stripes Forever	368
Start Your Engines	97
State Farm - Main Street Fire Station No. 1	377
State Farm - Main Street Memories	376
Statue Of Mark Twain	75
Steen's Maple House	209
Steeple Church	201, 203
Steepled Church	6
Steppin' Out On The Town	272
Sterling Jewelers	256
Stick Style House	45
Stillwaters Boathouse	355
Stone Bridge	366
Stone Church (1977)	7
Stone Church (1979)	10
Stone Cottage	128
Stone Curved Wall/Bench	404
Stone Footbridge	408
Stone Footpath Sections	361
Stone Holly Corner Posts And Archway	408
Stone Holly Tree Corner Posts	408
Stone Mill House	11
Stone Stairway	409
Stone Train Trestle	366
Stone Trestle Bridge	408
Stone Wall	404
Stone Wall With Sisal Hedge	404
Stonehurst House	28
Stonemason At Work	294
Stoney Brook Town Hall	206
Story For The Children, A	194
Strange Case Of Dr. Jekyll & Mr. Hyde, The	193
Strangers Beware	120
Stratford House	18
Street Car	14
Street Lamps	395
Street Merchants	190
Street Musicians	270
Street Sign	74
Streetcar	396
Streetlamp With Garland	395
Streetlamp Wrapped In Garland	395
String Of 12 Christmas Candy Lights	401
String of 12 Christmas Presents Lights	401
String Of 12 Pumpkin Lights	418
String Of 12 Santa Lights	401
String Of 12 Snowflake Lights	401
String Of 12 Snowman Lights	401
String Of 25 Mini LED Lights	398
String Of Spotlights	399
String Of Starry Lights	398
Stroll In The Park, A	356
Strolling Down Howard Street	195
Stucco Bungalow	20
Stuck In The Snow	81
Stump Hill Gatehouse	166
Sudbury Church	146
Summer Platform	414
Summertime Family Picnic	103
Summit House	19
Sunday Football With Dad	99
Sunday Morning At The Chapel	356
Sunday School Serenade	36, 82
Super Suds Laundromat	48
Susquehanna Station	212
Sutton Place Brownstones	244
Sutton Place Rowhouse	244
SV Garland Trim	407
Sweet Rock Candy Co. Gift Set	308
Sweet Roses	155, 186

Sweet Shop, The	57
Sweetbriar Cottage	163
Sweetheart Candy Shop	60
Swinging Disney Fab 5	334
Swinging Ghoulies	420
Swinging Under The Old Oak Tree	391
Swiss Chalet	15
T. C. Chester Clocks & Watches	169
T. Puddlewick Spectacle Shop	144
T. Smith Christmas Crackers	167
T. Wells Fruit & Spice Shop	132
Tacky Wax	407
Tailored For You	350
Taking Bones For A Walk	421
Taking Grain To The Mill	189
Taking The Tree Home	217, 229
Tall Stone Walls	404
Tallyho!	179
Tangled In Tinsel	325
Tap The First Barrel	242
Tapping The Maples	223
Tassy's Mittens & Hassel's Woolies	301
Tattyeave Knoll	149
Tavern In The Park Restaurant	257
Taxi	281
Taxi Cab	71
Teaching The Torah	279
Teaman & Crupp China Shop	150
Teddy Bear Training Center	317
Tee Time Elves	325
Telephone Poles	409
Television Antenna	409
Temple Bar	192, 341
Ten Pipers Piping - #X	181
Tending The Cold Frame	183
Tending The New Calves	180
Terry's Towing	84
Testing The Toys	321
Testing Video Games Is The Perfect Job!	335
Thanksgiving At Grandmother's House	65
Thatched Cottage	363
Thatched Cottage (DV)	128
Thatchers	178
Theatre Of The Macabre	165
Theatre Royal	136
These Are For You	187
This Looks Like A Good Spot	330
Thomas Kersey Coffee House	130
Thomas Mudge Timepieces	148
Thomas T. Julian House	208
Thornbury Chapel	160
Thoroughbreds	410
Three French Hens - #III	178
Through The Woods	74
Through The Woods Mountain Trail	399
Tillie's Tiny Cup Café	306
Timber Knoll Log Cabin	202
Timberlake Outfitters	51
Times Tower, The	253
Tin Soldier Shop	303
Tin Whistles - 25 Cents	262
Tin Whitles - 25 Cents	280
Tinker Bell's Treasures	347
Tinker's Caboose Cafe	319
Tinsel Ball Trees	417
Tinsel Trees	394
Tinsel Trims	409
Tis The Season	269
To Protect And To Serve	273
Toast To Our Anniversary, A	195
Today's Catch	227
Today's Specials	284
Tombstones	419
Toot's Model Train Mfg.	308
Totem Town Souvenir Shop	51
Tour The Village	80
Tower Bridge Of London	165, 168, 342, 343
Tower Cafe	244
Tower Guard & Garden Archway	291, 296
Tower Of David	291
Tower Of London	146, 340
Tower Restaurant	244
Towering Pines	391
Town Blacksmith	229
Town Church	12
Town Clock	407
Town Crier & Chimney Sweep	174
Town Gate	293
Town Hall	15
Town Meeting Hall	348
Town Square Carolers	142, 180
Town Square Gazebo	407
Town Square Market	196
Town Square Shops	142
Town Tinker	220
Town Tree (CIC)	248
Town Tree (GVA)	391
Town Tree Carolers	383
Town Tree Trimmers	270
Town Wall Sections	295
Town Well & Palm Trees	293
Townspeople	108
Toy Peddler, The	239
Toy Shop	25
Toy Shop And Pet Store	244
Toymaker Elves	321
Toys For Tots	384
Traffic Light	395
Traffic Policeman	28
Train And Lighted Station	130
Train Station	15
Train Station With 3 Train Cars	1
Train Trestle	36
Transport	26
Treasure From The Sea, A	18
Treasured Book, A	27
Treats for The Kids	11
Tree Brite Lites	39

Entry	Page
Tree For Me, A	76
Tree Lighting Ceremony, The	93
Tree Lot	73
Tree-Lined Courtyard Fence	403
Treetop Tree House	84
Trekking In The Snow	240
Trick Or Treat	357
Trick Or Treat Kids	119
Trim-A-Tree Factory	348
Trimming The North Pole	321
Trinity Church	19
Trinity Ledge	211
Trout Cabin	35
Trout Stream, The	411
Tudor Cottage	128
Tudor House (1979)	10
Tudor House (2001)	52
Turkeys/Geese In The Field	412
Turn Of The Century	16
Turn Of The Century Lamppost	395
Turner's Spice & Mustard Shop	168
Tutbury Printer	137
Tuttle's Pub	130
Twelve Drummers Drumming - #XII	183
Twig Snow Fence, Wood	404
Twin Peaks	21
Twinkle Brite Glitter Factory	311
Twinkling Lit Shrubs, Green	392
Twinkling Lit Shrubs, White	392
Twinkling Lit Town Tree	392
Twinkling Lit Trees, Green	392
Twinkling Lit Trees, White	392
Twinkling Tip Tree	392
Twirling Tea Cups	422
Twisty Glitter Pines	394
Two For The Road	88
Two For The Show	328
Two Lane Paved Road	409
Two Rivers Bridge	221
Two Turtle Doves - #II	178
Uncle Sam's Fireworks Stand	89
Under The Bumbershoot	184
Under The Mistletoe	223
Under The NCC Umbrella	375
University Club, The	253
Unloading Ice Blocks At The Dock	284
Untangle The Christmas Lights	323
Until We Meet Again	183
Up In The Apple Tree	392
Up On A Roof Top	407
Up, Up & Away	397
Up, Up & Away Witch	418
Uptown Motors Ford	45
Uptown Motors Ford Billboard	88
Uptown Shoppes - Set	248
Urban Landscape Set	394
Utility Accessories	269
Valentine Village Express	370
Valentine's Decorating Set	400
Van Guilder's Ornamental Ironworks	209
Van Tassel Manor	205
Variety Store And Barber Shop	245
Verna Mae's Boutique Gift Set	212
Victoria Station	134
Victoria Station Train Platform	175
Victorian	9
Victorian Christmas Scene	195
Victorian Cottage	16
Victorian Family Christmas House	167
Victorian Father Christmas	195
Victorian House	7
Victorian Skaters	164, 193
Victorian Wrought Iron Fence Extension	403
Victorian Wrought Iron Fence w/Gate	403
Village Autumn Trees	393
Village Bank & Trust	47
Village Bicycle And Tricycle	413
Village Boats	413
Village Church	16
Village Express Electric Train Set	398
Village Express Train - Black	395
Village Express Train - Red, Green	395
Village Express Van	270
Village Express Van (1992)	378
Village Express Van (1994)	379
Village Express Van (1995)	379
Village Express Van, Gold	378
Village Express Van, Silver	384
Village Fire Truck	88
Village Flea Market	412
Village Frosted Spruce, Sm	394
Village Gazebo (GVA)	409
Village Gazebo (SVA)	73
Village Greenhouse	31
Village Gumdrop Road	417
Village Harvest People	219
Village Junkyard	400
Village Lamppost And Sign	412
Village Legion Hall	54
Village Mail Box	77
Village Marching Band	77
Village Market	26
Village Memorial	370
Village Mill	127
Village Monuments	369
Village Moss	413
Village Mountain High	413
Village Musicians	62, 108
Village News Delivery	80
Village Parking Meter	75
Village Peppermint Sign	417
Village Pets - Sales & Service	66
Village Phone Booth	78
Village Police Station	38
Village Post Office	32
Village Public Library	34
Village Real Acrylic Ice, s/22	405
Village Realty	30

Village Roll Of Moss	414	We Don't Need Instructions!	336
Village Santa Sign	414	We Have A Deal!	110
Village Santa's Sleigh Sign	414	We'll Win For Sure!	108
Village Service Vehicles	89	We're Going By Train!	106
Village Sign and Bench	412	We're Going To A Christmas Pageant	79
Village Sign With Snowman	367	Weather & Time Observatory	303
Village Snow Clown	101	Weather Vane	409
Village Sounds Tape	407	Wedding Bells Chapel	309
Village Sounds Tape With Speakers	407	Wedding Chapel	36
Village Spring/ Summer Trees	393	Wedding Gallery, The	253
Village Square Clock Tower	368	Weekend Getaway	102
Village Square Snowman	370	Wegmans Delivery Wagon	384
Village Square Town Tree	371	Welcome Home	270
Village Station	34	Welcome To Elf Land Gateway Entrance	324
Village Station And Train	26	Welcome To Nettie's B&B	335
Village Stop Sign	75	Welcome To North Pole Woods Gateway Entrance	350
Village Street Peddlers	176	Welcome To Snow Village Population Sign	99
Village Swinging Skeleton	418	Welcome To The Congregation	90
Village Town Hall	50	Welcoming Christmas To Town	59, 105
Village Train	171	Well &Holy Cross	173
Village Train Station	60	Wells Fargo Historic Office	377
Village Train Trestle	366	West Village Shops - Set	248
Village Twinkle Brite Tree, Lg	393	Westminster Abbey	162
Village Twinkle Brite Tree, Sm	393	Weston Train Station	202
Village Twinkling Blanket Of Snow	401	Whale Tale Pub & Inn	214
Village Twinkling Snow Tree Skirt	401	What A Great Find!	110
Village Used Car Lot	78	White Horse Bakery	133
Village Utilities	102	White Picket Fence	40
Village Vet And Pet Shop	33	White Picket Fence Extensions	40
Village Warming House	29	White Picket Fence s/4	40
Village Well & Holy Cross	173	White Picket Fence With Gate	40
Village Winter Trees	393	Whitehill Round Barn	214
Vineland Estates Winery	62	Whittlesbourne Church	14
Vintage Christmas Lights Street Lights	401	Who's Walking Who?	10
Vintage Coca-Cola Truck	282	Whole Family Goes Shopping, The	8
Violet Vendor/Carolers/Chestnut Vendor	174	Wiener Roast	41
Violin Serenade	102	William Glen Delivery Truck	38
Vision Of A Christmas Past	177	William Glen Grocery Delivery	38
Visit With Santa, A	380	William Glen Taxi	38
Visiting The Nativity	274	Williams Gas Works	16
Volunteer Firefighters	223	Williamsburg House	2
W. M. Wheat Cakes & Puddings	140	Willow Trees	39
Wackford Squeers Boarding School	134	Windmill	8
Wagon Wheel Pine Grove	390	Windmill By The Chicken Coop	9
Walkway Lights	398	Windsor Castle	168, 34
Walpole Tailors	133	Wingham Lane Parrot Seller	15
Walter's Hot Dog Stand	371	Winter Birch	39
Warming Up	282	Winter Birch Tree	38
Warren Homestead And Walden Cottage	215	Winter Display Platforms	41
Washington Street Post Office	250	Winter Fountain	
Watching For Ducks	412	Winter Frolic	160, 19
Water Tower	73	Winter Green Spruce	39
Waterbury Button Company	216	Winter Oak Tree With 2 Red Birds	3
Waterfall In The Wilderness	296	Winter Oak, Lg	3
Waterfall W/Electric Pump	397	Winter Oak, Sm	3
Waverly Place	21	Winter Park Warming House	
Waving Flag Brite Lites	396	Winter Pine Trees With Pine Cones	3
Wayside Chapel	6	Winter Playground	
WCCO Radio	48		

Entry	Page
Winter Scene Backdrop	412
Winter Sled Ride	401
Winter Sleighride	177
Winter Trees	362
Winter Trimmings	414
Winter Village Accessories	219
Winter Wonderland Landscape Set	414
Wintergarten Café	253
Wintergreen Pines, s/2	391
Wintergreen Pines, s/3	391
Wise Men From The East	289, 293
Witch By The Light Of The Moon	418
Witch Crash	419
Witch Way?Flight School	116
Witchs' Brew Pub	117
Wm. Walton Fine Clocks & Pocket Pieces	213
Wolves In The Woods	410
Wong's In Chinatown	246
Wood Carvings For Sale	61, 108
Woodbridge Gazette & Printing Office	217
Woodbridge Post Office	208
Woodbridge Town Hall	217
Woodbury House	34
Woodcutter And Son	219
Wooden Canoes	411
Wooden Church	17
Wooden Clapboard	13
Wooden Pier	410
Wooden Rowboats	410
Woodlake Chapel Starter Set	53
Woodland Animals At Cliff's Edge	411
Woodland Animals At Mill Creek	409
Woodland Carousel	400
Woodland Landscape Set	413
Woodland Wildlife Animals, Lg	411
Woodland Wildlife Animals, Sm	411
Woodshed & Chopping Block, The	412
Woodsman And Boy	72
Woodsmen Elves	322
Woodworker, The	224
Woody Station Wagon	73
Woody's Woodland Crafts	61
Wool Shop, The	132
Work A Little, Play A Little	105
Wrap And Roll	329
Wreaths For Sale	77
Wrenbury Baker	143
Wrenbury Shops - Set	143
Wright Bike Shop	59
Wrigley Field	258
Wrought Iron Fence	403
Wrought Iron Fence Extensions	403
Wrought Iron Gate And Fence	403
Wrought Iron Park Bench	408
WSNO Radio	48
Yankee Jud Bell Casting	206
Yankee Stadium	256
Yard Lights	396
Ye Olde Lamplighter Dickens' Village Sign	179
Year Round Holiday House	59
Year Round Lighted Lawn Ornaments	401
Yeomen Of The Guard	180
Yes, Virginia...	271
Yesterday's Tractor	93
You Go First!	115, 121
Young Love	56, 100
Yummy Gummy Gumdrop Factory	317

Notes:

Notes:

The Marketplace

Enjoy collecting the villages more than ever with these great products. These are items that we have selected, including those that will help you display like the experts.

Whether you call toll-free, visit us on-line, or order by mail, you will be ordering from the people you know you can trust ... Greenbook.

HOT WIRE FOAM FACTORY 2-IN-1 HOT KNIFE/SCULPT KIT
This verstile kit includes the famous Hot Wire Foam Factory Hot Knife, the very popular Sculpting Tool, AC Power Supply, handy carrying case, and an instructional video. It has everything you need to begin building villages displays like the pros create.
NEW FOR 2005 ... On/Off switch and paddle handle!

Quickly cut through foam, make realistic hills, mountains, waterways, walls, and more. Be amazed at what you can create. Order your kit today. $74.95

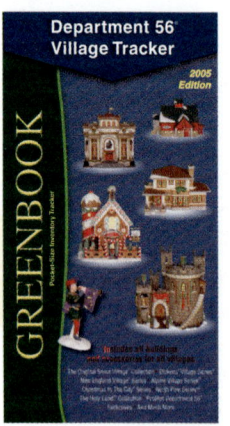

GREENBOOK VILLAGE TRACKER
The perfect pocket companion for the Greenbook Village Guide, this handy Tracker makes it possible for you to keep track of your collection everywhere you go. They contain lists of every design in each collection so you always know what you own and what you want. No more buying duplicates! $2.95

continued on next page
order information on page 464

The Marketplace

COME TO LIFE SOUND EFFECTS (CD)
Add another dimension to your village displays with these unique CDs and their clear, varied, and imaginative sounds of everyday life. It's just what your display needs to be even more realistic than you could have imagined. *(Please specify Vol. I - Dickens Village or Vol. II - Christmas in the City/Snow Village.)* $12.95 each

VILLAGE DISPLAY TIPS
This book provides hundreds of helpful ideas to incorporate into your displays; topics include finding room to display, creating mountains and water, hiding cords, adding animation, developing backgrounds, and much, much more. $21.95

VILLAGE DISPLAY TIPS II
This book takes display-making even further with more ideas, more techniques, and more color photos of collectors tips and methods. It's perfect for both the novice and experienced display-maker. $21.95

CHRISTMAS WITH DICKENS
Written by Cedric and David Dickens, Charles' great-grandsons, brimming with recipes, Victorian games, 27 original line engravings and the story of A *Christmas Carol*. $13.95

CHRISTMAS WITH DICKENS BOOKMARK
Designed to complement *Christmas With Dickens* (above), this red leather bookmark is a wonderful addition. $4.95

GREENBOOK HAT
This is a two-tone, stone-washed green and gray hat, featuring the Greenbook logo. $7.95

GREENBOOK MUG
This mug is deep green, featuring the Greenbook logo. $5.95

continued on next page
order information on page 464

The Marketplace

continued from previous page

PLACE & PLUG
Place & Plug is a completely customizable light cord system that does away with the "rat's nest" of cords that accumulates behind or under a display. With this system, you place lights only where they are needed. And you can change where the lights are year-after-year. You'll wonder how you ever displayed without it!

PLACE & PLUG 25' MULTI-OUTLET CORD
Connect up to 100 outlets and mantle stems to this cord. It includes 6 outlets to get you started. $21.00

PLACE & PLUG 12' MULTI-OUTLET CORD
Connect up to 100 outlets and mantle stems to this cord. It includes 4 outlets to get you started. $15.95

PLACE & PLUG OUTLET PACKS (4 OUTLETS PER PACK)
Place these outlets anywhere along the lengths of the 25' and/or 12' multi-outlet cords. Just snap them in place and add the mantle stems, and you're done. $8.95

PLACE & PLUG 6" MANTLE STEMS (6 STEMS/PACK)
Use these 6" stems to light buildings that are close to the multi-outlet cord. Each stem attaches to an outlet. $12.95

PLACE & PLUG 12" MANTLE STEMS (5 STEMS/PACK)
Use these 12" stems to light buildings that are between 6" and 12" from the cord. Each stem attaches to an outlet. $12.95

TO ORDER:

Call: 1-877-212-4356
(Toll-Free in U.S.)
401-467-9359 (Fax)

Mail: Greenbook
56 Freeway Drive
Cranston, RI 02920

Web: www.greenbooks.com

SHIPPING:

ORDER TOTAL	U.S.	CANADA
Under $10	$1.95	$2.95
$10 - $20	$3.95	$5.95
$21 - $30	$5.95	$7.95
$31 - $50	$7.95	$10.95
$51 - $150	$9.95	$12.95
Over $150	$0.00	$12.95